the
PROPHET'S
DEVOTIONAL

Jennifer LeClaire

the
PROPHET'S
DEVOTIONAL

365 Daily Invitations
to Hear, Discern, and
Activate the Prophetic

DESTINY IMAGE® PUBLISHERS, INC.
P.O. Box 310, Shippensburg, PA 17257-0310
"Promoting Inspired Lives."

This book and all other Destiny Image and Destiny Image Fiction books are available at Christian bookstores and distributors worldwide.

Cover design by Eileen Rockwell

For more information on foreign distributors, call 717-532-3040.

Reach us on the Internet: www.destinyimage.com.

ISBN 13 HC: 978-0-7684-5762-9

ISBN 13 eBook: 978-0-7684-5763-6

ISBN 13 LP: 978-0-7684-5764-3

For Worldwide Distribution, Printed in the U.S.A.

1 2 3 4 5 6 7 8 / 25 24 23 22 21

DEDICATION

The Prophet's Devotional is dedicated to modern-day prophets who have a "more" in their heart—to the ones who are sensitive to His Spirit and want to walk accurately in the prophetic. The only perfect prophet was Jesus, but together we can pursue a pure prophetic ministry and movement that edifies, comforts, exhorts, directs, warns, and, at times, course corrects the Body of Christ through repentance. I applaud you for your heart of service as unto the Lord in prophetic ministry, with all the persecution and the high cost of the anointing.

ACKNOWLEDGMENTS

I'm grateful for the Sauls in my life, who taught me how not to operate in prophetic ministry, and the Samuels in my life, who have provided counsel and covering along the way. This devotional would not be possible without the bumps and bruises, the breakthroughs and victories, that I've experienced over decades of standing in the office of the prophet. This book is also made possible by my dear friend Larry Sparks and my Destiny Image family who understand that prophets need to be encouraged, inspired, and challenged to pursue God's heart in all they do. Thank you.

CONTENTS

FOREWORD

You are about to embark on a life-changing journey on a daily basis. Jennifer LeClaire has accomplished the difficult task for all of us in the Body of Christ of giving us the opportunity to increase our ability to hear the voice of God every day as well as grow in the Lord.

One of the many things that I love about this book is the link between prayer and the prophetic.

When I wrote my first book, *Possessing the Gates of the Enemy,* which first came out in 1991, (before some of you were born!), God had shown me this powerful verse:

But if they are prophets, and if the word of the Lord is with them, **let them now make intercession** to the Lord of hosts, that the vessels which are left in the house of the Lord, in the house of the king of Judah, and at Jerusalem, do not to go Babylon. (Jeremiah 27:18 NKJV)

Jennifer calls prayer, the prophet's oxygen. She makes the excellent point that we need to be prayed up on a personal level so we can provide life-giving intercession for others.

An aspect of a mature prayer life includes waiting on God. Many of us are so busy talking *at* God, that we miss the need to *wait and listen* to Him. In fact, as you delve more deeply into *The Prophet's Devotional,* you will find that you are growing day-by-day in your walk with the Lord. This book could be aptly subtitled, "A year to increase your life as a believer!"

Another huge subject that Christians wrestle with is that sometimes God is silent. He is not talking! If we are truthful with one each other, I think we can all concur that this has happened to us, and, oftentimes, it is when we feel the neediest, and desperate to hear God's answer on a matter. This is a subject that the devotional takes on! I have often quipped that God is never late, but He misses a lot of great opportunities to be early. He seems like an 11th-hour God. This makes for wonderful and inspiring testimonies later but can be stressful to one's nervous system!

This is not an ordinary, sweet devotional book. Jennifer is not afraid to dig deep into one's soul and, while she doesn't pull any punches, her statements are also wrapped in love. In fact, she takes quite a bit of time to emphasize how important it is that we manifest the love of God in every aspect of our lives. Some prophets are rather harsh, and do not consider the possible damage they do to a person's soul when they do not speak from a broken heart. Strong things do need to be said, but it is important to ask God how to say them as well as what to say. I told someone once, "I can take correction as long as

I know the person loves me." After all, it is His kindness which leads us to repentance. (Romans 2:4)

This is a devotional book, a prayer book, and a mentoring book, all rolled into one! It is well worth your time, even though you might have used other daily devotionals. You will not be sorry!

—Cindy Jacobs
Dallas, Texas
Generals International

INTRODUCTION

When I stepped into the office of the prophet, I didn't realize I was stepping into a realm with so much breaking, persecution, spiritual warfare, diverse trials, and sufferings. Prophets are cut from a different cloth than other believers—not a better cloth, just different cloth. Prophets see the world through a different lens. Prophets have a different mandate and mission.

"To us a single act of injustice—heating in business, exploitation of the poor—is slight; to the prophets, a disaster. To us injustice is injurious to the welfare of the people; to the prophets it is a deathblow to existence: to us, an episode; to them, a catastrophe, a threat to the world," Abraham Joshua Heschel, author of *The Prophets*, wrote.

Few understand the plight of the prophet. I dare say the prophet often doesn't truly understand his own plight. What we understand—or come to understand after enough suffering—is that prophets are utterly dependent on God not just for the prophetic words they prophesy but for every breath they breathe. With spiritual and natural enemies and a message that often goes against the grain of an anything-goes society, true prophets are usually hated more than they are loved—at least while they live.

On top of the world's hate, the church is often skeptical of the prophetic voice. Many no longer believe prophets speak for God today. There are many misunderstandings about the prophet's office and many unfortunate stereotypes about the prophet's mantle. And prophets are seemingly held to a higher standard. I get it. If we propose to speak for God, our words—and even our character—must be judged.

Leonard Ravenhill once said, "Prophets are a strange breed of men. They are God's emergency men for crisis hours. And the price of being a prophet is that a man has to live alone. All God's great men have been very, very lonely men." Indeed.

As such, prophets have different struggles and different joys. Prophets have different ups and different downs—different valleys and different mountaintops. It's a different journey and a different devotion. *The Prophet's Devotional* aims to speak into the life of the prophet. This unique devotional is an invitation to hear God's words, discern God's ways, and activate in you a more accurate prophetic voice.

At times, *The Prophet's Devotional* will offer words that convict your heart and spur you to change the way you think—or even the way you operate in prophetic ministry. At times, it will offer words you need to read to keep from giving up. At times, it will challenge you to lay aside wrong teachings. At times, it will give you revelation, wisdom and understanding to advance in your calling.

The Prophet's Devotional is over twenty years in the making. After writing books like *The Heart of the Prophetic*, *A Prophet's Heart*, *The Making of a Prophet*, and *Becoming a Next-Level Prophet*, I realized the prophetic movement needed something more—something different. *The Prophet's Devotional* hopes to be that something different.

I wish I had something like this when I was rising up in prophetic ministry. It will answer a lot of your secret questions you are too afraid to ask anyone, correct some of your inaccurate assumptions that dull your prophetic edge, call you deeper still into intimacy with God, and otherwise ready you to advance to the next level—if you take these words to heart.

If you ponder the words on these pages, some of which offer practical wisdom, some of which are soothing to the soul, some of which deal with prophetic ministry itself, and some which deal with the prophet's heart, you'll grow stronger as a person and a prophet. And that's my prayer for you. I am committed to seeing a stronger prophetic movement—and that means raising up stronger prophets and strengthening seasoned prophets.

JANUARY

"Then the Lord reached out and touched my mouth and said, 'Look, I have put my words in your mouth! Today I appoint you to stand up against nations and kingdoms. Some you must uproot and tear down, destroy and overthrow. Others you must build up and plant'" (Jeremiah 1:9-10).

The Prophet's Oxygen

"Now return the woman to her husband, and he will pray for you, for he is a prophet. Then you will live. But if you don't return her to him, you can be sure that you and all your people will die" (Genesis 20:7).

The first time we see the word *prophet* in the Bible, it is closely coupled with prayer. This is no accident and is a powerful connection, especially if you understand the "law of first mention," a hermeneutical method suggesting the way a word or concept is first used in Scripture (especially the Book of Genesis) informs how the word is understood in future mentions. Genesis 20:7 is the first time we see both words—*prophet* and *prayer*—forever tying the prophet to the critical ministry of intercession.

Old Testament or New, you simply can't separate the prophet from prayer. Prayer is the life blood of prophetic ministry. Prayer is our connection with God that sparks the revelation of His will. Understanding prayer is first and foremost a conversation with God is imperative to the prophet's personal relationship with Him. And understanding intercession is the prophet's duty is imperative to the prophet walking worthy of his vocation (see Eph. 4:1).

The prophet's prayer duty is twofold: to pray for himself and to pray for others (see 1 Tim. 2:1). If we're not praying for ourselves we may not confidently and competently discharge our prophetic ministry. To be sure, the prophet who does not pray for his own needs will quickly dry out and then burn out. Consider how flight attendants tell passengers to put the oxygen mask on themselves first before helping others in an emergency. As prophets, we must pray for ourselves effectively so we can tap into the strength and prophetic intelligence to make intercession for others. Prayer is the prophet's oxygen.

Prophets should also pray for authorities (see 1 Tim. 2:2) spiritual leaders, family and friends, and those who work for us and with us—and even those who work against us. Yes, we should pray for those who persecute us—and prophets will have plenty of opportunity because of the rejection, mocking, and criticism we face. Remember, Moses prayed for Miriam when she was stricken with leprosy for criticizing him (see Num. 12).

Ultimately, prophets should pray as the Holy Spirit leads. The prophet's passion should be more than prophesying a weighty word. The prophet's passion should be prayer that touches God's heart. Ask the Holy Spirit to give you a passion for prayer.

— *Prayer* —

Father, in the name of Jesus, give me a passion for prayer and intercession. Help me seek You early and receive from You daily the strength and revelation I need to succeed in this office in which You have installed me. Inspire me to engage in intercession for all men.

Waiting on God to Reveal You

"As Samuel grew up, the Lord was with him, and everything Samuel said proved to be reliable. And all Israel, from Dan in the north to Beersheba in the south, knew that Samuel was confirmed as a prophet of the Lord" (1 Samuel 3:19-20).

When God calls you to prophetic ministry, it's at the same time exhilarating and frightening. I've met many people who want to be prophets but don't begin to understand the making process, which can be beyond brutal even though the transformation is worth the trials. When God begins to raise up a prophet, the character-building process accelerates to overdrive. There is warfare. There is persecution. There is rejection. There are temptations—and more.

One temptation prophets face is the need for everyone to know just how accurate they are. In the social media age, striving prophets post news stories that work to prove their prophetic utterance came to pass so as to be admired by men. But the prophet who engages in these types of behaviors is in danger of raising himself up rather than letting the Lord raise him up. He is in danger of exalting himself instead of waiting for the Lord to exalt him in due season. Striving to prove oneself accurate demonstrates the lack of maturity to stand and withstand the warfare, persecution, rejection and temptations that come against the prophet—and may ultimately lead to an embarrassing public fall.

When you consider 1 Samuel 3:19-20, don't focus on how everyone knew Samuel was an accurate prophet without considering the process that prepared and established him in ministry behind the scenes. Samuel didn't start his ministry with this reputation. He quietly served in the house of God from the time he was old enough to hold a broom and sweep the temple. Samuel grew in the things of God and was faithful to his spiritual father Eli before he ever uttered a public prophetic word. And he learned to hear the voice of the Lord and how to overcome the fear of man when God told him he was about to judge his mentor's house.

Indeed, before Samuel came to the point in his ministry where the Lord "did let none of his words fall to the ground" (1 Sam. 3:19 KJV) and exalted him to international influence, Samuel had to be raised up in the Word of God and the ways of God. So if you've been called into prophetic ministry, be patient and don't look to emerge from the wilderness until God establishes you in your character. Like Samuel, you can be sure that your time of revealing will come.

— *Prayer* —

Father, in the name of Jesus, help me not to strive in prophetic realms. Help me to embrace the developmental work You are doing in my character before You launch me into more visible platforms. Teach me the value of waiting on You to promote me in Your perfect timing.

Strengthening the Bride

"Then Judas and Silas, both being prophets, spoke at length to the believers, encouraging and strengthening their faith" (Acts 15:32).

Prophets have a keen sense of the heart of God for His people. While prophets go beyond personal prophecy which seeks to edify, comfort, and exhort, prophets should remember that their assignments to people groups often demand a strong focus on the 1 Corinthians 4:3 mandate. Believers need to be strengthened and encouraged. God Himself promises strength throughout the Scriptures.

God told Isaiah, "Encourage my people! Give them comfort" (Isa. 40:1 CEV). And God prophesied to the Israelites through Isaiah: "Don't be afraid, for I am with you. Don't be discouraged, for I am your God. I will strengthen you and help you. I will hold you up with my victorious right hand" (Isa. 41:10). He also promised, "But those who trust in the Lord will find new strength. They will soar high on wings like eagles. They will run and not grow weary. They will walk and not faint" (Isa. 40:31).

People faint in the day of adversity because their strength is small (see Prov. 24:10). Prophets are in a unique position to release strength through prophetic words, sharing the Lord's love, pleasure, direction, comfort, and joy with them. Through a prophetic word, Isaiah 40:29 can manifest in your midst: "He gives power to the weak and strength to the powerless." There is a satisfaction in encouraging God's people prophetically.

But there's another part of this: As a prophet, you too need strength. You are pouring out and pouring out prophetically and sometimes you will feel empty, even spiritually bankrupt, if you don't stay filled up. You may feel like the war against you is raging and everybody is pulling on you for ministry. You may feel like no one sees you. But God sees your labor of love for His Bride.

Before he stepped into his office and took on his difficult assignment, God encouraged Jeremiah, "They will fight you, but they will fail. For I am with you, and I will take care of you. I, the Lord, have spoken!" (Jer. 1:19). Listen for the Lord's encouragement in those times and prophesy to yourself!

— *Prayer* —

Father, in the name of Jesus, help me seek Your heart for words that strengthen Your Bride. Give me words of life that strengthen people in spirit and soul to stay the course You've given them. Help me love people the way You do and prophesy out of Your unfailing love.

Your Jeremiah 1:10 Mandate

"See, I have this day set you over the nations and over the kingdoms, to root out and to pull down, to destroy and to throw down, to build and to plant" (Jeremiah 1:10 NKJV).

Jeremiah, though young, was given a tremendous responsibility as a prophet to the nations. He had a mission, a mandate, and a mantle from God. Notice how God set him in place. If God doesn't set you, the enemy can move you. But when God sets you in a position in His unshakeable Kingdom, He is also able to make you stand.

This is why it's critical that we don't ordain ourselves as prophets to the nations, but we allow God to set us in that level of authority and oversight. Again, when God sets you—when He appoints you rather than you appointing yourself—no devil in hell can move you. When you set yourself, the enemy will work to upset your self-appointment.

Jeremiah's mandate was serious Kingdom business. Four parts of his mission were destructive and two were constructive, and we'd do well to understand these aspects of prophetic ministry. If our prophetic ministries deconstruct but don't reconstruct, we're missing the heart of God.

At the same time, if all we do is work to build and plant with words of edification we may, at times, be leaving the enemy's leverage in place. When it comes to evil nations, the Kingdom of God can only be fully established after demonic kingdoms are torn down and the demon powers are evicted.

Here we learn that the prophet's mandate is to destroy enemy trees by plucking them up by the root. Enemy trees that are not pulled up by the root may seem to disappear for a time but will grow back. Once the root is pulled up, the trees of unrighteousness—the principalities—can be pulled down from the heavenlies and their influence destroyed and thrown down. This is a territorial warfare function. Only after the enemies in a land are dispossessed of can you begin to build and plant God's purposes there.

— *Prayer* —

Father, in the name of Jesus, give me insight into how to walk in the Jeremiah 1:10 mandate in my life. Teach me to walk in balance so that I am not merely tearing down and destroying but building and planting Your Kingdom through my prophetic ministry.

The Day of Small Beginnings

"Do not despise these small beginnings, for the Lord rejoices to see the work begin..." (Zechariah 4:10).

It's easy to despise the day of small beginnings. *Small beginnings* often come with hard work and little help. Small beginnings usually offer tall resistance and modest encouragement. Small beginnings typically see limited budgets and abundant setbacks.

I remember when God told me to make prayer my life's work. I didn't even understand what that meant. In obedience, I set out to launch a house of prayer. I expected it to be an immediate and overwhelming success because I was in the will of God. On most meeting times, I stood alone and prayed. Today, I oversee hundreds of churches, houses of prayer, and prayer hubs under the Awakening House of Prayer banner all over the world. But that was only after a small beginning.

How about you? What has God called you to do? Are you in the day of small beginnings even now? The Lord is rejoicing to see the work begin and He will help you every step of the way. Don't take my word for it. Look at the Bible—King David had a small beginning in a field tending sheep and experienced more intense *warfare* than you or I will probably ever witness. Nehemiah rebuilt the wall of Jerusalem with a remnant despite the opposition and the odds.

The Bible is full of examples of God using the foolish things of the world to confound the wise. If you are in the day of small beginnings, take heart. He who called you to the work is faithful to strengthen your hands to do it, faithful to send workers into the field He called you to, faithful to help you overcome even the devil's best shot, faithful to encourage you by His Spirit and with His Word, faithful to provide all of your needs according to His riches in glory by Christ Jesus, and faithful to lead you into victory if you keep pressing toward the prize. "He who calls you is faithful, who also will do it" (1 Thess. 5:24 NKJV).

— *Prayer* —

Father, in the name of Jesus, help me not to despise the day of small beginnings. Help me avoid the tendencies of impatience, frustration, and disappointment that my ministry is not growing at the pace I desire. Teach me to wait on You for the growth, knowing You will sustain the work.

When God Is Silent

"When the Lamb broke the seventh seal on the scroll, there was silence throughout heaven for about half an hour" (Revelation 8:1).

It seems some prophets always have something to say about everything—even when it's clear God is not speaking when they open their mouths. It's a dangerous practice and a temptation any of us can fall into. Considering there is coming a time when even heaven is silent, we should consider being silent in some seasons. We don't have to continually press and press for a word. God is quite capable of speaking to us clearly without the striving.

Prophets would do well to keep their mouths tightly shut when they don't have an unction from the Holy Spirit. Yet too many prophets feel the people pressure—the natural expectation that comes with the office—to prophesy profusely in public meetings. And too many prophets feel they must offer up a "prophetic word" about the latest natural disaster, governmental shift, or economic crisis in order to stay relevant.

Yes, God surely does nothing unless He reveals it to His servants the prophets (see Amos 3:7). But that doesn't mean prophets and prophetic people should move beyond the unction and into presumption, does it? We can prophesy according to the proportion of our faith all day long, but that doesn't necessarily make it accurate, does it? Prophetic ministry is not an exercise that is ego-boosting—or at least it shouldn't be.

If you are not secure in your calling, you may succumb to requests and offer up something that may or may not be coming from the Holy Spirit just to preserve your "reputation." But we should be far more concerned about our reputation in heaven as a faithful steward of the gifts of God than we are about our reputation with man. Noteworthy is the Scripture that says, "In the multitude of words sin is not lacking, but he who restrains his lips is wise" (Prov. 10:19 NKJV). Also, "I have purposed that my mouth shall not transgress" (Ps. 17:3 NKJV).

Scriptures abound on the mouth. All believers, but prophets in particular, should pray this Scripture: "Set a guard, O Lord, over my mouth; keep watch over the door of my lips" (Ps. 141:3 NKJV).

— *Prayer* —

Father, in the name of Jesus, help me to embrace the silent seasons when You are not sharing with me earth-breaking revelation and applause-driving prophetic words. Teach me to dig a well in my spirit during the silent seasons so I can water Your people when You send me forth.

The Prophet's Primary Task

"Now these are the gifts Christ gave to the church: the apostles, the prophets, the evangelists, and the pastors and teachers. Their responsibility is to equip God's people to do his work and build up the church, the body of Christ" (Ephesians 4:11-12).

This may surprise you, but the primary function of the New Testament prophet is not to prophesy. Think about a dog. The primary purpose of a dog is not to bark. The primary purpose of the dog is to be a companion to man. Of course the dog is going to bark. Of course, the prophet is going to prophesy—and regularly.

When I ask people what the purpose of a New Testament prophet is, I get a myriad of answers. That tells me that most believers—even some prophets—don't understand the key assignment of prophets in the church today. Some, for example, say it's to encourage the Body to stay in the Word. But that's more of the teacher's vein. Others say to spread the gospel. But that's more of an evangelist's task. Still others say to dig wells of revival. That's an admirable venture, but it's not the primary function of the New Testament prophet.

If we don't understand the purpose of something, we may abuse it—and that's just what has happened to many modern-day prophets. Many people abuse prophets because they believe it's the prophet's job to have a word for them on demand. Many prophets allow themselves to be pushed to the edge of burnout because they believe it's their responsibility to spit out prophecy at will like a gum ball machine pops out candy.

In the New Testament, the primary purpose of the prophet is found in Ephesians 4:11-12. Speaking of fivefold ministers, *The Passion Translation* puts it this way: "And their calling is to nurture and prepare all the holy believers to do their own works of ministry, and as they do this they will enlarge and build up the body of Christ."

Jesus taught His disciples. He prepared them for the ministry they would inherit after He ascended to the right hand of the Father. Prophets will do many things—prophesy, call people to repentance, even preach the gospel—but the primary function is to equip believers to hear the voice of the Lord and cultivate an intimacy with God that propels them into their destiny.

— *Prayer* —

Father, in the name of Jesus, would You root out of my heart any misconceptions I have about my role as a prophet so I can walk accurately in the ministry You've given me? Help me understand my primary function so I can activate Your people in their destiny.

Obadiah Is Not Your Friend

"Was it not reported to my lord what I did when Jezebel killed the prophets of the Lord, how I hid one hundred men of the Lord's prophets, fifty to a cave, and fed them with bread and water?" (1 Kings 18:13 NKJV).

In this scene in Israel's history—during King Ahab and Queen Jezebel's infamously wicked reign—we find a kingdom servant named Obadiah explaining to the prophet Elijah what a good work he had done by protecting the true prophets from Jezebel. He felt like he was saving the lives of these one hundred prophets because Jezebel was on a quest to shut God's voice out of the land.

I am quite sure Obadiah's motives were pure. The name Obadiah means "servant of Yahweh." He seemed sincere in his efforts. Think about it for a minute. He was aiding and abetting Jezebel's arch enemies in one sense—and at his own peril. Ahab and Jezebel would have considered Obadiah's protection of the prophets of the Lord a treasonous act.

However, in another sense Obadiah inadvertently aided Jezebel in her wicked plot to cut off the true prophetic voice in the land. Jezebel didn't care if Jehovah's prophets lived their lives somewhere outside Jezreel as long as they didn't get in her way. I'm sure many prophets fled from Israel when she started slaughtering the prophets—and she didn't chase them down. She let them go. The prophets in the caves were essentially imprisoned. Obadiah was not truly their friend.

Jezebel killed the prophets because she didn't want them to speak out. She didn't want God's voice to be the loudest in Israel. She served Baal and Asherah and had her own prophets at her table. The true prophets were an obstacle to her plans for Israel.

Think about it for a minute. Jezebel didn't have to go to all the trouble to murder the prophets in order to silence them. If the prophet will willfully go into hiding, that makes Jezebel's job easier. Remember, Jezebel threatened to kill Elijah but never did. When he went into hiding she dropped it.

Here is the lesson: Don't let Obadiah put you into hiding. In other words, don't shrink back in fear and run to what you think is a safe place to avoid spiritual warfare or persecution. God doesn't have much use for a cowardly prophet.

— *Prayer* —

Father, in the name of Jesus, help me not go run and hide in the face of Jezebel's death threats. Deliver me from the cave I've made my home and give me the boldness I need to accomplish my assignment in a culture of compromise, immorality, idolatry, and death. Make me a voice.

A Prophet After God's Own Heart

"But God removed Saul and replaced him with David, a man about whom God said, 'I have found David son of Jesse, a man after my own heart'" (Acts 13:22).

David was a man after God's own heart. As prophets, we should likewise seek to be people after His own heart. A more modern way of saying that is "a man who always pursues my heart" (TPT). Only a person after God's heart will ultimately "accomplish all that I have destined him to do." Only a person after God's heart will seek one-hundred-fold obedience, even though he is sure to stumble along the narrow path.

In order to be a person after God's own heart we have to understand God's heart. David was a student of God's emotions. He understood what touched God's heart, what moved God's heart, and what grieved God's heart. We, too, can become students of God's emotions, which are displayed, in part, in the pages of the Bible. God has revealed His emotions to us in how He deals with His friends and His enemies.

When we understand God's emotions and how much He loves us, it renews our mind to who He is and who we are in Him. Instead of finding our identity in being a prophet, we find our identity in being His beloved ones. That changes the way we view everything, including the sin that so easily besets us. While Saul was sorry he got caught for his sin, David was sorry that he offended his heart. Big difference!

God does have a spectrum of emotions, from anger to compassion, from grief to joy, from love to hate and beyond. David understood what pleased God and sought to obey his Maker. Like us, David wasn't a perfect man. Nevertheless, God still called him a man after His own heart.

Jesus would later say these words that described the difference between Saul and David: "So why do you keep calling me 'Lord, Lord!' when you don't do what I say?" (Luke 6:46). When you understand the Lord's emotions, your heart will seek to obey.

— *Prayer* —

Father, in the name of Jesus, I want to know Your heart. Help me understand Your emotional makeup so I can love what You love and hate what You hate. Help me understand what grieves Your Spirit so I can honor Your heart. Teach me how You think and feel about people.

The Prophet's Primary Duty

"Then the Lord said through his servants the prophets" (2 Kings 21:10).

Over and over again, the Bible clearly calls God's prophets "servants." The familiar Amos 3:7 reveals, "Indeed, the Sovereign Lord never does anything until he reveals his plans to his servants the prophets." And in Jeremiah 44:4, God tells us, "Again and again I sent my servants, the prophets, to plead with them...."

Remember, you are first and foremost a servant of the Lord. Prophets are not immune to serving in any capacity the Lord chooses. Before Samuel emerged as a prophet, he was a servant in the house of the Lord, helping Eli the priest with tasks such as opening the doors of the tabernacle each morning (see 1 Sam. 3:15).

If we are not careful, we focus too much on the prophet part and forget about the servant part. The Hebrew word for "servant" in these verses is *ebed*. It has three basic definitions: servant, subject, and worshiper.

As servants, we serve His purposes in the earth as His mouthpiece whether or not it brings popularity or persecution. We say what He tells us to say even if we're afraid of what it might cost us. We keep our mouths quiet if He doesn't tell us to speak even though we have a deep revelation from heaven we'd love to share.

As obedient subjects, we perform the duties He calls us to perform, whether delivering a prophetic word, performing a prophetic act, making intercession, sounding the alarm, engaging the enemy—or anything else. As loyal subjects, we are completely subservient to His will and His influence. That means we go where He tells us, and we do what He tells us to do when He tells us to do it. When Jonah was not subject to the King's will, he found himself repenting in the belly of a whale.

But it's that last definition for servant that really grabs my heart's attention—worshiper. Prophets should be worshipers. King David is a prime example. David was a worshiping warrior. Many times, prophets embrace the warrior aspect of the calling but neglect the call to worship. Decide to be a worshiping warrior.

— *Prayer* —

Father, in the name of Jesus, teach me to identify as a servant. Grace me to embrace the call to worship with joy the One whose words I speak. Make me willing and able to walk in a prophetic ministry that is not always glamorous but that glorifies You.

I've Been Delivered of You

"Obviously, I'm not trying to win the approval of people, but of God. If pleasing people were my goal, I would not be Christ's servant" (Galatians 1:10).

I'm known for speaking out what others refuse—or are too afraid—to say. Some churches bring me in just because I am willing to "tell it like it is." We don't need more sugar-coated prophecies in the Body of Christ. We need bold, redemptive truth telling. I'm willing to deliver those wake-you-up, grow-you-up words in love because, well, I've been delivered of you.

What does that mean? It's a phrase a friend of mine from Kansas City used to say. Basically, it means I am free from man-pleasing. I am free from bowing to what people want me to say because I only bow to God. You can't bow to man and bow to God at the same time. "I've been delivered of you" means I don't care if you invite me to speak at your conference, sow into my ministry, or even follow me. My concern is what God thinks.

Prophet, when you do things to impress people, you have your reward—and you may have to live with knowing you compromised to get it. Large crowds, fancy titles, and handsome honorariums should not move us. We should ultimately be motivated by eternity. When we look at our actions through an eternal lens, we see what really matters and what really doesn't. When we behave as if an eternal God is watching—and He is—then we become aware of what truly matters in this life and what truly doesn't.

The applause of man may feel good in the moment, but even man's greatest rewards are fleeting. And we're not mouthpieces for man. We're mouthpieces for God. Ultimately, only God's rewards can truly satisfy our hearts. That's why I choose to pursue the rewards of obscurity. Anything that's not motivated by love won't last in eternity.

Jesus put it this way, "No one can serve two masters. For you will hate one and love the other; you will be devoted to one and despise the other" (Matt. 6:24). Say it with me, "I've been delivered of you."

— *Prayer* —

Father, deliver me from my insecurities. Deliver me from people pleasing. Deliver me from the opinion of man. Help me, Lord, to make what You think about me my primary concern and what You speak to me my primary message.

Walking in Prophetic Wisdom

"When Asa heard this message from Azariah the prophet, he took courage and removed all the detestable idols from the land of Judah and Benjamin and in the towns he had captured in the hill country of Ephraim. And he repaired the altar of the Lord, which stood in front of the entry room of the Lord's Temple" (2 Chronicles 15:8).

True prophets offer words that edify, comfort, and exhort. But the prophet's prophetic wisdom from above sometimes demands someone change to walk in God's best path. In 2 Chronicles 15 we see the spirit of God come upon Azariah, who went out to meet King Asa as he was returning from battle—the first battle of his kingship after many years of peace. Asa was known as a reformer, and the Lord gave him rest from his enemies in the early days of his reign.

It was in this context—after his first warfare victories as a king dependent on God's power to overcome—that Azariah delivered a prophetic word warning God's people not to abandon God, reminding them of dark times of the past and encouraging them to seek the Lord. The prophetic wisdom may have seemed to come at an odd time, given Asa's desperate cries to God in a battle despite his army of one million men and thirty chariots. Asa had done well.

From a natural perspective, Asa may have expected a prophetic word congratulating him on his humility in battle. Instead, he got a warning and then a promise: "But if you abandon him, he will abandon you," and "But as for you, be strong and courageous, for your work will be rewarded" (2 Chron. 15:2,7). Asa knew exactly what God meant. Over his reign of peace, idolatry had slipped back into the land. In fact, that's probably why the enemy attacked him in the first place—there was an open door.

The prophetic warning was not a condemnation—it was an invitation to pick up his reformation mantle once again. Azariah's prophecy gave King Asa courage to bring new religious reforms to Israel. The Lord used Azariah to convict the king to rid the land of false gods—those false objects of worship that stood in the way of a true relationship between Jehovah and the people He loved.

Prophets are called to root out, tear down, overthrow, and destroy, but they need God's wisdom on how to address the difficult issues. Azariah did not come to the king with a word of rebuke but a reminder of his purpose in his generation to reform.

— *Prayer* —

Father, in the name of Jesus, teach me to walk in prophetic wisdom when I receive difficult words for Your people. Impart to me the prophetic wisdom and grace you gave Azariah when he delivered Your prophetic warning with the king.

When You Feel Dusty

"If any household or town refuses to welcome you or listen to your message, shake its dust from your feet as you leave" (Matthew 10:14).

"Shake the dust off your feet." I wasn't really surprised when I heard the Holy Spirit say those six words—but when I read the Scripture in context it sent me into intercession for the ones who rejected the word of the Lord. The sad story begins in a local church where I was serving on the pastoral staff.

Soon enough, I discerned spirit of compromise invading the hearts of leadership. Decision after decision was made to please man rather than please God. Over the course of a year, I gently but directly pointed out areas of compromise. The senior pastor tolerated a woman with a spirit of Jezebel wreaking havoc in the church. He frequently attended "rock star" megachurch conferences and brought the seeker-friendly principles he learned back to the congregation. He refused to confront sin of all sorts, from adultery to homosexuality and beyond.

The day finally came when the compromise was so blatant that it sent me into weeping and travail for the church. After consulting with ministers more experienced and wiser than me, I boldly confronted the growing cancer in love with scriptural backing that could not be denied. Over the course of a year, my prophetic words of warning were pooh-poohed time and time again. I was told, in subtle terms, that I was missing God's heart in these matters.

Jesus said, "If any household or town refuses to welcome you or listen to your message, shake its dust from your feet as you leave" (Matt. 10:14). Sometimes we have to shake the dust off our feet and even shake out our garments (see Acts 13:51; Acts 18:6). But before we do, we must have a clear conscience. We must do everything we can to reach those God sends us to. We must not leave with self-righteousness or anger but with weeping and intercession for those who refuse to hear God's truth. Only then can we say, "Your blood is upon your own heads—I am innocent" (Acts 18:6).

— *Prayer* —

Father, in the name of Jesus, give me the grace to labor in love with people who don't see Your truth. Show me ways to be more effective in delivering prophetic instructions and perspectives so Your truth can break into pieces the lies of the enemy that put Your Bride in danger.

The Imposter Syndrome

"So do not throw away this confident trust in the Lord. Remember the great reward it brings you! Patient endurance is what you need now, so that you will continue to do God's will..." (Hebrews 10:35-36).

I was preaching at a conference on the topic of Jezebel. Although the congregation was saying hearty "amens" throughout the message, I could feel the strong resistance. That didn't surprise me because I know Jezebel doesn't like to be exposed. So I preached on.

After the message a man came up to the altar and started verbally attacking me, calling me a false prophet in front of the whole church. He was accusing me of misquoting Scripture. I stood my ground and suggested he needed to open his Bible and read the passage. He came back later and repented privately, but that was after making a very public scene.

Even though I knew I was right, I struggled the rest of the night with vain imaginations. That "false prophet" accusation brought on what is called the imposter syndrome. Every self-aware, reflective prophet will be plagued with this phenomenon at some point in their ministry. It's not a matter of if, but when. Imposter syndrome is essentially feeling like a fraud. The voice of imposter syndrome makes you question your calling and abilities.

I started wondering back to my original commissioning. Did they lay hands on me and anoint me just because of what I could do for their church or because I'm really a prophet? Am I really hearing from the Lord or am I making this stuff up? I struggled with this until morning, then I spoke with an apostle and told him what happened.

What he shared with me set me free. He told me the pastor's wife was operating in a Jezebel spirit and hated the message. She inspired one of her eunuchs to come up and attack me publicly to discredit the message and cause me to second-guess myself. Although he repented privately, the public damage was done.

At the same time, the witchcraft coming against my mind was so fierce that I started questioning myself even though I knew it was ridiculous. I broke through the imposter syndrome by breaking the silence on the voices that were coming against me. I separated my thoughts and feelings from the truth. And the voice crying "phony" finally shut up. When imposter syndrome attacks you, expose it.

— *Prayer* —

Father, in the name of Jesus, help me root my identity deeply in You. Help me to make my calling and election sure by standing firm against the vain imaginations that would have me believe You did not choose me as Your mouthpiece. I bind the voice of Jezebel!

Prophesying Amid Persecution

"God blesses you when people mock you and persecute you and lie about you and say all sorts of evil things against you because you are my followers" (Matthew 5:11).

When I first starting writing articles for *Charisma*, the floodgates of persecution were opened against me. I had no idea Christians were so vitriolic. Some readers didn't believe in prophets, so I am not sure why they were even reading the magazine. Others persecuted me because I'm a female and the Lord "suffereth not a woman to teach." Others were flat out heresy hunters who twisted my words, demonstrating their ignorance of Scriptures.

Yes, people have made satirical videos about me, created cartoon memes about me, written scathing articles about me, mocked me while I was in the pulpit, confronted me vehemently when I came down from the pulpit, sent me nasty letters pronouncing judgment over my life and more. At first, this used to bother me, but then I learned to rejoice. You need also rejoice in the persecution.

Jesus said, "God blesses you when people mock you and persecute you and lie about you and say all sorts of evil things against you because you are my followers. Be happy about it! Be very glad! For a great reward awaits you in heaven. And remember, the ancient prophets were persecuted in the same way" (Matt. 5:11-12).

Throughout history, God sent prophets who were persecuted and even killed. Second Chronicles 36:15-16 recites, "The Lord, the God of their ancestors, repeatedly sent his prophets to warn them, for he had compassion on his people and his Temple. But the people mocked these messengers of God and despised their words. They scoffed at the prophets until the Lord's anger could no longer be restrained and nothing could be done."

The true prophets didn't lash out in the midst of persecution. They didn't defend themselves. And they didn't stop prophesying. They stayed the course. We can do better than stay the course. We can rejoice—and we should. The ancient prophets are seeing great rewards in heaven for not giving up—and so will we. Ask the Lord to help you keep an eternal perspective in the face of persecution.

— *Prayer* —

Father, in the name of Jesus, help me not to lash out at my persecutors. Help me not to defend my rights. Help me not to stop prophesying boldly just because people don't like what You have to say. Give me the strength to keep going in the face of the opposition by focusing on eternity.

Deactivating Baal's Influence

"The priests did not ask, 'Where is the Lord?' Those who taught my word ignored me, the rulers turned against me, and the prophets spoke in the name of Baal, wasting their time on worthless idols" (Jeremiah 2:8).

The church was in a mess. The priests were the spiritual leaders of the nation—those who were supposed to bring blessing upon the nation—and they were falling down on the job. (That's actually an understatement, but you get the point.)

The law-handlers did not know the Lord. The pastors were sinning against the Lord. One would hope that the prophets would rise up and speak a word of correction. But the prophets failed Israel at a critical time. They were listening to the wrong spirit.

Specifically, the Lord said the prophets prophesied by Baal—a false god—and walked after things that do not profit. In other words, they strayed from the one true God and chased after idols, to the point of gaining prophetic intelligence from them. This is a tragedy and it's still happening today. Many in prophetic ministry are following Baal and other false gods. Their words are not only worthless—they are leading people astray.

How can you discern if you are prophesying out of a Baal spirit? Baal was the god of prosperity, weather, harvest, sex, and fertility. Baal prophets prophesy almost exclusively in these realms—promising peace where there is no peace (see Ezek. 13:10), promising prosperity with a motive to raise a huge offering for their ministry, prophesying weather predictions for the sake of demonstrating their accuracy, prophesying marriages and babies.

Don't get me wrong, any true prophet can prophesy prosperity, weather, harvests, marriages, or babies. But a balanced prophet will not merely prophesy things people want to hear. Remember, King Ahab was surrounded by Baal prophets who told him he would reign victorious in a war in which he ultimately died. Baal prophets are yes-man prophets who want to tickle people's ears for personal gain.

Ask the Holy Spirit to help you rid your life—and your heart—of Baal's tendencies and to overcome Baal's temptations in your prophetic ministry. Determine to stay focused on the one true God so that even if the priests, the pastors, and the law-handlers fail you will have the authority to rise up and prophesy what the Lord says.

— *Prayer* —

Father, in the name of Jesus, show me if I have any Baal tendencies in me. If I was taught wrong, re-teach me the truth about prophetic ministry I need to know. If I have spoken Baal's words, forgive me and cleanse me from this unrighteousness.

Healing Spiritual Eye Infections

"So I advise you to buy gold from me—gold that has been purified by fire. Then you will be rich. Also buy white garments from me so you will not be shamed by your nakedness, and ointment for your eyes so you will be able to see" (Revelation 3:18).

The enemy specifically targets the eyes of seers. The wicked one especially likes to traumatize the eyes of young seers with nightmares and scary visions long before they even know the gift of God they carry. The assignment is to convince the young seer to shut down their gift because it scares them. If the seer survives these attacks, the enemy changes his strategy. He works to inflict the seer with spiritual eye infections that hinder the ability to see—or at least to see accurately.

As I wrote in my book *Power Seers*, some seers have spiritual cataracts and need the Great Physician to do surgery. Naturally speaking, a cataract is a clouding of the normally clear lens of your eye according to the Mayo Clinic. "For people who have cataracts, seeing through cloudy lenses is a bit like looking through a frosty or fogged-up window," Mayo explains.

"Clouded vision caused by cataracts can make it more difficult to read, drive a car (especially at night) or see the expression on a friend's face." Spiritual cataracts cause you to see in part what God wants you to see in full. You can't quite make out the entire picture.

Some seers have spiritual glaucoma. Again, speaking naturally, "glaucoma is a group of eye conditions that damage the optic nerve, the health of which is vital for good vision. This damage is often caused by an abnormally high pressure in your eye." Seers and seeing people who feel pressure to see can wind up blinded by their own ambition.

God is removing spiritual eye infections from the seers who will submit their eyes to Him fully. He's healing blurred vision. He's healing tunnel vision. He's healing eye strain. He's healing vision loss. I see Him now putting His hands on the eyes of seers and seeing people. Dare to look up again as He restores your eyesight so you can see clearly again (see Mark 8:25).

— *Prayer* —

Father, in the name of Jesus, heal my seer eyes of fear and trauma. Help me stand and withstand the onslaught that comes against my mind, even in my dreams. Help me with my eyes wide open, fearless, knowing that whatever I see You are with me.

A Faithful Witness

"Let these false prophets tell their dreams, but let my true messengers faithfully proclaim my every word. There is a difference between straw and grain!" (Jeremiah 23:28)

Jesus is called the Faithful Witness (see Rev. 1:5). Other translations call him the Loyal Witness and the Trustworthy Witness. He is all of those things. As our prototype prophet, Jesus was full of grace and truth, loyal to the Father's will, and faithful to speak what the Father was saying without compromise, even with the penalty of a painful death staring Him in the face.

Prophets need to be careful not to speak when the Lord is not speaking. But there's a flip side to that truth: prophets need to be faithful to share the dreams and visions the Lord gives them. Prophets need to be faithful to speak His word—and ready to speak that word in season and out of season (see 2 Tim. 4:2). Prophets need to obey the voice of the Lord to speak when He says speak no matter who might like it or who might not like it. That is the gold standard in the prophetic.

Of course, that's not always as easy as it sounds. It's easy to prophesy a word of prosperity. It's simple to prophesy according to the party line. It's easy to edify, comfort, and encourage. It's easy to prophesy something that will garner applause from people and make you popular in the prophetic community. But the Bible proves God is not one-dimensional. He's not a bless-me-only God. He disciplines those He loves (see Heb. 12:6). He warns us of danger coming down the pike. He convicts us of wrong so we can repent.

It's not always so easy to speak a prophetic word of warning. It's not always fun to prophesy a word that goes against the grain of popular opinion. It's not always easy to prophesy something that runs contrary to what everyone else is insisting is the will of the Lord. But the willingness to speak what the Lord says to speak when the Lord says to speak it is what sets apart a mature prophet from an immature one—an obedient prophet from a disobedient one.

Ask the Lord to give you boldness and wisdom to move with Him in prophetic ministry. Ask the Lord to deliver you from the fear of man and exchange that fear for a spirit of the fear of the Lord so you can walk in a pure prophetic ministry.

— *Prayer* —

Father, in the name of Jesus, mature me. Help me live, move, and have my being—and my entire prophetic ministry—in You. Deliver me from the spirit of fear and let the spirit of the fear of the Lord rest upon me all the days of my life. Make me Your faithful witness.

Finding Your Prophetic Expression

"May the words of my mouth and the meditation of my heart be pleasing to you, O Lord, my rock and my redeemer" (Psalm 19:14).

Though a prophet is a prophet, the prophetic ministry has many unique expressions. A prophetic expression is how you release your prophetic gifting, or how the prophetic gift manifests through you. I always say it this way, "You can't put a prophet in a box." Some prophets prophesy prolifically in the context of prayer. Others in the context of scribing. Still others through prophetic preachers, who express their gift through their own personalities and life experiences.

When it comes to prophetic expressions, prophetic psalmists are another strong example. God is speaking to the heart of these minstrels, but how they express what God is speaking to them varies—and thank God it does. Would you like to hear the same song forever or don't you enjoy a little variety? This concept holds true for prophetic teachers, prophetic artists, and prophetic people of all sorts.

It's important to determine your prophetic expression. Although we want to be prophetically diverse, hearing and expressing prophecy in many ways, we want to build on our strengths, and we do not want to go beyond the grace of God in our gifting. Understanding your prophetic expression or expressions gives you confidence in releasing your gift. If you are consciously aware of how God moves through you accurately, then you will be bolder in releasing the prophetic words or visions God gives you.

Your prophetic expression is not just the way you convey or show forth a prophetic word. It could be the medium by which you deliver your prophetic gifting or your function and operation. Your prophetic expression is not completely unique to you as others will have similar expressions of prophetic giftings, but you can't force an expression that the Holy Spirit isn't manifesting through you.

In other words, you can't try to be someone you are not or release your prophetic anointing in a way the Holy Spirit isn't leading you. If you do, your prophetic gift may not be received or if it is received it may not be as effective. Ask the Holy Spirit to help you find your most accurate prophetic expression. This is where your gifting really comes alive.

— *Prayer* —

Father, in the name of Jesus, help me identify my primary, secondary, and tertiary prophetic expressions. I want to understand how You express Your mind, will, and emotions through me. Help me not to try to be someone I am not, but to be everything You've called me to be.

Walking in Your Prophetic Destiny

"'For I know the plans I have for you,' says the Lord. 'They are plans for good and not for disaster, to give you a future and a hope'" (Jeremiah 29:11).

When God first called me into prophetic ministry, I couldn't see the forest for the proverbial trees. In fact, I didn't even get it. The Holy Spirit was dropping prophetic puzzle pieces along my path, but because I didn't have any real understanding of modern-day prophetic ministry at the time, I continued to walk around as if I was clueless.

Soon, I began to see a running theme in my dealings with the Lord. He was showing me through books I was reading the earmarks of my calling. I was still unsure and didn't mention it to anyone. Within months, someone prophesied over me in a prayer line, proclaiming that I was a "voice of governing authority." I had no earthly idea what that meant. So I went home and researched each word in the Bible and the dictionary.

In order to get glimpses of your destiny, you often have to connect the prophetic dots, so to speak. That can take years because when we first catch on that God is calling us, we're typically only catching on to the first season of our calling. Sure, God can open your spiritual eyes and show you the end from the beginning. But more often than not your calling will progress and evolve much like a child's dot-to-dot coloring book. In other words, you may see the outline of the image but the intricate details that make it a picture worthy of hanging on the refrigerator are yet missing.

The Bible says, "But as it is written: 'Eye has not seen, nor ear heard, nor have entered into the heart of man the things which God has prepared for those who love Him.' But God has revealed them to us through His Spirit. For the Spirit searches all things, yes, the deep things of God" (1 Cor. 2:9-10 NKJV).

God reveals our progressive calling to us through His Spirit. Sure, He may use a person to prophesy over you. He may use a sermon or book to open your eyes. He may use divine appointments to get your attention. The Holy Spirit is actively offering you clues to your destiny. It's up to us to connect the prophetic dots.

— *Prayer* —

Father, in the name of Jesus, teach me how to walk worthy of my calling. Show me what You want me to see and help me avoid the temptation to see more and do more than You've called me to do in any given season of my life.

When God Tells You His Secrets

"Surely the Lord God does nothing, unless He reveals His secret to His servants the prophets" (Amos 3:7 NJKV).

Prophets love to quote Amos 3:7 and for good reason. We all love to think we have a special connection to God—and we all do. Here, though, we clearly see that God chooses to share some of His plans with the prophets, who then share them with the rest of the Body of Christ.

Yes, God does reveal His plans before He executes them in the earth. Remember when God planned to destroy Sodom and Gomorrah? Genesis 18:17 records God asking, "Should I hide my plan from Abraham?" Abraham was a prophet, so he was the natural candidate with whom to share His secret plans for destruction. God wants to share His secrets with somebody. Likewise, God told Moses He planned to wipe out the Israelites before He did it. Exodus 32:8-10 reveals the harrowing scene:

"How quickly they have turned away from the way I commanded them to live! They have melted down gold and made a calf, and they have bowed down and sacrificed to it. They are saying, 'These are your gods, O Israel, who brought you out of the land of Egypt.'" Then the Lord said, 'I have seen how stubborn and rebellious these people are. Now leave me alone so my fierce anger can blaze against them, and I will destroy them. Then I will make you, Moses, into a great nation.'"

Why does God tell the prophets His secrets? God shares His secrets with us first and foremost so we can pray for mercy or prepare the hearts of the people for what He is about to do. Abraham and Moses launched into intercession immediately. Although God still destroyed Sodom and Gomorrah, Abraham's intercession rescued Lot and his family from a fiery fate. God sent angels to lead righteous Lot out of the city. Moses' intercession pacified the Lord and He relented. God never wants to destroy anyone. He's always looking for a prophet to stand in the gap (see Ezek. 22:30).

God's secrets aren't always about pending destruction. And God sharing His secrets with His servants the prophets doesn't make the prophet elite. It's merely a function of the prophet to hear, see, and say—and then lead the rest of the Bride in the way they should go.

— *Prayer* —

Father, in the name of Jesus, teach me to incline my ear to You day and night. Show me how to position myself to hear the secrets You want to share with me. I am determined to go beyond the surface into the deeper revelations.

Singing the Song of the Lord

"Sing a new song to the Lord, for he has done wonderful deeds. His right hand has won a mighty victory; his holy arm has shown his saving power!" (Psalm 98:1).

The first time I heard the prophetic song of the Lord was in Nicaragua. The house prophet from our church back home was preaching and suddenly burst out into song with a strong prophetic anointing that caused some to weep and others to cheer despite the fact that she was speaking English and they couldn't understand a word she was saying.

I had never even heard of the song of the Lord, but it's scriptural. Deborah sang the song of the Lord, or what some call a victory hymn. Miriam also sang the song of the Lord after Moses led the people through the Red Sea (see Exod. 15). Later, Mary sang the song of the Lord after visiting Elizabeth and discovering she, too, was pregnant.

> *For the Mighty One is holy, and he has done great things for me. He shows mercy from generation to generation to all who fear him. His mighty arm has done tremendous things! He has scattered the proud and haughty ones. He has brought down princes from their thrones and exalted the humble. He has filled the hungry with good things and sent the rich away with empty hands. He has helped his servant Israel and remembered to be merciful. For he made this promise to our ancestors, to Abraham and his children forever* (Luke 1:49-55).

Let Him put a new song in your mouth (see Ps. 40:3). You don't have to be a singing prophet to release the song of the Lord. Listen for the Lord's songs of deliverance. Shout for joy in the Lord (see Ps. 33:1). Make a joyful noise to the rock of our salvation (see Ps. 95:1). Zephaniah 3:17 tells us, "For the Lord your God is living among you. He is a mighty savior. He will take delight in you with gladness. With his love, he will calm all your fears. He will rejoice over you with joyful songs."

Again, you don't have to be a singer to sing the song of the Lord. We can all address each other in psalms and hymns and spiritual songs, singing and making melody to the Lord with our hearts (see Eph. 5:19). Release the song!

— *Prayer* —

Father, in the name of Jesus, help me praise You with my mouth whether or not I feel like I am walking in victory. Help me to model the way of praise and worship in the prophetic movement and release songs of breakthrough that glorify You as Deliverer.

Don't Kill Your Prophetic Ministry

"But any prophet who fakes it, who claims to speak in my name something I haven't commanded him to say, or speaks in the name of other gods, that prophet must die" (Deuteronomy 18:20 MSG).

These words of the Lord are more intense than the eight woes Jesus pronounced on the scribes and Pharisees in the gospels. Although prophets who fake it and claim to speak in the name of the Lord or who speak in the names of other gods will not be stoned or otherwise die as they did in the Old Testament, it is nevertheless a dangerous practice that should spur in us a fear of the Lord.

There is so much in this one verse to unpack as it relates to prophetic ministry today. First, notice the Lord is concerned about the prophet who presumes. While the King James Version of the Bible only mentions the words *presume, presumed, presumptuous*, and *presumptuously* 11 times, it almost always leads to death. This is one of those times.

Prophets must never—never—presume to speak a word in His name that did not come from His heart. We need to be sure we are hearing His voice and not the voice of a stranger. We must judge prophetic utterances before we release them to the masses. We must not treat prophecy lightly, as if it is a common thing. This is the mind and will of God we're transmitting to hungry people who may be hanging on the words coming out of our mouth.

The Hebrew word for "presume" in Deuteronomy 18:20 means "to boil, boil up, seethe, act proudly, act presumptuously, at rebelliously, be presumptuous, be arrogant, be rebelliously proud." Can you see why He hates when a prophet presumes to speak in His name? A presumptuous prophet does not have the heart of God and should not speak for Him. The Lord puts presumptuous prophets on par with those who "speak in the name of other gods."

We live in an age of grace, and we will not die if we presume to speak a word in His name that He has not commanded us to speak—but He still hates it. And it will, over time, diminish the godly impact of your prophetic ministry. You may make an impact, but not inspired by God. Decide not to let anyone put words in your mouth besides God.

— *Prayer* —

Father, in the name of Jesus, search me and show me if there is any presumptuous way in me. Help me to never move in presumption and assumption and release words that come from another voice—or even my own heart. I submit to Your leadership.

Prophetic Leadership 101

"For even the Son of Man came not to be served but to serve others and to give his life as a ransom for many" (Mark 10:45).

Leadership is influence. Throughout the Bible, we see prophets as leaders. Not every prophet was a leader and not every leader was a prophet, but when we see the prophets leading we see miraculous provision and prosperity.

Joseph was a prophet who became prime minister of Egypt and led the nation—and the nations—through worldwide famine. Through Joseph's leadership, lives were saved and the riches of Egypt multiplied. Moses was a prophet who led the Israelites out of the bondage of an idolatrous Egyptian system hundreds of years later. Samuel was the leader of schools of prophets, as were Elijah and Elisha, and served as Israel's last judge.

Deborah was a prophet who led the Israelites into victorious war with a bold courage that even some of her male contemporaries didn't possess. David was a prophet who led Israel into victory in every battle he fought. Daniel was a prophet who advised several kings throughout his lifetime in an example of leading up that cannot be denied.

Prophetic leadership brings with it prophetic insight. So how do we develop leadership skills as prophets? Learn to prioritize the Kingdom. Demonstrate prophetic integrity. Find solutions to problems that escape the natural mind. Raise up younger prophets who can go beyond you. Carry a vision that's larger than life. Understand the power of self-discipline and self-control as you model the way.

Above all, be a servant. Jesus said in Matthew 20:25-28:

> *"Kings and those with great authority in this world rule oppressively over their subjects, like tyrants. But this is not your calling. You will lead by a completely different model. The greatest one among you will live as the one who is called to serve others, because the greatest honor and authority is reserved for the one with the heart of a servant. For even the Son of Man did not come expecting to be served but to serve and give his life in exchange for the salvation of many"* (TPT).

— *Prayer* —

Father, in the name of Jesus, teach me how to lead the way Jesus led. Help me take on the mind of Christ and demonstrates a servant's heart as I seek to walk in the measure of influence that You have afforded me.

Write This Down

"...And then he said to me, 'Write this down, for what I tell you is trustworthy and true'" (Revelation 21:5).

Imagine if John didn't write down the epic vision he received that we know as the Book of Revelation. John the Revelator wasn't the only one God commanded to write what he heard. In Jeremiah 30:2 we read, "This is what the Lord, the God of Israel, says: Write down for the record everything I have said to you, Jeremiah."

If those were the only two times God stressed the importance of writing down what He said, that would be enough for me. But it wasn't. He told Habakkuk, "Then the Lord said to me, 'Write my answer plainly on tablets, so that a runner can carry the correct message to others'" (Hab. 2:2).

All prophets should be scribes in the sense that we need to record what the Holy Spirit is saying and showing us. It would be irresponsible not to write down the revelation you receive because you may forget vital details. I've found, in fact, when you write down the revelation you position yourself to receive more revelation. I heard the Lord say:

> I am calling My scribes to describe what they see and hear before they say. I am calling chroniclers to rise up and write down what I show them in the day and what they dream at night. For I am releasing My anointing on a new generation of seers and scribes and they will be faithful to write down the visions, the visitations, and the views of the future I show them.

> They will be articulate with a pen and in speech. Their tongues shall be pens of ready writers. They will distribute what I show them, what they have scribed and chronicled, far and wide through digital media that reaches the nations of the earth. I am calling the scribes to describe My heart, My ways, My precepts, My principles, My presence, My love, and more through the power of the pen and the anointing of My Spirit. I am looking for a few good scribes.

— *Prayer* —

Father, in the name of Jesus, inspire me to record the revelations You share with my heart so I can release then to Your Bride with accuracy even down to the minute details of Your prophetic instructions. Make me a strategic scribe who stewards Kingdom revelation.

Releasing the Prophet's Reward

"He who receives a prophet in the name of a prophet shall receive a prophet's reward. And he who receives a righteous man in the name of a righteous man shall receive a righteous man's reward" (Matthew 10:41 NKJV).

Not everyone is going to receive your prophetic ministry, but there is a reward for those who do. The prophet's reward is the prophetic word itself. The reward is the gift of edification, exhortation, comfort, knowledge, warning, direction, correction, inspiration, or whatever else the message of God through the prophet intends to accomplish. God loves the person so much that He chooses to speak to them through His messengers.

Understanding this truth, a true prophet wants people to receive their ministry for the glory of God and the advancement of the Kingdom through the lives of the people who hear the word. A true prophet wants people to receive their prophetic utterance with faith that inspires action to do what the Lord wants to do in them and through them. A true prophet wants to see people receive the fullness of God's reward, not for his own reputation but for God's glory.

With this in mind, what does that mean for prophetic operations? If you are delivering God's reward, you want to handle it with care. You want to be careful how you say the words and be mindful of God's timing of releasing the words. Proverbs 15:23 tells us, "And a word spoken in due season, how good it is!" (NJKV). And Proverbs 25:11-13 advises:

> *A word fitly spoken is like apples of gold in settings of silver. Like an earring of gold and an ornament of fine gold is a wise rebuker to an obedient ear. Like the cold of snow in time of harvest is a faithful messenger to those who send him, for he refreshes the soul of his masters* (NKJV).

When God gives you a reward for someone, handle it with care. If it is a difficult word, take your time with it. Make intercession over the person so they will be prepared to accept the reward of the word of the Lord when it might come as an unwelcome correction. Prophetic announcements are often shocking, and corrections can be discouraging if they are not delivered in love.

— *Prayer* —

Father, in the name of Jesus, help me do my part to make sure the people I minister to receive the prophet's reward. Help me deliver prophecy in a way they can receive it. Would You give me the grace that was on the prophet's Nathan's life to deliver Your Word with kid gloves?

A Black and White Perspective

"Moreover, they shall teach My people the difference between the holy and the common, and teach them to distinguish between the unclean and the clean" (Ezekiel 44:23 NASB).

A key role of the prophet is to separate the profane from the holy. Every prophet I know has a black and white perspective. Sin is sin, with no gray areas. We can't afford to shut our eyes to profanity, or worse yet engage in it. We have to separate ourselves so we can bring a spiritual winnowing that separates the holy from the profane and discerns the wheat from the tares.

The Lord tells us to be holy even as He is holy (see 1 Pet. 1:16). To be holy is to be devoted entirely to God and His work, to be consecrated for His purposes. The word "profane" simply means unsanctified, secular, or irreverent. It doesn't take a prophet to discern the difference, yet it does take a prophetic anointing to separate the holy from the profane when the two have grown up together. This is part of the prophetic anointing to root out (see Jer. 1).

But that's just one way to separate the holy from the profane. The second way prevents demonic strongholds in the first place by calling a sin a sin before the devil takes up residence in the believer's soul. Prophets carry a grace that convicts people of their sin.

We know that Jonah went to Nineveh with a message of repentance. The people believed God, and proclaimed a fast, and put on sackcloth, from the greatest of them even to the least of them (see Jon. 3). We know that the Lord told Isaiah to "cry aloud...lift up thy voice like a trumpet, and shew my people their transgression" (Isa. 58:1 KJV). And we know that the Lord told Ezekiel to "cause Jerusalem to know her abominations" (Ezek. 16:1-2 KJV).

How can you separate the holy from the profane if your own heart is impure? If you have sin in a certain area of your life, how can you boldly speak against it? We've seen some of the staunchest advocates against abominations have been found out to be partakers of the same sin. That brings a reproach on the name of Jesus and pain to those who trusted them.

— *Prayer* —

Father, in the name of Jesus, I want to be holy even as You are holy. Help me rid my life of besetting sins so I can speak boldly to the profanity in my generation, spurring repentance with prophetic words of kindness that hate sin but love the peopled trapped in its grip.

Resisting Religion's Attacks

"Even so you also outwardly appear righteous to men, but inside you are full of hypocrisy and lawlessness" (Matthew 23:28 NKJV).

Once I received an email, which is too long to reprint here. In essence, it was a doom and gloom prophet with a directional word insisting I should move to Dallas. The conclusion of the e-mail read, "Also the Lord is bringing true biblical holiness back to the church. Jesus says He wants you to stop cutting your hair short. First Corinthians 11:15, 'But if a woman have long hair, it is a glory to her: for her hair is given her for a covering'" (KJV).

The letter continued, "Jesus is also saying to all His women no more fake hair, painted or fake nails, and no more makeup which as we read in the Bible was used by wicked women. Also no more earrings or jewelry, which were associated with idolatry in the Bible. A watch and wedding ring are all Jesus wants his women and men to wear. We have to be the example of what holiness looks and acts like."

As you can see, the religious spirit manifests in many ways. One of those ways is to focus on the outward appearance rather than the heart. Jesus said, "What sorrow awaits you teachers of religious law and you Pharisees. Hypocrites! For you are so careful to clean the outside of the cup and the dish, but inside you are filthy—full of greed and self-indulgence!" (Matt. 23:25).

Religious spirits are nefariously nasty and accusatory. The spirit of religion works to murder reputations, pervert the revelation of who we are in Christ, put us in bondage to legalism, and much more. We need to discern the operations of this wicked spirit in whatever form it reveals itself and resist it. Religion always attacks prophets. Jesus reminded the religious leaders they were the descendants of those who murdered the prophets (see Matt. 23:31).

The religious spirit is alive and well today. At its extreme, religion denies the reality of modern-day prophets, but religion has also infiltrated the prophetic ministry with extreme behaviors. Ask the Holy Spirit to help you resist religion's attacks against your ministry and your soul, so you don't become like the thing Jesus hated.

— *Prayer* —

Father, in the name of Jesus, deliver me from every root of religion that has been modeled to me. Deliver me from hard, callous, rulemaking, condemning religious mindsets that prevent me from walking—and prophesying—in love.

JANUARY 29

Align to the Cornerstone

"Together, we are his house, built on the foundation of the apostles and the prophets. And the cornerstone is Christ Jesus himself" (Ephesians 2:20).

Ancient buildings were made up of many stones, and all served a purpose. Capstones, for example, served as protective stones at the top of a wall to prevent water damage. Keystones are wedge-shaped stones at the center of arches to make sure the weight of the structure is evenly distributed. Then there's the cornerstone. Every architect knows the cornerstone is the most important stone in any building, ancient or modern.

The cornerstone is the first stone set in the foundation of a building. Every other stone in the foundation is set to or aligned to this stone. Without a cornerstone, the foundation would be unstable. The cornerstone holds the building together. Without it, the structure would collapse. Jesus Christ is the cornerstone of the church—and your life. He can handle the weight and the warfare associated with your prophetic ministry, even when it seems too much for you to carry.

There's a lot of talk about alignment in the Body of Christ—and rightly so. We need proper spiritual alignment just as our vehicles need proper wheel alignment. Without the right alignment, you will have a rougher ride, spend more energy on the journey, and wear yourself out prematurely.

We find the word *alignment* in the New Testament 13 times in the form of the Greek word *katartizo*. According to *The NAS New Testament Greek Lexicon*, it means "to render, i.e. to fit, sound, complete; mend (what has been broken or rent), to repair; to complete; to fit out, equip, put in order, arrange, adjust; and ethically to strengthen, perfect, complete, and make one what he ought to be."

Alignment is a proper positioning. Alignment can bring a birthing. Alignment can bring resurrection. Alignment can bring direction. Alignment can bring restoration. There are many other biblical benefits to alignment, and there's no better alignment than Jesus. As prophets, our lives must be aligned to His will, His ways, and His character. At times, we need an adjustment.

— *Prayer* —

Father, in the name of Jesus, give me a divine adjustment when I am out of line with Your will. Help me to willfully and intentionally adjust my mind, mouth, and attitudes to the Chief Cornerstone. Thank You for being the Rock who holds my foundation steady.

Making Wedding Plans

"He will also go before Him in the spirit and power of Elijah, 'to turn the hearts of the fathers to the children,' and the disobedient to the wisdom of the just, to make ready a people prepared for the Lord" (Luke 1:17 NKJV).

Luke not only records an angelic announcement about the birth and purpose of Jesus to save mankind (see Luke 7:28), he also record's Gabriel's announcement concerning the birth and purpose of John the Baptist to prepare a people for the coming of the Lord. John prepared a people for the first coming of the Messiah.

As modern-day prophets, we are called to prepare a people for Christ's Second Coming. Indeed, prophets are called to prepare a way for the Lord and to prepare people for the Lord. John the Baptist, a transitional prophet who served as the last of the major Old Testament prophets, was called to prepare a way for the Lord, to make His paths straight (see Matt. 3:2-4). Luke 1:17 spells out what this preparation looks like:

It is he who will go as a forerunner before Him in the spirit and power of Elijah, to turn the hearts of the fathers back to the children, and the disobedient to the attitude of the righteous [which is to seek and submit to the will of God]—in order to make ready a people [perfectly] prepared [spiritually and morally] for the Lord (AMP).

John the Baptist was a messenger, and this was his message: "Repent!" Repentance isn't saying sorry. Repentance comes at the revelation of a wrong and the damage the wrong has done to our relationship with God. Repentance is changing the way we think, which eventually leads to a change of heart because we become what we think about (see Prov. 23:7).

The prophet prepares the Bride of Christ for the Bridegroom by preparing their spirit and their soul. The spiritual preparation is prophetic wisdom and revelation in the knowledge of Him that strengthens their inner man. And the soul must be prepared to resist the temptations of the enemy to live a carnal life that may cause them to ultimately deny Him before He returns.

Of course, the prophet who prepares a people must first himself be prepared by God. Ask the Lord to examine your heart and show you any areas where your soul is not aligned with His will. Then you will have the authority to call others to repentance in the right spirit.

— *Prayer* —

Father, in the name of Jesus, help me to examine myself and reveal to me any area of my soul that is not aligned with Your will for my life. Prepare me to be one who prepares Your people for Your wedding feast. Ready me to convincingly declare Your Second Coming.

Where's Your Well?

"Jesus said to her, 'Go, call your husband, and come here.' The woman answered and said, 'I have no husband.' Jesus said to her, 'You have well said, 'I have no husband,' for you have had five husbands, and the one whom you now have is not your husband; in that you spoke truly.' The woman said to Him, 'Sir, I perceive that You are a prophet'" (John 4:16-19 NKJV).

These verses come from the woman at the well's encounter with Jesus. Jesus started the conversation, but He didn't enter the dialogue announcing Himself as a prophet. He appeared at first to be a thirsty Jew asking a Samaritan for a drink of water. That got her attention because Jews and Samaritans didn't mix well, and she entered into a prophetic dimension she wasn't expecting.

Instead of pointing to Himself, Jesus pointed back to the Father: "If you only knew the gift God has for you and who you are speaking to, you would ask me, and I would give you living water" (John 4:10). The woman didn't catch on to His prophetic innuendos. All she knew was He didn't have a rope or a bucket. She even insulted Him, asking, "And besides, do you think you're greater than our ancestor Jacob, who gave us this well? How can you offer better water than he and his sons and his animals enjoyed?" (John 4:12).

Jesus wasn't offended and didn't assert His prophethood. He kept speaking prophetic truths, sharing, "Anyone who drinks this water will soon become thirsty again. But those who drink the water I give will never be thirsty again. It becomes a fresh, bubbling spring within them, giving them eternal life" (John 4:13-14). Finally, she decided she wanted some of the water, and that's when Jesus started revealing His knowledge about her life and her husbands.

What's the point? Jesus ministered as a prophet without a title. He wasn't concerned with a crowd. He went after the one. He didn't care that she didn't know He was a prophet and didn't feel the need to announce Himself or prove Himself. He was manifesting spiritual gifts, but He wasn't trying to make a name for Himself. He always pointed back to the Gift Giver, His heavenly Father. Jesus did most of His ministry outside the temple, which is the equivalent today of the church. In that context, there are times we need to drop our titles but keep using our gifts.

— *Prayer* —

Father, in the name of Jesus, put me in the path of people who need a word from a prophet, even if they don't know what a prophet is. Show me people into whom I can speak prophetic words of life. Lead me to my well of ministry in the marketplace.

FEBRUARY

"If I could speak all the languages of earth and of angels, but didn't love others, I would only be a noisy gong or a clanging cymbal. If I had the gift of prophecy, and if I understood all of God's secret plans and possessed all knowledge, and if I had such faith that I could move mountains, but didn't love others, I would be nothing. If I gave everything I have to the poor and even sacrificed my body, I could boast about it; but if I didn't love others, I would have gained nothing" (1 Corinthians 13:1-3).

A Prophet to Prophets

"Before David got up the next morning, the word of the Lord had come to Gad the prophet, David's seer" (2 Samuel 24:11 NIV).

Maybe you've heard it said, "She's a prophet to prophets." Have you ever wondered what that meant? The one who is a prophet to prophets is greatly gifted with strong character and maturity that gives them the ability, the right, and even the responsibility to speak and prophesy into the lives of other prophets.

I've said many times every prophet needs a pastor, someone to demonstrate the Shepherd's heart. Well, I believe every prophet needs another prophet in their life because nobody understands a prophet like a prophet. Prophets need to be edified, comforted, and exhorted. Prophets need to be encouraged, lifted up, and prayed for. Sometimes, prophets need to be corrected privately before their public ministry suffers.

King David was a prophet and had prophets around him. David had three prophets around him at different stages of his life. Those prophets were Samuel, Nathan, and Gad. Samuel was a prophet to David in his youth, the one who edified him by anointing him as king in the presence of his family (see 1 Sam. 16). Later, when David was running from the wicked Saul, he ran to Samuel for advice (see 1 Sam. 19:18).

Samuel eventually died and God assigned David a new prophet. Gad the seer was David's peer. We see Gad providing David with prophetic counsel before he was king. Saul was still chasing him through the wilderness, but with Gad's help David escaped. Later, though, Gad delivered a prophetic rebuke to David for taking a census (see 2 Sam. 24:13).

God sent Nathan the prophet to help David the prophet. Nathan was younger than David and had the tough assignment of rebuking him over his sin with Bathsheba (see 2 Sam. 12) and prophetically forbidding him to build the temple (see 2 Sam. 2).

Every prophet needs a prophet who can guide them and, when necessary, correct them. As you mature, you should be a prophet's prophet. Ask the Holy Spirit to send the right prophets into your life and to send you into the life of the right prophets.

— *Prayer* —

Father, in the name of Jesus, help me remember my fellow prophets and their need for strategic counsel and prophetic insight into their lives—and help me receive the ministry of the prophet so I can tap more fully into the prophet's reward.

Great Awakening Prophets

"The Sovereign Lord has given me his words of wisdom, so that I know how to comfort the weary. Morning by morning he wakens me and opens my understanding to his will" (Isaiah 50:4).

God woke me up at midnight in April 2007 and told me He was bringing a great awakening to America. He later told me that awakening would spill out beyond the borders of my nation and sweep through other nations. I've been prophesying those words ever since. By some measure, I'm an awakening prophet. And I'm not alone.

At a time when some prophets are releasing curses on their nations, a new breed of prophetic people—some younger, some older—are declaring and decreeing the greatest-ever great awakening. It's an awakening that will touch the nations of the earth with great signs, wonders, and miracles—and mass salvations and deliverances—that demonstrate Jesus is alive.

As you've discerned, I call these awakening prophets. Awakening prophets are equipping a generation of prophetic people who see, hear, and say what the Lord is doing in their cities and regions—and have the persistence to contend to the end for more than a summer revival. They have the wherewithal to intercede for transformation and reformation that only comes from a spiritual awakening.

These awakening prophets trumpet a call for repentance mixed with hope for God's mercy that triumphs over judgment (see James 2:13). They are prophetic messengers who recall nation-shaking revivals like the First and Second Great Awakening, Azusa Street, the Voice of Healing Movement, and the Toronto Blessing and fervently cry out, "Do it again, Lord!"

Despite all the talk of awakening, some prophets are holding to words of judgment—and even cursing America with foretelling of disasters that are breeding fear in the hearts of believers. I do believe God gives us warning of impending judgments, but He doesn't give us a spirit of fear. The awakening prophet acknowledges judgment when it comes but stands on the promise of the coming awakening. What kind of prophet are you? Even Isaiah, a prophet who pronounced much doom and gloom, was known as a prophet of hope.

— *Prayer* —

Father, in the name of Jesus, wake me up! Help me see what You want to do in my city, my state, and my nation—and the nations of the earth. Help me agree with Your glory covering the earth like the water covers the sea. Amid judgment, help me remember grace and mercy.

Your Invitation to Revelation

"You shall hang up the veil under the clasps, and shall bring in the ark of the testimony there within the veil; and the veil shall serve for you as a partition between the holy place and the holy of holies" (Exodus 26:33 NASB 1995).

Few visit the holy of holies, but prophets must make a habit of getting on their faces before a holy God in anticipation of an invitation. In the holy of holies, His glory surrounds you as He reveals His heart to you. You feel more than alive. You feel like you've entered into another dimension—and you have. When you get there, time seems to stand still, and you never want to leave.

When Jesus died on the cross, God supernaturally tore the veil in the temple from top to bottom (see Matt. 27:50-51). Man was no longer separated from entering the presence of God. We can have confidence to enter the holy place through the blood of Jesus (see Heb. 10:19-20).

I heard the Lord say: "Press and keep on pressing because pressing is not for the faint of heart. You cannot just press one time like you'd press a button, as if you've waved a magic wand, and expect your life to change. It's not about pressing a button. It's about pressing past your flesh. It's about pressing past your past. It's about pressing past all those things I am putting before you, showing you, to get rid of them."

Some are content to stay in the outer court. Some dare to move into the inner court. Fewer press into the holy of holies. In the holy of holies, you find yourself engulfed by the presence, power, and love of God. You freely surrender your will, your pain, your past temptations, your fear—and everything that hinders love—to the Almighty One.

This is the place where deep truly cries unto deep (see Ps. 42:7). This is the sacred place where your spirit communes with His Spirit at a level your mind cannot comprehend. Mere words cannot do justice to the holy of holies experience.

Of course, entrance costs something. It requires you to shift your appetites, to lay aside childish things, set aside carnal desires, and seek Him with your whole heart (see Jer. 29:13). But the reward is worth the price. Will you accept the challenge? Will you RSVP?

— *Prayer* —

Father, in the name of Jesus, give me the grace to press past my flesh and into Your Spirit. I want to make my home in the holy of holies, not just visiting Your presence but abiding in Your heart all the days of my life. I am awaiting Your invitation.

Seeking Prophetic Feedback

"Let the prophets speak two or three, and let the other judge" (1 Corinthians 14:29 KJV).

In 1 Corinthians 14:29, Paul the apostle wrote the Spirit-inspired words above. Oh, that we would follow this protocol! The word "judge" in this verse comes from the Greek Word *diakrino*. According to *The KJV New Testament Greek Lexicon*, it means "to separate, make a distinction, discriminate, to try, decide, to determine, give judgment, and decide a dispute."

Other translations of 1 Corinthians 14:29 say, "the others should weigh carefully what is said" (NIV); "let the others evaluate what is said" (NLT); "let the others discern" (BLB); "Everyone else should decide whether what each person said is right or wrong" (GW); "let the others pass judgment" (NASB 1995); "while the rest pay attention and weigh and discern what is said" (AMPC).

Benson Commentary says, "Let the prophets speak—In succession; two or three—And not more, at one meeting; and let the others judge—And compare one doctrine with another for the further improvement of all. Or, the sense may be, Let the others, who have the gift of discerning spirits, discern whether they have spoken by inspiration or by private suggestion."

This is a serious issue and a serious command with serious words.

Who are these "others" of whom Paul speaks? These "others" are other prophets. While you can ask your pastor or wise elders to judge your prophecy, prophets ideally need other prophets to judge their significant prophetic utterances. That's because prophets don't just walk in an anointing, they stand in an office. It's a higher ranking in the spirit and a different level of hearing.

Of course, even a true prophet can miss it, but letting the other prophets judge keeps you from missing it in front of the masses and helps you gain understanding into what went wrong. On the flipside, the best ones to judge your serious words are other prophets who may be hearing the same thing or who can add wise insights that help you communicate God's heart in a way the greatest number of people will receive it.

— *Prayer* —

Father, in the name of Jesus, lead me to prophets who can help me obey 1 Corinthians 14:29. Show me who to share my prophetic intelligence with to get trusted Holy Ghost feedback that inspires in me greater confidence in my gift or corrects me before I make a mistake.

Accepting the Love Challenge

"Prophecy and speaking in unknown languages and special knowledge will become useless. But love will last forever!" (1 Corinthians 13:8)

A few months before the 2020 pandemic swept the nations, the Holy Spirit told me to study love for an entire year. I didn't wait to find out why, I just started studying. A few weeks later, He told me to challenge the Body of Christ to walk in love. The result was *The Love Challenge*, months of teaching on what true love is and how we should respond.

God is love; therefore, everything He does is motivated by love. God can't think, say, or do anything that is not inspired by love because it would violate His nature and His character. God never changes, so He will never stop loving us.

Prophets can be hard-edged at times. I was told early in my walk with God that prophets bite. However, just because our words can bite (convict) doesn't give us the excuse of being harsh. In fact:

> *Love is patient and kind. Love is not jealous or boastful or proud or rude. It does not demand its own way. It is not irritable, and it keeps no record of being wronged. It does not rejoice about injustice but rejoices whenever the truth wins out. Love never gives up, never loses faith, is always hopeful, and endures through every circumstance* (1 Corinthians 13:4-7).

Those verses should mark your prophetic ministry. God, who is love, is conforming us into the image of Christ, who is love, by the Holy Spirit, who is love. As you are rooted more deeply in love, you will flow more accurately in the prophetic.

Consider Paul's words in 1 Corinthians 13:2: "If I had the gift of prophecy, and if I understood all of God's secret plans and possessed all knowledge, and if I had such faith that I could move mountains, but didn't love others, I would be nothing." We can walk in all manner of revelation and prophesy prolifically, but if love is not our motivation we may as well be quiet.

— *Prayer* —

Father, in the name of Jesus, teach me to love. Teach me to walk in love and to prophesy in love. Teach me to live, move, and have my being in love. Let love always motivate my prophetic ministry in all of its manifestations.

If You Claim to Be a Prophet...

"If you claim to be a prophet or think you are spiritual, you should recognize that what I am saying is a command from the Lord himself" (1 Corinthians 14:37).

The apostle Paul wrote a long letter to the church at Corinth explaining spiritual gifts, urging unity in the spirit, expressing the importance of love, explaining guidelines for tongues and prophecy, and offering outlines for order in prophetic ministry. At the conclusion of this important teaching he wrote these words, "If you claim to be a prophet or think you are spiritual, you should recognize that what I am saying is a command from the Lord himself" (1 Cor. 14:37).

Prophets need to be especially careful to discern and obey the commands of the Lord. Prophets are held to a higher standard of obedience because they are speaking on behalf of God Himself. Disobedient prophets are not credible prophets.

The prophet Samuel understood this and tried to live it out and share it with others. He told Saul, "What is more pleasing to the Lord: your burnt offerings and sacrifices or your obedience to his voice? Listen! Obedience is better than sacrifice, and submission is better than offering the fat of rams" (1 Sam. 15:22). Saul prophesied among the prophets more than once, but his disobedience caused him to lose his anointing.

Obedience is a baseline trait for prophets. And rebellion is as the sin of witchcraft (see 1 Sam. 15:23). I am convinced the practice of prophetic witchcraft is rooted in a rebellious heart—and God strictly forbids witchcraft. When prophets begin operating in witchcraft, they are in danger of walking on the broad path that leads to destruction. Remember Jesus' words in Matthew 7:21-23 and let them put the fear of the Lord in your soul:

> *Not everyone who calls out to me, "Lord! Lord!" will enter the Kingdom of Heaven. Only those who actually do the will of my Father in heaven will enter. On judgment day many will say to me, "Lord! Lord! We prophesied in your name and cast out demons in your name and performed many miracles in your name." But I will reply, "I never knew you. Get away from me, you who break God's laws."*

Again, obedience is a baseline trait for prophets. Rebellious or unwilling prophets do not finish well in Scripture. Consider Jonah, whose disobedience landed him in the belly of a whale and his inability to accept the will of the Lord left him sitting under a tree wishing he was dead. There is no joy or peace in disobedience. Ask the Lord to give you the grace of obedience.

— *Prayer* —

Father, in the name of Jesus, help me see obedience like You see it—and like Samuel saw it. Give me a revelation of how my prophetic power is tied to my heart-felt obedience, and give me the grace of obedience so I can follow Jesus wholly. I repent of all disobedience.

The Prophet's Inescapable Reality

"For examples of patience in suffering, dear brothers and sisters, look at the prophets who spoke in the name of the Lord" (James 5:10).

James, inspired by the Holy Spirit, made a specific connection between prophets and suffering. Many prophets wish we could scratch James 5:10 out of the Bible, but we have to accept this truth along with other truths we prefer not to quote. The reality is, if you want to go deeper into prophetic realms, you are going to suffer.

The Greek word "suffering" in that verse is *kakopatheia*, which specifically means the suffering of evil, i.e. trouble, distress, afflicted, according to *The KJV New Testament Greek Lexicon*. Suffering implies pain—and in prophetic ministry it is both inevitable and unavoidable. It can't be escaped. It has to be endured.

The Passion Translation of this verse reveals: "My brothers and sisters, take the prophets as your mentors. They have prophesied in the name of the Lord and it brought them great sufferings, yet they patiently endured."

Suffering is part of the prophet's making process, and it never ends. Prophets are rejected, persecuted, misunderstood, and more. When you go through seasons of suffering, understand there is a promotion waiting on the other side of your pain.

God moves us from glory to glory (see 2 Cor. 3:18), but the prophet suffers between glories. Suffering is an indication of the depths God wants to take you to. I've never suffered so much in my life since I went into prophetic ministry, and if you've walked in the prophetic life for any length of time you can probably say the same.

When you are suffering, try to put it into perspective. Jesus suffered more than any prophet who walked the earth, and other prophets like Jeremiah, Isaiah, and Micaiah endured plenty of suffering in their own right. Like Jesus in the midst of His suffering, try to keep your eyes on the prize. The greater the suffering, the greater the glory. Ask God for the grace to endure the pain, and soon you will find yourself walking in greater accuracy, greater anointing, and greater authority.

— *Prayer* —

Father, in the name of Jesus, help me suffer with style and a smile on my face, rejoicing because I know that suffering is working things out of me and working things in me so You can do more of Your prophetic work through me. Give me perspective in the face of my suffering.

The Weeping Prophets

"A time to cry and a time to laugh. A time to grieve and a time to dance" (Ecclesiastes 3:4).

Jeremiah was the original weeping prophet. We see the word *weep* over 30 times in the Book of Jeremiah alone. We haven't even considered his other book, Lamentations, which means "expressing grief." Jeremiah mourned for idolatrous Israel in the midst of harsh words of judgment he knew would come to pass. Jeremiah was ordained in Jeremiah 1, and by Jeremiah 4:19-20 he was weeping:

> *My heart, my heart—I writhe in pain! My heart pounds within me! I cannot be still. For I have heard the blast of enemy trumpets and the roar of their battle cries. Waves of destruction roll over the land, until it lies in complete desolation. Suddenly my tents are destroyed; in a moment my shelters are crushed.*

And again in Jeremiah 8:18, "My grief is beyond healing; my heart is broken."

He wept so much, God twice told him to stop. God said, "Pray no more for these people, Jeremiah. Do not weep or pray for them, and don't beg me to help them, for I will not listen to you" (Jer. 7:16). And again, "Pray no more for these people, Jeremiah. Do not weep or pray for them, for I will not listen to them when they cry out to me in distress" (Jer. 11:14).

Jeremiah wasn't the only weeping prophet. Samuel mourned for Saul so long that God told him, too, to stop. David was known for watering his bed with tears (see Ps. 6:6). Even Jesus wept (see John 11:35). Weeping is part of the prophet's prayer life. The very definition of "weep" in these Scriptures is a ringing cry of entreaty or supplication.

You may not be a weeper in the natural, but when the Spirit of God's grief comes over you, tears may fall from your eyes. Don't quench the spirit. Sometimes your prayers look like tears.

— *Prayer* —

Father, in the name of Jesus, thank You for the gift of tears. Help me to yield to Your Spirit to express the grief of Your heart, but not to get swept away with the grief of my own heart in the face of spiritual tragedies. Teach me how to steward weeping and travail.

Casting Out the Miriam Spirit

"Miriam the prophetess, the sister of Aaron, took the timbrel in her hand; and all the women went out after her with timbrels and with dances. And Miriam answered them, 'Sing to the Lord, for He has triumphed gloriously! The horse and his rider He has thrown into the sea!'" (Exodus 15:20-21 NKJV).

Miriam is one of the few female prophets mentioned in the Old Testament—but we can learn plenty from her victories and defeats. Unfortunately, she is often remembered best for siding with her brother Aaron against Moses. Moses' siblings spoke against the man of God because he married a Cushite woman. Numbers 12 recounts the event in which the Lord's anger burned against them and Miriam became leprous as snow and was shut out of the camp for seven days. Imagine the shame!

Earlier, in Exodus 15, we saw Miriam in a better light. She led the women in praise and worship to the God who led them out of Egypt. She broke out into a prophetic song of victory. She was prophesying with the timbrels and with dancing, singing, "Sing to the Lord, for he has triumphed gloriously; he has hurled both horse and rider into the sea." We see in churches today prophetic expressions that glorify God as did the prophetess Miriam.

How did Miriam go from singing the song of the Lord in Exodus to being cast out of the camp just a few years later? How did she go from prophesying celebratory words to criticizing the man Moses, whom God used as a great prophet and deliverer?

Unfortunately, Miriam regressed in her relationship with Jehovah while she was in the wilderness. Like many of the Israelites, she adopted a wilderness mentality and adopted the habit of complaining against Moses. She allowed the pressure of the wilderness to pollute her speech. Prophets, no matter how long you are in the wilderness remember this: you won't complain your way out.

Prophets—or prophetesses—you have a choice what you do with your mouth. You can use it to judge and curse people or bless and honor God. You can use it to prophesy God's will or criticize other prophets. Ask the Holy Spirit to deliver your mouth from complaining so you can purify your prophetic flow.

— *Prayer* —

Father, in the name of Jesus, help me stay strong in my wilderness seasons so I don't curse what You have blessed. Teach me to keep my mouth off my leaders when I don't get the opportunities I want so I don't operate out of a Miriam spirit.

FEBRUARY 10

Dig a Well

"And Isaac dug again the wells of water which they had dug in the days of Abraham his father, for the Philistines had stopped them up after the death of Abraham" (Genesis 26:18 NKJV).

Because of my international travels, when I am on the road I don't always have the time to press into the Word or wait up on the Lord for hours upon hours like I do when I am home. Indeed, long flights, jet lag, and busy ministry schedules make lengthy private devotions a challenge.

That said, I have learned a key to sustaining a deep, accurate prophetic ministry despite the very real challenges of travel: I dig a well while I'm home so I can draw from it when my pace is more hectic. Then I prime the pump on the well while I'm on the road. Let me explain.

Your well is your capacity to receive prophetic intelligence from God and pour it out to others. The reality is you have a well within you. Praying in tongues expands your spiritual capacity. It adds depth to your well. So does meditating on the Word of God, praise and worship, or just sitting in His presence, where you can tap into fullness of joy, peace, courage, or whatever else you need on your journey.

But let's focus on praying in tongues, because it's easy enough to do that anywhere you are. It's one way you can literally pray without ceasing (see 1 Thess. 5:16-18). Jesus said:

> He who believes in Me [who cleaves to and trusts in and relies on Me] as the Scripture has said, From his innermost being shall flow [continuously] springs and rivers of living water. But He was speaking here of the Spirit, Whom those who believed (trusted, had faith) in Him were afterward to receive. For the [Holy] Spirit had not yet been given, because Jesus was not yet glorified (raised to honor) (John 7:38-39 AMPC).

The enemy wants to stop up your well with business, stress, fatigue, or even fleshly desires. He'll do anything he can to dry up your well. We see the concept in the life of Isaac. He kept trying to re-dig the wells of his father Abraham, but the locals kept tempting him into strife. Isaac persevered despite enemy opposition and succeeded in cultivating a well that would leave him and his camp well-watered. Make digging a well your priority in the quiet times so you can draw from its depths in the busy times.

— *Prayer* —

Father, in the name of Jesus, remind me to take advantage of the time I have in Your presence. Remind me to pray in tongues, knowing that I am expanding my capacity to receive from You so I can continue to minister to Your people when the pace seems too frenzied to dig.

Overcoming Prophetic Overwhelm

"From the ends of the earth, I cry to you for help when my heart is overwhelmed" (Psalm 61:2).

When God called me into prophetic ministry, I was completely overwhelmed by the reality of what that meant. How would that change my life? What would be required of me? What kind of warfare would I get from the enemy—or even a church world that still largely does not accept prophets. Why me?

Sometimes your calling or assignment seems overwhelming—even when we are the one who cried out for the new thing. When God called me into prophetic ministry, He told me, "Think back to the petitions you have made of Me and this won't seem so overwhelming. You showed yourself willing. I will make you able. Lean and depend on Me and not on your own understanding. Thus do the prophets."

"Overwhelm" is an enemy I've fought many times over the years. The enemy likes to work in our naturally overwhelming circumstances to apply spiritual pressure. When that spiritual pressure mounts, too often we look for a way of escape rather than trusting in the Lord for His sufficient grace to meet the situation at hand.

Don't feel ashamed in your battle against overwhelm. David understood these feelings all too well. He once wrote:

> *My heart is severely pained within me, and the terrors of death have fallen upon me. Fearfulness and trembling have come upon me, and horror has overwhelmed me. So I said, "Oh, that I had wings like a dove! I would fly away and be at rest. Indeed, I would wander far off, and remain in the wilderness. Selah. I would hasten my escape from the windy storm and tempest"* (Psalm 55:4-8 NKJV).

The first step in battling overwhelm is to recognize it and acknowledge the situation you find yourself in. Denying feelings of overwhelm won't help you conquer your flesh or the devil. Once you've acknowledged the reality of an overwhelmed heart, you can work with the Holy Spirit to get to the root of these feelings.

What is causing this overwhelm, really? Is the enemy blowing it out of proportion? Is it really as bad as it looks, or is this pressure demonic? Put your circumstances—and your emotions—into perspective. Is there anything you can do right now in the natural to relieve some of the burdens you feel?

— *Prayer* —

Father, in the name of Jesus, help me discern the root cause of this feeling of overwhelm. I know You will never allow more to come upon me than I can bear. You are my way of escape.

Standing Before Kings

"If you are uniquely gifted in your work, you will rise and be promoted. You won't be held back—you'll stand before kings!" (Proverbs 22:29 TPT).

When I was ordained, Bishop Bill Hamon prophesied over me that I would stand before kings. That's a big word! I did have the opportunity to prophesy over a queen once and sat in the quarters of a president of a foreign nation and made decrees. I did prophesy to a governor once in his mansion.

While these are not everyday occurrences in our times, standing before governors and kings was not an unusual circumstance in the lives of Old Testament prophets. Samuel stood before Israel's first king, Saul. Nathan and other prophets stood before King David. Elijah stood before King Ahab. And the list goes on.

Today, there are fewer kings in the earth, but we translate the notion of prophesying before kings to mean those in high authority. Not every prophet will stand before governors or kings—but some prophets will. Consider the trust the Lord would need to place in you to give a prophetic direction to a governor or king. The Lord trusted Gad—and David, who had been anointed king over Israel, also trusted his words.

How do you earn the privilege to prophesy to governors and kings? You don't. God has to appoint you to that level of authority. However, you can be diligent in the Father's business. Proverbs 22:29 says, "Do you see a man who excels in his work? He will stand before kings; he will not stand before unknown men" (NKJV). In the last days, Jesus said His disciples would be "brought before governors and kings for My sake, as a testimony to them and to the Gentiles" (Matt. 10:18 NKJV) in the context of persecution.

Standing before governors and kings is not something you should set your heart on. You can't make yourself a prophet to the nations or a prophet to presidents or a prophet to prime ministers. Lay aside any prophetic ministry ambitions that distract your heart from God's true purpose for you. You don't want to enter into a realm He hasn't called you because you won't have the grace to walk there. Excel in your God-given prophetic ministry and leave the rest up to Him.

— *Prayer* —

Father, in the name of Jesus, prepare me to prophesy at the highest levels at which You've called me to operate. Teach me scriptural truths and practical protocols that will prepare me to speak a word in due season to someone in high ranks of authority.

Guarding Your Voice

"Once when Jezebel had tried to kill all the Lord's prophets, Obadiah had hidden 100 of them in two caves. He put fifty prophets in each cave and supplied them with food and water" (1 Kings 18:4).

Before I started walking in prophetic ministry or even understood the call of God on my life, I had a run-in with Jezebel in the form of a man who was stalking me. (Yes, men can operate in a Jezebel spirit the same as women.)

I met this young man at my church and he quickly decided I was the one for him. Instead of pursuing a healthy relationship, he became controlling. At one point when I didn't call him back, he stealthily creeped around my condo waiting for me to come home at night so he could talk to me. It was actually a frightening experience to see him pop out from behind the wall.

Because he refused to stop the controlling behavior, the church leaders excommunicated him. Then they explained to me Jezebel was trying to take me out before I could even get started. I didn't even know there was such a thing as a Jezebel spirit and certainly did not understand how it operated. Many still don't.

However, if you've walked in prophetic ministry any length of time, you have probably caught on to the reality that Jezebel wants to cut off your voice. Jesus warned us the enemy comes to steal, kill, and destroy (see John 10:10). That's the agenda of every demon, but Jezebel does it through seduction. Jezebel, at its essence, is a seducing spirit (see Rev. 2:20).

Dogs ate the remains of the wicked Queen Jezebel mentioned in this verse but make no mistake—the spirit of Jezebel is alive and well. I've written several books about this spirit and its many facets, including the *Spiritual Warrior's Guide to Defeating Jezebel*, *Satan's Deadly Trio*, and *Jezebel's Puppets*. Every prophet needs to get informed and equipped about the strategies and tactics of this spirit.

The bottom line—Jezebel wants you to keep your mouth shut. This spirit doesn't want you to release the word of the Lord. If Jezebel cannot shut your mouth, this spirit will work overtime to pervert the prophetic voice you carry so that you will lack the credibility you need to bring true reform or lead people into true repentance.

— *Prayer* —

Father, in the name of Jesus, show me any open doors in my life the spirit of Jezebel could creep in. If there are open doors through hurts and wounds, heal me. And, Lord, show me if I am operating with any Jezebelic tendencies so I can repent. I want nothing to do with Jezebel.

God's Love Language

"But anyone who does not love does not know God, for God is love" (1 John 4:8).

Some say prophets have a hard edge. I was once warned that prophets bite. While it's true that God uses prophets to deliver hard words at times, mature prophets walk in love and minister in love. As I write in my book, *The Making of a Prophet*:

> When the true prophetic manifests, it is manifests in love. Prophets who walk in love—patience, kindness, not envious, not boastful or proud, not dishonoring others, not self-seeking, not easily angered, quick to forgive, not delighting in evil but rejoicing in truth, protecting, trusting, hoping and persevering—cannot ultimately fail. And they will grow in grace and maturity much more quickly.

Paul the apostle spoke to the importance of prophets walking in love: "If I had the gift of prophecy, and if I understood all of God's secret plans and possessed all knowledge, and if I had such faith that I could move mountains, but didn't love others, I would be nothing" (1 Cor. 13:2). Meditate on that. You can be the most accurate prophet in the world with the deepest revelations and the most spectacular encounters, but if you don't have love none of it really matters.

Love motivates every thought God thinks, every action God takes, and every word He speaks. God cannot operate contrary to love because God is love. If God motivates your prophetic ministry, love will mark your walk. What does love look like? Paul offers us an outline in 1 Corinthians 13:4-8:

> *Love suffers long and is kind; love does not envy; love does not parade itself, is not puffed up; does not behave rudely, does not seek its own, is not provoked, thinks no evil; does not rejoice in iniquity, but rejoices in the truth; bears all things, believes all things, hopes all things, endures all things. Love never fails. But whether there are prophecies, they will fail; whether there are tongues, they will cease; whether there is knowledge, it will vanish away* (NKJV).

Ask the Holy Spirit to help you live, move, and have your being in love.

— *Prayer* —

Father, in the name of Jesus, make me into a prophet of love. Deliver me from anything that hinders love. Show me Your people through the eyes of Your perfect love. Help me prophesy words that demonstrate Your unconditional love to Your people.

What We Can Learn from Micaiah

"Meanwhile, the messenger who went to get Micaiah said to him, 'Look, all the prophets are promising victory for the king. Be sure that you agree with them and promise success'" (1 Kings 22:13).

King Ahab had plenty of prophets around him who were more than willing to tell him anything he wanted to hear. I call them yes-man prophets, or in the case of Jezebel it would be yes-ma'am prophets. Either way, these prophets only prophesied Ahab's political party line. They were only there to prop him up as he pursued his evil desires.

I'm not sure if Ahab's prophets merely wanted to get into his pocket or if they were already on Jezebel's payroll like many others, but the false prophets who surrounded the king warned the true prophet Micaiah to stand in agreement with their misguided words. Micaiah was implored to agree with the yes-men.

Micaiah had two choices: He could cave to the pressure of the company of false prophets who had already primed the king's pump with smooth words he wanted to hear or he could stay true to what the Lord was telling him to say and risk his life. Interestingly enough, at first he went along with the yes men, even though he vowed he would not.

"As surely as the Lord lives, I will say only what the Lord tells me to say." When Micaiah arrived before the king, Ahab asked him, "Micaiah, should we go to war against Ramoth-gilead, or should we hold back?" Micaiah replied sarcastically, "Yes, go up and be victorious, for the Lord will give the king victory!" (1 Kings 22:14-15).

When Ahab pressed him for the truth, Micaiah told the truth. Micaiah prophesied Ahab would die in the battle and was thrown into prison. There will come times when there is pressure to come into agreement with prophecies that you know in your spirit are not true. What will you do in that hour? Pray for the Holy Spirit to engrain a love for the truth so deep in your heart that you will not cave in to the prophetic pressure.

— *Prayer* —

Father, in the name of Jesus, deliver me from the status quo. I don't want to be a puppet prophet, so teach me to handle the pressure and temptation that comes my way to go along with the prophetic crowds and prophesy what I know is false.

Embracing Your Wilderness

"In those days John the Baptist came preaching in the wilderness of Judea" (Matthew 3:1 NKJV).

John the Baptist was prepared in the wilderness. Like John the Baptist and Jesus, prophets must go through a period of preparation before they step into their highest prophetic calling. John the Baptist was a voice crying in the wilderness for many years before he made his public debut. That doesn't mean you can't express your prophetic gift in the wilderness.

I'm convinced some prophets are supposed to live in the wilderness for long seasons. John the Baptist did. Indeed, the wilderness can be a place of fruitful ministry. John never walked through Israel ministering, like Jesus did. He didn't teach in the synagogue (church) or have thousands of people listen to him prophesy from a mountaintop like Jesus. John spent most of his life in the wilderness and did most of his ministry on the edge of the wilderness.

You may think the enemy is keeping you in the wilderness, but it's God who leads you there and God who leads you out. The enemy may meet you there, but he's not putting you in the wilderness or keeping you there longer than God allows. You may keep yourself there by not cooperating with God. But the enemy doesn't have power over your times. Your times are in God's hands.

Yes, there are stages and levels of preparation, and I believe the Lord will use us where we are to do what He can trust us to do. And, yes, I believe that the times have accelerated. Still, sometimes you feel like you are going to die in the wilderness while waiting for your release.

That's how the Israelites felt: "They said to Moses, 'Why did you bring us out here to die in the wilderness? Weren't there enough graves for us in Egypt? What have you done to us? Why did you make us leave Egypt?'" (Exod. 14:11). Don't despise your wilderness. Ask the Holy Spirit what He wants you to learn—and who He wants you to minister to—while you are in your wilderness season.

— *Prayer* —

Father, in the name of Jesus, give me the grace to embrace the wilderness place You've assigned me. Help me not to resent it and try to leave the desert before Your appointed time. Teach me everything You want me to learn before You bring me out with more power.

Binding the Voice of Mammon

"So Gehazi set off after Naaman. When Naaman saw Gehazi running after him, he climbed down from his chariot and went to meet him. 'Is everything all right?' Naaman asked. 'Yes,' Gehazi said, 'but my master has sent me to tell you that two young prophets from the hill country of Ephraim have just arrived. He would like 75 pounds of silver and two sets of clothing to give to them.' 'By all means, take twice as much silver,' Naaman insisted. He gave him two sets of clothing, tied up the money in two bags, and sent two of his servants to carry the gifts for Gehazi" (2 Kings 5:21-23).

In the story of Naaman, we find a proud captain who repented and was healed and a greedy prophet who pursued rewards that never belonged to him. The latter was stricken with an incurable disease of which the former was healed. Indeed, Naaman's humility ultimately saw him cleansed of leprosy and Gehazi's greed made him and his descendants lepers.

Here's what happened: Elisha gave Naaman a healing strategy and it worked, despite his initial prideful objections. When his skin miraculously cleared up, the military officer tried to reward Elisha. The prophet declined. Elisha's servant Gehazi didn't understand his mentor's reasoning and, in his greed, decided to go after the offering himself. Yes, Gehazi lied to Naaman for greedy gain. What happens next is astounding. Elisha pronounced that Naaman's leprosy would cling to Gehazi and his descendants forever.

This is a disturbing story but one that should strike the fear of the Lord in the hearts of prophets, especially those who minister publicly. There is nothing wrong with receiving an offering. There is scriptural basis for this. The issue here is the heart. Gehazi was greedy for gain. Paul the apostle says greed amounts to idolatry (see Col. 3:5).

There are too many prophets in the Body of Christ today with spiritual leprosy that comes from the wrong ministry motive. It can happen to anyone, and we should all beware. Take the time right now to ask the Holy Spirit to keep your heart free from the love of money, greed, and idolatry before you face a temptation like the one that led Gehazi astray.

— *Prayer* —

Father, in the name of Jesus, help me not to forfeit my spiritual inheritance for natural increase. Teach me to keep my mind set on things above and to keep my eyes set on eternity and the great rewards for Your good and faithful servants that outlast the riches of this world.

A Word of Warning

"The Lord, the God of their ancestors, repeatedly sent his prophets to warn them, for he had compassion on his people and his Temple. But the people mocked these messengers of God and despised their words. They scoffed at the prophets until the Lord's anger could no longer be restrained and nothing could be done" (2 Chronicles 36:15-16).

My prophetic ministry was birthed in warnings that nobody wanted to hear. When the pastor saw me coming, he would walk in the other direction because he knew it was likely another word of warning in my mouth.

Thankfully, I was in a ministry that understood they needed to listen anyway—but that's not always the case. God sends warnings about enemy attacks and about sin in the camp hoping His people will respond to His messengers because He has compassion and wants to show forth His mercy.

Unfortunately, many don't receive prophetic warnings. They may wrongly perceive a merciful prophetic warning as judgment and reject it vehemently. They may mock and slander your name for delivering the sure word of the Lord. Either way, they are essentially despising His prophetic word and there are always consequences to willfully despising God's Word.

This is not a new thing. Over and again in Scripture we see people rejecting God's warnings. Jeremiah 25:4 shares, "Again and again the Lord has sent you his servants, the prophets, but you have not listened or even paid attention."

Jesus Himself warned, "Therefore, I am sending you prophets and wise men and teachers of religious law. But you will kill some by crucifixion, and you will flog others with whips in your synagogues, chasing them from city to city" (Matt. 23:34). We are not likely to be hung on a cross, flogged, and chased—but we may meet with severe rejection and word-based persecution for releasing words of warning.

If God has given you a prophetic ministry that includes warnings, be careful when and how you deliver the warnings. You need to be led by the Spirit of God. Be careful with whom you share the warnings. You need only share it with the one to whom God directs you. And, by all means, bathe the warning in intercession that it may be received as our compassionate God intends it.

— *Prayer* —

Father, in the name of Jesus, give me confidence to deliver Your urgent warnings and help me deliver them in a way people will listen. But if they don't listen, help me understand that the blood is not on my hands—and inspire me to keep praying to stop the danger You showed me.

FEBRUARY 19

Find Your Apostle

"As you read what I have written, you will understand my insight into this plan regarding Christ. God did not reveal it to previous generations, but now by his Spirit he has revealed it to his holy apostles and prophets" (Ephesians 3:4-5).

I believe every prophet needs an apostle—and every church needs both apostles and prophets. Ephesians 2:20 tells us apostles and prophets are the foundation of the church. Prophets will be most effective when they find an apostle to work with and vice versa. I once put it this way: Just as Batman needs Robin, apostles need prophets. (We won't argue about which one is Batman and which one is Robin!)

Prophets may announce a new direction. Apostles execute the prophetic word. Don't get me wrong. I am not saying that the tail is wagging the dog. Apostles themselves can be very prophetic and set direction without a prophet. Apostles may get the vision, but many times the prophet gets the direction and timing to guide the vision.

Apostles may wrestle in warfare over the assignment. Prophets discern the root of the attack. Apostles and prophets are both warriors, but they war from different perspectives. The apostle may be looking at the big picture vision and the sweeping details of the attack against it while the prophet will discern the specific roots of the demonic assignment against the vision. This way, the apostle can still pioneer, build, and plant while the prophet stands in the gap with prophetic intelligence to close the open doors.

Apostles pioneer. They have the master plan and go into new territories to advance the Kingdom of God. Prophets see the pitfalls along the road and warn the apostles of the territorial demons they may be up against. Apostles have wisdom. Prophets have revelation. Of course, either office can move in wisdom and revelation, but in a team context the prophet may have the revelation from God and the apostle may have the wisdom to apply the revelation. Apostles strategize. Prophets advise on timing and teams.

We're talking about apostolic-prophetic synergies, and you can't tap into those synergies without an apostle. Not every prophet is fortunate enough to work alongside an apostle in the church, but that doesn't mean you shouldn't pursue apostolic relationships. Ask the Lord to help you find the right apostolic relationships in your life so you can tap into those synergies.

— *Prayer* —

Father, in the name of Jesus, help me find my apostle. Give me a revelation of the synergies I can tap into and the benefits to Your Kingdom when I co-labor with apostolic leaders to bring Your will into the earth. Make me a team player.

How to be an Unpopular Prophet

"You brood of snakes! How could evil men like you speak what is good and right?
For whatever is in your heart determines what you say" (Matthew 12:34).

It seems like every time I talk about sin, the quiet in the church is deafening. You could
hear a pin drop. Thankfully, my congregation is not afraid of the topic, even though it's
uncomfortable. But, of course, my church is not the most popular in South Florida (and
I don't even talk about sin every week!).

Here's the point: True prophets are not always the most popular fivefold ministry gift on
the block because they are bold enough to release a word of the Lord that deals with sin
or that warns the local church of potentially unpleasant circumstances coming down the
proverbial pike. People would prefer a feel-good message from God.

Prophets obsessed by the fear of man or unholy desires will not fulfill God's ultimate
plan. We must be careful, then, not to prophesy according to the party line in order to
establish and preserve popularity in ministry circuits. If we fall into this trap we find ourselves in danger of perverting the gift of God by building walls of religion.

True prophets may not always have the flare, charisma, or appeal of their false twins, but
who said they are supposed to? Jeremiah wasn't the most popular prophet in his time,
nor was Ezekiel in his day. John the Baptist had his head served up on a silver platter for
warning the people of the looming decision between everlasting life and eternal hellfire.
But they were the unadulterated mouthpieces of God. And so it should be.

Prophets are called to separate the profane from the holy. They aren't into candy-coated
prophetic words and they aren't afraid to confront sin. They are jealous for God's Word
and God's Spirit. Nathan confronted David's sin with Bathsheba. Elijah called for a
showdown at Mount Carmel. He took on 850 false prophets all by himself.

Just be sure you're not a fire-and-brimstone prophet. John the beloved said, "But if we
confess our sins to him, he is faithful and just to forgive us our sins and to cleanse us
from all wickedness" (1 John 1:9). Balance out your call for repentance with the truth of
forgiveness. In this way, you'll be popular in heaven where it really counts.

— *Prayer* —

Father, in the name of Jesus, I don't want to be a popular prophet by man's standards. I want to be popular by heaven's standards. Show me how to adjust my
ministry to represent You accurately even if my words fall on deaf ears. Remind
me that I am just the messenger.

Discovering Your Prophetic Jurisdiction

"We will not boast about things done outside our area of authority. We will boast only about what has happened within the boundaries of the work God has given us, which includes our working with you" (2 Corinthians 10:13).

Paul the apostle was very careful not to move beyond the boundaries of his authority and assignment. He was a *sent* one, not a *went* one. That Greek word for "authority" in 2 Corinthians 10:13 is *metron*, which means a measure. In modern language, we would call it a jurisdiction. A jurisdiction is an area in which one has power, right, and authority to operate. In 2 Corinthians 10:14-15 Paul continues:

We are not reaching beyond these boundaries when we claim authority over you, as if we had never visited you. For we were the first to travel all the way to Corinth with the Good News of Christ. Nor do we boast and claim credit for the work someone else has done. Instead, we hope that your faith will grow so that the boundaries of our work among you will be extended.

This is a vital principle in both apostolic and prophetic ministry. Prophet, you need to determine your area of authority by the leadership of the Holy Spirit. You need to understand your *metron*, the boundaries of your ministry, and your jurisdiction by His direction. Paul was careful not to reach beyond those boundaries because he understood the laws of the spirit and the grace of God. He would not presume to minister to people or in places God did not call him to.

Practically speaking, that means understanding what you have a right to publicly prophesy into. Are you a house prophet? A house prophet's authority and ministry is to a local church body. Are you prophet to a people group or a denomination? Are you a prophet to a network or to a nation? If we exceed the God-ordained boundaries for our ministry, two things can happen: we can bring unnecessary warfare on ourselves and we can find ourselves prophesying out of presumption or out of some other spirit.

Ask the Holy Spirit to help you find your prophetic jurisdiction. This is the place in which your gifts will be most effective in ministry. And remember, it may not be the assignment you choose, but when you embrace your prophetic jurisdiction and faithfully exercise your gifts there, God can promote you to another assignment in His timing. You are not likely to start out as a prophet to the nations. But you are a prophet to somebody.

— *Prayer* —

Father, in the name of Jesus, show me who and where my assignment is. Reveal to me the boundaries of my prophetic jurisdiction. I don't want to behave presumptuously and step beyond the measure assigned to me, so help me walk circumspectly.

Diffusing Prophetic Illusions

"For this is a rebellious people, lying children, children who refuse to listen to the law of the Lord; they say to the seers, 'You must not see visions,' and to the prophets, 'You must not prophesy to us right things; speak to us pleasant things, prophesy illusions" (Isaiah 30:9-10 MEV).

God spoke to Isaiah about prophets who prophesy illusions. That's an interesting phraseology. An illusion, by definition, is a misleading image. An illusion, by definition, is something that deceives and misleads people. These verses show us why false prophets are so popular. There are actually people in the church who don't want to know about true visions and only want to hear pleasant things. False prophets are glad to oblige. True prophets speak the truth no matter what the consequences.

In Isaiah's day, he was faced with a rebellious church, a lying people, those who refused to obey the Word of God. Those same people would have stricken the seers blind if they could have—they didn't want to hear about the visions God was giving them because those visions were more likely to convict their hearts than tickle their ears. They wanted the prophets to offer pleasant prophesies—illusions—rather than speaking the truth.

Some translations of these verses use the words, "Tell us lies" (NLT). King James translates it "Prophesy deceits." Brenton says, "speak and report to us another error." The Contemporary English Version says, "Just say what we want to hear, even if it's false." The Douay-Rheims Bible says, "See errors for us." This is shocking! But this is the state of some prophetic camps today. And you don't want any part of it. *The Message* version of Isaiah 30:9-11 reads:

"Don't bother us with irrelevancies." They tell their preachers, "Don't waste our time on impracticalities. Tell us what makes us feel better. Don't bore us with obsolete religion. That stuff means nothing to us. Quit hounding us with The Holy of Israel."

Don't fall into this trap. This generation we live in is wicked and growing darker. True prophetic voices, true seers, must share what the Lord shows them when He shows them no matter how rebellious, stubborn, or blind the people are. You will be tempted at some point to report a blessing when God is issuing a rebuke. Fear of man hits every prophet at some time or another.

— *Prayer* —

Father, in the name of Jesus, help me not to allow the voice of the people and the idolatry of a generation influence my ministry. Deliver me from the evil temptation to prophesy illusions and strengthen me to prophesy the words and visions You give me without compromise.

A Prophet to the Nations

"I knew you before I formed you in your mother's womb. Before you were born I set you apart and appointed you as my prophet to the nations" (Jeremiah 1:5).

Jeremiah was truly called as a prophet to the nations. Twice in his commissioning, the Lord told Jeremiah his jurisdiction and assignment included nations. That's a huge calling for a prophet of any age, much less a young man who hadn't been trained for ministry. Jeremiah serves as a reminder that God can use anyone to do anything at any time for His glory.

That said, many in prophetic circles today like to promote themselves as a prophet to the nations without truly understanding what that means. When Jehovah called Jeremiah as a prophet to the nations, He was really calling the young man as a prophet against the nations. His assignment was ultimately to bring healing to the land, but that couldn't happen until he rooted out the disease.

Matthew Henry's Commentary expounds on this: "the nation of the Jews in the first place, who are now reckoned among the nations because they had learned their works and mingled with them in their idolatries, for otherwise they would not have been numbered with them.... He is still in his writings a prophet to the nations (to our nation among the rest), to tell them what the national judgments are which may be expected for national sins. It would be well for the nations would they take Jeremiah for their prophet and attend to the warnings he gives them."

If you look at Jeremiah as a prophet to the nations—or a prophet against the nations—you see a ministry of warnings and calls to repentance. Some in modern-day prophetic circles use "prophet to the nations" in the sense of being called to preach and prophesy all over the world. These prophets may be called to preach and prophesy all over the world, but a true prophet to the nations in the context of this oft-quoted verse will weep over the warnings he has to bring.

Be careful not to step out in the name of a prophet to the nations without the burden of the Lord. The persecution that lands on a prophet to the nations is more severe. Just look at the life of Jeremiah.

— *Prayer* —

Father, in the name of Jesus, help me not to step beyond the boundaries You have given me in this season of my prophetic development. But prepare me for the next level You are calling me to so I can advance Your Kingdom agenda on the earth without delay.

Dealing with Demons from Your Past

"...But I press on to possess that perfection for which Christ Jesus first possessed me"
(Philippians 3:12).

Some of us have dramatic testimonies of how God delivered us from dark places into which even your typical sinner doesn't venture. But if we aren't truly free from the demonic influences that held us in bondage, we could fall back into the snare of the enemy once again. We are forgiven from our past sins, but sometimes we must deal with our past demons.

Demons from the past are often recognizable as persistent issues that hold you back from God's best. When you encounter one, it's like hitting a wall that you can't leap over, get around, dig under, or break through. It's a bondage. Often, deliverance ministry is required. But even then, you have to do your part.

I believe the same Holy Spirit by whom we prophesy is faithful to bring to our attention the issues that we need to deal with, if we don't already see them. He may do that one on one or use a trusted person in your life to point out a problem in love. When we can see a demonic stronghold, whether subtly in our thoughts or fully manifest through our actions, we need to get help. If we are well aware that demons from our past are leading us into dangerous temptations, and especially if we are falling into the trap, we need to get help. We need to deal with the demons of our past.

If we don't deal with the demons from our past, the devil will come at a more opportune time and try to steal, kill, and destroy us. So how do you deal with demons from your past? Acknowledge that there is a problem. Confront it courageously. Stop running from it. Don't deny it's there. Don't try to build your walls higher. Take off the mask you've been using to disguise the pain you are going through.

That requires humility, but humility opens the door to God's grace. Get some help from trusted Christians in your life who are equipped to help you find the deliverance and healing you need in Christ. Don't worry about what other people are going to think if they know the truth. If they are discerning people, they probably already know you are struggling.

— *Prayer* —

Father, in the name of Jesus, would You show me if there is anything holding me back in my soulish realm so I can deal with it now? Would You expose the demons from my past and deliver me from this evil? I humble myself before You, my Deliverer. Please set me free.

Beware Prophetic Plagiarists

"'Therefore,' says the Lord, 'I am against these prophets who steal messages from each other and claim they are from me. I am against these smooth-tongued prophets who say, "This prophecy is from the Lord!" I am against these false prophets. Their imaginary dreams are flagrant lies that lead my people into sin. I did not send or appoint them, and they have no message at all for my people. I, the Lord, have spoken!'" (Jeremiah 23:30-32)

That's a heavy word worth consideration. Read that passage a few times. The Lord says He is against the prophets who steal His words. He says He's against them not once, not twice, but thrice in a row. This is serious business. But what exactly does the Lord mean and why does it grieve Him?

In the modern context, that looks like this: A prophet prophesies a powerful, true word from the Lord at a meeting or over a Facebook Live, YouTube video, blog post, or magazine article. Another prophet picks up that word and begins prophesying it at his own meetings—as if the Lord spoke it to him directly. He gives no credit to the original prophecy and he never heard that word himself. But since it seemed popular, he copied it.

Although I don't believe anyone owns a prophetic word—God speaks for the edification, exhortation and comfort of all men—I do believe it's dangerous to pick up prophetic words that were spoken in a time, at a place, or in a season and re-prophesy them in your own time, at a different place, or in another season when you never heard those words. In other words, just because God said it once doesn't mean He's saying it to the next group who gathers. Just because it sounds deep doesn't mean it's the right word in another setting.

Prophets should not prophesy if the Lord is not speaking. Bottom line. And the Lord makes it clear in this verse that He is against the prophets who steal prophecies. God is more than willing to give you fresh revelation if and when He wants to release it through your ministry. Until then, avoid parroting the prophetic words of others unless the Lord moves on your heart to share what you've heard Him say elsewhere—and even if He does, don't pretend you were the first one to hear it.

— *Prayer* —

Father, in the name of Jesus, make me an original prophet. Help me avoid, even subconsciously, picking up prophetic words I heard somewhere else and releasing them as if You spoke them directly to me. Help me press in for fresh manna every day so I don't release stale revelation.

Withholding Nothing

"Then all the military leaders, including Johanan son of Kareah and Jezaniah son of Hoshaiah, and all the people, from the least to the greatest, approached Jeremiah the prophet. They said, 'Please pray to the Lord your God for us. As you can see, we are only a tiny remnant compared to what we were before. Pray that the Lord your God will show us what to do and where to go.' 'All right,' Jeremiah replied. 'I will pray to the Lord your God, as you have asked, and I will tell you everything he says. I will hide nothing from you'" (Jeremiah 42:1-4).

In his writings, Jeremiah reveals the heart of a true prophet. When the people came to him asking for prayer and prophetic wisdom, it touched God's heart—and it touched Jeremiah's heart. Unlike many others whom Jeremiah dealt with over the course of his prophetic ministry, these men were serious about the word of the Lord. They said to Jeremiah:

"May the Lord your God be a faithful witness against us if we refuse to obey whatever he tells us to do! Whether we like it or not, we will obey the Lord our God to whom we are sending you with our plea. For if we obey him, everything will turn out well for us" (Jeremiah 42:5-6).

How refreshing these words must have been to the persecuted prophet whose words were despised, rejected, and even destroyed!

Notice the people didn't come to Jeremiah like a diviner, seeking a prophecy to tickle their ears. No, they truly wanted to the Lord to show them how to walk rightly before Him and anything else they needed to do to please Him. Jeremiah heard their heart's cry and empathized with them.

Notice also how Jeremiah did not immediately start a prophetic pontification; rather, he committed to making intercession for them and vowed to share with them anything he heard from the Lord with regard to his situation. Jeremiah went off to prayer and waited on the Lord. He returned to them ten days later with a significant prophecy.

This is a proper order in prophetic ministry. It's not healthy for people to run to you—depending on you—to give them a prophetic word all the time. But it is appropriate for people to ask the prophet to make intercession. True prophets will not hold back what the Lord tells them to share.

— *Prayer* —

Father, in the name of Jesus, teach me to hold nothing back. Make me into a prophet who is at least as quick to seek and pray as I am to preach and prophesy so I can be confident that the word birthed in my heart is from Your Spirit and will accomplish what You are sending it to do.

Build Your Prayer Circle

"And for me, that utterance may be given to me, that I may open my mouth boldly to make known the mystery of the gospel" (Ephesians 6:19 NKJV).

Warfare is a way of life for me. I am careful to put my armor on, stay alert to the spirit realm, and walk as closely to the Holy Spirit as I possibly can. Still, there are seasons when the battle rages and I grow weary. There are times when I need reinforcements in the face of surging enemies that are intent on stealing what is rightfully mine, killing me, and destroying my family and ministry. Part of the Ephesians 6 dress code goes beyond the pieces of armor. Paul wrote in Ephesians 6:11-19:

> *Put on the whole armor of God, that you may be able to stand against the wiles of the devil. For we do not wrestle against flesh and blood, but against principalities, against powers, against the rulers of the darkness of this age, against spiritual hosts of wickedness in the heavenly places. Therefore take up the whole armor of God, that you may be able to withstand in the evil day, and having done all, to stand.*
>
> *Stand therefore, having girded your waist with truth, having put on the breastplate of righteousness, and having shod your feet with the preparation of the gospel of peace; above all, taking the shield of faith with which you will be able to quench all the fiery darts of the wicked one. And take the helmet of salvation, and the sword of the Spirit, which is the word of God; praying always with all prayer and supplication in the Spirit, being watchful to this end with all perseverance and supplication for all the saints—and for me, that utterance may be given to me, that I may open my mouth boldly to make known the mystery of the gospel* (NKJV).

Paul was always asking for prayer. Paul asked for prayer that God would provide an opportunity to speak, be heard, and spread the gospel message clearly (see Col. 4:3-4); that people would accept his message and believers would accept his God-given wisdom (see 2 Thess. 3:1-2); for deliverance from the Jews (see Rom. 15:30); for deliverance from challenging circumstances and prison (see 2 Cor. 1:11); that he could see in person those to whom he was writing (see Rom. 1:8).

Prophet, build your prayer circle. You need it.

— *Prayer* —

Father, in the name of Jesus, would You send intercessors my way? Would You show me how to connect with tight-lipped prayer warriors who will stand in the gap for me, warn me of enemy attacks I don't see, and otherwise lift up my arms as I press in to do Your will.

Don't Make Excuses to Stay Silent

"'O Sovereign Lord,' I said, 'I can't speak for you! I'm too young!'" (Jeremiah 1:6)

While there are some prophets who speak too freely—even prophesying words that God never said—apparently, it seems some prophets are equally as good at making excuses as to why they can't speak in the name of the Lord. Indeed, this is a pattern in Scripture among God's prophets. Maybe you can relate.

Moses was the first prophet to hem and haw in the face of God's charge to prophesy. He used his speech impediment as an excuse. But Jeremiah and Isaiah also put up a pretty good case against prophesying the word of the Lord. Or at least they thought they put up a good case. Exodus 4:10-14 reads:

> But Moses pleaded with the Lord, "O Lord, I'm not very good with words. I never have been, and I'm not now, even though you have spoken to me. I get tongue-tied, and my words get tangled." Then the Lord asked Moses, "Who makes a person's mouth? Who decides whether people speak or do not speak, hear or do not hear, see or do not see? Is it not I, the Lord? Now go! I will be with you as you speak, and I will instruct you in what to say." But Moses again pleaded, "Lord, please! Send anyone else." Then the Lord became angry with Moses....

Finally, the Lord assigned Aaron to be Moses' prophet until, finally, Moses got over his case of the nerves and found his own voice.

Jeremiah's excuse was that he was too young to prophesy. God wasn't buying that excuse either. He said, "'O Sovereign Lord,' I said, 'I can't speak for you! I'm too young!' The Lord replied, 'Don't say, "I'm too young," for you must go wherever I send you and say whatever I tell you'" (Jer. 1:6-7). His excuse didn't pan out for him any more than Moses'.

Isaiah made his excuse before God even had a chance to call him: "I have filthy lips, and I live among a people with filthy lips" (Isa. 6:5). What's your excuse? God may put hard words in your mouth, but who are you to make excuses for releasing them?

— *Prayer* —

Father, in the name of Jesus, would You show me what excuses I make for not answering the fullness of Your call on my life? If I am holding back because of fear or insecurity, would You root out these undesirable traits so I can speak Your word boldly?

Staying in Tune to God's Voice

"In the first year of his reign I, Daniel, understood by the books the number of the years specified by the word of the Lord through Jeremiah the prophet, that He would accomplish seventy years in the desolations of Jerusalem" (Daniel 9:2 NKJV).

Daniel was not only a student of the Word—he was a student of God's prophetic words to his contemporaries and was well-versed in the words of prophets in generations that went before him. We know, specifically, how Daniel studied the prophecies Jeremiah left behind.

Daniel's awareness of Jeremiah's prophetic words helped him perceive accurately the times and seasons Israel found itself in during the reign of King Darius. With this prophetic intelligence, he was able to intercede accurately. Daniel read these prophetic words from Jeremiah:

"And this whole land shall be a desolation and an astonishment, and these nations shall serve the king of Babylon seventy years. Then it will come to pass, when seventy years are completed, that I will punish the king of Babylon and that nation, the land of the Chaldeans, for their iniquity," says the Lord; "and I will make it a perpetual desolation" (Jeremiah 25:11-12 NKJV).

The next 16 verses record the prophet's intercession, starting with these words: "Then I set my face toward the Lord God to make request by prayer and supplications, with fasting, sackcloth, and ashes" (Dan. 9:3 NKJV). Daniel pressed into prayer for a nation under judgment, but he used another prophet's prophetic intelligence to inform his prayer. His prayer was more accurate because he had the timeline on the judgment.

Daniel's wise practice offers important lessons for modern-day prophets. We need to understand the signs of the times. Beyond direct revelation, one way we can do this is by studying biblical prophecy. Another way is by getting into agreement with what the Lord is saying through our contemporaries.

But we can and should take a step beyond that. We can review the prophecies from prophets and prophetic voices from past generations—prophecies from the likes of Smith Wigglesworth and William Seymour and A.A. Allen and Kenneth E. Hagin. We can, like Daniel, observe the prophecies and make more relevant intercession. What you find will help you see what others are missing.

— *Prayer* —

Father, in the name of Jesus, help me not to be an island to myself with regard to what I know about what You know. Lead me and guide me to the prophetic intelligence I need, whether from the past or present, in order to effectively pray for current situations.

MARCH

"But if they are prophets, and if the word of the Lord is with them, let them now make intercession to the Lord of hosts, that the vessels which are left in the house of the Lord, in the house of the king of Judah, and at Jerusalem, do not go to Babylon" (Jeremiah 27:18 NJKV).

Prophesying Christ's Return

"Moses said, 'The Lord your God will raise up for you a Prophet like me from among your own people. Listen carefully to everything he tells you.' Then Moses said, 'Anyone who will not listen to that Prophet will be completely cut off from God's people.' Starting with Samuel, every prophet spoke about what is happening today" (Acts 3:22-24).

This is a fascinating passage and one that modern-day prophets would do well to consider long and hard. Peter is reminding us that every prophet since the days of Samuel prophesied about the coming Christ. Prophet after prophet between Samuel's day and John the Baptist's pointed people prophetically to the soon coming Messiah. It was a vital part of their ministry to announce the coming paradigm shift.

What are we to take away from this New Testament observation? Peter wasn't talking about date setting—predicting the date at which Christ will crack the sky and come to earth for the Battle of Armageddon with a saints-and-angels army. Jesus Himself told us no man knows the day or hour of His return—not even the angels. Only the Father in heaven knows when Jesus will come back (see Matt. 24:36).

Nevertheless, Peter was pointing out a critical part of the modern-day prophet's role—to point people to the soon-coming revelation of Jesus Christ. While the Old Testament prophets pointed people to the birth, death, and resurrection of Jesus through dozens of printed Messianic prophecies recorded in Scripture, New Testament prophets should likewise point people to His imminent return that spurs an urgency in the Bride to ready herself for the wedding feast.

Although we do not know the timeframe, we can discern the signs of the times and prophesy what Christ is saying to His church in the moment. We can teach people what the Bible says about the Second Coming and prophesy into the preparation. We can prophesy the promise of His coming to a people who are weary in the world (see 2 Pet. 3:4).

As prophets, we are releasing the testimony of Jesus. Revelation 19:10 tells us the essence of prophecy is to give a clear witness of Jesus. Is your prophetic ministry accomplishing this mission? Are you exalting Jesus in the earth while we wait for His ultimate return? Ponder these questions and ask the Holy Spirit if you need to refocus your eyes and refine your ears to hear what He is saying to His church about His return.

— *Prayer* —

Father, in the name of Jesus, teach me to operate in a prophetic anointing that speaks what Jesus is saying to His Bride about Himself today. Help me avoid getting wrapped up in prophesying about things in the earth that perish and neglect the eternal perspectives.

Pray for Prophetic Windbags

"God's prophets are all windbags who don't really speak for him. Let their predictions of disaster fall on themselves!" (Jeremiah 5:13)

You've probably met a prophetic windbag, but if you aren't sure what the Lord meant when He spoke to Jeremiah let's offer some definition here. A windbag is someone who talks and talks and talks and talks. *Merriam-Webster* defines *windbag* as "an exhaustively talkative person."

In the context of prophetic ministry, a windbag would be someone who prophesies and prophesies and prophesies but the wind of God is not on it. Remember, one of the symbols of the Holy Spirit is wind. The Holy Spirit came at Pentecost like a mighty rushing wind. With prophetic windbags, God may have stopped speaking before the prophet did. Perhaps the second half of their prophetic pontification was not inspired. You can discern it if you listen closely.

A prophetic windbag may also be defined this way: The prophet who always has a prophetic word about everything all the time and won't let anyone else get a prophetic word in edgewise. It's one thing to be prepared to prophesy in season and out of season. It's another thing to dominate a setting without regard to others' prophetic ministries and voices.

Prophetic windbags eventually end up walking a fine line instead of a narrow path. Indeed, there's a fine line between prophecy and presumption. Prophetic windbags may be people pleasers or attention seekers. They may be puffed up in pride because of the prophetic knowledge they carry (see 1 Cor. 8:1). Nobody likes a prophetic windbag.

If you see these tendencies in others, don't compete for the microphone. Don't resent them for taking away an opportunity you thought was yours. Pray for them because they may end up on a broad path that leads to destruction. If you see these tendencies in yourself, ask the Holy Spirit to deliver you because pride comes before destruction (see Prov. 16:18).

— *Prayer* —

Father, in the name of Jesus, knock the fleshly wind out of me if I start prophesying out of competition, jealousy, or pride. Help me to follow Paul the apostle's advice and prophesy in turn, accepting the reality that I don't always have to be the one in the spotlight.

Honing Prophetic Versatility

"And the Lord said to them, 'Now listen to what I say: "If there were prophets among you, I, the Lord, would reveal myself in visions. I would speak to them in dreams"'" (Numbers 12:6).

While there are many different types of prophets—and many different prophetic expressions—I am convinced the Lord wants His people to diversify their spiritual receptivity. Another way to say it is prophetic versatility. Versatile prophets can prophesy out of what they see, decree the revelation in their dreams, and otherwise move from one prophetic mode to another seamlessly.

God communicates in many, many different ways. You might say God is a multi-media God. He speaks through many different mediums. Elijah saw God answer by fire, but later heard Him speak in a still small voice. God thunders and lightnings, but He also whispers to us in our dreams. God can give us epic visions or show us quick pictures. God can give us a check in our spirit or let us feel what He feels.

Prophetic versatility is becoming more important as we progress in the end times. If we can only receive God's communications through one medium—or one channel—we could be missing the message. Imagine if you only had a radio. You would never see images on a TV screen. God is opening the ears of seers and opening the eyes of hearers.

God is stretching His prophets and leading us outside our prophetic comfort zones for a prophetic purpose. He wants us to be as comfortable sharing a spontaneous prophetic word as we are writing down a prophetic message. He wants us to be as accurate with the right hand and the left. Don't be surprised, dreamers, if your dreams dry up because He's trying to open your ears. Don't be surprised, prophetic psalmists, if you start seeing visions during worship.

Ask the Holy Spirit to help you discern His mode of communication accurately even if He is delivering a message to you to deliver through you in a new way. Ask Him to teach you how to handle prophetic insight in whatever medium He chooses. You'll be better for it.

— *Prayer* —

Father, in the name of Jesus, lead me outside my prophetic comfort zone. I don't want to be a one-dimensional prophet. Teach me to receive Your prophetic revelations though various means and modes, fine tuning my spirit to Yours.

When the Word of the Lord Is with You

"But if they are prophets, and if the word of the Lord is with them, let them now make intercession to the Lord of hosts, that the vessels which are left in the house of the Lord, in the house of the king of Judah, and at Jerusalem, do not go to Babylon" (Jeremiah 27:18 NJKV).

Jeremiah 27:18 is an often-overlooked verse in the prophetic community. Consider these words and consider them well. There are two major "ifs" in this verse. *If* is a word that precedes conditions. *If* is the bridge to *then*. *If* assumes an activity on the part of the one receiving the promise or position. You can't have the *then* if you don't embrace the *if*.

Look at Jeremiah 27:18 in the New Living Translation: "If they really are prophets and speak the Lord's messages, let them pray to the Lord of Heaven's Armies." And *The Message* really drives it home: "If they are real prophets and have a Message from God, let them come to God-of-the-Angel-Armies in prayer."

Now look at this from the perspective of today's prophet. If you are a prophet and you expect the word of the Lord to be in your mouth, intercession needs to be a priority in your life. Put another way, don't expect the Lord to use you in a mighty way in prophetic ministry if you don't spend time in prayer. Sure, your prophetic gifting will function because it's a gift of God, but if you want to make the impact the Lord wants you to make, you'll make intercession.

You will be more powerful as a prophet if you pray—and not just for yourself but for the gaps in which God has called you to stand. Intercession is proof of your prophethood as much as is an accurate prophecy. If you truly have the word of the Lord in your mouth, you'll have intercession in your heart and it will flow with as much power as your prophetic word.

Let's make this practical: If you receive a prophetic word over a person, city, or nation, you should make intercession for that person, city, or nation. You should partner with the Lord to bring His will to earth as it is in heaven. If your prayer life isn't what it should be—if you are not making intercession—then ask the Lord to help you come up higher in this area. Your prophetic ministry will be more effective and you will honor the Lord.

— *Prayer* —

Father, in the name of Jesus, make me the intercessor You've called me to be. Help me to enjoy the ministry of intercession for people at least as much as I enjoy prophesying to people. Teach me to listen for Your prayer prompts and to pray effectively for what's on Your heart.

Prophesying over People You Don't Like

"But King Jehoshaphat of Judah asked, 'Is there no prophet of the Lord with us? If there is, we can ask the Lord what to do through him.' One of King Joram's officers replied, 'Elisha son of Shaphat is here. He used to be Elijah's personal assistant'" (2 Kings 3:11).

Is there a prophet of the Lord here? King Ahab was content with listening to his false prophetic puppets, mouthpieces who told him what he wanted to hear when he wanted to hear it—and so did his son Joram. But King Jehoshaphat had a different spirit. This wise king wanted to hear what the Lord really had to say before they went into battle. He understood the danger of going to war without a clear word from the Lord.

Jehoshaphat asked, "Is there a prophet of the Lord here, through whom we may inquire of the Lord?" Indeed, there was. His name was Elisha and the king recognized that "the Lord speaks through him" (2 Kings 3:12). With that, the two kings went down to Elisha seeking his prophetic wisdom on the battle.

What happened next is interesting. Elisha wanted nothing to do with Israel's King Joram, Ahab's son, but had regard for Judah's King Jehoshaphat and asked for a musician to minister and delivered a warfare strategy that enabled them to defeat the Moabites.

There may be times when the Lord calls you to prophesy over those for whom you have no regard. Elisha wanted nothing to do with Joram, the son of the wicked king whose wife tormented his spiritual father Elijah. In that moment, you nevertheless have to be obedient to the Holy Spirit's unction to share His heart with honesty and purity.

Interestingly, Elisha had a good word for the son of the king that Elijah once rebuked as the troubler of Israel:

> *But this is only a simple thing for the Lord, for he will make you victorious over the army of Moab! You will conquer the best of their towns, even the fortified ones. You will cut down all their good trees, stop up all their springs, and ruin all their good land with stones* (2 Kings 3:18-19).

I've had this happen. I have found myself prophesying deeply impactful words to people who have wronged me, irritated me, or are just generally cantankerous. It never surprises me because I know God has something good to say to everyone. Ask God for a word for someone you don't especially like.

— *Prayer* —

Father, in the name of Jesus, help me take on Your character with the unlovely. Make me no respecter of persons like You are no respecter of persons. Teach me to press into Your heart to understand what You feel about people—even those I don't like—and to share it with them.

Communicating with Angels

"Then I raised my eyes and looked, and there were four horns. And I said to the angel who talked with me, 'What are these?' So he answered me, 'These are the horns that have scattered Judah, Israel, and Jerusalem'" (Zechariah 1:18-19 NKJV).

Throughout the pages of the Bible, prophets communicated with angels. Angelic interventions, encounters, and interactions are not rare. Hebrews 1:14 tells us, "What role then, do the angels have? The angels are spirit-messengers sent by God to serve those who are going to be saved" (TPT). At their essence, though they take on many divine assignments, angels are messengers.

The more we are aware of the presence of God, the more we will be aware of His angels on assignment. There are over 300 verses in Scripture on angels. It's far too many to ignore. And it's not enough to agree they exist. Prophets are to work with angels and sometimes that means interactions, including communication.

Jesus had interaction with angels. Angels ministered to Him at least twice that we know of. After Jesus' temptation (see Matt. 4:11) and his prayer in Gethsemane (see Luke 22:43), angels came to Jesus and ministered to or strengthened Him.

In Daniel 8 and 9, the prophet Daniel had a conversation with the angel Gabriel. Isaiah interacted with seraphim, who put a coal of fire to his mouth. How would you like that kind of angelic encounter? In the Book of Revelation, John spoke to angels about his prophetic visions. And Zechariah talked to angels over and over again in conjunction with the visions he had. Zechariah 4:1-5 reads:

> *Then the angel who had been talking with me returned and woke me, as though I had been asleep. "What do you see now?" he asked. I answered, "I see a solid gold lampstand with a bowl of oil on top of it. Around the bowl are seven lamps, each having seven spouts with wicks. And I see two olive trees, one on each side of the bowl." Then I asked the angel, "What are these, my lord? What do they mean?" "Don't you know?" the angel asked. "No, my lord," I replied.*

Don't ask the Lord to send angels to converse with you, but do be prepared to engage with them if Jesus sends them to help you interpret a dream or a vision or to deliver to you a prophetic message. Study angels and learn how to cooperate with their ministry.

— *Prayer* —

Father, in the name of Jesus, teach me what I need to know about the ministry of angels. Root me and ground me about the truth of angels as revealed in Your Word and show me the principles of communicating with angels in my prophetic ministry.

Escaping Religion's Witchcraft

"Woe to you! For you build the tombs of the prophets, and your fathers killed them" (Luke 11:47 NKJV).

For all the talk of Jezebel—and it's necessary—fewer talk about religion's impact on prophets. I've seen many prophets' voices cut off by Jezebel, but I've seen just as many cut off by the spirit of religion.

Let's start with denominationalism. Some prophets are stuck in denominations that don't believe in prophets. They can never fully be who God called them to be because the denomination and its unbelief serves as a lid over their life. They never have a chance to develop their voice because they are effectively muted. (I say leave.)

Other prophets are stuck in churches that only allow one prophet to prophesy. They may have a sure word of the Lord in their mouth but the head prophet won't acknowledge their voice so the power of life in their tongue is neutralized if not paralyzed. (I say leave.)

If you think that's a bold suggestion, just look at the strong words Jesus offered religious leaders of His day:

> *What sorrow awaits you! For you build monuments for the prophets your own ancestors killed long ago. But in fact, you stand as witnesses who agree with what your ancestors did. They killed the prophets, and you join in their crime by building the monuments! This is what God in his wisdom said about you: "I will send prophets and apostles to them, but they will kill some and persecute the others"* (Luke 11:47-49).

Jesus also charged:

> *Go ahead and finish what your ancestors started. Snakes! Sons of vipers! How will you escape the judgment of hell? Therefore, I am sending you prophets and wise men and teachers of religious law. But you will kill some by crucifixion, and you will flog others with whips in your synagogues, chasing them from city to city* (Matthew 23:32-34).

Prophet, you will make religious spirits nervous and the result is witchcraft. Religious witchcraft attacks not just your voice but your very identity in the Kingdom. Religious witchcraft bullies and threatens you if you don't conform to its legalistic image. Religious witchcraft batters your mind with condemnation if you dare to break out of its box. Take your stand!

— *Prayer* —

Father, in the name of Jesus, help me to discern the operation of religious witchcraft so I can resist it! I submit my calling and election to You, not some religious structure or organization who defies the reality of prophets for today. Deliver me from religious bondage.

What Are You Discerning?

"Yes, if you cry out for discernment, and lift up your voice for understanding" (Proverbs 2:3 NKJV).

Just because you're a prophet doesn't mean you are discerning. The gift of prophecy and the gift of discerning of spirits are two completely separate endowments. Although many prophets come equipped with the ability to discern between good and evil, just as often I meet prophets who have little or no spiritual discernment. They may hear from the Lord with perfect accuracy, but they don't see Jezebel under their nose.

Discernment is "the quality of being able to grasp and comprehend what is obscure," also "an act of perceiving or discerning something" according to *Merriam-Webster's* dictionary. *Discerning* means "able to see and understand people, things, or situations clearly and intelligently."

Webster's Revised Unabridged Dictionary offers this definition: "The power or faculty of the mind by which it distinguishes one thing from another; power of viewing differences in objects, and their relations and tendencies; penetrative and discriminate mental vision; acuteness; sagacity; insight; as, the errors of youth often proceed from the want of discernment."

Joshua was a man who heard directly from the Lord. He got his battle plans from the Lord. He got his marching orders from the Lord. He had great success in warfare, but he demonstrated very little discernment. Joshua did not discern the grief of the Lord over Achan's sin and sent Israelites into Ai to battle and they died because the Lord did not help them gain the victory (see Josh. 7).

Joshua did not discern the Gibeonites were lying to him and made a covenant with them too quickly and had to go to war on their behalf (see Josh. 9). Joshua did not discern the Captain of Hosts standing before him with a sword in his hand and had the audacity to ask the Lord, "'Are you friend or foe?' 'Neither one,' he replied. 'I am the commander of the Lord's army'" (Josh. 5:13-14).

Don't assume you have good discernment because you hear from the Lord. Hearing is not always the same thing as discerning. Ask the Lord to increase your discernment and begin to practice discernment in everyday life so you can grow in this vital area.

— *Prayer* —

Father, in the name of Jesus, give me discernment so I can recognize the demon powers that are working to derail my ministry. Give me discernment so I can accurately see the spirit behind prophetic words. Give me discernment to see things the way You do.

Post-Prophetic Stress Disorder

"...If God is for us, who can ever be against us?" (Romans 8:31)

Have you ever heard of post-prophetic stress disorder? Probably not, but you may have experienced it. Post-prophetic stress disorder is a condition of the soul that's triggered by demonic assault—whether through principalities and powers or through persecuting people. Post-prophetic stress disorder may occur after a season of terrible spiritual warfare or severe trials. When it does, healing is in order.

Maybe when you entered prophetic ministry your denomination gave you the left foot of fellowship, expelling you from the congregation. Maybe when you stepped out into your prophetic calling, Jezebel terrorized your family—and you lost your marriage, your money, or your job. Maybe you prophesied with a genuine belief that your word was absolutely accurate, then missed it badly and met with public persecution and blackballing in certain camps.

These are just a few examples of post-prophetic stress disorder. I'm sure Jeremiah suffered from this phenomenon in his ministry. Jeremiah was often ignored. When he wasn't ignored he was mistreated. He was called a liar (see Jer. 43:2). The religious rulers of the day beat him and put him in stocks (see Jer. 20:1-2). A king burned his scroll with record of his prophetic words (see Jer. 36:23). A death sentence was issued against him (see Jer. 26:11). He was left to die in the mud (see Jer. 38:6).

Jeremiah complained to the Lord more than once. In Jeremiah 20:7, he exclaims, "O Lord, you misled me, and I allowed myself to be misled. You are stronger than I am, and you overpowered me. Now I am mocked every day; everyone laughs at me."

Understand, the trauma is not to your spirit but your soul. It's an emotional response to some sort of conflict, whether in the natural or in the spirit, with resulting behavior that can fracture your prophetic stream. Walking in the office of the prophet is not easy. Ask the Lord to heal your soul of any prophetic-traumatic stress or trauma you've received prophesying to His people. He is for you, even when nobody else is. And He wants to heal you.

— *Prayer* —

Father, deliver me from post-prophetic stress disorder. Deliver me, too, from the trauma of my past at the hand of the enemy and at the hand of flesh and blood. Heal me from the wounds that carnal and demon-inspired people have inflicted on my soul.

Don't Cave in to the Pressure

"Obviously, I'm not trying to win the approval of people, but of God. If pleasing people were my goal, I would not be Christ's servant" (Galatians 1:10).

The pressure to prophesy is off the charts. That pressure has contributed to too many prophets putting out a constant stream of prophecy in order to keep their audiences. We must reject the pressure to prophesy—and reject building our ministries on a gift rather than on the Gift-Giver, Jesus Christ.

The pressure to prophesy is insidious. Once someone sees you prophesy accurately, you may find people will request or even urge you to prophesy at meetings or even in private. I have had that happen time and time again. I've been taken in back rooms under the guise of seeing a beautiful painting only to be cornered for a prophetic word. Don't give in to this pressure. Resist the pressure to prophesy like you'd resist the devil. If God is not speaking, we do not have anything to say.

Consider this: Pressure is a burden of physical or mental stress, according to *Merriam-Webster*'s dictionary. It's stressful when people always expect you to prophesy on demand, even at the dinner table or while you are driving away in your car after ministering all day. (Yes, this happens to me frequently.)

People should not be putting a demand on you to prophesy. If God is not speaking, you don't have anything to say. Remember, sometimes God is not speaking anything new to someone because they didn't obey the last thing He instructed them to do.

Taking on pressure to prophesy because people expect you to have a word can lead you into compromise or error. If you strain and stress to prophesy you could tap into a familiar spirit or divination. Don't worry about what could happen to your reputation if you don't prophesy. Be more concerned about what could happen to your reputation if you succumb to pressure and speak something the Holy Spirit is not saying.

If you are distressed and stressed by this pressure, take a play from David's prayer book: "In my distress I prayed to the Lord, and the Lord answered me and set me free. The Lord is for me, so I will have no fear. What can mere people do to me?" (Ps. 118:5-6).

— *Prayer* —

Father, in the name of Jesus, help me walk the fine line between a willingness and eagerness to share prophetically what You are saying and falling into a pressure cooker that can compromise my prophetic ministry. Help me stay quiet when You are quiet, despite the pressure.

Pursuing the Issachar Anointing

"And of the children of Issachar, which were men that had understanding of the times, to know what Israel ought to do; the heads of them were two hundred; and all their brethren were at their commandment" (1 Chronicles 12:32 KJV).

God anointed the tribe of Issachar to see prophetically into times and seasons—and to tap into the wisdom to know what to do. The Hebrew word for "understanding" in this verse is *yada*. According to *The KJV Old Testament Hebrew Lexicon*, it means to know, to perceive and see, find out and discern. Sounds very prophetic to me!

God anointed this tribe of Israel to see prophetically into times and seasons. *Benson Commentary* says of the tribe of Issachar: "They understood public affairs, the temper of the nation, and the tendencies of the present events." Prophets should not just be predictors of the future but interpreters of the current times to lead a people along God's path to wisdom in the moment.

The Issachar anointing is a vital part of the prophetic makeup for several reasons. First, when we understand the times we come to better understand the ways of God and how He moves. Second, when we understand the season we're entering into we can be spiritually and naturally prepared to respond in a godly manner and disallow the enemy access.

Third, we need to understand the times so we can pray and come into agreement with what God is about to do or what He is currently doing. Fourth, understanding the times and knowing what to do guards us from deception and spurs in us a fervency for holiness. Finally, many believers are so busy with the affairs of life they do not discern the times or seasons they are in or the world is in. Prophets can help fill that gap by prophesying the time, the season, and the wisdom in how to move ahead in victory.

Of course, not every prophet will walk in a strong Issachar anointing, but every prophet should pursue that anointing in the times in which we live. God is anointing tribes of seers today to see into times and seasons, but He can also allow you to enter into the Issachar dimension as He wills. We need to discern the signs of the times and the seasons in the earth as we prepare a people for the Second Coming of Christ. Ask the Holy Spirit to show you times and seasons—and give you practical wisdom. Ask the Holy Spirit to give you an Issachar anointing.

— *Prayer* —

Father, in the name of Jesus, would You impart to me the Issachar anointing? Teach me how to interpret the seasons and help me emerge in the midst of trying times with prophetic wisdom and insight into how Your people should respond. Show me what to do.

Healing the Prophet's Hurts and Wounds

"I am weary with my groaning; all night I make my bed swim; I drench my couch with my tears" (Psalm 6:6 NKJV).

Sadly, there are too many wounded prophets limping around the church trying their level best to serve God. Maybe you are one of them. Jezebel loves to wound prophets so she can get a stronghold on their soul and use them like puppets.

Like anyone else, prophets get wounded at times—and prophets need the healing balm of Gilead, spiritual medicine to heal their souls. But they also need natural, practical help to break free. That's because rather than walking in their Christ-given victory, wounded prophets walk in emotional defeat that oft holds them in bondage to enemy lies.

So what do you do with a wounded prophet who is so hurt and exhausted both physically and emotionally that they can't take another step forward? Some in the church today would offer a scriptural platitude and a dose of condemnation for failing to rejoice in the midst of their trials. Others would pressure the wounded prophet to get back up and prophesy despite the gaping, oozing wound in their soul. Still others would insist on casting out the devil.

Well, prophet, you know as well as I do it's not always so easy to count it joy or to get back in the fight. And it's not always a devil. I mean, yes, the devil is ultimately behind many of the attacks that leave the prophet wounded. But that doesn't mean a wrestling match in a deliverance session will put the wounded prophet back on his feet. And it doesn't mean we need to encourage a pity party and help the wounded prophet lick his wounds, either. So what do you do?

If you know a wounded prophet, be quick to listen and slow to speak. Don't offer them pat answers from the Bible because you don't know their pain. Don't judge them for where they are because you don't know what you would do if you took the hits they took. If they hurl accusations against you, don't retaliate. Walk in love and pray. If you are a wounded prophet, find someone who can be that person for you. Ask the Holy Spirit to help you heal.

— *Prayer* —

Father, in the name of Jesus, help me be a healer prophet, who can see the wounds in the soul of another and bring words of life that release Your healing power. And help me, Lord, to heal from the wounds that Jezebel and her cronies have inflicted on my soul. Set Your prophets free!

The Diplomatic Prophet

"A gentle answer deflects anger, but harsh words make tempers flare" (Proverbs 15:1).

Prophets aren't always the most diplomatic of the fivefold, but we need to learn to be. What is diplomacy, you ask? *Merriam-Webster's* dictionary defines it as skill in handling affairs without arousing hostility. Being a diplomatic prophet means you are "exactly reproducing the original" and "employing tact and conciliation especially in situations of stress." Tact is "a keen sense of what to do or say in order to maintain good relations with others or avoid offense."

Now, sometimes a prophetic word will offend people. But sometimes it's offensive or hurtful because of the way you say it. As ambassadors of God, we have to be good diplomats for the Kingdom of Heaven. Deliver prophetic words with diplomacy. How you deliver a word can make a difference in whether or not someone receives it.

If you have to deliver a corrective word, for example, it should be released only after much prayer and even grieving or weeping. Delivering words of warning must also be done with diplomacy to avoid perceptions of judgment on a person, as if they are in some way to blame, etc.

Diplomacy in the prophetic begins with the way we listen to God. In order to express God's heart in a matter, we need to hear His heart and not just His voice. If we miss God's heart, we can miscommunicate His will and lead people astray or cause them to shut their ears to the message.

When we listen well, we will share responsibly. If we listen to God through the lens of our bias, we will speak with prejudice. If we listen to God through the filter of bitterness, we will speak with judgment. If we listen to God through the ears of grace and mercy, we will speak the bold truth in love.

Ask the Holy Spirit to teach you diplomacy. That doesn't mean watering down or sugar coating the word. It means prophesying the truth in love.

— *Prayer* —

Father, in the name of Jesus, help me listen to Your heart not just Your words. Teach me to speak with tact not just boldness. Show me how to navigate sensitive matters with Your wisdom, grace, and mercy. I want people to receive Your life-changing words.

No Blood on Your Hands

"But if you warn righteous people not to sin and they listen to you and do not sin, they will live, and you will have saved yourself, too" (Ezekiel 3:21).

All watchmen are not prophets, but all prophets are watchmen. Some have a very strong calling to the watchtower while others will occasionally receive a word of warning. Ezekiel 3 and Ezekiel 33 were two Scriptures God used to call me into the watchman's ministry. I tell the whole story in my book *The Making of a Watchman*, but suffice it to say these passages about blood on my hands for failing to release timely warnings have struck a fear of the Lord in my heart.

As a watchman, it's not enough to see what's coming down the pike. If you don't warn the people, we are not walking in full obedience to the Lord. While God won't literally hold us responsible for the deaths of those who aren't warned like He did in Ezekiel's day, God can't trust us to walk in higher levels of the watchman anointing if we're not obedient at the level we're at.

Since part of the watchman's ministry is releasing warnings, if the watchman prophet doesn't release the warning God will look for someone else who is willing to risk the persecution and rejection to sound the alarm and blow the trumpet. The watchman prophet has a serious calling and needs to take it seriously despite the individual believer's own mandate to watch and pray.

Part of the watchman prophet's mandate is to pray. You may not have a significant platform from which to warn. Perhaps your influence is not far and wide at this point in your ministry. Nevertheless, you can write a blog post, tell those in authority and, above all, you can lift up your voice to heaven and pray. You can stand in the gap and make up the hedge. The point is: take the calling seriously. Do something with the warning you receive.

Now you can see why the spirit of the fear of the Lord came upon me when God called me as a watchman. This is not a game or a joke. In the Bible, it was one man's prayer who rescued Lot and his family from Sodom and Gomorrah. Never underestimate the power of prayer. Take responsibility through intercession. Cry aloud to the Lord who wants to intervene and does so at the sound of the voice of a man or woman in the earth who is willing to yield to His Spirit.

— *Prayer* —

Father, in the name of Jesus, help me take my responsibility as a watchman seriously. If and when I receive words of warning, help me to pray them through and wait for Your instruction on how and to whom to release them to thwart the plans and purposes of the enemy.

Entering the Secret Place

"For in the time of trouble He shall hide me in His pavilion; in the secret place of His tabernacle He shall hide me; He shall set me high upon a rock" (Psalm 27:5 NKJV).

Everyone—even God—has secrets. Choosing whether or not—and to whom—to reveal a secret rests solely in the power of the secret holder. In the secret dimension, God is the revealer of secrets (see Dan. 2:47). We know God reveals His secrets to two different types of people—His servants the prophets (see Amos 3:7) and those who fear Him (see Ps. 25:14).

As I write in my book *The Seer Dimensions*, you have the inherent potential to enter the secret dimension of the seer realm. Deuteronomy 29:29 tells us, "The secret things belong to the Lord our God, but those things which are revealed belong to us and to our children forever, that we may do all the words of this law" (NKJV).

The unfortunate reality is few will enter into the secret dimension because they are unaware of its existence or they won't pay the price to cultivate a lifestyle that gains them access. God can share His secrets with us through a still small voice or through the seer dimensions, including encounters, trances, dreams, and visions.

We find many types of secrets spoken of in the pages of the Bible—and there are many more we can discover through our pursuit of the Holy One of Israel. Understanding what's scripturally available to you builds faith to access the secret dimension of the seer world.

Many Scriptures point us to this secret place. Psalm 91:1 assures us, "He who dwells in the secret place of the Most High shall abide under the shadow of the Almighty" (NKJV). When you enter the secret place of God's presence in the seer dimensions, you may see strong angelic activity. You will no longer hear the strife of tongues, you will hear the song of the Lord, the sounds of angels, or one of the many diverse and otherworldly sights and sounds. Several times I have entered into this secret dimension and heard angels singing or spiritual frequencies I cannot describe. I often hear high-pitched frequencies in the spirit that alert me to significant angelic activity.

The secret place of thunder is a phenomenon few seem to experience—and it's fascinating. In Psalm 81:7 the Lord says to David, "You called in trouble, and I delivered you; I answered you in the secret place of thunder" (NKJV). The word "thunder" in that verse literally means *thunder*. Think about it for a minute. A secret place that is so loud that there's a reverberating rumble. Given thunder always follows lightning, meditate on the awesome sights of the secret place of thunder.

— *Prayer* —

Father, in the name of Jesus, would You escort me into the secret place of thunder? Would You teach me how to walk on the path that leads me to the secret dimension where I can learn of the deeper things of Your Spirit? I want to understand the mysteries of the Kingdom.

Prophetic Reform Begins with You

"Jehoshaphat lived in Jerusalem, but he went out among the people, traveling from Beersheba to the hill country of Ephraim, encouraging the people to return to the Lord, the God of their ancestors. He appointed judges throughout the nation in all the fortified towns" (2 Chronicles 19:4-5).

Old Testament or New, the spirit of reformation charges prophetic ministry. The prophetic ministry is called to bring change—positive change. This reforming spirit—the spirit that brings divine change—brought hope to the people whose stories we read in the pages of the Bible.

Elijah is a prime example. He challenged the people of Israel to declare whom they would serve—Jehovah or Baal (see 1 Kings 18:21). His reformation message, along with the courage to confront false prophetic operations, sought to turn the hearts of men away from pagan gods. He succeeded. At the end of the day, there was a reformation. The Israelites chose to serve the one true living God (see 1 Kings 18:39).

The Old Testament is filled with prophetic reformers like Ezekiel, Jeremiah, Isaiah, and Malachi. A reformer mentality is a common characteristic that accompanies the prophetic anointing in any era. Haggai's reforming message challenged Israel to rebuild God's temple so they could receive His blessings. Don't forget the prophetess Deborah. She united the Israelites against the Canaanites during a time when the leading man was unwilling to lead. She led her nation in victory, bringing freedom to Israel.

Moving into the New Testament, we see John the Baptist with his reformation message—better known as "repent!"—and, of course, Jesus, the mighty Reformer, who came to reform religion as His day knew it. You can't divide a reformation mindset from the prophetic. Prophets have reformation in their DNA.

The prophet's goal is to see God's best for people and nations. Reformer prophets take action to bring change, whether that is in the heart of man, through spiritual warfare, or in building and planting. The apostles, remember, aren't the only fivefold ascension gift called to build. The prophetic ministry builds and plants. The apostle and prophet build in different ways, but their desire is the same—to see the glorious Church without spot or wrinkle filled with equipped, triumphant saints. You can't take on every ill in the Body of Christ, but God gives reformers a cause and a message. What's yours?

— *Prayer* —

Father, in the name of Jesus, help me recognize the reformation assignment You've ordained for me. Give me prophetic messages for society sectors You've called me to impact. Teach me to look beyond the church to understand what grieves Your heart. Give me a burden.

Pursuing Prophetic Accuracy

"Every word of God proves true..." (Proverbs 30:5).

When God speaks, He's always right in what He says. When God speaks, the word cannot fail or fall to the ground. In fact, Jehovah once told Isaiah, "It is the same with my word. I send it out, and it always produces fruit. It will accomplish all I want it to, and it will prosper everywhere I send it" (Isa. 55:11).

This concept of God's Word never failing is repeated throughout Scripture. Second Samuel 22:31 tells us: "As for God, His way is perfect; the word of the Lord is proven; He is a shield to all who trust in Him" (NKJV). David wrote, "The words of the Lord are pure words, like silver tried in a furnace of earth, purified seven times" (Ps. 12:6 NKJV).

Bear with me while I drive this point home. Numbers 23:19 assures, "God is not a man, that He should lie, nor a son of man, that He should repent. Has He said, and will He not do? Or has He spoken, and will He not make it good?" (NKJV). And Isaiah penned these truths, "The grass withers, the flower fades, but the word of our God stands forever" (Isa. 40:8 NKJV).

In Isaiah 45:23 we read again, "I have sworn by my own name; I have spoken the truth, and I will never go back on my word." And Jesus said, "Heaven and earth will disappear, but my words will never disappear" (Matt. 24:35).

Are you getting the picture? If God really said it, it will always be accurate. The problem is we have a soul that filters prophetic messages. In other words, the Holy Spirit shares the testimony of Jesus with our spirits. Our spirts transmit that prophecy to our soul. If our souls are out of line with the Word of God, we may release a prophetic word that is less than 100 percent accurate.

The only perfect prophet was Jesus. Any of us can miss it because of our biases, emotional wounds, or warfare against our mind. Nevertheless, we must pursue prophetic accuracy. Commit yourself to prophetic accuracy and you will become more accurate.

— *Prayer* —

Father, in the name of Jesus, help me value prophetic accuracy more than I value prophetic productivity. I don't want to be an assembly line prophet, pumping out words that sound good but may not be right. Help me deal with issues that skew my prophetic perspective.

Uprooting Demonic Weeds

"Here is another story Jesus told: 'The Kingdom of Heaven is like a farmer who planted good seed in his field. But that night as the workers slept, his enemy came and planted weeds among the wheat, then slipped away. When the crop began to grow and produce grain, the weeds also grew. The farmer's workers went to him and said, "Sir, the field where you planted that good seed is full of weeds! Where did they come from?" "An enemy has done this!" the farmer exclaimed'" (Matthew 13:24-28).

Although Matthew 13 applies to false believers, there is another principle we can glean from this. The enemy sows weeds in our souls. Those weeds choke the written Word out of our hearts and may cause us to release imperfect prophetic words out of our mouths. So what are these weeds? Weeds grow from seeds. Therefore, the weeds are the manifestation of the seeds the enemy planted in our souls—seeds we did not root out.

These seeds can come in the form of vain imaginations we don't cast down (see 2 Cor. 10:5). These seeds can come in the form of lies that leave us deceived. These seeds can come in the form of worldly temptations, such as lust of the eyes, the lust of the flesh, and the pride of life—or, as the New Living Translation puts it, "For the world offers only a craving for physical pleasure, a craving for everything we see, and pride in our achievements and possessions..." (1 John 2:16).

When the enemy's seeds grow, they turn into weeds that compete with the fruit of the Spirit—love, joy, peace, patience, kindness, goodness, faithfulness, gentleness, and self-control—in our lives. Because the gifts of God are irrevocable (see Rom. 11:29), the gifts of the Spirit may still manifest without the fruit of the Spirit. At best our influence will wane. At worst we stray down the broad path that leads to destruction and lead others down that path with presumptuous or false prophecy.

Prophets, spend some time with the Holy Spirit and ask Him to help you root out any seeds the enemy planted in your life before they sprout up as weeds. Then ask Him to help you see the weeds that are hiding in your soul so you can repent for allowing the enemy into your headspace. Finally, ask the Holy Spirit to pull the weeds. Do this periodically. The enemy sows seeds when our guard is down.

— *Prayer* —

Father, in the name of Jesus, help me see the enemy's seeds and weeds in my soul so I can renounce them specifically and You can free me completely. I repent for not tending the garden of my mind more diligently. Help me be a good steward of my soul. Renew my mind.

MARCH 19

Prophets Bring Warfare

"Praise the Lord, who is my rock. He trains my hands for war and gives my fingers skill for battle" (Psalm 144:1).

Prophets bring warfare. One of my mentors from many years ago shared that truth with my heart. Of course, I already knew that but when she put it that way—"Prophets bring warfare"—it resonated a little more deeply. Maybe because I was going through some extreme warfare at the time. The sooner you accept these three words—"Prophets bring warfare"—the better prepared you'll be for the attack.

There will be times—and probably many times—when you feel that all hell is breaking loose against you. Maybe you are under spiritual attack even as you read these words. You are not the first prophet and you will not be the last prophet to endure warfare. Besides David and Deborah, prophets in the Bible usually were not the ones to lead the charge in warfare. Kings typically went to battle after the prophets gave them strategies for attack.

Nevertheless, prophets in the Bible experienced spiritual warfare whether or not they saw it as such. When Elijah called the showdown at Mount Carmel, it was as much a spiritual confrontation with Baal as it was a natural confrontation with the false prophets. Elijah called on the God who answers by fire and there was a supernatural manifestation in what was really a supernatural war.

When Jezebel threatened to have Elijah murdered within 24 hours, this was as much a spiritual attack as it was a natural threat. In the realm of the spirit, a word curse carrying witchcraft and a spirit of death attacked Elijah's mind. He left his servant behind and went into hiding. The spiritual warfare Daniel faced in Babylon manifested in the lion's den. The spiritual warfare Isaiah faced ended with him being sawn in two.

While you're not likely to wind up in a lion's den, make no mistake, the enemy is roaming about like a roaring lion seeking someone to devour (see 1 Pet. 5:8). As a prophet, you are a threat to the kingdom of darkness because you carry the living word of God, which brings light and life into the earth. Know your God but know your enemy.

— *Prayer* —

Father, in the name of Jesus, train my hands for war and my fingers to fight. Teach me to gird up the loins of my mind so the enemy attack bounces off my helmet of salvation if I forget to lift up my shield of faith. Show me the root of the attacks against me so I can prevail.

Divine Fire in Your Bones

"For when I spoke, I cried out; I shouted, 'Violence and plunder!' Because the word of the Lord was made to me a reproach and a derision daily. Then I said, 'I will not make mention of Him, nor speak anymore in His name.' But His word was in my heart like a burning fire shut up in my bones; I was weary of holding it back, and I could not" (Jeremiah 20:8-9 NKJV).

Jeremiah wasn't just a weeping prophet. He was also a fiery prophet. Early in Jeremiah's ministry, when God sent Jeremiah to look for even one honest person in Jerusalem so He didn't have to destroy the city, God told him, "Because the people are talking like this, my messages will flame out of your mouth and burn the people like kindling wood" (Jer. 5:14). It's no wonder he was so persecuted.

God told Jeremiah His words were like fire (see Jer. 23:29). So it only made sense that the prophetic word the prophet received was like fire in his bones. Jeremiah felt the fire before God gave the explanation of what he was experiencing. Of course, this was a supernatural fire kindled by the God who answers by fire. Maybe you've experienced that fire in your bones. It's a sign of God's urgency.

The prophet Amos felt a similar stirring in his spirit. Right after God told him he doesn't do anything without revealing His secrets to His servants the prophets, He said, "The lion has roared—so who isn't frightened? The Sovereign Lord has spoken—so who can refuse to proclaim his message?" (Amos 3:8). Again, there is a sense of urgency in that fire. Amos described it as a roar on the inside he was charged with releasing.

There are times when you will receive a word from the Lord that you know will not be popular. There are times when you know the prophetic word goes against the party line, your tribe's preferences, or your pastor's theology. God's Word trumps party lines, preferences, and theologies.

The mature prophet will stand in the face of hard-headed people with a forehead like flint and release the fiery word of God. The fire will be your sign. Remember, it's not a fire in your soul but a fire in your spirit lit by the Lord. If you do not obey the unction to release the word, you will wear yourself out trying to hold it in. This is one of the ways of God with the prophet.

— *Prayer* —

Father, in the name of Jesus, please help me discern between an urgency in my soul and the urgency of Your Spirit within my spirit. Would You give me the courage and confidence to release fiery words to a hard-headed people? Teach me to set my face like flint.

Cleansing Your Mouth

"Then I said, 'It's all over! I am doomed, for I am a sinful man. I have filthy lips, and I live among a people with filthy lips. Yet I have seen the King, the Lord of Heaven's Armies.' Then one of the seraphim flew to me with a burning coal he had taken from the altar with a pair of tongs. He touched my lips with it and said, 'See, this coal has touched your lips. Now your guilt is removed, and your sins are forgiven'" (Isaiah 6:5-7).

Prophets love to talk about their encounters with God, and we see spectacular encounters prophets like Ezekiel, Zechariah, and Isaiah had in the pages of Scripture. Fewer of us would welcome the type of encounter Isaiah had during the year King Uzziah died. It started out as a breathtaking vision of the Lord sitting on a lofty throne and the train of His robe filled the temple. Isaiah wrote:

Attending him were mighty seraphim, each having six wings. With two wings they covered their faces, with two they covered their feet, and with two they flew. They were calling out to each other, "Holy, holy, holy is the Lord of Heaven's Armies! The whole earth is filled with his glory!" Their voices shook the Temple to its foundations, and the entire building was filled with smoke (Isaiah 6:2-4).

When Isaiah saw the Lord, he immediately understood his own weaknesses. Apparently, his greatest perceived weakness was his mouth. He understood that he could not walk in the highest levels of his prophetic calling without a deliverance of the mouth. Remember, out of the abundance of your heart your mouth speaks (see Luke 6:45). What comes out of your mouth is a sign of what's in your heart, so your mouth issue could really be rooted in a heart issue.

Prophet, the good news is God can deal with our heart issues that lead to our mouth issues. Before He calls you to prophesy over nations, He will purify your heart and cleanse your mouth. Before God puts fire in your bones, He may put fire on your mouth.

Proverbs 13:3 assures, "He who guards his mouth preserves his life, but he who opens wide his lips will have destruction" (NKJV). And Proverbs 16:23 tells us, "The heart of the wise teaches his mouth, and adds learning to his lips" (NKJV). Ultimately, we know death and life are in the power of the tongue (see Prov. 18:21).

— *Prayer* —

Father, in the name of Jesus, purify my heart and cleanse my mouth from all evil thoughts and words. Help me tame my tongue that's vulnerable to speaking forth the enemy's plans instead of Your plans. Deal with my filthy lips so I can release a clean prophetic river.

Rejecting the Spirit of Rejection

"To the praise of the glory of His grace, by which He made us accepted in the Beloved" (Ephesians 1:6 NKJV).

My first mentor in the prophetic shared with me a powerful truth that I have never forgotten and will never forget: You can't have a prophet with rejection. What she meant was, prophets need to get delivered from rejection. Her words were on point for me then. Maybe they are on point for you now.

Rejection used to have a tight rein on my soul—and I didn't even know it. All I knew was that I always felt like there was something wrong with me. I often felt like nobody really cared. And I sometimes felt like people were talking about me behind my back. If I walked past people who were laughing, I assumed they were laughing at me. It was all in my mind.

Rejection works subtly to destroy your self-esteem and your purpose. Rejection causes you to feel sorry for yourself. Rejection spurs you to reject other people before they have an opportunity to reject you. Rejection wants you to base your worth on what you do instead of who you are in Christ.

There is true rejection, but there is also imagined rejection. Indeed, rejection often works through imaginations. The spirit of rejection can twist your perception of circumstances so it looks and feels like you are being rejected even when you aren't. In the natural, it's called a misunderstanding. But if you don't cast down the imaginations that ride on the back of misunderstandings, the spirit of rejection will work to form a stronghold in your mind that controls your thought patterns and makes it easy for this demon to hold you in bondage.

Whether you are in full-blown bondage to rejection or just have an occasional battle with this spirit, the remedy is the same: Reject rejection and accept your God-given identity. You can't walk in your highest prophetic calling if you have a spirit of rejection because you will wind up bowing to fear of rejection instead of the Prophet Jesus.

— *Prayer* —

Father, in the name of Jesus, cause me to despise rejection the way You do. Give me a deep revelation that I am accepted in the beloved. Help me discern the voice of rejection and to cast it off and cast it out in the name of Christ and by the power of the Holy Spirit.

Prophesying into Revival

"The high and lofty one who lives in eternity, the Holy One, says this: 'I live in the high and holy place with those whose spirits are contrite and humble. I restore the crushed spirit of the humble and revive the courage of those with repentant hearts'" (Isaiah 57:15).

Prophets are spiritually equipped to serve as the eyes, ears, and voice to the Body of Christ. Although prophets have many functions, one of the most vital in this hour from a revival and awakening perspective is the John the Baptist mandate to lead the church into repentance—to prepare a people for the Second Coming of the Lord. Matthew 3:1-3 says:

In those days John the Baptist came to the Judean wilderness and began preaching. His message was, "Repent of your sins and turn to God, for the Kingdom of Heaven is near." The prophet Isaiah was speaking about John when he said, "He is a voice shouting in the wilderness, 'Prepare the way for the Lord's coming! Clear the road for him!'"

Let's face it: There is no revival without repentance—and it's not just repentance from sins like lying, gossiping, and prayerlessness. It's a change in the way we think about church, the gifts of the Spirit, and even Jesus Himself. The spirits of religion and Jezebel that killed the prophets in former days are still working to silence the voices of the prophets of revival today. These spirits have watered down the gospel, shut out—or perverted—the gifts of the spirit, and skewed our perspective of Jesus as Bridegroom, King, and Judge.

Meanwhile, some prophets in this hour are prophesying judgment and curses—doom and gloom. Clearly, God has lifted some of His hedge of protection from many nations, but using our anointed mouths to continually confess judgment over mercy will bear fruit we don't want to eat. When God wanted to judge Sodom and Gomorrah, Abraham interceded (see Gen. 18–19).

God is a God of hope, and in this emerging move of God prophets sent out as individuals, in teams, or in companies need to be sober-minded and warn of the wages of sin and the law of sowing and reaping sin, but the prophetic voices most closely aligned with God's heart in this hour are carrying a message of hope against hope. Will you prophesy into revival?

— *Prayer* —

Father, in the name of Jesus, help me embrace my responsibility to call the church to repentance, even though it may not make me a popular prophet. Teach me to balance calls for repentance with promises of revival as I prophesy about the next great move of God.

Cultivating Prophetic Boldness

"The wicked flee when no one pursues, but the righteous are bold as a lion" (Proverbs 28:1 NKJV).

Boldness eluded me for many years. I was shy, timid. I am naturally an introvert, so I don't like to be seen to begin with. But I was so timid I would run and hide if I thought someone was going to call on me to pray or prophesy publicly. My first mentor in the prophetic gave me some keen advice—pray for boldness.

Throughout the pages of the Bible, we see boldness as part of the prophetic DNA of many men of God. Moses confronted Pharaoh and delivered millions of Israelites from Egyptian bondage after releasing a series of plagues. And remember when King Ahab called Elijah a troubler of Israel? Elijah didn't back down or run away. Instead, the prophet boldly replied:

> *"I have made no trouble for Israel. ...You and your family are the troublemakers, for you have refused to obey the commands of the Lord and have worshiped the images of Baal instead. Now summon all Israel to join me at Mount Carmel, along with the 450 prophets of Baal and the 400 prophets of Asherah who are supported by Jezebel"* (1 Kings 18:18-19).

Elijah was so bold he not only confronted a wicked king but called a showdown with 850 prophets. Operating in the spirit of Elijah, John the Baptist called the religious leaders to the carpet: "But when he saw many Pharisees and Sadducees coming to watch him baptize, he denounced them. 'You brood of snakes!' he exclaimed. 'Who warned you to flee the coming wrath?'" (Matt. 3:7). Jesus as prophet was at least as bold.

Now, remember, boldness and harshness are not the same thing. Boldness is fearless in the face of danger. Boldness is a daring spirit. Boldness is freedom. When the apostles were filled with the Spirit of God, they spoke the word of God with boldness (see Acts 4:31). Prophets filled with the Spirit of God should be equally as bold. That's how people will know we've been with Jesus (see Acts 4:13). The righteous are as bold as lions. Know who you are and boldness will come.

— *Prayer* —

Father, in the name of Jesus, would You give me the boldness of the Lion of the Tribe of Judah? Deliver me from the spirit of timidity and cowardice that keeps my tongue cleaving to the roof of my mouth when I should be prophesying a bold word.

Overcoming Prophetic Stage Fright

"For God has not given us a spirit of fear, but of power and of love and of a sound mind" (2 Timothy 1:7 NKJV).

God told Ezekiel not to look at the people's faces as he prophesied. Why? Well, have you ever stood up in front of a congregation and actually looked at the people's faces?

Many of them look mad. Some of them look like they are going to fall asleep. Others just look completely blank. It can be scary from up there! If the emotion of fear isn't anguish enough, the devil follows it up with a heavy dose of condemnation for being too timid to step out in faith and speak what you believe the Lord is saying.

Oh sure, I remember being in an intercessory prayer meeting and feeling the unction of the Holy Spirit bubbling up. I knew the Lord was speaking to me, but when the prayer leader called for anyone who had a prophetic word to step forward I was suddenly paralyzed with fear.

Keep in mind that just a minute before that I was praying boldly with the rest of them, binding up principalities and powers and wreaking havoc on the enemy's camp. Then "the word of the Lord came unto me saying" and I ran to my cave (a.k.a. the women's restroom). Or I stood there struggling within myself, trying to convince my soul to yield to the Spirit.

The root of prophetic stage fright is the fear of having your performance evaluated negatively. The bottom line is that it's the fear of man, of what man might think of you, or any persecution it may bring you. We can't walk in the fear of God and the fear of man at the same time. Overcoming prophetic stage fright at the highest level means fearing God more than you fear man. Fear of man will prevent us from prophesying the will of the Lord. If we are concerned about what people will think of us, then how can we deliver a word boldly?

Ask the Lord to deliver you completely from fear. The effectiveness of your prophetic ministry depends on it.

— *Prayer* —

Father, in the name of Jesus, deliver me from prophetic stage fright. Help me to overcome those nervous jitters that rise up when You are leading me to prophesy publicly. Help me to avoid looking at the faces of the people who I am afraid are judging and criticizing me.

Embracing Your Cross

"Then Jesus said to his disciples, 'If any of you wants to be my follower, you must give up your own way, take up your cross, and follow me'" (Matthew 16:24).

Caught up in the spirit during prayer, I saw a road in the seer dimensions—a pathway. As I kept on looking I noticed something curious. Crosses were lying on the ground. One after another, I saw crosses strewn along this narrow path.

These crosses belonged to people who started down the path to self-denial. These crosses belonged to people who started down the road to the knowledge of the holy. These crosses belonged to people who started down the lane of life—that narrow road that's constricted by pressure—and when that pressure became too great, when the cost became too much, they abandoned the cross and turned back. I am reminded of Christ's words in Matthew 16:24-27:

> *If anyone desires to be My disciple, let him deny himself [disregard, lose sight of, and forget himself and his own interests] and take up his cross and follow Me [cleave steadfastly to Me, conform wholly to My example in living and, if need be, in dying, also].*
>
> *For whoever is bent on saving his [temporal] life [his comfort and security here] shall lose it [eternal life]; and whoever loses his life [his comfort and security here] for My sake shall find it [life everlasting].*
>
> *For what will it profit a man if he gains the whole world and forfeits his life [his blessed life in the kingdom of God]? Or what would a man give as an exchange for his [blessed] life [in the kingdom of God]?*
>
> *For the Son of Man is going to come in the glory (majesty, splendor) of His Father with His angels, and then He will render account and reward every man in accordance with what he has done* (AMPC).

You can't walk in the highest levels of prophetic ministry if you do not embrace the work of the cross—and embrace your own cross. The good news is if you've left your cross on the side of the narrow road, you can still pick it up and follow Christ again.

— *Prayer* —

Father, in the name of Jesus, help me deny myself and pick up my cross and truly follow You wherever You lead me, knowing You may lead me to a place I do not want to go. I am Your servant, Your prophet, and Your friend. Give me the grace of surrender.

Releasing Prophetic Decrees

"Thou shalt also decree a thing, and it shall be established unto thee: and the light shall shine upon thy ways" (Job 22:28 KJV).

Just as prophets are called to a priesthood, prophets are also called to a kingship. Remember, Peter tells us we are a royal priesthood (see 1 Pet. 2:9). Priests make intercession. Kings make decrees. We have to know when to shift from interceding on our knees to standing with decrees. Prophets are well equipped to follow the Holy Spirit's leadership to make that shift, but we need to understand the power of a decree.

Different translations shed interesting light on Job 22:28. For example, the New International Version tells us, "What you decide on will be done, and light will shine on your ways." The Contemporary English Version puts it this way: "He will do whatever you ask, and life will be bright."

The Amplified Bible, Classic Edition expounds on this truth a little more: "You shall also decide and decree a thing, and it shall be established for you; and the light [of God's favor] shall shine upon your ways." And *The Message* assures, "You'll decide what you want and it will happen; your life will be bathed in light."

Prophetic decrees are decrees that emanate from your anointed mouth through a Holy Spirit-inspired utterance. It could be a Scripture the Holy Spirit drops in your spirit. Or it could be prophetic wisdom that He fills your mouth with as you set out to pray. In a moment, you could be in a priestly role petitioning, and in the next moment you could be in a kingly role decreeing.

When we decree the written Word of God or release prophetic decrees, we are standing on solid ground and results are guaranteed because, again, God's Word does not return to Him void. It accomplishes what He sends it to do through you (see Isa. 55:10-11). Your carnal nature will decree what it wants, what the devil wants—anything but what God wants. Your spirit man will decree the will of the Lord.

— *Prayer* —

Father, in the name of Jesus, help me navigate the realm of intercession with an understanding of the power of a decree. Lead me to exchange the priest's mantle for the king's mantle when I need to shift an atmosphere with Spirit-inspired words that enforce Your rule of law.

Breaking Jezebel's Back

"Judah, your brothers will praise you. You will grasp your enemies by the neck..."
(Genesis 49:8).

In one season, my throat was under such attack it felt like every sip of water was running over shards of glass on the way down my esophagus. I started asking around and, lo and behold, many prophets were experiencing major throat issues as well. In that, God showed me a pattern of a Jezebelic attack and how to fire back.

While Jezebel, a seducing spirit, often attacks our minds, this nefarious spirit will also release subtle attacks on prophetic voices by targeting the throat. The throat is home to your vocal cords, so when witchcraft—the power of the enemy—is targeted at your throat it becomes difficult to release your voice. Instead of a strong, clear, bold voice, throat attacks leave the voice weak, scratchy, and with painful spasms.

This is not a new strategy. The wicked Queen Jezebel in the Old Testament was known for slaughtering the prophets at the edge of the sword, slicing through the vocal cords and leaving them voiceless in the last moments of their life so they were unable to prophesy her demise.

In the Bible days, warriors put their foot on the neck of the enemy, crushing their throat and silencing their voice. Jezebel is mimicking that strategy. Jezebel may also put a yoke of bondage around your neck to keep you silent. When the enemy was attacking David, he uttered these words: "My mouth is dried up like a potsherd, and my tongue sticks to the roof of my mouth; you lay me in the dust of death" (Ps. 22:15 NIV).

It's time to flip the script. You break these Jezebelic attacks against the throat by praising God through the pain until you reach a crescendo in the spirit where boldness arises for you to take authority over the attacks. Psalm 149:6 puts it this way, "Let the praises of God be in their mouths, and a sharp sword in their hands."

God told Judah his hand will be at the throat of his enemies (see Gen. 49:8). You put your hand to Jezebel's throat by pressing through the dryness, the scratchiness, and the painful spams with praise. But don't stop there. Put your foot on the neck of your enemy and declare victory with a shout of thanksgiving.

— *Prayer* —

Father, in the name of Jesus, help me praise and worship You in spirit and in truth when the enemy is attacking my throat with lies and witchcraft. Help me press past the attack with the spirit of Judah that overcomes the spirit of Jezebel. No matter what, I will yet praise You.

When You Are Rebuked for Prophesying

"So he told it to his father and his brothers; and his father rebuked him and said to him, 'What is this dream that you have dreamed? Shall your mother and I and your brothers indeed come to bow down to the earth before you?'" (Genesis 37:10 NKJV)

When Joseph was 17 years old, he dreamed a dream and apparently told his brothers immediately. Joseph's brothers already hated him because their father Jacob favored the young man more than his elder brothers. In fact, Jacob even presented Joseph with a special coat of many colors, making him the envy of the family. The Bible says that his brothers "hated Joseph because their father loved him more than the rest of them. They couldn't say a kind word to him" (Gen. 37:4).

Joseph must have known his brothers didn't like him, so why he would share this prophetic dream is beyond me. It's possible he was operating in pride, and he was certainly unfamiliar with prophetic protocol. After all, there was no school of the prophets. On the other hand, he could have just been excited about the dream and wanted to share. In any case, it wasn't wisdom to prophesy this to his brothers:

"We were out in the field, tying up bundles of grain. Suddenly my bundle stood up, and your bundles all gathered around and bowed low before mine!" (Gen. 37:7). It doesn't take a prophet to figure out that this would only cause his brothers to hate him more—and it did, according to verse 8.

That didn't seem to deter young Joseph, though. He had another dream, made the same mistake of telling his brothers, and this time he shared the prophecy with his father also: "Listen, I have had another dream," he said. "The sun, moon, and eleven stars bowed low before me!" (Gen. 37:9). Jacob wasn't having it. Jacob immediately rebuked Joseph, which probably really stung given his special bond with his father and his strained relationship with his brothers. Shortly thereafter, his brothers conspired to kill him.

Have you ever been rebuked for sharing a true prophetic dream? Many prophetic people have experienced criticism—from people they know and from people they don't—for sharing prophetic dreams. It stings and can make you second-guess whether you really heard from the Lord if you meditate on it too long.

Don't adopt a spirit of rejection. Just wait it out. Time is on your side and God will vindicate your true dreams. Ask God to help you respond to rebukes with humility. Remember, Jacob kept the dream in mind despite the rebuke (see Gen. 37:11).

— *Prayer* —

Father, in the name of Jesus, give me wisdom in what to share and what not to share so I don't walk into a strong rebuke for releasing a true prophetic word with wrong timing, the wrong way, and to the wrong people. Help me embrace rebukes as learning experiences on my journey.

The Spirit of the Fear of the Lord

"And the Spirit of the Lord will rest on him—the Spirit of wisdom and understanding, the Spirit of counsel and might, the Spirit of knowledge and the fear of the Lord" (Isaiah 11:2).

Isaiah 11:2 speaks of the spirit of the fear of the Lord. Prophets who do not walk in the fear of the Lord are more likely to be presumptuous in speaking a word in His name or, alternatively, not speaking forth what He commands them to say. Either side of this equation is dangerous. The fear of the Lord is vital to the prophetic ministry.

What is the fear of the Lord? It's not being afraid of Him. God doesn't want us to be afraid of Him like we would be afraid of an abusive father. The fear of the Lord is to reverence Him, to honor and respect Him. For starters, the fear of the Lord is to hate evil (see Prov. 8:13). Fear in that verse is the Hebrew word *yare*, which means "to fear, to respect, to reverence."

Jesus, our prototype Prophet, once said: "Don't be afraid of those who want to kill your body; they cannot touch your soul. Fear only God, who can destroy both soul and body in hell" (Matt. 10:28). The Greek word for fear in this verse is *phobos*, which can be translated "reverential fear." *Vine's Complete Expository Dictionary* defines it as "not a mere 'fear' of His power and righteous retribution, but a wholesome dread of displeasing Him." That's intense!

Prophets need great wisdom, and Proverbs 9:10 tells us plainly, "Fear of the Lord is the foundation of wisdom." Prophets need knowledge from the Lord, and Proverbs 1:7 assures, "Fear of the Lord is the foundation of true knowledge." Prophets long to hear God's secrets, and Psalm 25:14 promises, "The Lord is a friend to those who fear him." Prophets must depend on God for everything, and Psalm 34:9 says, "Fear the Lord, you his godly people, for those who fear him will have all they need."

Solomon once said, "Here now is my final conclusion: Fear God and obey his commands, for this is everyone's duty" (Eccles. 12:13). If there is one thing I have going for me, I consistently walk in the fear of the Lord. He doesn't expect us to be perfect, He just expects us to respect Him. Ask the Father to give you the spirit of the fear of the Lord.

— *Prayer* —

Father, in the name of Jesus, teach me to walk circumspectly. Help me not to fear man who can kill the body but give me a revelation of the benefits of walking in a reverential fear of the One who gives me life, love, and prophetic words.

Discerning the Prophetic Prima Donna

"For the world offers only a craving for physical pleasure, a craving for everything we see, and pride in our achievements and possessions. These are not from the Father, but are from this world" (1 John 2:16).

An encounter with a prophetic prima donna got me thinking: How do Christians with international ministries, book deals, and large staffs become such drama queens (and kings) who think more highly of themselves than they ought?

Did they start their journey as part of the nameless, faceless generation only to fall victim to pride's puffery? Or were they always secretly striving for the spotlight? Were they always willing to climb over (and even trample on) anyone and everyone to get to the top of the ministry ladder? How does it happen? And how can we keep from falling into this trap as God promotes us to more visible roles in the kingdom or in society?

Every time I run into one of these prophetic prima donnas I walk away with the fear of God. I know anyone can be deceived by the pride of life, especially when no one is willing to hold you accountable for the pattern of pride that consistently manifests in your life.

I've come to this conclusion: There is not any one formula for the making of a prophetic prima donna. Any of us can fall into pride any number of ways. I've come to the conclusion that in order to avoid falling into the sins of prophetic prima donnas—the ones who mistreat people and begin to think they deserve a measure of the glory for running the ministry the Lord assigned them—we need to frequently check our own hearts. And we need to be open to hear those who labor with us if they suggest we may have an "issue" to deal with.

We need to ask ourselves: How are we treating people? How do we think about people? Do we take God's glory? Walk in false humility? I think if we all focused on walking in humility and love, we'd be more ready to hear and obey the Holy Spirit to help others whose pride may be setting them up for a fall. Ask the Lord to help you see the pride of life in your heart.

— *Prayer* —

Father, in the name of Jesus, help me not to follow the path of the prophetic prima donnas I see on television networks and major conference platforms. Teach me to walk in humility, with the revelation that everything I carry comes from You. Deliver me from selfish ambition.

APRIL

"At the usual time for offering the evening sacrifice, Elijah the prophet walked up to the altar and prayed, 'O Lord, God of Abraham, Isaac, and Jacob, prove today that you are God in Israel and that I am your servant. Prove that I have done all this at your command. O Lord, answer me! Answer me so these people will know that you, O Lord, are God and that you have brought them back to yourself.' Immediately the fire of the Lord flashed down from heaven and burned up the young bull, the wood, the stones, and the dust. It even licked up all the water in the trench! And when all the people saw it, they fell face down on the ground and cried out, 'The Lord—he is God! Yes, the Lord is God!'" (1 Kings 18:36-39).

Deliverance from Foolishness

"And the word of the Lord came to me, saying, 'Son of man, prophesy against the prophets of Israel who prophesy, and say to those who prophesy out of their own heart, "Hear the word of the Lord!" Thus says the Lord God: "Woe to the foolish prophets, who follow their own spirit and have seen nothing! O Israel, your prophets are like foxes in the deserts"'' (Ezekiel 13:1-4 NKJV).

This is a sobering word. God is calling out the foolish prophets who follow their own spirit and haven't really seen anything at all. Prophets are called to prophesy out of God's heart, not their own minds or spirits. Our human spirit has good things in it, but a good thing isn't necessarily a God thing. Our vain imaginations should not inform our prophetic utterances.

Ezekiel 13 offers verses we don't like to read, but we need to stay sober-minded and remember that although we can all innocently miss it there is danger in following temptations to prophesy out of our soul when we haven't heard or seen anything. Let's break down verse 3 using the Hebrew words that show just how dangerous that really is.

"Foolish" in this verse comes from the Hebrew word *nabal*. It translates "foolish, senseless, fool." The Bible has plenty to say about the fool and none of it is good. Fools take no pleasure in understanding (see Prov. 18:2). Fools give full vent to their spirit (see Prov. 29:11). Fools despise wisdom and instruction (see Prov. 1:7). A fool's mouth is his ruin (see Prov. 18:7). Doing wrong is like a joke to a fool (see Prov. 10:23). The Bible goes on and on about fools.

What about this woe? Woe is an expression of grief or regret. Prophets who act like fools should grieve over their behavior. Paul called it godly sorrow:

For godly sorrow produces repentance leading to salvation, not to be regretted; but the sorrow of the world produces death. For observe this very thing, that you sorrowed in a godly manner: What diligence it produced in you, what clearing of yourselves, what indignation, what fear, what vehement desire, what zeal, what vindication! In all things you proved yourselves to be clear in this matter (2 Corinthians 7:10-11 NKJV).

If you've behaved foolishly in word or deed, repent to God and repent to the people you may have harmed. It's vital to keeping a pure prophetic flow.

— *Prayer* —

Father, in the name of Jesus, forgive me if I have prophesied a good thing out of my spirit instead of a God thing out of Your heart. I repent if I have misrepresented You and behaved foolishly with my mantle. Teach me to divide between my spirit and Yours.

Ready, Set, Shift

"And He changes the times and the seasons..." (Daniel 2:21 NKJV).

Before we can shift spiritual atmospheres around us, we have to shift our own personal spiritual atmosphere. And that means creating a climate that sets the stage for God to move in our lives. Scientists will tell you that the earth's seasons have shifted in recent years—and they point to climate change as the foundation for the shift.

If we translate this to a spiritual reality—as natural surroundings often correspond to spiritual conditions—it's clear that changing our spiritual climate sets the stage for a shift in spiritual seasons. We can't shift our seasons—God does that. But we can create a climate that invites Him to do the work in our hearts that prepares us for the next season.

What is the spiritual climate over your life? If you are angry, ungrateful, complaining, greedy, controlling, critical, impatient, indifferent, discouraged, jealous, frightened, frustrated, unforgiving, resentful, bitter, selfish, or something of the like, you're creating a spiritual climate over your life that repels the Holy Spirit. He loves you, yes, but your flesh is warring against His Spirit.

If, by contrast, you are thankful, peaceful, prayerful, joyful, generous, forgiving, loving, content, selfless, hopeful, faithful, inspired, worshipful, you are creating an atmosphere that attracts the presence of God. And the presence of the Holy Spirit is the ultimate key to spiritual change and growth. Put another way, we need to cultivate the fruit of the Spirit in our lives and reject the works of the flesh. In doing so, we position our hearts for God to shift us into fruitful seasons of harvest.

We know that if we meditate on the Word day and night we will stand like trees planted by the rivers of water, bringing forth fruit in its season and prospering in whatever we do (see Ps. 1:2-3). But we must also know that it is God who changes the times and seasons (see Dan. 2:21). We can't change our own season, but we can position ourselves for a season shift.

— *Prayer* —

Father, in the name of Jesus, give me the grace to cultivate a spiritual climate in my life that invites Your presence. Open the eyes of my heart so I can gain heaven's perspective and release the Kingdom to shift atmospheres in the places You've called me to walk.

Remnant Prophets Rising

"The remnant will return, the remnant of Jacob, to the Mighty God" (Isaiah 10:21 NKJV).

Elijah is a strategic example of a remnant prophet. A remnant is a part of the greater lot. You may be familiar with the term *remnant* if you've ever had carpet installed in your home. There are always pieces and scraps left over. Sometimes, people use the remnant as a doormat. It's the same in prophetic. We see remnant prophets treated like doormats while celebrity prophets have a red carpet rolled out for them.

Elijah knew he was a remnant prophet and felt the isolation of that status. In 1 Kings 19:10, he said, "I have been very zealous for the Lord God of hosts; for the children of Israel have forsaken Your covenant, torn down Your altars, and killed Your prophets with the sword. I alone am left; and they seek to take my life" (NKJV).

At two other occasions in Scripture, Elijah says similar words. Finally, God corrected him and informed him he was part of a larger remnant. God said He had 7,000 other prophets in the land who had not bowed a knee to Baal or kissed his face.

We can't be too hard on Elijah. He didn't see any other prophets around. When Jezebel started murdering the prophets, they either sold out and started serving her, hid in caves, or ran away. He didn't see any other prophets around him. When you are a remnant prophet, sometimes you feel like you are the only one—but you have to look for the rest of the remnant.

So what does a remnant prophet look like? For one thing, remnant prophets make themselves of no reputation. Philippians 2:5-7 tells us, "Let this mind be in you which was also in Christ Jesus, who, being in the form of God, did not consider it robbery to be equal with God, but made Himself of no reputation..." (NKJV).

Paul wasn't suggesting that prophets don't have a reputation. The lesson here is that remnant prophets don't set out to make their name known. They set out to make Christ's name known. It seems the boldest prophets are part of the remnant. Ask the Lord to help you find the rest of the remnant.

— *Prayer* —

Father, in the name of Jesus, help me find the rest of the remnant so I can run with a company of prophets who are uncompromising in the face of Jezebel's attacks. Lead me to the remnant so we can encourage each other to stand strong in a perverse society.

What Is the Lord Really Saying?

"Knowing this first, that no prophecy of Scripture is of any private interpretation, for prophecy never came by the will of man, but holy men of God spoke as they were moved by the Holy Spirit" (2 Peter 1:20-21 NKJV).

Prophets see, hear, and say what the Lord wants to share with people. But it's important to interpret what you see and hear before you open your holy mouth and say a thing that's going to shift an atmosphere or a person's life in the wrong direction. One of the ways prophets miss it is in the interpretation—and not just with dreams and visions but also in the realm of the still small voice of God.

In other words, it's important to understand first that you've heard from the Lord—to judge the revelation you receive as truly prophetic—and then ask the Lord what He is saying. This entire process can take place in seconds or take months.

At times, the unction will be strong to release without understanding. But without that unction, you need to press in for interpretation. Interpretation means understanding. You can have an accurate prophetic revelation and interpret it wrongly by not understanding the intended audience or the symbols.

The Passion Translation of 2 Peter 1:20 says, "You must understand this at the outset: Interpretation of scriptural prophecy requires the Holy Spirit, for it does not originate from someone's own imagination." *The Message* says, "The main thing to keep in mind here is that no prophecy of Scripture is a matter of private opinion."

We must be careful not to speak rashly. Proverbs 12:18 says, "There are those who speak rashly, like the piercing of a sword, but the tongue of the wise brings healing" (AMPC).

Was there a time when you had a right word and the wrong interpretation, the wrong timing, or the wrong setting? What did you learn from that? If this happens, be sure to ask the Lord how you missed it. He is the best teacher and you will learn and grow through humility. Ask the Holy Spirit to help you interpret what you hear rightly.

— *Prayer* —

Father, in the name of Jesus, remind me to test the prophetic revelation I receive, judging it thoroughly and seeking understanding from Your Spirit. Give me the courage to take responsibility when I miss it so I can learn and grow.

When You're Misunderstood and Maligned

"Moses assumed his fellow Israelites would realize that God had sent him to rescue them, but they didn't" (Acts 7:25).

It seems I've been misunderstood my whole life. I was an extremely shy kid, but some thought I was just a snob. As a prophetic voice, I'm attacked, maligned, and otherwise misunderstood on a weekly basis. Maybe you can relate. Nobody likes to be misunderstood. Indeed, it can be downright discouraging to be doing your utmost for His highest and have people wrongly judge your message and your motives.

So, what causes these misunderstandings and what can we do to help avoid them? Timing is key. If we are talking about spiritual things to someone who has their mind on natural things, we are often going to be misunderstood. Sometimes we are misunderstood by people who have hidden motives that cloud their ability to understand what we are doing or saying. Often someone operating in pride will accuse us of being conceited or exclusive. Someone with a Jezebel spirit will accuse us of being controlling. People can project on you what's in their own heart.

Sometimes we feel misunderstood when, in reality, others understand us better than we think they do. We have to remember that being misunderstood is a feeling. We "feeeeel misunderstood." But we may not be misunderstood at all. We could just feel that way because we don't get the response out of the person that we wanted.

The "misunderstood syndrome," as I call it, taps into self. It's our "self" that needs to feel understood. It's our "self" that feels rejected. It's our "self" that feels lonely. It's our "self" that gets depressed and wants to have a pity party. We need to get our minds off our self and on somebody else, helping others who are in much worse spots than we are. It's amazing how the burdens lift when you get your mind off yourself.

Jesus was misunderstood—and it didn't seem to bother His soul one bit. Remember that Jesus understands you perfectly (see Heb. 4:15). His understanding is inexhaustible and boundless (see Ps. 147:5). He is able immediately to run to the cry of those who are suffering (see Heb. 2:18). These Scriptures will help you stay steady in the midst of the pain of misunderstanding and the persecution that sometimes goes along with it.

— *Prayer* —

Father, in the name of Jesus, thank You that You understand me completely and love me thoroughly. I decree my feelings will not rule my life and my joy does not depend on people understanding me. I break the misunderstood syndrome off my life.

Beware Your Biases

"But the Lord said to Samuel, 'Don't judge by his appearance or height, for I have rejected him. The Lord doesn't see things the way you see them. People judge by outward appearance, but the Lord looks at the heart'" (1 Samuel 16:7).

If your eye is biased, you may see what other people want you to see rather than what God wants you to see. A bias is a bent or a tendency to favor one thing over another. It could be a prejudice but it could also just be a preference. Not all biases are evil. I prefer vanilla ice cream over chocolate. I prefer Adidas sneakers over Nikes. I prefer filet mignon over liver.

Although not all biases are evil, some biases can be destructive. We can fail to prophesy accurately over someone because of their appearance. We might have a hard time believing the Lord is really saying such words to someone who looks "that way." How we've been trained to operate in prophetic ministry can become a bias that can hinder the purity of our flow. What we've been taught about the Bible and our traditions can also skew our prophetic perspective.

Samuel was a seer with a bias. In 1 Samuel 16, God told the prophet to stop mourning for Saul and go to Bethlehem to anoint a new king. He told Samuel the king would be a son of a man named Jesse. Let's look at 1 Samuel 16:4-7 to see Samuel's bias:

So Samuel did as the Lord instructed. When he arrived at Bethlehem, the elders of the town came trembling to meet him. "What's wrong?" they asked. "Do you come in peace?"

"Yes," Samuel replied. "I have come to sacrifice to the Lord. Purify yourselves and come with me to the sacrifice." Then Samuel performed the purification rite for Jesse and his sons and invited them to the sacrifice, too.

When they arrived, Samuel took one look at Eliab and thought, "Surely this is the Lord's anointed!"

But the Lord said to Samuel, "Don't judge by his appearance or height, for I have rejected him. The Lord doesn't see things the way you see them. People judge by outward appearance, but the Lord looks at the heart."

Samuel almost anointed the wrong person as Israel's next king because Eliab, who was the eldest, would have been the natural choice due to custom. Cry out to God to show you your hidden biases so you don't prophesy out of them.

— *Prayer* —

Father, in the name of Jesus, deliver me from my biases. Help me develop a self-awareness of my preferences and prejudices so I can be careful to correct my thinking and reject any automatic responses to prophesy out of a deep-down bias.

Searching for Your Gap

"And I sought for a man among them, that should make up the hedge, and stand in the gap before me for the land, that I should not destroy it: but I found none" (Ezekiel 22:30 KJV).

The Bible says we are priests and kings (see 1 Pet. 2:9). In fact, we are royal priests—kingly priests. Jesus is the King of kings and the High Priest of priests. He is also the Prophet of prophets. So, with that in mind, have you considered the priesthood of the prophetic? You might be asking, "What is the priesthood of the prophetic?"

A priest in the common sense of the word is one who is authorized to act as an intermediary between man and God. Sounds a lot like an intercessor, doesn't it? We know that Jesus is our mediator; nevertheless, God has chosen not to do anything in the earth unless someone in this realm makes a petition. Although Jesus is seated at the right hand of the Father ever making intercession for us (see Isa. 53:12), prophets are still charged with serving the priestly duty of praying His will from heaven to earth (see Matt. 6:10).

In other words, God won't work in the earth unless we pray. The Lord said, "I looked for someone who might rebuild the wall of righteousness that guards the land. I searched for someone to stand in the gap in the wall so I wouldn't have to destroy the land, but I found no one" (Ezek. 22:30). Let those words not escape the Lord's lips in this generation!

Every believer is called to intercede. In 1 Timothy 2:1, the apostle Paul exhorts us to offer supplications, prayers, intercessions, and giving thanks for all people. Jesus ever lives to make intercession for us, but that does not do away with our responsibility to pray. Still, there are those with special callings as intercessors and prophets. You've probably heard it said before that every prophet is an intercessor, but not every intercessor is a prophet. Thank God for all those who are doers of 1 Timothy 2:1 and 2 Chronicles 7:14.

With these truths established, we must move deeper into the heart of the prophetic priestly duty to make intercession. Ask the Lord to help you find your gap to stand in.

— *Prayer* —

Father, in the name of Jesus, help me fully embrace the priesthood of the prophetic. Teach me the value of making intercession on the earth just as Jesus is making intercession in heaven. Warn me if I am neglecting this aspect of my calling and inspire me to stand in the gap.

The Danger of Monthly Prognosticators

"You are wearied in the multitude of your counsels; let now the astrologers, the stargazers, and the monthly prognosticators stand up and save you from what shall come upon you. Behold, they shall be as stubble, the fire shall burn them; they shall not deliver themselves from the power of the flame; it shall not be a coal to be warmed by, nor a fire to sit before!" (Isaiah 47:13-14 NKJV)

I've been troubled in my spirit for some time over what I call the "monthly prophecy trend." We see prophets—and even those who don't claim to be prophets—releasing a brand-spanking-new shiny happy prophetic word chock full of super-duper life-changing promises each and every month. Not just one, but scores and scores and scores of monthly prophetic words circulate social media. Many people are anticipating them with great excitement!

The problem is most of those prophecies fail. They fall right to the ground with a loud thud that echoes. The prophetic word did not prosper because it did not come out of God's mouth. Rather, it returned void. And yet the very next month, these social media prophets, motivated by clicks, pontificate about prophetic promises that must surely come to pass in a 30-day window.

This "monthly prophetic word" trend has troubled me for a long while. I understand a sermon series based on a prophetic word. I did that for a few months several years ago. When the Lord stopped, I stopped. I also understand sending out prophetic encouragement to those who follow your ministry each month. That's healthy.

What troubles me is these grandiose promises from scores of people each and every month that come with an unspoken guarantee that it will happen in that thirty-day window. Without fail, every single September, someone prophesies it's a "September to remember." Some prophesy every October how it's the month of harvest with strong instructions to sow. The only one who got a harvest was the prophet who prophesied it.

Beware of these traps in prophetic ministry. They may make you popular with man, but they don't make you popular with God. Your reputation in heaven matters more than your reputation on earth. Ask the Lord to show you if you are tapping into any prophetic trends that grieve His heart.

— *Prayer* —

Father, in the name of Jesus, help me avoid the prophetic trends and winds that don't come from Your Spirit. I don't want to be a prophet with gimmicks. I want to be a prophet who glorifies Your name. Help me avoid the popularity tricks and rely solely on You.

Turning the Key to Your City

"Receive this truth: Whatever you forbid on earth will be considered to be forbidden in heaven, and whatever you release on earth will be considered to be released in heaven" (Matthew 18:18 TPT).

Among the many assignments of prophets is the gatekeeper. Although all prophets don't stand in the gate as a main thrust of their ministry, some prophets are strategic gatekeepers over cities and nations—and God is raising up more gatekeeper prophets as the gates of hell continue trying to prevail against the church in regions of the world.

What is a gatekeeper? Simply stated, a gatekeeper is one who guards the gate or one who controls access. A gatekeeper is a praying prophet who makes a wall. The goal of the gatekeeper prophet is to forbid access to unauthorized persons and demonic intruders and to let in the King of glory.

Gatekeepers are vital in the house of God. In Scripture, gatekeepers were set at every gate at the house of the Lord deciding what comes in and what goes out. Second Chronicles 23:19 tells us, "He also stationed gatekeepers at the gates of the Lord's Temple to keep out those who for any reason were ceremonially unclean."

But, again, prophets are not just gatekeepers in the house of God but also in their jurisdiction, whether that be a city, region, or nation. The greater the sphere of authority the gatekeeper prophet stewards, the greater responsibility to discern in prayer who is approaching the gate. Gatekeeping also demands a warrior's mentality as demons try to storm the gates of the city with force.

One weapon in the arsenal of the gatekeeper prophet is the collective keys of the Kingdom. Matthew 18:18 reads, "Truly I tell you, whatever you forbid and declare to be improper and unlawful on earth must be what is already forbidden in heaven, and whatever you permit and declare proper and lawful on earth must be what is already permitted in heaven" (AMPC). Gatekeeper intercessors have to understand the laws of the Kingdom and discern what God wants in and out.

Of course, gatekeeper prophets are not just opening and closing doors to demons, but also opening the door for the King of Glory to come in. All this is accomplished by the praying prophet at the gates. Ask God to give you a gatekeeper anointing for your city.

— *Prayer* —

Father, in the name of Jesus, give me the gatekeeper anointing for the jurisdiction You've called me to guard. Give me a persevering heart to stand in the gate and in the gap and a discerning spirit to determine if friend or foe is working to get into my region.

When God Speaks Judgment

"I pray that God, the source of hope, will fill you completely with joy and peace because you trust in him. Then you will overflow with confident hope through the power of the Holy Spirit" (Romans 15:13).

I'm not comfortable with the doom and gloom prophets who never have anything good to say. Although I do believe watchman prophets deliver more than the typical number of warnings compared to other types of prophets, God is not a doom and gloom God. God is a God of redemption.

Many nations are now seeing a measure of the judgment of God. That's a scary proposition and one that elicits a lot of emotion. My definition of judgment: We are reaping what we've sown and God isn't intervening without intercession. We're seeing the consequences of rebellion, and without repentance we can't stem the tide. The hedges of protection are eaten away and gaps are created by rebellion to God.

You might say, "Judgment is an old covenant thing." God is still a God of judgment. He just doesn't flood the earth, send fire and brimstone, or make nations servants to other nations. But God does not change. God still judges in the new covenant. Jesus is at the same time Bridegroom, King, and Judge.

Yes, God disciplines those He loves (see Heb. 12:6). That's a form of judgment. Why does He do that? To bring a wayward child back to His heart, to train us in righteousness and holiness, to produce an obedience in us that saves us from greater danger. And God still judges nations. Maybe you are as uncomfortable as I am with words of judgment. You should be. Any prophet who delights in releasing words of judgment does not have the heart of God.

Remember, God is not just a God of judgment. He's a God of hope. Even in the midst of judgment, God spoke these words to Israel:

"You will be in Babylon for seventy years. But then I will come and do for you all the good things I have promised, and I will bring you home again. For I know the plans I have for you," says the Lord. "They are plans for good and not for disaster, to give you a future and a hope" (Jeremiah 29:10-11).

If you receive words of judgment, ask the Lord to share with you His redeeming truth.

— *Prayer* —

Father, in the name of Jesus, help me understand Your heart in judgment and to remember always that mercy triumphs over judgment. Teach me how to deliver warning words—or even words of judgment—with redeeming truth, hope, and a way of escape. Inspire me to intercede.

When Mysteries Become Revelation

"As I briefly wrote earlier, God himself revealed his mysterious plan to me" (Ephesians 3:3).

Paul, who wrote two-thirds of the New Testament by direct revelation, spoke of mystic concepts again and again the Bible. If we are rooted and grounded in the Bible in the mystic realm, including trances, being caught up in the spirit, and transported in the spirit, we can engage with the whole counsel of God and understand better the mysteries of the Kingdom.

Mysteries are tied to the seer realm—and the Bible speaks of them over and over again. Although this devotional is not intended to give a deep explanation of the mystic realm, it's important that you understand some fundamentals as they relate to the seer realm. God makes mysteries known to us by revelation. Look at Ephesians 3:3-6:

> *As I briefly wrote earlier, God himself revealed his mysterious plan to me. As you read what I have written, you will understand my insight into this plan regarding Christ. God did not reveal it to previous generations, but now by his Spirit he has revealed it to his holy apostles and prophets.*
>
> *And this is God's plan: Both Gentiles and Jews who believe the Good News share equally in the riches inherited by God's children. Both are part of the same body, and both enjoy the promise of blessings because they belong to Christ Jesus.*

As I write in *Seer Dimensions*, the word *mystery* in that verse comes from the Greek word *musterion*. According to *The King James Version New Testament Greek Lexicon*, it means, "hidden thing, secret, mystery; generally mysteries, religious secrets, confided only to the initiated and not to ordinary mortals; a hidden or secret thing, not obvious to the understanding; a hidden purpose or counsel; the secret counsels which govern God in dealing with the righteous, which are hidden from ungodly and wicked men but plain to the godly; in rabbinic writings, it denotes the mystic or hidden sense, of an O saying; of an image or form seen in a vision; of a dream." Ask the Lord to help you tap into mysteries that become revelation.

— *Prayer* —

Father, in the name of Jesus, help me draw revelation out of the mysteries in Your Word. I want to understand the deep things of God, the secrets of Your Kingdom, and unlock the hidden counsel for my generation. Lead me into present-day truth.

Come Out of the Cave

"And there he went into a cave, and spent the night in that place; and behold, the word of the Lord came to him, and He said to him, "What are you doing here, Elijah?" (1 Kings 19:9 NKJV)

Prophets are called to see, hear, and say, but who can hear you when you are in a cave? In the Old Testament, they buried dead people in caves. It's time to stop letting the devil bury your voice in a cold place of rejection. It's time to stop letting the enemy bury your calling in a damp, dingy corner.

In the Old Testament, people hid from enemies in caves. It's time to stop hiding from Jezebel. It's time to stop hiding from the religious dogs. It's time to stop hiding from your persecutors. It's time to come out of the cave! A cave can quickly become a cage, locking up your voice.

You're not called to live in a cave, but many prophets have grown comfortable in the cave. They've grown complacent in the cave. They've even grown apathetic in the cave. Too many prophets have accepted the cave as their lot in life. They've settled down in the cave. They've decorated the cave—and redecorated the cave. They've wallpapered the cave with modern designs. They've hung pretty pictures of the outside world in the cave.

Elijah went running to the cave, escaping the wrath of Jezebel. God, knowing everything, asked Elijah a pointed question: "Why are you here?" (see 1 Kings 19:9). Of course, Elijah gave God a sob story about the death threat on his life. What did God say to the prophet in response? "Come out of the cave."

"Go out and stand before me on the mountain," the Lord told him (1 Kings 19:11). Elijah did not obey the word of the Lord. He apparently stayed in the cave. To get his attention, a windstorm, an earthquake, and fire manifested. Finally, Elijah responded to the voice of the Lord, wrapped his face in his cloak, and stood at the entrance of the cave, where God again asked Him what he was doing there and Elijah told Him his sob story again.

Finally, God gave him a new assignment that compelled him to leave the cave and return to ministry. Ask the Lord to give you the courage to come out of the cave.

— *Prayer* —

Father, in the name of Jesus, deliver me from the cave that I've holed up in running from Jezebel and religion. I don't want to be an echo in the cave; I want to be a voice to the nations. Give me the courage to step out of the cave and accept my assignment.

APRIL 13

A Prophet with Protocols

"All Scripture is inspired by God and is useful to teach us what is true and to make us realize what is wrong in our lives. It corrects us when we are wrong and teaches us to do what is right. God uses it to prepare and equip his people to do every good work" (2 Timothy 3:16-17).

Some prophets, seers, and otherwise prophetic people have never heard of prophetic protocols. Others have functioned under an unction, unaware of the need for protocols that serve as banks on the prophetic rivers. Still others have operated almost instinctively in some, if not many, wise protocols without anyone but the Holy Spirit leading, guiding, and teaching them.

What are prophetic protocols? A protocol is a code prescribing strict adherence to correct etiquette and precedence, according to *Merriam-Webster*'s dictionary. A protocol outlines the correct way something should be done.

Prophetic protocols are established by the Word and Spirit of God. Sure, some denominations may have established rigid and even ridiculous protocols for prophetic ministry that have given protocols a bad name. But the Bible does give us clear guidelines for operating in prophetic ministry and there is wisdom gained from experience.

Yes, there is a right way to operate in prophetic ministry. The right way blesses the Body of Christ through edification, exhortation, comfort, and at times direction and correction. Yes, there's more than one right way to operate in prophetic ministry, but there is a "right way." There's also a wrong way to operate in prophetic ministry that can bring harm. (For more, see my book *Prophetic Protocols & Ethics*.)

Practice prophetic responsibility by seeking to adhere to biblical ethics. Be unwilling to compromise, take shortcuts to promotions, or bring harm to people who believe in your utterance through presumptuous behavior or moving beyond the grace of God.

— *Prayer* —

Father, in the name of Jesus, help me see prophetic protocols rightly, not as restrictions to hold back my prophetic flow but as banks on the prophetic river that protect me from being accused or inadvertently causing people trouble. Let my prophetic ministry glorify Jesus.

The Ethical Prophet

"May integrity and honesty protect me, for I put my hope in you" (Psalm 25:21).

Doctors have ethics in the practice of medicine. Attorneys have ethics in the practice of law. Likewise, prophets should have ethics in the practice of prophetic ministry.

Ethics are different from protocols. What are ethics? Merriam-Webster's dictionary defines ethics as, "the discipline dealing with what is good and bad and with moral duty and obligation; a set of moral principles: a theory or system of moral values, the principles of conduct governing an individual or a group, a guiding philosophy, a consciousness of moral importance."

So protocols are the guidelines for safe and effective prophetic ministry. Ethics are the boundaries of what is right. Just because a method of prophetic ministry is effective doesn't make it ethical. You can get money from robbing a bank; that doesn't make it ethical. You can become a doctor by cheating on your exams, but that doesn't make it ethical. You can write a book by plagiarism, but that doesn't make it ethical.

Although there are many ethics to be considered, as I write in my book *Prophetic Protocols & Ethics*, we might sum up prophetic ethics in one verse: "No, O people, the Lord has told you what is good, and this is what he requires of you: to do what is right, to love mercy, and to walk humbly with your God" (Mic. 6:8). Yes, the manifestation of that threefold chord of ethics is diverse, but it boils down to this.

If that's too much to remember, Jesus further drilled down into one line, which many call the Golden Rule: "Do to others as you would like them to do to you" (Luke 6:31). If someone were ministering to you prophetically, how would you like them to treat you? How would you like them to deliver a hard word? How would you like them to treat your mother or your child? Would you want them to prophesy that to you publicly?

Ask the Holy Spirit to help you hold high ethics as a prophet. People notice that sort of integrity, and so does the Lord.

— *Prayer* —

Father, in the name of Jesus, help me walk in the highest ethics and integrity. Warn me if I am giving anyone any appearance of evil in my ministry. Help me take precautions so that I don't find myself in ethical binds that damage my prophetic reputation.

APRIL 15

Test Absolutely Everything

"But test everything that is said. Hold on to what is good" (1 Thessalonians 5:21).

Spontaneous prophecy is a beautiful thing, and seasoned prophets understand how to discern the strong unction of the Lord to prophesy at what seems to many almost on a whim. But not all prophecy should be released spontaneously. Directional words, words of judgment, and other serious prophecies should be judged before they are released.

Remember, judging your prophecy is first your responsibility, and you must learn the principles of testing the spirits. Before you take a prophecy to other people to judge—and before you release it publicly—take time to judge it yourself. Ensure it is in line with Scripture and that you aren't filtering through your own biases. You could judge wrongly, but you should make testing the spirit behind the prophetic word your first effort after hearing the prophetic word.

First John 4:1 exhorts believers: "Beloved, do not believe every spirit, but test the spirits, whether they are of God; because many false prophets have gone out into the world" (NKJV). *The Passion Translation* puts it this way: "Delightfully loved friends, don't trust every spirit, but carefully examine what they say to determine if they are of God, because many false prophets have mingled into the world."

This verse applies to testing the words, dreams, visions, and encounters of prophets, but if you are going to prophesy it also applies to testing the spirit that you are hearing, to make sure it is actually God.

When I was young in the prophetic, I would search out Scriptures that were in line with my prophetic words and ask the Holy Spirit to give me confirmation before releasing it publicly. As a matter of fact, with bold and significant national prophecies, I often still do.

Yes, there is grace to miss it, but by judging your own prophecy with the help of the Holy Spirit you can miss it privately rather than missing it publicly—and ask Him to show you where you went wrong. In other words, wouldn't you rather have the Holy Spirit show you privately how you missed it rather than bringing harm to someone or discrediting yourself publicly?

— *Prayer* —

Father, in the name of Jesus, help me discern the source of the voice I hear in my heart. Give me the grace and wisdom to test my own prophetic words before releasing them so I don't discredit my prophetic voice by allowing another spirit to speak through me.

Matters of the Heart

"Look, I am sending you the prophet Elijah before the great and dreadful day of the Lord arrives. His preaching will turn the hearts of fathers to their children, and the hearts of children to their fathers. Otherwise I will come and strike the land with a curse" (Malachi 4:5-6).

A critical aspect of prophetic ministry in today's world is found in these two verses of Malachi 4. It's a mandate shared by prophets operating under both the Old and New Covenants.

Think about it: If prophecy reveals the heart of God, then the prophetic ministry is called to turn the hearts of His children toward the matters of His heart. In other words, it is not enough to breeze through a congregation with a prophetic utterance on your way to the next meeting. Too many times, prophetic words are delivered but not prayed through. I believe this is because the hearts of the children were not completely turned toward the heart of the Father in the matter. The prophetic word evoked a shout and a few goose bumps, but soon found its way into a drawer, waiting half-heartedly for God to bring it to pass.

Prophets have a responsibility not just to declare the heart of God but to work with Him to turn the hearts of the people toward His heart in any matter He chooses to share.

Teaching the saints to meditate and pray the word through is one way to help ensure the hearts of the people are turned to the heart of the Father. And teaching them to wage a good warfare with the prophetic word is still another.

However, in order to turn the hearts of men to the Father, your own heart must be fully turned toward Him. Could it be possible that your heart is not turned toward Him in the area of finances or submission to authority? Could it be possible that your heart is not turned toward Him in the area of walking in love with the unlovely? Could it be possible that your heart is not turned toward Him in the area of patiently waiting for His will in your life? With the heart-turning ministry, make sure you turn your heart first.

— *Prayer* —

Father, in the name of Jesus, would You show me any area of my life where my heart—my will—is not submitted to You? Lead me in turning from any wicked ways in me, for I know my heart is deceitful above all things. Teach me to guard my heart in Your grace.

Renouncing Rock Star Status

"A young man ran and reported to Moses, 'Eldad and Medad are prophesying in the camp!' Joshua son of Nun, who had been Moses' assistant since his youth, protested, 'Moses, my master, make them stop!' But Moses replied, 'Are you jealous for my sake? I wish that all the Lord's people were prophets and that the Lord would put his Spirit upon them all!'" (Numbers 11:27-29)

Prophets have to be careful not to encourage idolatry, jealousy, or strife in any of its diverse manifestations. It was natural for the Israelites—and especially Joshua who sat outside the tent of meeting where God met Moses face-to-face—to admire the one who led them out of Egyptian bondage. It was natural for the children of Israel to look up to the one God used as a deliverer and a prophet. But admiration and idolatry—or the rock star syndrome, as I call it—are two different things.

As prophets, we have to continually point people to Jesus and make His name great rather than drawing people to ourselves to make our names great. That's what Moses did in Numbers 11. Joshua was upset that other people were prophesying. Perhaps Joshua was concerned that Moses' reputation as the leader would be dinged or that the prophesiers might fracture the leadership structure of Israel with their spiritual gifts. Joshua's heart was probably in the right place—to guard Moses. But Joshua was stepping close to the dangerous line of idolatry.

I love Numbers 11:29 because it shows that Moses had a different spirit. He was not jealous or upset in any way that others in the camp were speaking the mind and will of God to the nation. Moses did not set himself up as a rock star prophet. In fact, the Bible says he was the meekest person on the face of the earth (see Num. 12:3). As a prophet, Moses was completely dependent on God and demonstrated that dependence to the people who followed him, continually steering them away from idolatry to love the Lord with all of their hearts, all of their minds, and all of their strength.

Moses was tempted to enter into jealousy and strife. It was a test of the prophet's humility and allegiance to God. And look at who the temptation came from—someone close to him. Joshua suggested that Moses forbid Eldad and Medad from prophesying in the camp.

Thankfully, Moses rejected the notion. It seems long before James wrote his epistle to the church, Moses knew in his heart this truth: "For wherever there is jealousy and selfish ambition, there you will find disorder and evil of every kind" (James 3:16). When prophets enter into strife, they enter into confusion and evil works.

— *Prayer* —

Father, in the name of Jesus, help me guard Your heart from envy and strife that will hinder the prophetic anointing You have poured out on my life. Help me keep my ear to Your mouth and my heart bowed down before You.

Bring Me a Minstrel

"But now bring me a minstrel. And it came to pass, when the minstrel played, that the hand of the Lord came upon him" (2 Kings 3:15 KJV).

Elisha was doing the work of the ministry when three kings suddenly showed up at his doorstep. Elisha was not pleased. He rejected the kings' request to prophesy to them about their plans to go to battle with enemy nations:

"Why are you coming to me?" Elisha asked the king of Israel. "Go to the pagan prophets of your father and mother!" (2 Kings 3:13)

Why the harsh word? Well, there was no love lost between Elisha and Ahab. He had doubtless heard his spiritual father Elijah tell him about how Ahab and his wife Jezebel troubled Israel, bringing a famine on the land by provoking the Lord through idolatry. Ahab's son Joram was now king of Israel, and Elisha didn't want any part of it. Joram said to Elisha, "No! For it was the Lord who called us three kings here—only to be defeated by the king of Moab!" (2 Kings 3:13).

Elisha replied, "As surely as the Lord Almighty lives, whom I serve, I wouldn't even bother with you except for my respect for King Jehoshaphat of Judah. Now bring me someone who can play the harp." While the harp was being played, the power of the Lord came upon Elisha, and he said, "This is what the Lord says..." (2 Kings 3:14-16).

Elisha went on to prophesy a victory for the three kings against the king of Moab. It was a good word!

Why did Elisha ask for a minstrel, or what modern translations call a harpist or a musician? Music sets an atmosphere. Worship attracts the Holy Spirit. Psalm 22:3 tells us God inhabits the praises of His people.

If you need to shift an atmosphere or if you are feeling personally dry, press into worship and praise as it not only shifts the atmosphere around you—sometimes it shifts the atmosphere within you. And it makes it easier for you to hear what the Holy Spirit is saying.

— *Prayer* —

Father, in the name of Jesus, I want to worship You in spirit and in truth. Would You give me an appreciation for worship, even if there is not a minstrel in sight? Would You teach me how to leverage music to shift demonic atmospheres and create prophetic atmospheres?

Avoid Dangerous Heresies

"But there were also false prophets in Israel, just as there will be false teachers among you..." (2 Peter 2:1).

The church needs prophets who can rightly discern the moving of the Lord—and the moving of the enemy. We need prophets who will stand in the gap and make up the hedge so the enemy cannot infiltrate. We need warrior prophets to embrace the whole armor of God.

Anyone with a sensitive spirit can pick up on the rising level of spiritual warfare in this hour. Just look at the attacks on major cities in our nation. Just look at the persecution of Christians. Just look at the number of church leaders who have fallen. Just look at how many churches are closing. Just look. Clearly, darkness is raging against the church.

Spiritual warfare is real, despite some who insist we don't have to fight because the devil is already defeated. Spiritual warfare is biblical, despite those who argue we should ignore the operations of the devil. Spiritual warfare is necessary because principalities, powers, rulers of the darkness of this age, spiritual hosts of wickedness (see Eph. 6:12), and other forces are raging against all those who call Christ Lord.

I understand why some denominations don't believe in spiritual warfare, even though I don't agree. But prophets who insist we should not put any focus on spirits like Jezebel, Python, Absalom, or other demonic culprits that work to wreck lives, ministries, cities, and nations puzzle me. After all, spiritual warfare is part of the prophet's mantle.

Look at Elijah in the showdown at Mount Carmel (see 1 Kings 18:17-39). He engaged in natural warfare to slay 850 false prophets who were propagating Jezebel's false religion. This is a mirror of the spiritual warfare we fight against wicked spirits today. Elijah also battled the spirit of death in his ministry—as did Jesus Himself—raising someone from the dead. Elisha battled the spirit of infirmity. I could go on and on. You can't separate a prophet from spiritual warfare realities.

— *Prayer* —

Father, in the name of Jesus, show me the truth about Your role as a warrior and help me shun any anti-biblical notions that I don't have to fight the good fight of faith or engage in wrestling matches with demonic powers through intercession. Teach my hands to war and my fingers to battle.

Know in Part, Prophesy in Part

"For we know in part and we prophesy in part" (1 Corinthians 13:9 NKJV).

"Now our knowledge is partial and incomplete, and even the gift of prophecy reveals only part of the whole picture!" That's how the New Living Translation translates 1 Corinthians 13:9. *The Passion Translation* says, "Our prophecies are but partial."

This reality should not discourage you. Rather, it should cause you to rely on other prophets in humility to discern the fullness of what God may be saying. Think about it for a minute. If God gave any one prophet the whole picture, that prophet would fall into pride. Paul said, "Knowledge [alone] makes [people self-righteously] arrogant" (1 Cor. 8:1 AMP). The only one who knows everything is God, and we are on a need-to-know basis.

That said, this Scripture also points to a powerful dynamic among prophets. In my experience, I've discovered when prophets run in companies the picture of what God is saying is more complete. Each prophet gets a part of the puzzle. Each one gets revelation that oftentimes, when shared with other prophets, fills in the corners and the middle parts until you can see the big idea God is sharing. When everybody puts their word on the table, the pieces come together.

There's yet another side of this verse worth considering. First Corinthians 13:9 reveals: "For we know in part, and we prophesy in part [for our knowledge is fragmentary and incomplete]" (AMP). At times, the prophecy is an invitation for exploration. God wants us to seek out the rest of what He is saying. Are we curious enough? Yet another reason for prophesying in part is that if we saw the whole picture we might try to make it happen, or the prophecy might be daunting.

— *Prayer* —

Father, in the name of Jesus, make me spiritually curious and biblically proficient so I can press in to all that You have to say. Lead me to a company of prophets and prophetic people where I can share my revelations and, together, unlock the fullness of the message You are speaking.

A Prophetic Stretch

"...So after you have suffered a little while, he will restore, support, and strengthen you, and he will place you on a firm foundation" (1 Peter 5:10).

I work out five days a week, lifting heavy weights and doing all sorts of crazy new exercises with my personal trainer in my home gym. My trainer is not physically present, so he trusts me to do the stretching on my own after each session is over. I always plan to stretch but sometimes I get distracted and forget.

When that happens, I'm always sorry later. I wake up the next day with muscles so tight I can barely walk—and sometimes with excruciating pain. That soreness makes me want to skip the next workout. You might say my muscles are "weary in well-doing."

Lately, I've found myself in God's gym—lifting heavy spiritual weights and doing all manner of uncomfortable new exercises. I don't have to worry about the stretching part. He's doing that too. God's stretching is sometimes as painful on our souls as working over a sore muscle—I'm reminded of Lurch from *The Addams Family* on that medieval-looking stretching machine in the dungeon.

Remember this: there's a purpose for the stretching. Stretching is for your own good, even though it's inconvenient and it hurts. God's stretching leaves you with a spiritual capacity great enough to move into the next season He's ordained for you.

That may mean He's stretching your faith in a trial. This benefits you in the end because you prophesy according to the proportion of your faith (see Rom. 12:6). It may mean He's stretching you in trust. It may mean He's stretching you in some area of your character.

You may feel like you are a rubber band ready to snap, but God knows how far you can stretch—and it's further than you think. There's a scientific fact about rubber bands that should encourage you: Once it's stretched it never goes back to its original condition. When God stretches you, you will never be the same prophet.

— *Prayer* —

Father, in the name of Jesus, give me the grace to yield to the stretching. Help me recognize Your hand in the stretching so I am not tempted to resist You instead of resisting the enemy of my soul. Show me how to cooperate with the prophetic stretch.

Letting God Establish You

"Now may our Lord Jesus Christ Himself, and our God and Father, who has loved us and given us everlasting consolation and good hope by grace, comfort your hearts and establish you in every good word and work" (2 Thessalonians 2:16-17 NKJV).

Many people think I came out of nowhere. I didn't come out of nowhere. I was being established for well over a decade before God revealed me on an international scale. Since then, many people have introduced me on platforms around the world with kind words of affirmation before I release the word of the Lord. But make no mistake, God's introduction is the best introduction.

When God calls you into prophetic ministry, there's a time between the calling and the commissioning. But even after the commissioning, there's an establishing. Many people don't understand that until God establishes you, you don't have the authority, credibility, or at times even the wisdom to say certain things. Until God establishes you, you don't have the divine opportunity to do certain things. Until God establishes you, you have to wait or risk being out of God's order. It's in the waiting that you undergo the character development that qualifies you for establishment.

Jezebel and Baal will seduce you if you are not firmly established in your commitment to the Lord. If you are blown about by every wind of doctrine, you'll be deceived by a spirit of error. God has to make sure you are not unstable or double-minded before He can fully establish you in prophetic ministry—or establish you at the next level—so He works instabilities out of your soul through the renewal of your mind. God has to work out of you anything that is not set on His purpose. It takes time.

There will be many temptations to establish yourself by trying to get on other people's platforms or by buying Instagram likes or by prophesying flattering words to leaders who can give you a leg up. All of that will fail. Whatever is not born of the Spirit cannot prosper (see John 3:6). But when God establishes you, it's effortless. He introduces you and causes you to grow and multiply.

— *Prayer* —

Father, in the name of Jesus, establish me. Do what only You can do in my life. Warn me when I am straying away from Your establishing plans in my ministry. Restrain me when I seek to step out into a territory I'm not ready for. I don't want step out of Your will.

Casting Down the Voice of Offense

"John the Baptist, who was in prison, heard about all the things the Messiah was doing. So he sent his disciples to ask Jesus, 'Are you the Messiah we've been expecting, or should we keep looking for someone else?'" (Matthew 11:2-3)

Matthew 11 reveals a sad moment in John the Baptist's ministry. He was a great prophet and greatly persecuted. Days before he met with his ultimate fate of beheading, I am sure he felt immense pressure. As a result, he started questioning what he thought he knew. I can only imagine the vain imaginations that were attacking his mind. Maybe the enemy infused his mind with thoughts like:

"I sacrificed my whole life as a Nazirite in the wilderness. Why won't my cousin Jesus save me? I paved the way for His ministry and didn't complain when my disciples left me and started following Him. Where is He now?" At some point right before his untimely death, John sent his remaining disciples to Jesus to ask Him the burning question on his heart: "Are You the Messiah or should we find another?"

As I read these verses in Matthew, it occurs to me that the voice of offense was speaking to John. He expected Jesus to come and open the prison doors or at least send an angel on his behalf. John seems somewhat disillusioned. We shouldn't be too hard on John. He was under massive spiritual attack. And it's in those times when we feel someone could alleviate our suffering that we have to beware the voice of offense.

Offense is dangerous because "a brother offended is harder to be won than a strong city, and their contentions are like the bars of a castle" (Prov. 18:19 MEV). But love is not touchy or easily provoked (see 1 Cor. 13:5-6). We know that "good sense makes one slow to anger, and it is his glory to overlook an offense" (Prov. 19:11 ESV). And the Preacher offers some really good advice: "Do not give heed to everything people say, lest you hear your servant cursing you. Your heart knows that many times you have spoken a curse against others" (Eccles. 7:21-22 MEV).

An offended prophet is in danger of losing the right perspective of Jesus, whose testimony we're called to prophesy. An offended prophet can turn into a condemning prophet and start operating in presumption and spreading strife.

— *Prayer* —

Father, in the name of Jesus, make me unoffendable. Deliver me from any tendency in my soul to take things personally that I should process objectively. If I carry any offense in my heart, root it out before it seeps deeply into my soul and perverts my prophetic voice.

Dealing with Spiritual Frustration

"Even though I have received such wonderful revelations from God. So to keep me from becoming proud, I was given a thorn in my flesh, a messenger from Satan to torment me and keep me from becoming proud. Three different times I begged the Lord to take it away. Each time he said, 'My grace is all you need. My power works best in weakness.' So now I am glad to boast about my weaknesses, so that the power of Christ can work through me" (2 Corinthians 12:7-9).

Once someone asked me, "Is there such a thing as spiritual frustration? If so, can you explain, and what would you suggest as a solution?" That was a good question because it's a reality many prophets face in their journey.

Years later, my answer is the same. Yes, I believe there is such a thing as spiritual frustration. Paul was frustrated about the thorn in his flesh. Frustration, in its simplest terms, is a deep and chronic sense of being dissatisfied because of long-term warfare, challenges, persecution, or unfulfilled needs, such as recognition, promotion, or appreciation.

So how do you deal with spiritual frustration? You first have to discern if the frustration is a godly or satanic frustration. Sometimes the devil comes with discontent to try to move us out of or ahead of God's will. We all face frustration in the wilderness, but if we leave ahead of God's timing we'll just end up right back in the desert we despise. We all want that spiritual promotion, but we can't go after it the devil's way. God is the one who promotes and demotes (see Ps. 75:7).

Other times, it's a spiritual frustration from God that moves us more toward His will. We don't always know it, but sometimes spiritual frustration is a sign of spiritual hunger. We need to get in His Word and get in His presence so peace can replace frustration. He is the unfilled need, but He's ready to fill you.

Much of our spiritual frustration comes from not trusting His timing or not knowing what His will is. So what do you do? Don't stay frustrated. Ask God what's causing your spiritual frustration and believe Him for a revelation. Pray in tongues a lot. Confess Scriptures over your life that have to do with wisdom and revelation and watch God expose the root of that spiritual frustration so you can deal with it.

— *Prayer* —

Father, in the name of Jesus, will You show me what's really frustrating me? Since I know I will find my satisfaction in doing Your will, please make Your will crystal clear to me in every season. Make me sensitive to Your movements so I can follow You every step along the way.

The Psalm 137:6 Prophetic Boundary

"May my tongue stick to the roof of my mouth if I fail to remember you, if I don't make Jerusalem my greatest joy" (Psalm 137:6).

Prophets should adapt Psalm 137:6 to the prophetic ministry. That's because not everything we hear in the secret place is supposed to be shouted from the rooftops. Far too often I've heard public prophetic words that make me cringe on behalf of the recipient. You might adapt the Psalm 137:6 prayer like this: "May my tongue stick to the roof of my mouth if I fail to remember to wait for Your unction to release prophecy."

Before you release a prophetic word—particularly something beyond the bounds of edification, exhortation, and comfort (such as a word that will strike fear in the hearts of people or stir controversy in the church)—consider the consequences and the ripple effect. It's not even a matter of being accurate. You can have an accurate prophetic word, dream, vision, or encounter but that doesn't give you the right to release it. The Holy Spirit gives you that right.

Consider this: You may think you are right, but if the word brings fear or controversy and you are wrong you could hurt a lot of people. Let's filter our prophetic revelation through the lens of wisdom. Ask yourself, who will this help? Does it ultimately exalt Jesus? If the prophecy brings more attention to you than to God, something is wrong with the prophetic picture.

Even if we receive a directional or corrective word, we need to pray before the release so the Lord can prepare the recipient to receive it. Charles Spurgeon once said, "Even Christ's own seed of the word, pure from His own hand, brings forth no fruit when it falls on unprepared hearts."

Let's consider the consequences of our prophetic utterances. Death and life are in the power of the tongue (see Prov. 18:21), and sincere prophets can curse God-fearing ministries, bring a lot of heartache to suffering families, and breed strife and division in the body unintentionally.

— *Prayer* —

Father, in the name of Jesus, would You help me remember to slow my flow when I receive words that could do more harm than good if I release them in the wrong way, through the wrong media, to the wrong people, or at the wrong time? Help me wait on Your unction.

The Ambidextrous Prophet

"...The Lord told the donkey to speak..." (Numbers 22:28 CEV).

For years, my prophetic ministry was marked predominantly by audible revelation—and that was the emphasis in the early days of the restoration of the office of the prophet. Even until today, many prophets have only experienced, "the word of the Lord coming unto them saying." In other words, they are hearing prophets but they don't experience many visions, dreams, or other encounters in the seer dimensions.

At the same time, seer prophets can experience dramatic visual revelation but may not hear the word of the Lord as freely. Although all seers are prophets, all prophets are not seers. The hearing prophet and the seeing prophet are two streams that come from the same river. Nevertheless, God is cultivating what I call ambidextrous prophets.

Just as an ambidextrous artist can use both hands equally well to paint, God is raising up prophets who can both see and hear so they can say in multiple dimensions. Although seers will still predominantly see and prophets will still predominantly hear, this ambidextrous thrust will expand the anointings of prophets around the world.

Remember Balaam's donkey? The rebellious prophet was going in the wrong direction. The donkey stopped suddenly several times, and the prophet beat him for it. We find out why the donkey got so stubborn when the animal started talking to Balaam.

"This time when the donkey saw the angel, it lay down under Balaam. In a fit of rage Balaam beat the animal again with his staff. Then the Lord gave the donkey the ability to speak" (Num. 22:27-28). The donkey saw in the spirit what the prophet could not. Then the donkey rebuked the prophet for his rebellion. Only then did the prophet's eyes open to the angel in front of him, who then rebuked him for beating his donkey.

Here's the point: If a donkey can both see and hear in the spirit, so can you. If God can give a donkey the ability to speak and see, He can do the same for you. And He wants to. If you are a seer, it's time to press into hearing. If you are a hearer, it's time to press into seeing.

— *Prayer* —

Father, in the name of Jesus, help me to be ambidextrous in the spirit. Stretch me so I can expand my faith to receive revelation in whatever package You send it. Make me more sensitive to Your Spirit so I can catch what You are pouring out.

Prophesying Over Dry Bones

"Again He said to me, 'Prophesy to these bones, and say to them, "O dry bones, hear the word of the Lord!"'" (Ezekiel 37:4 NKJV)

Imagine this scene when God picked up Ezekiel and put him in the Valley of Dry Bones. The bones weren't just dry—they were "very dry." There weren't just a few bones lying around. The valley was full of bones. In this hour, much of the church finds herself in the Valley of Dry Bones instead of on the mountaintop.

As He did with Ezekiel, the Lord is asking us a question: "Can these bones live?" (Ezek. 37:3 NKJV). Many are responding just like Ezekiel did, uncertain if it's too late for their church, their city, or their nation. They are answering, "O Lord God, You know" (Ezek. 37:3 NKJV). Let's listen in to what happens next:

> *Again He said to me, "Prophesy over these bones and say to them, O dry bones, hear the word of the Lord. Thus says the Lord God to these bones: I will cause breath to enter you so that you live. And I will lay sinews upon you and will grow back flesh upon you and cover you with skin and put breath in you so that you live. Then you shall know that I am the Lord"* (Ezekiel 37:4-6 MEV).

In this hour, when so much of the church is lukewarm, dry, or even apostate, we need to rise up and prophesy God's will instead of tapping into the doom, gloom, judgments, and cursing. God is in the restoration business. He is in the resurrection business. He is in the transformation business. We need to prophesy His will over our lives, churches, cities, and nations with endurance. That's what Ezekiel did (see Ezek. 37:7-8).

When we're obedient to say what God tells us to say and to do what God tells us to do, we can expect things to change. We must prophesy what He commands. Prophesying to the dry bones will breathe new life into the Body of Christ and inspire them to stand up on their feet, an "exceeding great army."

— *Prayer* —

Father, in the name of Jesus, help me discern the dry bones and choose not to decree what I see in the natural but to pray in what You see in the spirit. Show me dry churches and dry cities and give me a prophetic prayer strategy to prophesy life into what You want to restore.

Waging War with the Prophecies

"This charge I commit to you, son Timothy, according to the prophecies previously made concerning you, that by them you may wage the good warfare" (1 Timothy 1:18 NKJV).

We see many warfare strategies in Scripture. The key is to discern and execute the warfare strategy God is breathing on during any given season and for specific situations. Prophets in particular do well to adopt the strategy Paul gave his spiritual son Timothy: "This charge I commit to you, son Timothy, according to the prophecies previously made concerning you, that by them you may wage the good warfare" (1 Tim. 1:18 NKJV).

The Amplified translation of that verse exhorts us to be "inspired and aided" by the prophetic words so that "you may wage the good warfare." The New Living Translation tells us that the prophetic words "help you fight well in the Lord's battles." And *The Message* tells us the prophecies should make you "fearless in your struggle, keeping a firm grip on your faith and on yourself. After all, this is a fight we're in."

Indeed, this is a fight we're in—it's a good fight of faith against unseen enemies. "For our fight is not against flesh and blood, but against principalities, against powers, against the rulers of the darkness of this world, and against spiritual forces of evil in the heavenly places" (Eph. 6:12 MEV). Thankfully, the unseen God and unseen angels are on our side. The angels are an important part of this spiritual warfare equation.

Prophets, if you are going to prophesy you may have to engage in prophetic warfare to see the word come to pass. Of course, I'm not suggesting we have to go to battle over every prophecy we release. That would not be realistic.

That said, if you are a house prophet, a prophet to a network, or a prophet to the nations, your job is usually not done when you release the prophetic word. If you have responsibility to a people or organization, you should feel compelled to wage war with the prophecy you released until you see it come to pass. Because God gave you the word, you have a unique authority to stand in the gap and thwart enemy attacks against God's will.

— *Prayer* —

Father, in the name of Jesus, would You give me a burden for the prophecies with which I should wage a good warfare? Would You show me when a prophetic word is so pivotal to Your will that my assignment is to push back the powers that are trying to hold back Your promise?

Walking Through the Dark Night of the Soul

"I affirm, by the boasting in you which I have in Christ Jesus our Lord, I die daily"
(1 Corinthians 15:31 MEV).

Although this happy night brings darkness to the spirit, it does so only to give it light in everything; and that, although it humbles it and makes it miserable, it does so only to exalt it and to raise it up; and, although it impoverishes it and empties it of all natural affection and attachment, it does so only that it may enable it to stretch forward, divinely, and thus to have fruition and experience of all things, both above and below, yet to preserve its unrestricted liberty of spirit in them all.

These are the words of St. John of the Cross, who wrote a book called *The Dark Night of the Soul* in the 1500s. There is no evidence that John was a prophet. History describes him as a Spanish mystic and reformer. The concept of the dark night of the soul is popular in prophetic circles because it describes the process many prophets go through. It's different from a breaking. It's more of a stripping or a purging process. John writes:

This darkness should continue for as long as is needful in order to expel and annihilate the habit which the soul has long since formed in its manner of understanding, and the Divine light and illumination will then take its place.

It is meet, then, that the soul be first of all brought into emptiness and poverty of spirit and purged from all help, consolation and natural apprehension with respect to all things, both above and below. In this way, being empty, it is able indeed to be poor in spirit and freed from the old man, in order to live that new and blessed life which is attained by means of this night, and which is the state of union with God.

Prophets, if you are walking through a dark night of the soul—and if you are not, you will—submit to the purging. It's a process of dying to self where you question everything you know. Let Him remove from you everything that hinders love and you will come out with more prophetic accuracy.

— *Prayer* —

Father, in the name of Jesus, prepare me in the seasons when I seem to bask in Your glory for the dark night of the soul that may follow in the future. Root me and ground me so deep in Your love that when I can't feel Your presence I will remain confident You are with me.

Pray for Those Who Persecute You

"But I say, love your enemies! Pray for those who persecute you!" (Matthew 5:44)

When someone is gossiping about you, slandering you, or otherwise cursing you behind your back, the devil will do everything he can to make sure those words get back to your ears. Much of the time, the gossip, slander, and curses just make your accuser look like a fool. Mature, discerning Christians recognize evil speech for what it is, refuse to give an ear to it—and wouldn't think of spreading it.

When you find out someone is speaking gossip, slander, or Christian curses over you or your family, you have two choices: You can react in the same wicked spirit as your persecutor, or you can resist the temptation to act like the accuser of the brethren and respond like your Father in heaven instead. Jesus said:

Love your enemies, bless those who curse you, do good to those who hate you, and pray for those who spitefully use you and persecute you, that you may be sons of your Father in heaven; for He makes His sun rise on the evil and on the good, and sends rain on the just and on the unjust (Matthew 5:44-45 NKJV).

So, what does this look like in action? How do we love our enemies and bless those who curse us and do good to those who hate us, practically speaking? How do we pray for those who purposefully, knowingly use and abuse us? How do we act like sons and daughters of our Father in heaven?

Pray God would forgive them. They may know what they did and said, but they don't really understand what they are going to reap from that seed. Pray for God to root them and ground them in love (see Eph. 3:17-19). Pray for God's love to abound in them (see Phil. 1:9-11). Pray for God to show them His will (see Col. 1:9-10).

Beyond that, intercede as the Holy Spirit leads you until you feel a release in your spirit. And remember, Paul admonishes us to "Bless those who persecute you. Don't curse them; pray that God will bless them" (Rom. 12:14).

— *Prayer* —

Father, in the name of Jesus, would You help me walk in a Sermon on the Mount lifestyle that goes the extra mile and turns the other cheek? Would You help me adopt an attitude of forgiveness and mercy that drives me to my knees to bless and pray for my enemies?

MAY

"And Elijah said to Elisha, 'Stay here, for the Lord has told me to go to Bethel.' But Elisha replied, 'As surely as the Lord lives and you yourself live, I will never leave you!' So they went down together to Bethel. The group of prophets from Bethel came to Elisha and asked him, 'Did you know that the Lord is going to take your master away from you today?' 'Of course I know,' Elisha answered. 'But be quiet about it.' Then Elijah said to Elisha, 'Stay here, for the Lord has told me to go to Jericho.' But Elisha replied again, 'As surely as the Lord lives and you yourself live, I will never leave you.' So they went on together to Jericho" (2 Kings 2:2-4).

Releasing the Red Alert

"When the watchman sees the enemy coming, he sounds the alarm to warn the people" (Ezekiel 33:3).

Prophets release words of warning, not just words of blessing. But the way in which you sound the alarm is critical. The mature prophet understands how to release warnings with clarity and wisdom that inspires Jesus' followers to take swift, God-informed action. Paul wrote these words, which prophets would do well to remember: "For if the trumpet makes an uncertain sound, who will prepare for battle?" (1 Cor. 14:8 NKJV).

As I write in my book *The Making of a Watchman*, some warnings seem too hot to handle. But the wisdom of God and common sense can help you sound the alarm clearly, boldly, and loudly to get people's attention. Of course, you first have to judge the warning before you release the word. When we sound a false alarm because the warning came from our souls instead of from our Savior, we can lose credibility. We don't want to accidently become like the boy who cried wolf, lest a true warning in the future be ignored.

Remember, look—or listen—for the redemption of God in the warning before you sound the alarm. Yes, ultimately there are times when God's judgment will fall. There comes a day when enough is enough and there's no averting God's decision. We see this with Nineveh. God sent Jonah the prophet to release a warning to the ancient city, knowing the king and his people would repent. God was right. But later Nineveh backslid and judgment came.

Don't release a warning without a clear call to action. In other words, take the time to hear what the Holy Spirit wants us to do, how He wants us to pray, and any other prophetic intelligence that would help to stop the enemy's plans about which you are warning God's people. Ask the Holy Spirit to show you the big picture—not just the problem but the solution—or people will start to tune you out. Become a prophetic solutionist.

— *Prayer* —

Father, in the name of Jesus, make me the watchman You've called me to be. Help me see the danger or the glory through Your wise eyes and wait for Your divine wisdom and instruction about what to do next. Help me cultivate a reputation for accuracy in my watching.

Wading Through a Dream Drought

"And the Lord said to them, 'Now listen to what I say: "If there were prophets among you, I, the Lord, would reveal myself in visions. I would speak to them in dreams"" (Numbers 12:6).

Many prophets and prophetic people tell me their dream life dries up from time to time—or that it dried up a long time ago and has never returned. This can be upsetting, especially if you are used to God sharing profound revelation with you while you sleep. But this reality doesn't have to be upsetting if you gain understanding as to what is going on. There are at least two reasons your dream life may have ceased.

First, understand God may be trying to speak to you in a different way. Everyone loves the dream world, but God wants us to be well-versed in His communication vehicles. He doesn't want us to only hear His still small voice or receive dreams or see visions. He wants us to be able to receive His message in whatever medium He decides to share it. If we master or get too comfortable with one way He speaks, He may start teaching us a new way.

Second, if you are not a good steward of your dreams He may stop sharing with you while you sleep. In other words, if you don't take the time to write your dreams down, process them with the Holy Spirit to get an accurate interpretation, and apply the revelation the way He leads, why would He talk to you that way? It's like speaking to someone and having the words go in one ear and out the other.

Third, if you aren't able to understand what He is saying to you in your dreams despite your best efforts, God may switch the mode of communication to another format until you gain more skill in interpretation because He really wants you to get the message. That's how much He loves you. Finally, you may have had some trauma in your soul that is preventing you from receiving the dreams of God. In this case, you may need inner healing or deliverance. Ask God why your dream life has dried up.

— *Prayer* —

Father, in the name of Jesus, will You show me the root of my sparse dream life? Help me not to get anxious or upset because I am not receiving nocturnal revelation. Please show me what You are doing or what the enemy is doing so I can respond appropriately to the dream drought.

Developing Your Unique Prophetic Voice

"John replied in the words of the prophet Isaiah: 'I am a voice shouting in the wilderness, clear the way for the Lord's coming!'" (John 1:23)

I was a freelance writer before I found the Lord. When I learned to write, I had to find my voice. What does that mean, exactly? The writer's voice is an individual style of word choice and delivery. In the prophetic, how you deliver the word is part of your voice. Since we're all different, we sound different when we prophesy—sometimes even when we prophesy the same things!

John the Baptist was not just a voice crying in the wilderness—he was a unique voice. So unique that people came from all over out to the wilderness to hear him speak. John never swayed from his God-given voice, despite the persecution he endured for his strong stance for truth and cries for repentance.

You, too, have a unique prophetic voice. You just have to find it. Too many prophets and preachers emulate a style or voice that is not natural to them. In doing so, they water down the power of their prophetic ministry. Your voice may be similar to another prophet's voice and that's OK, as long as it's truly you.

Consider the Bible itself. It has a number of authors, all chronicling the oracles of God. But if you know the Bible well, you can easily distinguish the Holy Spirit-inspired writings of John from the Holy Spirit-inspired writings of Paul from the Holy Spirit-inspired writings of Isaiah.

Although the Holy Spirit inspired them all to write the words they recorded, there is some uniqueness in their voices because it flowed through their individual beings. In other words, God didn't turn John, Paul, Isaiah, and others into monotone robots to record His words. You'll find their voice in writings. Their personal stories are woven through the pages of the Old and New Testament. And the language they use is unique to their level of education and understanding of God's past words.

Ask the Holy Spirit to help you tap into your original prophetic voice. Don't try to copy someone else's style. Be who He called you to be and prophesy from that place, speaking His words with confidence.

— *Prayer* —

Father, in the name of Jesus, make me aware of the temptation to mimic a voice I admire and parrot the prophetic styles of others. Help me discover and release the prophetic voice with confidence that You created me to share.

When You're Reluctant to Prophesy

"Don't be afraid, for I am with you. Don't be discouraged, for I am your God. I will strengthen you and help you. I will hold you up with my victorious right hand" (Isaiah 41:10).

When I was young in prophetic ministry, I was a nervous Nelly. I was afraid of missing it—afraid of the reactions from the people even if it was a good word. I was afraid. I didn't want to misrepresent God. I'm sure you know exactly what I mean.

Speaking in His name is a big deal and we should have a fear of the Lord as a baseline of our prophetic ministry if we are going to speak in His name. But we have to be careful that the fear of the Lord and a reverence for His name doesn't turn into a spirit of fear that causes us to shut up when God is leading us to prophesy.

An elder prophet in my church once visited my home and said a few words to me that set me straight. He said, "You better start prophesying what the Lord gives you to say or He will find someone else and you'll sit on a shelf until you get over that fear." The apostle of the church later told me, "God wants to use your voice in the nations, but you have to get over that fear first." I got hit from both sides.

That fear of missing it—putting words in the Lord's mouth He didn't say—was then balanced with the fear of being disobedient because I was too afraid to open my mouth. When God tells you to speak, you need to speak. If you are afraid to prophesy what the Lord has put in your mouth, you need to get to the root of the matter—and fast.

You might be reluctant to prophesy for fear of offending people. Prophesy anyway. You might be reluctant to prophesy because you don't think people will receive the word in the spirit in which it is given. Prophesy anyway. You may be reluctant to prophesy for any number of reasons. Prophesy anyway if the Holy Spirit is stirring you. It's boring to sit on a shelf.

— *Prayer* —

Father, in the name of Jesus, deliver me from the fear of missing it, the fear of mispresenting You, the fear of being criticized and judged, and every other fear that is more powerful in my life than the fear of the Lord. Give me the courage to speak what You are saying accurately.

Finding Your Company

"Simon Peter, a servant and an apostle of Jesus Christ, to them that have obtained like precious faith with us through the righteousness of God and our Saviour Jesus Christ" (2 Peter 1:1 KJV).

We see companies of prophets in the Bible, and we recognize the synergies of running with prophets in groups, nests, tribes, and prophetic families. Nobody understands prophets quite like other prophets.

So, with that in mind, who's your company? Think about it for a minute. Not all churches and corporations in the world are the same. They have different missions, cultures, values, and structures. Likewise, not all companies of prophets are the same. You need to know something about the company you are joining before you join it. Just as you wouldn't take just any job without knowing more about what you were getting into, don't just join any prophetic network.

Indeed, it's critical to find the right company to run with because when the battle is on, you want to know they've got your back. When Peter and John were arrested for healing the man at the gate beautiful, the priests, the religious leaders threatened them not to preach in the name of Jesus ever again. They decided right then and there—and make it known to the religious rulers—that they would only bow to Jesus.

You'll remember what they did next: "And being let go, they went to their own company, and reported all that the chief priests and elders had said unto them. And when they heard that, they lifted up their voice to God with one accord" (Acts 4:23-24 KJV). Notice that they immediately drew in the apostles and prayed in unity. This was a similar picture to the upper room on the Day of Pentecost. The place where they were praying shook and they were all filled with the Holy Spirit.

The right company has the right mission, values, and culture—and is unified. The right company is a praying company. The right company is a place where you are filled continually, sharpened, and fired up for the call of God on your life. Ask God to help you find the right company—and when you find it be sure to value it. Good companies can be hard to find.

— *Prayer* —

Father, in the name of Jesus, help me find the right company of prophets to run with, to work with, and to share my life with. Help me find those of like precious faith who will understand the uniqueness of my anointing, and teach me to be grateful for my tribe and honor them rightly.

What Do You See?

"Then the Lord said to me, 'Look, Jeremiah! What do you see?'" (Jeremiah 1:11)

When the Lord asks, "What do you see?" He's trying to activate your spiritual vision. Many times the word of the Lord comes to a seer after he or she sees. This happened to Jeremiah more than once. Beyond his introduction to the prophetic and the seer dimensions, God asked the young prophet a second time in Jeremiah 24:3-7:

> *Then the Lord said to me, "What do you see, Jeremiah?" I replied, "Figs, some very good and some very bad, too rotten to eat." Then the Lord gave me this message: "This is what the Lord, the God of Israel, says: The good figs represent the exiles I sent from Judah to the land of the Babylonians. I will watch over and care for them, and I will bring them back here again. I will build them up and not tear them down. I will plant them and not uproot them. I will give them hearts that recognize me as the Lord. They will be my people, and I will be their God, for they will return to me wholeheartedly."*

Throughout Scripture, we see this trend. God asked Amos "what do you see?" twice. He asked the same question to Zechariah. On all accounts, the Lord was trying to open the prophet's eyes to something they were not yet seeing, but it required a hearing ear to listen to the Lord's voice, a willing heart to look at what He wanted to show them.

Again, many times audible revelation followed the seer revelation. Other times, the prophet will see something in the spirit and then the Lord or an angel will ask him what he sees. Zechariah 5:1-3 reads, "I looked up again and saw a scroll flying through the air. 'What do you see?' the angel asked. 'I see a flying scroll,' I replied. 'It appears to be about 30 feet long and 15 feet wide.' Then he said to me, 'This scroll contains the curse that is going out over the entire land....'"

It's important to pay attention in the spirit because visual revelation can come just as spontaneously as audible revelation. Ask the Holy Spirit to make you sensitive to what He is trying to show and tell you.

— *Prayer* —

Father, in the name of Jesus, I want to see in the spirit like Jeremiah, Zechariah, and the other prophets in the pages of the Bible. Would You open my eyes to the seer dimensions and help me navigate the visual revelation? Will You level up my seer anointing?

When Signs Follow the Prophet

"These miraculous signs will accompany those who believe: They will cast out demons in my name, and they will speak in new languages. They will be able to handle snakes with safety, and if they drink anything poisonous, it won't hurt them. They will be able to place their hands on the sick, and they will be healed" (Mark 16:17-18).

Through the pages of the Bible we see prophets walking in the miraculous—though some had a more visible miracle ministry than others. We see Moses making prophetic declarations of plagues on Egypt, parting the Red Sea with his staff at God's instruction, and bringing water out of a rock. We see Elijah bringing a provision miracle to the widow of Zarephath and raising the dead.

Elisha did twice as many miracles than Elijah. We see Elisha healing waters, multiplying a widow's oil, curing deadly food, feeding a hundred men with fifty loaves, curing a captain's leprosy—even Elijah's bones raised someone from the dead. But most of the prophets in the Bible didn't walk in the type of miracle anointing that turns heads.

Though God did miracles in Isaiah's ministry—he prayed for the for a sign that Hezekiah would live and the shadow defied time by moving backward ten steps—the miracles in his ministry were not nearly as dramatic as the miracles of Moses, Elijah, or Elisha.

And consider this: Many prophets in the Bible didn't seem to do any miracles at all. Jeremiah didn't heal anyone. Hosea didn't do multiplication miracles. And, in fact, John the Baptist performed no sign (see John 4:1). You get the picture. Still, prophets and the miracle anointing go hand in hand.

Modern-day prophets have something our Old Testament counterparts didn't—the infilling of the Holy Spirit. Christ the Prophet is the miracle worker in us, working signs and wonders by the power of the Holy Spirit just like He did when He walked the earth. Jesus said signs would follow those who believe. It's time for modern-day prophets to press in to the miracle realm. Ask the Holy Spirit to give you the spiritual gift of working of miracles.

— *Prayer* —

Father, in the name of Jesus, would You give me the spiritual gift of the working of miracles? When it serves Your purpose, cause me to move in the miracle realm to confirm Your prophetic words with signs following. Open the eyes of unbelievers through Your wonder working power.

Count the Costs

"But don't begin until you count the cost..." (Luke 14:28).

When God called me into prophetic ministry, one of the things He told me was "to count the costs and don't look back." Some years later, the Lord asked me if I was willing to pay the price to do what He had called me to do. I answered quickly, "Yes, Lord. I am willing." After all, I had already counted the costs when He called me—or at least I thought I had. The Lord admonished me, "Don't answer too quickly. Consider the costs."

I went off to pray. After about a week, I returned to the Lord with a solid answer: "Yes, Lord, I am willing to pay the price." I sensed the pleasure of the Holy Spirit at my sincere answer, but I never anticipated what He would tell me next: "It will be a very dear price."

Before too long, I started paying a dear price indeed. Had he not warned me of what was about to happen through that one line—"It will be a very dear price"—I would have been devastated at what happened next. I was in a spiritually abusive church and left. When I did, I lost all my ministry opportunities, all my friends—everything I knew.

Leonard Ravenhill, a British evangelist and author of many books including *Why Revival Tarries*, said this: "Few believers have paid the price of laying down their lives and being fully committed to Christ. Even fewer are willing to consider taking up the cross daily. Few pay the price because they are too comfortable in this world... We need to come to the point where we know we cannot do without a mighty move of God."

There is a price to pay to walk in high levels of the prophetic anointing. The cost of taking the time to prepare yourself for the higher calling may seem too much to bear now. Impatience clouds the realities of readiness. But I guarantee this: If you put off reconciling your character debts today you'll pay the piper with compounded interest later.

— *Prayer* —

Father, in the name of Jesus, help me to consider the costs—to count the costs of going to the places in the prophetic dimensions that I pray about. I don't want to step into realms I'm not prepared for, so ready me for the realms You've called me into. Prepare me to pay the price.

The Spirit of the Prophets

"But if someone is prophesying and another person receives a revelation from the Lord, the one who is speaking must stop. In this way, all who prophesy will have a turn to speak, one after the other, so that everyone will learn and be encouraged. Remember that people who prophesy are in control of their spirit and can take turns. For God is not a God of disorder but of peace, as in all the meetings of God's holy people" (1 Corinthians 14:30-33).

I was in a meeting once where I was prophesying over the congregation and a woman stood up and began shouting out a prophetic word very loudly. It was jarring, shocking, and hard to believe. I had about a split second to decide whether I was going to stop her, which would have been extremely embarrassing for her, or let her continue in this disorder.

Of course, I didn't want to embarrass her, but I could not allow the disorder. I was concerned if she had no self-control she may not have accuracy in her utterance either. I processed all this in about two seconds and chose to begin to pray in tongues loudly to drown out what she was saying. Most everyone else in the meeting caught on and began praying loudly in the spirit too. She stopped.

Self-control is one of the fruits of the Spirit, and it's important in the context of prophetic ministry. A prophet who can't exercise self-control is a prophet who should keep their mouth shut until the fruit manifests as often as the prophetic unction.

Self-control is restraint over your own wants, emotions, and even prophetic impulses. Just because you have a prophetic word doesn't mean you need to share it. God can show you many things for the sake of prayer, or to share privately at a later time.

Imagine a meeting in which everyone who felt like they had a word from the Lord was allowed to share it. There may be little time for anything else and some of those words may not be from the Lord—doing more harm than good.

Paul wrote, inspired by the Spirit, to let two or three prophets prophesy (see 1 Cor. 14:9). Prophecy is valuable but it's not the only form of ministry we need to see manifest in meetings. We need to worship. We need to hear the Word of God. We need time to take communion. Though prophetic ministry is vital to the church, the church is more than prophetic ministry. We need to have God control rather than no control if we want to earn prophetic respect.

— *Prayer* —

Father, in the name of Jesus, give me the grace and self-awareness to cultivate and exercise the fruit of self-control in my life and ministry. Teach me to hold my tongue until Your Spirit gives me permission to repeat the words You spoke to me in the secret place.

The Unsung Prophet

"Meanwhile, Elisha the prophet had summoned a member of the group of prophets. 'Get ready to travel,' he told him, 'and take this flask of olive oil with you. Go to Ramoth-gilead, and find Jehu son of Jehoshaphat, son of Nimshi. Call him into a private room away from his friends, and pour the oil over his head. Say to him, "This is what the Lord says: I anoint you to be the king over Israel." Then open the door and run for your life!"' (2 Kings 9:1-3)

Remember when Jehu was anointed king of Israel? Can you tell me who anointed him? You can't remember, can you? That's because the Bible does not record the name of the prophet who accepted this important assignment.

This unnamed prophet obeyed Elisha's command. He sought out Jehu, anointed him as king over Israel, and commissioned him to destroy the house of Ahab. This unnamed prophet went on to deliver a powerful prophetic word about the fate of Jezebel—dogs would devour her in Jezreel—and then he opened the door and ran, giving no one an opportunity to applaud his powerful prophetic announcement or pat him on the back for a job well done.

After receiving this behind-the-scenes prophetic commissioning, Jehu would ride his chariot furiously to Jezreel. Jezebel's fate was just as the unnamed prophet had announced. Jehu gets all the recognition, but it was the unsung prophet's faithfulness to complete his mission that sparked a major turning point for Israel.

There are other examples of unnamed prophets who accomplished important works in the Bible—and there are hundreds of modern-day prophets following in those humble footsteps. Thank God for the prophets who seek to honor the One who sent them instead of vying for self-glorification.

The reality is, if you are operating in your God-given ministry and completing your God-given assignments, you are a hero in the Kingdom of God whether or not anyone ever knows your name in the earth. The most important thing is that your name is known in heaven and written in the Lamb's Book of Life.

— *Prayer* —

Father, in the name of Jesus, help me to forfeit my need for recognition and prophesy as unto You—never for my glory and always for Your glory. Rid me of the need to be applauded, celebrated, and even appreciated by the church. Help me prophesy from a place of purity.

Confronting False Prophets

"Then Elijah commanded, 'Seize all the prophets of Baal. Don't let a single one escape!' So the people seized them all, and Elijah took them down to the Kishon Valley and killed them there" (1 Kings 18:40).

Just like Elijah confronted the prophets of Baal, the time is coming when God's New Testament mouthpieces will confront modern day merchandisers. The true will defy the false. The holy will challenge the unholy. Until that day, spirits of divination, with a little help from the lust of the eyes, the lust of the flesh, and the pride of life, are working overtime to woo God's true prophets to the side of error.

Some merchandising prophets, with their miracle water, prophetic soap, and prosperity oil, are catching naïve Christians hook, line, and sinker. Other gospel gainsayers are profiting with urgent announcements that God will heal the first five people who run up to the altar with a $100 bill in hand.

But perhaps the most dangerous merchandisers are those who use their gift to tap into divination. These prophets announce what the believer wants to hear in order to sow a false seed of faith in his heart and reap an improper financial reward, inappropriately earned position, or wrongly received recognition.

Elijah threw down the prophetic gauntlet and challenged the false camp to bring fire down from heaven by calling upon their god. The merchandising diviners cried to Baal from dawn to dusk with no answer.

When the false camp had finally exhausted itself, Elijah built an altar holding a sacrifice to Jehovah, drenched it with four barrels of water, said a simple prayer, and watched as the fire of God fell from heaven and consumed the sacrifice, the wood, the stones, the dust, and even the water in the trench. Then Elijah slew his false counterparts one by one.

There's a boldness coming on true prophets of God who, like Elijah, will begin to confront their false counterparts. False prophets will continue to rise anyway, just as Jesus said they would. But there will be times when true prophets have to confront the false for the sake of the sheep. Ask the Lord to give you wisdom to know when to speak out about a false prophet deceiving people in your care and when to confront them privately.

— *Prayer* —

Father, in the name of Jesus, give me boldness and courage to stand against the atrocities in the prophetic movement in my day. Teach me to confront the prophetic malpractice with wisdom and boldness so the victims of prophetic abuse can be set free from false operations.

Tapping into Prophetic Synergies

"When Saul and his servant arrived at Gibeah, they saw a group of prophets coming toward them. Then the Spirit of God came powerfully upon Saul, and he, too, began to prophesy" (1 Samuel 10:10).

God is the God of synergies. For example, you've probably heard it said one can put a thousand to flight and two can put ten thousand to flight in the context of spiritual warfare. But synergies are not just a reality in spiritual warfare. They are a reality in prophetic ministry as well.

Before you can tap into prophetic synergies, you need to understand what synergy really is. Let's look first at the dictionary definition: "the interaction of elements that when combined product a total effect that is greater than the sum of the individual elements, contributions, etc.," according to Dictionary.com.

My definition of prophetic synergy may be a little easier to remember: the harmony among prophetic people that creates a spiritual atmosphere that makes it easier to accurately see, hear, and say what the Lord is doing.

Even people who are not particularly prophetic can tap into prophetic synergies. Saul is a prime example. The king tapped into prophetic synergies more than once, and quite by accident. The first time around, Samuel prophesied to Saul about an encounter with a company of prophets that would turn him into another man. And it happened just as Samuel prophesied. Saul stepped into prophetic synergies and started prophesying so accurately people wondered, "Is Saul also among the prophets?" (1 Sam. 10:12 NKJV). Clearly, Saul was not a prophet.

If that had only happened once, it would have been interesting, but because it happened twice it points to a principle. And it didn't just happen to Saul. It happened to everyone who stepped into the atmosphere prophetic synergy created. When Saul's messengers stepped into the atmosphere, they prophesied. And when Saul encountered the company of prophets a second time, he prophesied all day and all night naked!

Wouldn't you like to tap into prophetic synergies like that! (Minus the naked part!) This is why it's important to be in a prophetic church and among prophetic people. It makes you more prophetic! It's like you put your prophetic anointing with the prophetic anointings of others and there's a prophetic explosion.

— *Prayer* —

Father, in the name of Jesus, give me an appreciation for prophetic synergies that create atmospheres in which it's easier to discern Your will, prophesy Your word, and see what You are showing me. Teach me how to cultivate harmony that brings in the glory.

Throw Jezebel Down

"Jehu looked up and saw her at the window and shouted, 'Who is on my side?' And two or three eunuchs looked out at him. 'Throw her down!' Jehu yelled. So they threw her out the window, and her blood spattered against the wall and on the horses. And Jehu trampled her body under his horses' hooves" (2 Kings 9:32-33).

After ministering at the Watchman Leadership conference at Christian International, Bishop Bill Hamon led me through the back where I ran into Chuck Pierce. Chuck was glad to see me, because he had a word for me. He proceeded to wrap a mantle around me and prophesied that God was raising me up to send me into many nations to throw Jezebel off the wall.

Soon after that, I was getting calls from all over the world to do just that. God sent me to seven nations in one year to train prophets how to deal with Jezebel. Thank God, He had prepared me. How do you prepare to throw Jezebel down? One key is building walls of prayer in your ministry.

Prophets who build walls of prayer have a distinct authority to throw down spirits that try to penetrate that wall or erect a stronghold on that wall. Prophets who live on the wall of intercession incline their ear to the Lord's command to throw Jezebel—or other demons—down at the right moment. Prophets who live on the wall—those who watch and pray day and night, night and day—gain a position of authority to throw Jezebel down.

God is always looking for prophets who will make a wall, stand on it, and actually dwell on it to prevent Jezebel from gaining further inroads of destruction in families, churches, and cities. You can't dwell on the wall until you build the wall or, put another way, your tower of prayer.

There comes a time to throw Jezebel down in your life, your ministry, your family, your church, and your workplace. Again, you do this in the place of prayer. And after you throw her down, bury all memory of her. Move on with your life in victory!

— *Prayer* —

Father, in the name of Jesus, teach me how to build prayer towers—walls of intercession—that position me to see Jezebel's attack and cast down her witchcrafts coming against me. Weave warfare intercession into my mantle so that building prayer walls becomes my first response.

When Your Prophetic Promotion Is Delayed

"Humble yourselves before the Lord, and he will lift you up in honor" (James 4:10).

There's nothing fundamentally wrong about hoping God notices your faithfulness, increases your prophetic anointing, and gives you greater influence. But striving for promotion only leads you to unhealthy competition, envy—and perhaps even error.

Maybe you're hoping to prophesy from the platform in your church, get invited to the conference with all the prophetic rock stars, sign a best-selling book deal, get published in an online magazine, or some other indicator of promotion. Maybe you feel you are being overlooked and even feel you are more accurate than, humbler, or even more anointed than the ones you see surpassing you in popularity.

Regardless of the circumstances, our true character is on display when we feel like God has overlooked us for a promotion. And sometimes our character reveals to us and others we were not ready for the promotion.

Even before the Holy Spirit fell on the Day of Pentecost, believers in the early church refused to allow jealousy to distract them from their mission. After Judas betrayed the Lord and committed suicide, Peter pointed out Scripture that a new witness to Jesus' resurrection must be appointed. Two men were proposed: "Joseph called Barsabas, who was surnamed Justus, and Matthias" (Acts 1:23 NKJV).

> *Then they all prayed, "O Lord, you know every heart. Show us which of these men you have chosen as an apostle to replace Judas in this ministry, for he has deserted us and gone where he belongs." Then they cast lots, and Matthias was selected to become an apostle with the other eleven* (Acts 1:24-26).

We don't see Justus getting jealous, making false accusations against Matthias, or throwing him in a deep well to die. Justus didn't pitch a hissy fit to the other disciples or seek to prove why he was better suited for the promotion. He didn't storm of out the Upper Room and spread rumors about the apostles. We don't know what happened to Justus, but I believe he went on to do great things for God. If you respond in humility when someone else gets the promotion you want, so can you.

— *Prayer* —

Father, in the name of Jesus, deliver me from jealousy and envy that causes me to be more concerned with what You are doing in someone else's life instead of what You are doing in mine. Help me instead to lean into the preparation for the promotion You have for me.

Freedom from Man-Pleasing

"Fearing people is a dangerous trap, but trusting the Lord means safety" (Proverbs 29:25).

I have never been a man pleaser (or people pleaser). I've had a lot of fears in my life, but fear of man is not one of them. I'm not bragging, I'm grateful. Solomon told us the fear of man brings a snare. Fear of man shuts your mouth when you should be speaking out.

God warned His seers and prophets not to fear man. Why? Because He knew they would be tempted to fear man. God told Jeremiah in Jeremiah 1:8, "Do not be afraid of their faces" and told Ezekiel in Ezekiel 2:6, "Do not be afraid of their words or dismayed by their looks" (NKJV). I assure you, looks really can't kill and sticks and stones may break your bones but words can't hurt you—unless you let them. Jesus put it plainly:

> *Don't be afraid of those who want to kill your body; they cannot touch your soul. Fear only God, who can destroy both soul and body in hell* (Matthew 10:28).

Fear of man could prevent us from prophesying the will of the Lord.

We disqualify ourselves from our highest prophetic calling if we bow to this man-made structure. If we aren't willing to share exactly what we see because we are afraid of what man will do to us, then we will never get to the level of seeing into high level situations.

Paul boldly declared, "Obviously, I'm not trying to win the approval of people, but of God. If pleasing people were my goal, I would not be Christ's servant" (Gal. 1:10). And God told Isaiah, "I, yes I, am the one who comforts you. So why are you afraid of mere humans, who wither like the grass and disappear?" (Isa. 51:12).

The Bible says we prophesy according to our faith. Faith overcomes fear. If we believe that the Lord is truly showing us something in the spirit, then we can overcome the fear of man and get to the next level.

— *Prayer* —

Father, in the name of Jesus, deliver me from the fear of man. Deliver me from people pleasing. Deliver me from caring what other people think. Help me prophesy to the masses as if I am prophesying to an audience of the One who gave me the prophetic words to speak.

Prophetic Soap Operas

"Then Elijah stood in front of them and said, 'How much longer will you waver, hobbling between two opinions? If the Lord is God, follow him! But if Baal is God, then follow him!' But the people were completely silent. Then Elijah said to them, 'I am the only prophet of the Lord who is left, but Baal has 450 prophets'" (1 Kings 18:21-22).

Elijah was as bold a prophet as they come. He confronted King Ahab for his sin without apology. He challenged the false prophets and defeated them singlehandedly in a prophetic showdown of epic proportions (see 1 Kings 18:20-40). He turned the heart of Israel back to Jehovah. Elijah must have felt the pleasure of the Lord after a history-making day of ministry.

Then came the plot twist. Jezebel found out Elijah killed her yes-men prophets and sent a messenger to deliver a death threat. Mighty Elijah started spinning out. He ran a day's journey into the wilderness, sat down under a juniper tree, and prayed that God would let him die.

"I have had enough, Lord," he said. "Take my life, for I am not better than my ancestors who have already died." Then he lay down and slept under the broom tree... (1 Kings 19:4-5).

This is what I call a prophetic soap opera. Some prophets have a tendency to get melancholy and even overly dramatic about the persecution and spiritual warfare they face— or when people reject their prophetic ministry. Elijah and Jonah are two prophets who come to mind. You'll remember Jonah pulled a similar stunt with God, sitting under the gourd wishing he was dead after Nineveh escaped judgment (see Jon. 4:9 KJV).

Have you ever been in a place where you said, "God, just take me on to heaven now? I can't deal with this anymore?" It's not that you want to die, it's just that you want to escape the current reality. I'll admit that I have felt that way many times. If God was listening (later, I always hope He wasn't), He didn't even dignify my whining with an answer.

After the great victory and the Jezebel attack, Elijah wanted to die right then and there— or so he said. Elijah took his focus off God and put it on himself. He fell into the trap of self-pity. He felt lonely. From there, Elijah went to a cave and isolated himself. He felt like he was fighting alone. In a sense he was, because when he fled from Jezebel he left his servant behind (see 1 Kings 19:3).

If this happens to you—if you face a spiritual attack that makes you feel alone and unable to keep fighting the good fight of faith—seek those of your own company. Don't let Jezebel or any other spirit isolate you from your tribe. You are not alone. God is with you and He has assigned people to walk with you and war with you.

— *Prayer* —

Father, in the name of Jesus, help me resist the temptation to organize a pity party when I am overwhelmed by Jezebel's attacks. Teach me to keep my eyes on You instead of on myself. Show me how to escape the prophetic soap opera in which I've scripted myself.

Enoch's Secret to Walking in Revelation

"If we live in the Spirit, let us also walk in the Spirit" (Galatians 5:25 NKJV).

Prophets love to quote Amos 3:7 and for good reason. We all love to think we have a special connection to God—and we all do. Here, though, we clearly see that God chooses to share some of His plans with the prophets, who share them with the rest of the Body of Christ.

The Hebrew word for "secret" in this verse is *cowd*. It means connotes a council of familiar conversation, a circle of close companions, and intimacy with God. That suggests that all prophets may not have the same level of prophetic intelligence, but what He shares depends on how close you walk with Him.

I imagine Enoch walked in great revelation. Genesis 5:21-24 reads, "When Enoch was 65 years old, he became the father of Methuselah. After the birth of Methuselah, Enoch lived in close fellowship with God for another 300 years, and he had other sons and daughters. Enoch lived 365 years, walking in close fellowship with God. Then one day he disappeared, because God took him."

If you've read the Book of Enoch, you understand this man of God had many revelatory encounters. Later, we see Methuselah's son Noah walking with God in a similar way. Genesis 6:9 reads, "Noah was a righteous man, the only blameless person living on earth at the time, and he walked in close fellowship with God." Noah was the only person on the entire face of the earth with whom God shared the secret of the flood.

Paul told us in Galatians 5:16 to walk by the Spirit. But Paul didn't just teach it. Paul modeled it for his generation. And he, too, discovered the secrets of God and the mysteries of the Kingdom. He walked in so much direct revelation that two-thirds of the New Testament are made up of his Holy Spirit-inspired writing.

What about you? Are you willing to make some changes to enter into that council of familiar conversation and intimacy with God that qualifies you to steward His secrets and mysteries? Start by drawing near to God and He will draw near to you.

— *Prayer* —

Father, in the name of Jesus, would You encounter my heart and teach me the principles of unlocking and walking in the deep things of God? Would You show me how to walk like Enoch, Noah, and Paul into revelation that helps a generation know You better?

Don't Be a Blabber Mouth Prophet

"Set a guard, O Lord, over my mouth; keep watch over the door of my lips" (Psalm 141:3 NKJV).

God knows every secret of your heart, but He's careful about who He shares His secrets with. Let me be blunt: You can quote Amos 3:7—"Surely the Lord God does nothing, unless He reveals His secret to His servants the prophets" (NKJV)—over and over again without ever hearing the secrets of His heart. You can meditate on that verse day and night and never experience the privilege of hearing His secrets if you have a blabber mouth.

Sure, God is revealing His secrets to some prophets somewhere, but Amos 3:7 doesn't obligate Him to share them with you. Think about it for a minute. Who do you share your secrets with? Do you walk up to strangers on the street and share the intimate details of your life? Of course not. Do you share your secrets with people you are in loose relationship with? Probably not. At least you shouldn't.

No, you share your secrets with people you feel you can trust. You share your secrets with people who you feel will handle them with care. You share your secrets with people who will not blab them all over the world. So does God. God does not share His secrets with blabber mouths. He doesn't intend for you to share with the world—or sometimes with anybody at all—every secret He shares with you. Some things are just between you and Him. Some things are to be prophesied at a later time.

The preacher said, "Too much talk leads to sin. Be sensible and keep your mouth shut" (Prov. 10:19). It is tempting to want to share with the masses things the Lord is saying and showing you in the secret place. But without His express permission, it's sin to do so. James warns us to be quick to listen and slow to speak (see James 1:19). This should mark the prophet's ministry when it comes to revealing the mysteries of God. Ask the Holy Spirit to help you discern when to share and when to stay silent.

— *Prayer* —

Father, in the name of Jesus, help me discern when it's time to share and time to stay silent. Teach me to steward the prophetic intelligence You share with me responsibly. Deliver me from the need to be seen and known as one who walks in revelation.

Who's Your Elijah?

"...Elijah passed by him and threw his cloak on him" (1 Kings 19:19 MEV).

Who's your Elijah? In other words, who are the prophetic mentors in your life? Every Elisha needs an Elijah. Every prophet needs a mentor, a coach, someone who can show them the ropes, help them avoid the ditches of error and excess, and encourage them in righteousness.

Every Elisha needs an Elijah, someone who will help you build a platform so you can release your prophetic voice, someone who will stand with you and pray for you, someone who will help you hone your prophetic accuracy. You may have been waiting for an Elijah for a long time. Don't stop looking. They may appear suddenly.

> *So Elijah went and found Elisha son of Shaphat plowing a field. There were twelve teams of oxen in the field, and Elisha was plowing with the twelfth team. Elijah went over to him and threw his cloak across his shoulders and then walked away* (1 Kings 19:19).

If you are not paying attention you will miss your divine connection, you will miss your Elijah, and you will miss your release. You have to be discerning—especially those who are praying to God for a mentor, for the right training opportunities, and for healthy apostolic and prophetic alignments. You have to keep your spiritual ears and eyes open because God will send you an Elijah when you are ready to receive him.

Keep in mind, you might run into a Saul first. David served under a Saul. Saul celebrated him for a moment, but when David started rising Saul wanted to kill him. Saul threw javelins at him. Saul hunted him down in the wilderness. Saul was not interested in releasing David into his prophetic mantle. Saul wanted to stifle David.

Be careful when you pray for an Elisha that Saul doesn't come knocking on your door in disguise and you don't come into an alignment with a Saul who will crush you and try to kill you. Look for the Elijah. But also know this. <u>Sometimes God will put you under a</u> <u>Saul to get the Saul out of you.</u> Nevertheless, keep looking for your Elijah.

— *Prayer* —

Father, in the name of Jesus, help me not to grow weary and frustrated waiting for my Elijah. Help keep my hand to the plow You have assigned me to until You make the divine connections I am praying for. I bind all discouragement and decree my Elijah is coming.

Blending Grace and Truth

"Instead, we will speak the truth in love, growing in every way more and more like Christ, who is the head of his body, the church" (Ephesians 4:15).

The prophet must be willing to speak the truth, the whole truth, and nothing but the truth—so help you God. But truth without grace is not God's way. John described Jesus, the Prophet, as full of grace and truth (see John 1:4). That translates into our modern day as bold, redemptive truth-telling.

Walking in prophetic ministry demands speaking and acting boldly. Like Peter and John, people should be able to see our boldness and marvel, knowing that we have been with Jesus (see Acts 4:13). They should be able to recognize the Lion of the Tribe of Judah in us. If you look up variants of "bold" in your handy dandy concordance, you will quickly discover that the use of words like "bold," "boldly" and "boldness" in the King James Version are almost always—yes, almost always—used in conjunction with on-fire believers.

Take the apostle Paul, for example. He prayed that when he opened his mouth he would speak forth boldly (see Eph. 6:19). He preached boldly at Damascus in the name of Jesus (see Acts 9:27). He spoke boldly in the name of the Lord Jesus, and disputed against the Grecians who wanted to kill him (see Acts 9:28-29). He spoke boldly in the synagogue even though the people spoke evil about Jesus (see Acts 19:8). In fact, Paul "spake boldly" everywhere he went. Even when he was an ambassador in bonds he spoke boldly (see Eph. 6:20). Do you see the pattern yet?

All that said, boldness alone won't cut it. Grace is required. It is possible to speak the truth in love. God is the God of redemption. When we speak boldly, we must not just boldly declare the truth. We must also boldly declare God's redemptive purposes; otherwise, we stun people with our boldness and may leave them angry, upset, or discouraged—or thinking God is angry and upset with them. If you are especially bold, be especially careful that you prophesy God's redemptive purposes with difficult words.

— *Prayer* —

Father, in the name of Jesus, set me on fire and give me boldness that refuses to back down from or water down the truth You have spoken. But, Lord, let my speech be seasoned with grace and salt that makes people hungry to embrace the truth You are releasing through me.

Developing Thick Skin

"As an adamant harder than flint have I made thy forehead: fear them not, neither be dismayed at their looks, though they be a rebellious house" (Ezekiel 3:9 KJV).

If you don't have thick skin, you better start toughening up. I may have had an advantage. Before I knew I was a prophet, I was a journalist. When I started my career we sent in what are called query letters to editors via snail mail. It sounds archaic, I know.

I checked my mailbox every day, hoping for an answer much the same way a fisherman waits on still water hoping for the fish to bite. Most of the time, I never even got a response. Sometimes I got what they call a rejection letter. Every once in a while, an editor would take my pitch and assign me a story. Even after it was written, when I was young in my craft, editors would tear my story apart and ask for rewrites. I didn't like it, but I learned how to develop thick skin.

The prophet will be rejected in his day and perhaps celebrated in his legacy. You may have heard the phrase "set your forehead like flint." We find this twice in Scripture. Ezekiel tells us:

> *But look, I have made you as obstinate and hard-hearted as they are. I have made your forehead as hard as the hardest rock! So don't be afraid of them or fear their angry looks, even though they are rebels* (Ezekiel 3:8-9).

And this was Isaiah's confession:

> *Because the Sovereign Lord helps me, I will not be disgraced. Therefore, I have set my face like a stone, determined to do his will. And I know that I will not be put to shame. He who gives me justice is near. Who will dare to bring charges against me now? Where are my accusers? Let them appear! See, the Sovereign Lord is on my side! Who will declare me guilty? All my enemies will be destroyed like old clothes that have been eaten by moths!* (Isaiah 50:7-9)

You have to develop thick skin to stand in this office—or even to warn your inner circle of friends and family. Prophets must be more concerned with what God wants them to say than what other people say about them. Take on this mindset and it will shield you from the impact of the persecution.

— *Prayer* —

Father, in the name of Jesus, would You help me develop thick skin? Teach me not to take rejection personally. Give me a forehead like flint, a face like stone, and a determination to keep speaking Your Word even when people don't want to hear it.

Watch to See

"I will climb up to my watchtower and stand at my guardpost. There I will wait to see what the Lord says and how he will answer my complaint" (Habakkuk 2:1).

Habakkuk said he would "watch to see." The New International Version says, "I will look to see." The English Standard Version says, "look out to see." The New Living Translation says, "I will wait to see." The watchman prophet must be an expert not only at watching, but waiting.

As I write in my book *The Making of a Watchman*, in Bible days watchmen could watch days or weeks at a time and not see much of significance, but they were faithful to stand on their post regardless. See, it's not always about seeing something. Seeing nothing can be a good thing. If the coast is clear, that means the land is at peace.

> *I wait for the Lord, with bated breath I wait; I long for His Word! My soul waits for the Lord, more than watchmen for the morning, more than watchmen for the morning* (Psalm 130:5-6 MEV).

You can't separate the watchman prophet from waiting. The two go hand in hand. If we want to cultivate a watchman's eye—if we want to gain the Lord's perspective—we need to be willing to wait until He shows us something.

If you are going to cultivate a watchman's eye, you have to set aside the multi-tasking and the mind traffic and be still. Understand that the Hebrew word for "wait" is not a passive, boring waiting that tempts you to sleep and slumber. No, the Hebrew word for "wait" is *qavah*. It is an active word that means to "look for," according to *The KJV Old Testament Hebrew Lexicon*.

The watchman is looking for action in the spirit. Sometimes things happen so fast, if you aren't waiting, expecting, and looking for it you'll miss it. I liken watching to praying with your eyes. It's like your eyes crying out to God to show you what He wants you to see and demonstrating your faith for a prayer answer by continuing to look.

— *Prayer* —

Father, in the name of Jesus, help me pray with my eyes. Teach me to watch for my next prayer assignment carefully, being content when there is nothing to report but peace. Help me not to grow weary or bored in my watchtower when activity in the spirit realm is lacking.

MAY 23

Dishonor: Get Used to It   *'Dishonored' the game*

"Then they scoffed, 'He's just the carpenter's son, and we know Mary, his mother, and his brothers—James, Joseph, Simon, and Judas. All his sisters live right here among us. Where did he learn all these things?' And they were deeply offended and refused to believe in him. Then Jesus told them, 'A prophet is honored everywhere except in his own hometown and among his own family'" (Matthew 13:55-57).

Jesus is never wrong—never. So when Jesus said a prophet is honored everywhere except in his own city and his own family, He was right. This wasn't just a truth for His day. It's just as true today as it was 2,000 years ago. I can speak from experience. I can travel anywhere in the United States—or anywhere in the world—and people honor the gift of God in me. In my own city, though, I'm typically persecuted and disregarded.

I am not alone. Many prophets are downright dishonored, despised, and disdained in their own city and even in their own family. You've heard the old saying, "Familiarity breeds contempt." That's generally true of God's prophets or any ministry gift. Sometimes if you open your heart too much and people see you're flawed just like they are, they lose respect. The people in Jesus' hometown remembered when He learned to walk and talk. They remembered Him working with Joseph in carpentry. It was hard for them to see Him as a prophet.

Merriam-Webster defines honor as "respect that is given to someone who is admired; a good reputation; good quality of character as judged by other people; and high moral standard of behavior." So the question is, what kind of honor are you seeking? If you are looking for respect and admiration, you are missing the mark. Look at the prophets in the Old Testament—or look at John the Baptist and Jesus Christ, for that matter. They were persecuted, ridiculed and rejected. At one point, the people tried to run Jesus off a cliff! Ultimately, they crucified Him, the most shameful way to die in His era.

Now, there is a type of honor that you should seek—good quality character and high moral standards of behavior. That type of honor honors God. That type of honor draws people to God. That type of honor is honorable. Ask the Holy Spirit to search your heart to see if you are seeking praise and honor from men—and if you are, then repent and set your heart to develop character, morals, and behavior that honor God.

— *Prayer* —

Father, in the name of Jesus, I repent for the desire to be honored or admired. Help me balance the realities of praise and rejection. Help me seek to honor Your name more than I seek my own honor, and help me honor others whether they honor me or not.

Correcting Your Prophetic Punctuation

"Who is he who speaks and it comes to pass, when the Lord has not commanded it?" (Lamentations 3:37 NKJV)

Over decades of operating in prophetic ministry, I've discerned a difficult truth: If we are not careful, we can fall into one of two traps that may cause us to miss it—and cause people to spit out our revelation. Of course, there are many other ways prophets miss it. But these two are very common and can be especially difficult to discern because at least half the prophecy is accurate.

Let's see if you can relate: Have you ever prophesied something that was half right and half wrong? Have you ever prophesied something that started off accurate and ended in error? The scary part about those questions, especially if you prophesy a lot in travel, is you may not know the answer. That's why it's so important to understand this concept: Don't put a period where God puts a comma, and don't put a comma where God puts a period.

Here's what I mean: If we put a period where God puts a comma, we're essentially shutting down our listening before God is finished speaking. In other words, we got so excited at what God was saying that we interrupted the prophetic inflow and started our outflow with only half the message. We may put a period where God puts a comma when we get distracted while He's speaking or fail to press in to get the full revelation.

Alternatively, putting a comma where God puts a period means we keep talking after He finishes speaking. The word then is at least half our words, not His words. This is easy enough to do because our spirit carries truth—good things—but that doesn't mean it's an accurate picture of what God is saying. We have to be careful to shut our mouths when the river dries up or we can lead people astray. Seasoned prophets can tell when God is winding down, even during spontaneous prophecy.

— *Prayer* —

Father, in the name of Jesus, teach me to speak the truth, the whole truth, and nothing but the truth. Help me put the commas and periods in the right place so that I don't rob Your people of the revelation You are sharing or share out of my own spirit our soul after You stop speaking.

Jeremiah's Rebuke

"From the least to the greatest, their lives are ruled by greed. From prophets to priests, they are all frauds" (Jeremiah 6:13).

Greed—a selfish desire for more than you need—sullied the prophets in Jeremiah's day. God called these greedy prophets "frauds" because they misrepresented His heart to a people who depended on them for spiritual leadership. These prophets put their needs before the people God called them to serve and it grieved His heart.

The New International Version of Jeremiah 6:13 tells us these prophets were "practicing deceit" and apparently they had mastered their craft because the people were falling for it hook, line, and sinker. *The Message* version of this verse is a blunt strike at the character of greedy prophets: "Everyone's after the dishonest dollar, little people and big people alike. Prophets and priests and everyone in between twist words and doctor truth."

What an indictment! You've probably seen greedy, fraudulent prophets in the modern-day prophetic movement who practice deceit, twist words, and doctor truth. You would expect this descriptor for psychics in their little shops of horrors tempting desperate, unsuspecting victims, but unfortunately some who call themselves prophets fell into the greed trap Jeremiah describes and may not know how to get out.

Mind you, the prophets Jeremiah is prophesying about were not prophets who sincerely thought they heard from God but missed it. No, the Jeremiah-era prophets were practicing deceit the way a doctor practices medicine—by profession. It's a heart issue—and some of Jeremiah's contemporaries needed spiritual cardiac surgery.

The Bible beseeches all believers to lead a life worthy of our calling. Paul was literally begging us to "walk holy, in a way that is suitable to your high rank" (Eph. 4:1 TPT). How much more so should prophets rely on the grace of God to practice holiness rather than practicing covetousness? Be sure, the enemy will lay the trap of greed at some point in your ministry. Know this: God will provide for His prophets just like He provided for Elijah at the brook in a time of famine. Holiness pays eternal rewards.

— *Prayer* —

Father, in the name of Jesus, help me avoid greed and covetousness. Deliver me from anything that looks like the love of money, which is a root of all evil. Help me to walk holy, in a way that is suitable to Your high calling on my life.

Soaring to New Prophetic Heights

"I wait for the Lord, my soul waits, and in His word I do hope. My soul waits for the Lord more than those who watch for the morning—yes, more than those who watch for the morning" (Psalm 130:5-6 NKJV).

The eagle has long been a sign of prophets and prophetic ministry. In fact, if you look at the early books on the prophetic—and even some newer ones—many of them feature an eagle. In reality, there are eagle prophets and vulture prophets in the church.

What is an eagle prophet? Consider the natural eagle. Eagles fly at high altitudes, not with low-flying birds like sparrows or other small birds. Eagles have strong vision, with an ability to focus on objects up to three miles away. When storm clouds gather, eagles get excited. An eagle uses the storm's wind to lift himself higher, far above the clouds. In the meantime, all the other birds hide in the leaves and branches of the trees.

An eagle prophet is one who soars high in ministry. Our attitude toward God, His Word, and prophetic ministry determines our altitude. In order to succeed in God's call on your life, you need a clear vision and must remain focused on what God is saying and doing no matter what spiritual warfare comes your way. You have to learn to thrive in storms, to see through the breakthrough on the other side of the dark clouds.

Eagle prophets are different from vulture prophets. Vulture prophets are self-minded, money-minded, or platform-minded. Vulture prophets prey on people and go after dead things. Eagles never fly with vultures. They can discern them and avoid them. So what is the secret of eagle prophets? It's found in Isaiah 40:31:

> *But those who wait for the Lord [who expect, look for, and hope in Him] will gain new strength and renew their power; they will lift up their wings [and rise up close to God] like eagles [rising toward the sun]; they will run and not become weary, they will walk and not grow tired* (AMP).

When you wait on the Lord, you get the right perspective—a bird's eye view—of God, His Word, and prophetic ministry. Ask the Lord to help you wait on Him.

— *Prayer* —

Father, in the name of Jesus, help me to soar above life's circumstances to get heaven's perspective on the times, seasons, challenges, and spiritual warfare. Give me strong vision and focus on what You are doing so I can follow Your leadership. Help me develop a right attitude.

The Pollyanna Prophet

"For the leaders of the people have misled them. They have led them down the path of destruction" (Isaiah 9:16).

You've probably met one. I'm talking about a Pollyanna prophet. Who, you might wonder, is Pollyanna? *Pollyanna* was a 1913 novel about an 11-year-old orphan girl who has an unfailingly optimistic outlook. Pollyanna had a subconscious bias to see everything through rose-colored glasses. In the book, Pollyanna's philosophy of life was to play what she called "The Glad Game" to cope with problems in life.

This might be a good way to approach life, but it's not an accurate way to approach the prophetic. Yes, God is good, but the reality is everything He says is not rainbows, roses, and unicorns. The Holy Spirit convicts of sin, sometimes even through prophecy. The Holy Spirit warns of danger, sometimes even through prophecy. The Holy Spirit redirects us when we are going the wrong way, sometimes even through prophecy.

Think about it for a minute. A Pollyanna prophet would have never prophesied a crucified Messiah, but that was the reality. A Pollyanna prophet would never have prophesied Israel would go into Babylonian captivity for seventy years, but that was the realty. A Pollyanna prophet would never have prophesied the permanent destruction of a city, but that was the realty in Tyre.

If we take a Pollyanna approach to prophecy, unwilling to share anything that won't yield cheers from the crowds, we are in danger of misleading people. The Bible is filled with prophetic words that Pollyanna would never dare speak out of her mouth. Pollyanna prophets who play "The Glad Game" to make people happy may be leading them into misery after their feel-good prophecies fail to come to pass.

Yes, God is good, but He also tells it like it is. As prophets, if we are unwilling to share the true counsel of God we probably should hang our mantle in the closet until we can grow into it. We're responsible to Him for what we say, and unfortunately Pollyanna prophets often lead people astray.

— *Prayer* —

Father, in the name of Jesus, help me maintain a positive outlook on life but to refrain from speaking only feel-good words. Help me walk with a balanced eye, not a biased eye. Teach me to stand in Your presence and receive the full counsel of Your Spirit, with the good and bad.

Oily Prophets

"The smart virgins took jars of oil to feed their lamps" (Matthew 25:4 MSG).

If you want to be an oily—anointed—prophet, you need to cultivate the oil of intimacy in your life. That, of course, requires time in God's presence, renewing our minds about who we are in Christ and His love for us.

We gain intimacy with God by studying His emotions; through praising, worshiping, and fellowshipping with Him; and by determining to seek, obey, and please Him in our thoughts, words, and deeds. When we seek to abide in Him, we are cultivating the oil of intimacy. The Parable of the Ten Virgins in Matthew 25:1-12 is both a warning and an invitation.

> *Then the Kingdom of Heaven will be like ten bridesmaids who took their lamps and went to meet the bridegroom. Five of them were foolish, and five were wise. The five who were foolish didn't take enough olive oil for their lamps, but the other five were wise enough to take along extra oil. When the bridegroom was delayed, they all became drowsy and fell asleep.*
>
> *At midnight they were roused by the shout, "Look, the bridegroom is coming! Come out and meet him!" All the bridesmaids got up and prepared their lamps. Then the five foolish ones asked the others, "Please give us some of your oil because our lamps are going out." But the others replied, "We don't have enough for all of us. Go to a shop and buy some for yourselves."*
>
> *But while they were gone to buy oil, the bridegroom came. Then those who were ready went in with him to the marriage feast, and the door was locked. Later, when the other five bridesmaids returned, they stood outside, calling, "Lord! Lord! Open the door for us!" But he called back, "Believe me, I don't know you!"*

Many will prophesy in His name, and He will say, "I never knew you" (Matt. 7:23). Knowing is more than knowing His name and His Word. It's knowing His heart. An oily prophet is a wise prophet.

— *Prayer* —

Father, in the name of Jesus, I want to be an oily prophet. I want to walk in an anointing that breaks yokes and sets captives free with my prophetic ministry. Help me position myself in Your presence, worshiping with You. Ready me to obey You out of a heart of love.

Your Safety Net

"Obey your spiritual leaders, and do what they say. Their work is to watch over your souls, and they are accountable to God. Give them reason to do this with joy and not with sorrow. That would certainly not be for your benefit" (Hebrews 13:17).

Accountability can seem like a dirty word to some prophets because of bad experiences with controlling apostles, but in reality accountability is your friend. In fact, accountability is the prophet's safeguard and is critical to staying sharp in the Spirit. Some prophets take on the mindset that Jesus is their covering and they are accountable to God and God alone. That's not a wise stance. We all need a safety net.

Apostolic authority is the most strategic authority for a prophet to submit to. Paul wrote these words to the church at Corinth: "I may seem to be boasting too much about the authority given to us by the Lord. But our authority builds you up; it doesn't tear you down. So I will not be ashamed of using my authority. I'm not trying to frighten you by my letters" (2 Cor. 10:8-9). As I write in *Becoming a Next Level Prophet*:

> Prophets are undoubtedly vital to the end-time Church. Apostles recognize this truth and welcome prophets to work alongside them to build the Church and to equip believers for the work of the ministry (see Eph. 4:11). Where other ministry offices have been threatened by or misunderstood the prophet's gift, healthy apostles embrace the grace and seek to build a platform for the prophetic voice. That platform, however, is only accessible by stable prophets who are willing to be held accountable for their utterances.

Not every prophet has access to apostles, but that doesn't exempt us from accountability. Again, accountability is our friend. If I am about to a fall into a ditch, I want someone to tell me. If I am sliding into error, I want someone to correct me. If I am not living up to my prophetic potential, I want someone to challenge me. In order to reap those benefits, we have to allow the right people to speak into our lives.

So, again, even if you don't have apostles around you, you can still build an accountability team that can watch over your ministry. Ideally, they would understand the prophet's mindset, but some things are just a matter of truth and character that mature believers can see and share. And it's not all about correction. It's about wise counsel. Every prophet needs wise counselors in their lives. Solomon wrote, "Where there is no counsel, the people fall; but in the multitude of counselors there is safety" (Prov. 11:14 NKJV).

— *Prayer* —

Father, in the name of Jesus, give me Your perspective on accountability. Help me not to run from apostolic authority but to embrace it as the safety net that it is. But, Lord, lead me to the right leaders and help me discern the apostolic abusers who seek to control my voice.

Delivering Prophetic Announcements

"But the angel said, 'Don't be afraid, Zechariah! God has heard your prayer. Your wife, Elizabeth, will give you a son, and you are to name him John. You will have great joy and gladness, and many will rejoice at his birth, for he will be great in the eyes of the Lord. He must never touch wine or other alcoholic drinks. He will be filled with the Holy Spirit, even before his birth'" (Luke 1:13-15).

Some people argue every prophetic word is confirmation, but Scripture proves this is not true. While some prophetic words can be confirmation, and while recipients should bear witness to prophetic words in their spirit even if they don't fully understand them in their mind, there are prophetic announcements scattered throughout the pages of the Bible. And God still uses prophets to make prophetic announcements today.

For example, God announced to Pharaoh each plague before it happened—including the final judgment of death of every firstborn son. Not only were Moses' messages not confirmation to Pharaoh, but the ruler also did not believe the prophet despite the string of true prophetic announcements of judgment Moses released earlier.

When Samuel prophesied to Saul about his kingship, it was not confirmation. It was a prophetic announcement: "As they were going down to the outskirts of the city, Samuel said to Saul, 'Tell the servant to go on ahead of us.' And he went on. 'But you stand here awhile, that I may announce to you the word of God'" (1 Sam. 9:27 NKJV).

When Samuel announced and anointed David as the next king of Israel, it was news to the young shepherd boy and his family. I am sure they had a hard time believing the young boy would be the next ruler of Israel. When the angel Gabriel announced the birth of John the Baptist, it was not confirmation to Elizabeth—and her husband didn't even bear witness to it. In fact, he spoke against it. When Gabriel announced to Mary she would birth the Messiah, she asked how it could be so.

Are you seeing the pattern here? Yes, believers all have the ability to hear from God, but sometimes God chooses to make an announcement through a prophet. Sometimes people just can't hear from God on a matter because of emotional turmoil. Sometimes God knows they would not believe it was Him speaking because the word is so wonderful. Sometimes God chooses to make a public declaration over a person so that the people will see them differently and help them in their mission.

— *Prayer* —

Father, in the name of Jesus, use me as a herald to announce Your will in the earth. Send me as a prophetic messenger to decree, declare, proclaim, and prophesy the news of the new thing You plan to do. Let my prophetic words stir faith in the people to respond to Your heart.

Friendship with God

Jesus spoke these spectacular words to His disciples: *"I no longer call you servants, for a servant does not know what his master does. But I have called you friends, for everything that I have heard from My Father have I made known to you"* (John 15:15 MEV).

Wow! That's a huge statement! *The Passion Translation* sheds some additional light on the type of friendship Jesus had with the ones He walked closest with: "I call you my most intimate and cherished friends." *The Message* says, "I have let you in on everything I've heard from the Father." Mind you, the people Jesus was talking to weren't even prophets.

I believe prophets can expect the Lord to share His purposes—His secrets. But I believe the prophets who seek Him for true friendship will learn more of His secrets. Jesus is the Friend who sticks closer than a brother. If we stick close to Him, we can hear Him sharing His secrets.

Indeed, I believe the prophets who press in to discover His heart will find He reveals more than they expected. In other words, if we're seeking the Lord only to attain His secrets, He may reveal some hidden things. But if we seek the Lord for who He is, we will gain deeper understanding of His ways, His will, and His plans. It's all about the relationship.

Three prophets in the Bible were called friends of God. The prophet Abraham made "friend of God" based on his faith (see James 2:23; Isa. 41:8). Moses was called a friend of God. In Exodus 33:11 we read, "Inside the Tent of Meeting, the Lord would speak to Moses face to face, as one speaks to a friend."

David was a friend of God—and even more. God called David a man after his own heart. In Acts 13:22 we find this account: "But God removed Saul and replaced him with David, a man about whom God said, 'I have found David son of Jesse, a man after my own heart. He will do everything I want him to do.'"

— *Prayer* —

Father, I want to be a friend to You like You are a Friend to me. Teach me to be Your friend. Show me how to earn Your trust and steward Your heart. Create in me a heart that seeks to serve You and obey You as I get to know You more and more with each passing day.

JUNE

"You must understand this at the outset: Interpretation of scriptural prophecy requires the Holy Spirit, for it does not originate from someone's own imagination. No true prophecy comes from human initiative but is inspired by the moving of the Holy Spirit upon those who spoke the message that came from God" (2 Peter 1:20-21 TPT).

When Your Prophetic Insight Is Hindsight

"Cry out for insight, and ask for understanding" (Proverbs 2:3).

It never fails. After every major world event, prophets come out of the woodwork—and some even come out of caves—to deliver the word of the Lord. There's nothing inherently wrong with that. It can be very helpful to understand what the Lord is saying about a major world event or significant headline-making tragedy.

However, wouldn't it be far better to know about the tragedy before it struck so we could try to avert disaster? Wouldn't it be more strategic to get ahead of the enemy's plans with prayer to shut down the attack, or at least mitigate the damage?

Admittedly, we don't always see everything before it happens. We know in part and we prophesy in part (see 1 Cor. 13:9). But if we are going to continually tout Amos 3:7—if we are going to insist that God doesn't do anything unless He first reveals it to the prophets—then we shouldn't be satisfied with hindsight prophecy.

What is hindsight prophecy? It's after-the-fact prophecy. Sometimes it's even "I prophesied that" statements even though the word was far too obscure to connect directly to the event. Sometimes it's, "I had a feeling something bad was going to happen there." Thank God, He sees the end from the beginning (see Isa. 46:10).

When Agabus prophesied about a severe famine coming that would spread throughout the Roman world, he was foretelling not retelling (see Acts 11:28). When Jeremiah prophesied Israel would find herself in bondage to Babylon for seventy years, he was foretelling not retelling. When Jesus prophesied what would happen in the end times, He was foretelling not retelling.

As prophets, we should press into His prophetic intelligence to have foresight so we can foretell instead of retell. Retelling is appropriate when it's forthtelling what God has already said, but when our prophetic insight comes only after a tragedy we have to ask ourselves if we are really watching and praying or if we're just reacting. Hindsight is always 20/20. Let's press in for foresight.

— *Prayer* —

Father, in the name of Jesus, make me alert in the Spirit so I can pick up on the slightest whisper and warning from Your heart. Teach me to recognize how You are working to show me what is coming next so I can prepare Your people and pray without ceasing.

Positioned for a Double-Portion Anointing

"And so it was, when they had crossed over, that Elijah said to Elisha, 'Ask! What may I do for you, before I am taken away from you?' Elisha said, 'Please let a double portion of your spirit be upon me'" (2 Kings 2:9 NKJV).

Picture this: Elijah was running for his life from the wicked queen Jezebel. At a time when he needed all the friends he could get, Elijah found himself isolated in the wilderness battling fearful imaginations of Jezebel's henchmen making good on her death threat.

Elijah's servant was supposed to protect him, to stand with him—to run with him if necessary. Instead, this unnamed servant stayed behind in Beersheba (see 1 Kings 19:3). The Bible says Elijah left his servant there, but there's no indication that the servant even so much as tried to stay by his side like Ruth refused to leave Naomi.

That has always puzzled me. This servant had just witnessed Elijah call down fire from heaven. God only knows how many other miracles Elijah's servant witnessed. Yet at the first sign of trouble, the servant stayed behind in Beersheba, a fertile land of plenty, while Elijah isolated himself in the wilderness. Well, Elijah's servant missed out—that's the last we hear of Elijah's servant. He could have been in line for a double portion anointing, but he forfeited it by not sticking with Elijah through thick and thin.

On the other hand, Elisha served Elijah faithfully—and fervently. He was widely known in the kingdom of Israel as the one who poured water over Elijah's hands (see 2 Kings 3:11). Elisha was bold enough to ask Elijah for a double portion of his anointing before he went on to be with the Lord. He knew he would need it to continue the work of the ministry. Elijah told the young prophet if he saw him go up he would grant his request. Elisha stuck with him to the very end even when Elijah told him to leave.

As a result, Elisha received the double portion anointing for which he petitioned. And here's my point: Elijah's other servant, the one who stayed behind at Beersheba, was a candidate for this double portion anointing. At the very least, he was in line to receive a mighty impartation from Elijah. Humble service is a pathway to the double portion anointing all talk about. Ask the Holy Spirit to give you the grace of humility.

— *Prayer* —

Father, in the name of Jesus, make me into a faithful servant. Show me who to serve and help me go all in to cover, protect, and intercede for the leaders to whom You've assigned me so that I am positioned rightly to receive the spiritual inheritance You have ordained for me.

The Patient Prophet

"...Consider the farmers who patiently wait for the rains in the fall and in the spring. They eagerly look for the valuable harvest to ripen. You, too, must be patient..." (James 5:7-8).

Many years ago, the Holy Spirit spoke these words to me: "Impatience clouds the realities of readiness." Let that sink in. Impatience clouds the realities of readiness. In other words, when you look at your prophetic ministry through the eyes of impatience, you see that you are ready. But impatience is deceptive and therefore dangerous to the prophet.

While some prophets never think they are ready, some are too ready to step out before they are prepared—or to prophesy a true word of the Lord to the masses before God's ready to reveal them. The reality is patience in the prophetic truly is a virtue. By faith and patience we inherit the promises of God (see Heb. 6:12), and that includes the promises for the ministry He's called us to.

Patience is also a fruit of the Spirit. Paul explained, "But the Holy Spirit produces this kind of fruit in our lives: love, joy, peace, patience, kindness, goodness, faithfulness, gentleness, and self-control. There is no law against these things!" (Gal. 5:22-23). Prophets who stand in public ministry should demonstrate not just the gifts of the Spirit but the fruit of the Spirit. Again, patience is one of them.

At its root, impatience is a sign of pride in the prophet's heart. If you find yourself in a season of suffering, don't immediately look to the enemy. Look at your heart. God may be trying to root pride out of you and instill in you total dependence on Him in humility.

You're not ready to prophesy on the highest platforms until you are able to suffer with patience and let patience have its perfect work. Here's why: When you prophesy on the highest platforms you will suffer persecution. If you can't patiently endure the waiting for prophetic ascension, you won't endure the suffering that comes from the persecution at the level you hope to climb.

— *Prayer* —

Father, in the name of Jesus, help me cultivate patience in my heart. Root out the impatience in my mind, will, and emotions so that I do not get ahead of You in the journey. Teach me to depend on Your leadership, Your timing, and Your unction.

A Key to Being More Prophetic

"But you, beloved, building yourselves up on your most holy faith, praying in the Holy Spirit" (Jude 1:20 NKJV).

For many years, I would pray, "Lord, make me more prophetic." It was a consistent prayer, and it bore fruit. But I am convinced part of the reason it bore such fruit is because I was also praying in the Spirit—praying in my supernatural heavenly prayer language.

When we pray in tongues our spirit is praying with the help of the Holy Spirit and our mind has no idea what we are talking about (see 1 Cor. 14:14). When we pray in tongues, we're not speaking to men but to God and are uttering mysteries in the Spirit (see 1 Cor. 14:2). And, of course, when we speak in tongues we build ourselves up (see 1 Cor. 14:4). Paul said he spoke in tongues more than anyone, and he was certainly prophetic!

As prophets, we prophesy according to the proportion of our faith (see Rom. 12:6). We also prophesy by the Holy Spirit. If you want to be more prophetic, pray in the Spirit. *The Passion Translation* of Romans 12:6 makes it plain: "So if God has given you the grace-gift of prophecy, activate your gift by using the proportion of faith you have to prophesy."

Now, let me make a statement that may startle you. Being prophetic is more than prophesying. Being prophetic is living a life infused with the Holy Spirit's being. He is a prophetic Spirit. Being prophetic is knowing what you didn't know, being sensitive to what the Holy Spirit is leading you to do, praying what He wants you to pray. Being prophetic is walking with the ministry of the Holy Spirit activated in your life.

Yes, paying in tongues makes you more prophetic. But prophesying means speaking forth. Being prophetic doesn't require you to speak. *The Passion Translation* puts Jude 1:20 this way: "But you, my delightfully loved friends, constantly and progressively build yourselves up on the foundation of your most holy faith by praying every moment in the Spirit."

— *Prayer* —

Father, in the name of Jesus, make me more prophetic. Infuse my life with Your very being so I can know what You know, be sensitive to Your leadership, hear Your still small voice with crystal clarity, and pray with great efficacy. Help me release Your ministry in the earth.

Discerning the Obadiah Phenomenon

"For so it was, while Jezebel massacred the prophets of the Lord, that Obadiah had taken one hundred prophets and hidden them, fifty to a cave, and had fed them with bread and water" (1 Kings 18:4 NKJV).

You've probably never heard of the Obadiah phenomenon—but it's painfully real. So, what does the Obadiah phenomenon look like in the modern-day prophetic movement? There are a few issues we must watch.

First, it looks like prophets who hide in their own companies, never venturing out of their nest to synergize with prophets who have expressions different from their own. We see this even now, with prophets entrenched in specific camps—the doom and gloom camp, the grace camp, the glory camp, etc.—and it's not healthy.

The 1 Kings companies of prophets were isolated in two companies—and they were isolated from every other prophet in Israel. Even between the two companies in close-by caves, there was no intermingling. There was no connection or community. They couldn't pray together, worship together, share their prophetic words with one another. Their perspectives grew limited without any fresh revelation from prophets outside their own camp.

God is working to break down silos in the prophetic so we can truly work together. It's fine and good to have your own company, but when we deny the power of other expressions we're shutting out revelation that could add to our own view. Remember, we know in part and we prophesy in part (see 1 Cor. 13:9). We need all the parts to come together—all the streams to come together. Many streams make a great river.

Remember, Obadiah took 100 prophets and split them down the middle. Prophets—the voice of God—should not be divided. Although God is surely saying many things to many prophets at once, the Holy Spirit does not speak with a forked tongue. It's difficult for the Body of Christ to know what prophet to follow when there is so much contradiction. Part of the problem is a lack of communication. Hubs, companies, and nests—along with cross-pollination among prophetic camps—help solve that issue.

— *Prayer* —

Father, in the name of Jesus, help me not to take on an elitist spirit that believes my flow is the best flow. Show me who I can collaborate with in order to create new synergizes in the prophetic movement that paint a fuller picture of what You are doing in the earth.

When Prophets Deceive You

"...But the old man was lying to him" (1 Kings 13:18).

It's one of the most troubling stories in Scripture. I've meditated on it for years. It's found in 1 Kings 13:1-24. You have to read it for yourself to get the fullness of the picture, but let me paint some broad strokes. A young prophet was on assignment for the Lord to denounce the wicked King Jeroboam. He prophesied and the Lord manifested spectacular signs confirming his words. The king got angry and called for his arrest, but the Lord intervened.

When the young prophet completed his assignment, he set out to return home. That's when he ran into an old, deceitful prophet. The old prophet invited his younger counterpart to come home with him to eat, but the young prophet insisted the Lord commanded him not to eat or drink anything while he was in Bethel. (He was essentially fasting.) First Kings 13:18-22 tells the story:

> But the old prophet answered, "I am a prophet, too, just as you are. And an angel gave me this command from the Lord: 'Bring him home with you so he can have something to eat and drink.'" But the old man was lying to him. So they went back together, and the man of God ate and drank at the prophet's home.
> Then while they were sitting at the table, a command from the Lord came to the old prophet. He cried out to the man of God from Judah, "This is what the Lord says: You have defied the word of the Lord and have disobeyed the command the Lord your God gave you. You came back to this place and ate and drank where he told you not to eat or drink. Because of this, your body will not be buried in the grave of your ancestors."

The old prophet deceived the young prophet, who was torn apart by a lion. While we must honor our elders and respect our contemporaries, we must not disobey the word of the Lord. If we hear His command and do not obey His command, we set ourselves up for deception.

— *Prayer* —

Father, in the name of Jesus, help me to avoid deception by prophetic elders who have an agenda that defies Your prophetic directives for my ministry. Teach me to walk in love with the fathers and mothers in the faith without bowing to advice that did not come from Your heart.

The Jonah Syndrome

"Just kill me now, Lord! I'd rather be dead than alive if what I predicted will not happen" (Jonah 4:3).

You've probably run into a Jonah prophet—and I certainly hope you are not one. "Jonah" prophets—those prophets who would rather see a nation destroyed because they are bitter in spirit—are pontificating and prophesying about doom, gloom, cataclysmic disasters, catastrophic calamities, foreboding horrors, and the like.

What is a Jonah prophet? Jonah prophets are disobedient to God, bucking and fighting against His will. Just like Jonah fled to Tarshish from the presence of the Lord because he did not want to see Nineveh come to repentance (see Jon. 1:1-2), modern-day prophets run in the opposite direction when God is calling them on a mercy assignment. All they hear, see, and say is doom and gloom because they carry judgment in their heart.

Jonah prophets say they fear the Lord (see Jon. 1:9), but inwardly their actions do not line up with their words, and their prophecies are not in line with the Father's heart. I can just hear the Lord saying:

> *I have not sent these prophets, yet they run around claiming to speak for me. I have given them no message, yet they go on prophesying. If they had stood before me and listened to me, they would have spoken my words, and they would have turned my people from their evil ways and deeds* (Jeremiah 23:21-22).

Jonah prophets think their way is better than God's way. Jonah prophets are self-centered drama queens (and kings). These are just a few of the characteristics of Jonah prophets. Read the Book of Jonah and you'll see more. God is slow to anger and rich in mercy, but Jonah prophets are not. Still, God is longsuffering with the Jonah prophets. But consider this: The last time we hear anything about Jonah he's sitting under a tree wishing he was dead. God never used him again. Don't be a Jonah prophet.

— *Prayer* —

Father, in the name of Jesus, deliver me from the Jonah mindset. Teach me to recognize these evil tendencies in my heart before I act on them. If there is any wayward, stubborn way in me, show me that I can repent, change the way I think, and move in the right direction.

When People Don't Believe You

"Early the next morning the army of Judah went out into the wilderness of Tekoa. On the way Jehoshaphat stopped and said, 'Listen to me, all you people of Judah and Jerusalem! Believe in the Lord your God, and you will be able to stand firm. Believe in his prophets, and you will succeed'" (2 Chronicles 20:20).

Prophets beware. Second Chronicles 2:20 is another oft-quoted Scripture that can tempt you to tap into a spirit of pride or control. Yes, it's absolutely true believers who mix Spirit-inspired works with strong faith in accurate prophetic words will see success. Warfare may ensue, but those who plow through the opposition, waging war with the prophetic word according to 1 Timothy 1:8, will see prosperity.

Some prophets, however, have used 2 Chronicles 2:20 to manipulate naïve believers into following poor instructions and false prophecy. Be careful about the temptation to use the word as a weapon against the people you are called to edify, comfort, and exhort. Be careful not to fall into the trap of intimidating and threatening believers to agree with your prophetic word, judging their trust in God or their willingness to fight the good fight of faith if they don't choose to believe your prophetic utterance.

You can be sure of this: The spirit of Jezebel will tempt you to manipulate and control people with prophecy—even prophecy that is true. Put another way, even if your prophetic word is 100 percent accurate and everyone should believe it, they might not. That doesn't give you a right to be forceful and pushy out of passion or to save face. Prophets need to be on guard for the spirit of Jezebel in any way it manifests. Jezebel looks for a home in your heart through rejection, so don't take it personally if people reject your prophetic utterances. Know that they are not rejecting you, they are rejecting the Word of God.

If the person rejects the word—or rejects you—don't respond in kind. Instead, go into intercession for them. There's always a price to pay for rejecting the word of the Lord, when you know that you know that you know that God has given you a prophetic word for someone—and you know, too, that He wants you to actually deliver it, speak it forth boldly with humility, not fearing the consequences, not fearing rejection. This is the spirit of a true prophet. True prophets have a mercy gift and are intercessors.

— *Prayer* —

Father, in the name of Jesus, help me not to take the rejection of Your word personally. If they rejected Jesus, I know they will reject me. Make me secure in my identity in Christ as I prophesy Your will, despite the opposition, the deaf ears, and the unbelief.

The Counterfeit Holy Spirit

"One day as we were going down to the place of prayer, we met a slave girl who had a spirit that enabled her to tell the future. She earned a lot of money for her masters by telling fortunes" (Acts 16:16).

The girl in Thyatira—which, by the way, is the city in which the Revelation 2:20 Jezebel resided—was operating in divination. Divination is essentially witchcraft. *Baker's Evangelical Dictionary of Biblical Theology* tells us divination is "Communication with a deity for the purpose of determining the deity's knowledge, resulting in clarification of a decision or discernment of the future." The deities diviners communicate with are familiar spirits.

A familiar spirit is a specific class of spirit. As its name suggests, it is characterized by familiarity. *Familiar* means intimately acquainted with, like dear friends or family. When you know someone intimately, you know what they like, what they don't like, how to persuade them, what scares them, how to comfort them.

Familiar spirits are connected to witchcraft, but people who may never have practiced witchcraft can prophesy out of a familiar spirit. If you have dabbled in any kind of witchcraft, from Ouija boards to tarot cards to curses and spells, you could open the door to a familiar spirit. Familiar spirits are essentially a counterfeit Holy Spirit.

Jesus described many of the functions of the Holy Spirit in John 14:26:

> *But the Comforter (Counselor, Helper, Intercessor, Advocate, Strengthener, Standby), the Holy Spirit, Whom the Father will send in My name [in My place, to represent Me and act on My behalf], He will teach you all things. And He will cause you to recall (will remind you of, bring to your remembrance) everything I have told you* (AMPC).

The familiar spirit can deliver accurate words that edify, comfort, exhort, and predict. But the wisdom they offer is not coming from above. It's demonic and will lead people astray. In other words, just because your prophecy is accurate doesn't mean it came from the Holy Spirit. That's why you have to judge the source of your own prophecy. If you enter into regions and territories where witchcraft is raging, familiar spirits may be speaking to you—and if you aren't careful you may believe it's the Holy Spirit.

— *Prayer* —

Father, in the name of Jesus, show me if I am operating out of any other spirit than the Holy Spirit. Teach me to discern the voice of familiar spirits that mimic Your still small voice. I command every familiar spirit to loose me, now. Be gone!

Practicing Prophetic Statesmanship

"Now then, we are ambassadors for Christ, as though God were pleading through us: we implore you on Christ's behalf, be reconciled to God" (2 Corinthians 5:20 NKJV).

In some prophetic circles, we see a lot of showmanship. Showmanship should have no place in the prophetic, but the showman has staying power because of the theatrics, the hype, the spectacular, dramatic, and effective prophetic performance. The problem is there's a thin line between the showman and the shaman (a diviner using magic to control events). Think about that.

Jesus gave prophets to the church to be statesmen, not showmen. Another way to explain it is we are ambassadors for Christ (see 2 Cor. 5:20). An ambassador is "a diplomatic agent of the highest rank accredited to a foreign government" and "an authorized representative or messenger," according to *Merriam-Webster*'s dictionary. We are representing Jesus. We are messengers of the Most High God.

From that perspective, the prophet as statesman does more than prophesy—much more. The prophet as statesman understands the principles of the Kingdom of God. The prophet as statesman discerns the art and science of spiritual government. The prophet as statesman knows how to legislate in the spirit. The prophet as statesman is both wise and skillful, rightly dividing the word of truth and able to advance God's purposes in the earth even without a platform.

Raised in Egypt and trained in the wilderness, the prophet Moses goes down in Bible history as a statesman. He negotiated the release of the Israelites from Pharaoh's oppressive kingdom. He represented the King of Glory to a people who barely knew Him. He led a military campaign in a time of war in the wilderness on the way to the Promised Land.

Prophets, this world is not our home, and we are called to walk in the world but not behave like the world (see 1 John 2:15-17). As prophets speaking on behalf of the Creator of the universe, we need to behave in a way that glorifies the Chief Prophet, Jesus. When I think of ambassadors to nations, I think of stable, solid statesmen who understand the cultures they are entering. We need to do the same.

— *Prayer* —

Father, in the name of Jesus, form me into the prophetic statesman You created me to be. Teach me Your principles. Show me how to legislate in the spirit to see Your Kingdom come and Your will done in the earth. Make me wise and skillful in delivering Your prophetic words.

There's No Off Switch

"I therefore, the prisoner of the Lord, beseech you that ye walk worthy of the vocation wherewith ye are called, with all lowliness and meekness, with longsuffering, forbearing one another in love" (Ephesians 4:1-2 KJV).

When you are a prophet, you're always a prophet. You don't have an off switch. It's your vocation. A vocation in one sense is a calling, but in another sense your vocation is your full-time occupation. It's the work you do day in and day out. It's not a hobby you do on weekends. It's your job.

As a prophet, you have a calling and that calling translates into the work of the ministry—and equipping others to do the work of the ministry (see Eph. 4:11-13). While you might go on vacation to Hawaii or some other desired resting place in the earth, you can't leave your work mantle in the closet in exchange for island digs. In other words, even while you're on vacation you are still walking in your vocation.

Let me put it another way. You are always a prophet in the same way that a doctor is always a doctor. The doctor takes the Hippocratic Oath "to treat the ill to the best of one's ability, to preserve a patient's privacy, to teach the secrets of medicine to the next generation," and so on. When the doctor is on vacation in Hawaii eating a filet mignon with lobster in butter sauce and someone cries, "Is there a doctor in the house?" what does the physician do? By oath, he cannot pretend he did not hear the cry for help and keep enjoying his dinner. By oath, he must run to the rescue and practice his vocation.

It's the same with prophets. Don't get me wrong. I am not saying that you have to stop and prophesy to everyone who recognizes you as a prophet. I am saying when God tells you to speak to someone, you need to finish chewing that steak and go approach with the word of the Lord even if you are on vacation. When the Lord calls you to intercession, it doesn't matter if you planned to go see a movie. Prophet, walk worthy of your vocation.

— *Prayer* —

Father, in the name of Jesus, help me remember that there is no off switch. I am always on duty, serving prophetically at Your pleasure. Teach me how to stay in a state of readiness even while I'm resting. I give You permission to interrupt my vacation so I can walk in my vocation.

Dissecting a Word of Warning

"Now we see things imperfectly, like puzzling reflections in a mirror" (1 Corinthians 13:12).

Although the Holy Spirit speaks expressly, we see through a glass darkly. Sure, it's easy enough to understand the words of that still, small voice in your spirit. But impressions, dreams, and visions aren't always as clear as we'd like them to be—and reasoning blocks discernment.

I remember a time when a friend of mine was planning a trip to Los Angeles. She told me she was nervous about going, but I reasoned that it was a natural case of "the nerves" because she had an important meeting there. The week before she left, I started to get impressions that something bad was going to happen to her in Los Angeles.

Looking back, it's clear that the Holy Spirit was warning my friend that the devil had plotted an assignment against her in Hollywood. She reasoned herself out of Spirit-led wisdom and went on the journey anyway. It's also clear that the Holy Spirit was warning me about the impending danger. I reasoned myself out of Spirit-led wisdom and decided not to tell my "nervous" friend because I didn't want to make her more nervous.

Thoughts crossed my mind of a bad car accident. I cast down those imaginations. She was so set on going on the trip, believing this was going to see massive breakthrough, that I did not warn her because I didn't think she would listen. I did pray. She went. She got in a head-on collision. She did not die but had a long recovery.

So what's the lesson from all this? If you aren't sure something is the Holy Ghost, ask Him. When the Holy Ghost shows us something, press in to seek more details. When the Holy Spirit gives you an impression, ask Him if you are supposed to share it with someone else or just pray. And always pray. Pray always, and when you catch your mind trying to reason out a prophetic revelation, let your spirit man rise up and take control. And always remember, reasoning blocks discernment.

— *Prayer* —

Father, in the name of Jesus, I know I can't unlock supernatural revelation with my natural reasoning. Help me to avoid this pitfall that can lead me into confusion, inaction, and even error. Give me the grace to settle down and press in to understand what You are trying to tell me.

Let Iron Sharpen Iron

"As iron sharpens iron, so a friend sharpens a friend" (Proverbs 27:17).

Let's get real for a moment. Silly putty doesn't sharpen iron. Plastic doesn't sharpen iron. Not even sandpaper sharpens iron, although at times you may feel like a fellow believer is aggressively rubbing your soul with sandpaper. No, Solomon in his wisdom tells us that it takes iron to sharpen iron. Put another way, prophets need other prophets to sharpen them.

Prophets need iron-like strength that will break, pulverize, and bust up the kingdom of darkness. We need an iron-like will to continue to pursue God's will in the face of resistance from principalities and powers. But even with hard-as-steel spiritual traits, our souls can become weary in the day-to-day battle that's not merely against principalities and powers but also against flesh.

You can respond in one of two ways during the sharpening process. You can moan, groan, whine, complain, cry, pout, and pity yourself and extend your pain, or you can yield to the iron furnace of suffering and emerge as sparkling gold (see Jer. 11:3). Remember, blacksmiths have to put iron into fire to make it malleable before removing it and shaping it with quick repeated blows with a hammer.

Jesus often uses those closest to us as tools to show us the muck and mire in our souls that is hindering our success. But instead of becoming offended, angry, and unforgiving, apostolic living requires us to praise the Lord in the midst of the admittedly often unpleasant sharpening process. Do you have an axe to grind? Humbly iron out your differences with brothers and sisters and watch God work.

Are you ready to become that threshing instrument about which Isaiah prophesied? Submit yourself to the sharpening process at the hands of your fivefold ministers, friends, foes, and family—and, of course, the Spirit of God—and emerge from the iron furnace as a razor-sharp battle axe fit to cut through any spiritual opposition. From major trials and tribulations to life's everyday struggles, your fire-tested, apostolic metal will lead you into victorious living. Who is the blacksmith in your life?

— *Prayer* —

Father, in the name of Jesus, help me embrace the iron—those people in my life whom You have sent to show me what I can't see and even those people You allow in my presence to rub me the wrong way. Help me to take on an attitude of gratitude for my blacksmith.

Waiting for the Vision

"Write my answer plainly on tablets, so that a runner can carry the correct message to others" (Habakkuk 2:2).

God is looking for prophets who will stand watch, station themselves on the watchtower, and keep watch to see what the Lord will say—and answer when they are reproved.

God is looking for those with a Habakkuk spirit who will not only see and hear, but record and proclaim—and keep proclaiming until the people's ears and eyes open to what the Lord is saying and doing. Once, when Habakkuk stood on the wall, he heard the Lord say this:

> *Write my answer plainly on tablets, so that a runner can carry the correct message to others. This vision is for a future time. It describes the end, and it will be fulfilled. If it seems slow in coming, wait patiently, for it will surely take place. It will not be delayed* (Habakkuk 2:2-3).

It's important to understand that this oft-cited verse is not talking about just any vision. According to *The KJV Old Testament Hebrew Lexicon*, the word "vision" in that verse comes from the Hebrew word *chazown*, which means "vision (in ecstatic state); vision (in the night); vision, oracle, prophecy (divine communication), and vision (as title of book of prophecy)."

Because these prophetic visions will rock religious mindsets and shake the status quo, you'll have to be determined to write them down, meditate on them day and night, and, as Habakkuk 2:2 says, make it plain. In other words, you need to rely on the Holy Spirit to interpret the vision rightly so that you can declare it clearly so people can come into agreement with what the Lord is saying and doing—then pray accordingly.

Believe me, there's going to be a war over the prophetic vision God gave you. The enemy will always oppose the will of God. If you aren't clear, if it's not plain, you won't run with it or rise up and defend it from the enemy's abortive plans. Prophecy, in any way it comes, always brings warfare because the devil is after the word.

— *Prayer* —

Father, in the name of Jesus, give me a Habakkuk anointing. Teach me how to articulate the visions You share with me so people will be less likely to reject them—and more likely to make intercession concerning them. Use me as an agent to bring heaven's vision to pass.

Be a Sent One, Not a Went One

"One day as these men were worshiping the Lord and fasting, the Holy Spirit said, 'Appoint Barnabas and Saul for the special work to which I have called them'" (Acts 13:2).

Prophets shouldn't go without being sent. The same God who gifts prophets to preach, pray, and prophesy is the same God who will send prophets forth to exercise those gifts. Most often, prophets are appointed by earthly authority as the Holy Spirit leads. This is scriptural. Acts 13 reads:

Now in the church that was at Antioch there were certain prophets and teachers: Barnabas, Simeon who was called Niger, Lucius of Cyrene, Manaen who had been brought up with Herod the tetrarch, and Saul. As they ministered to the Lord and fasted, the Holy Spirit said, "Now separate to Me Barnabas and Saul for the work to which I have called them." Then, having fasted and prayed, and laid hands on them, they sent them away (Acts 13:1-3 NKJV).

So Barnabas and Saul were sent out by the Holy Spirit... (Acts 13:4).

They were sent. We don't know who prophesied the word of commissioning over Saul and Barnabas. The sending was attributed to the Holy Spirit. This is where some prophets, though, miss it. Many believe they were sent by the Holy Spirit but they really just went. That's why their mission is not fruitful. There were even times when the great apostle Paul went without being sent.

Next Paul and Silas traveled through the area of Phrygia and Galatia, because the Holy Spirit had prevented them from preaching the word in the province of Asia at that time (Acts 16:6).

If Paul can miss it, so can we. The problem is sometimes we're not sensitive enough to the Holy Spirit to discern that He is actually the one preventing us. We think it's the devil thwarting us.

Make no mistake. The most successful prophetic journeys are those the Holy Spirit leads. This requires a willingness to wait on the Lord, to mature in His Word and cultivate a strong relationship with the Holy Spirit. Paul put it this way, "For as many as are led by the Spirit of God, these are sons of God" (Rom. 8:14 NKJV). I believe Paul learned from his mistakes. I pray we learn from ours.

— *Prayer* —

Father, in the name of Jesus, I don't want to go where You are not sending me. Help me to enter into the apostolic sending dimension through Your leadership and the direction of those whom You have put in my life to watch over my soul. I will go where You send me.

Prophetic Timing Is Everything

"A man hath joy by the answer of his mouth: and a word spoken in due season, how good is it!" (Proverbs 15:23 KJV)

All my life, people have told me I have good timing. I can't take credit for that. The Lord leads me and guides me. I just try to listen. It takes a certain sensitivity and skill to deliver news, especially bad news, to someone in the right timing. You don't want to discourage them on the best day of their life, when they are flying high. By the same token, you don't want to bring discouraging news when they are already walking through a difficult season.

As important as good timing is in delivering good or bad news to family and friends, it's perhaps even more critical in the realm of the prophetic. Like Solomon said, "A word fitly spoken is like apples of gold in pictures of silver" (Prov. 25:11 KJV). The New Living Translation puts it this way: "Timely advice is lovely, like golden apples in a silver basket."

If that's true, and it is, so is the opposite—untimely advice is troublesome. An ill-timed prophetic word can land on deaf ears—or even angry ears. Someone may reject your prophetic word just because they were in the wrong state of mind when you delivered it. They may not be ready to hear even if what you discern is breakthrough news if they are not in the right headspace.

Prophet, you need to be as accurate in the timing of delivering a prophetic word as you are with the content of the word. Indeed, it's critical you not just learn how to discern times and seasons but also learn how to discern the right time to deliver a prophetic word. Even the most exciting prophetic word can be rejected if it's delivered prematurely or too late.

In fact, a late prophecy may be an irrelevant prophecy as the circumstances may shift by the time you complete the delivery. Your prophetic word is no longer prophetic if what you said came to pass last week, or, worse, you could have helped someone avoid a major mistake with the prophetic intelligence that was on your lips but failed to speak out.

— *Prayer* —

Father, in the name of Jesus, help me develop good timing—Your timing. Teach me to stay prophetically in lock step with Your Spirit, who is never early or late but always right on time. Remind me to seek You for the timing of my prophetic release before I open my mouth.

Open Your Mouth

"...Open your mouth wide, and I will fill it with good things" (Psalm 81:10).

In my early days of prophetic ministry, we tag teamed. A group of prophets would hand the mic one to another to prophesy to someone in a prayer line or out in the congregation. I didn't like that. I felt like I was being put on the spot. Of course, that's part of the point. When you train emerging prophets, many times you just have to put them on the spot.

Many times, emerging prophets want to wait until God gives them the entire prophetic word before they open their mouth. They want to know the fullness of what God is going to say before they say it—and they are only hearing one word. Here's the thing: Even if God gave you paragraphs in advance you could never remember all the words.

Psalm 81:10 is a popular Scripture among prophetic people. Although the original context had nothing to do with prophecy, there is a legitimate application here that is worth exploring. Prophecy can start off with an impression in your spirit, a visual picture, or just one word or phrase. As you open your mouth to share what He is showing you, He supernaturally fills in the rest of the pictures and paragraphs. That's part of prophesying by faith.

If you've ever primed a pump, you'll understand the water doesn't flow from the well immediately. Likewise, prophecy often starts out a drip, and then a trickle, and then the fullness of the river flows freely. With prophecy, you feel the unction—a bubbling up in your spirit—but may not have much in your mouth. And, again, that's where faith comes in. When you open your mouth, God will fill it.

The Passion Translation of Psalm 81:10 puts it this way: "Open your mouth with a mighty decree; I will fulfill it now, you'll see! The words that you speak, so shall it be!"

— *Prayer* —

Father, in the name of Jesus, help me get over the need to know it all before I prophesy. Teach me how to build up my faith to prophesy the trickle so You can release the river of prophecy through me. Give me a confidence that You will show me the rest as I open my mouth.

Don't Hide from Jezebel

"Elijah was afraid and fled for his life..." (1 Kings 19:3).

Queen Jezebel had a reputation. She was slaughtering God's true prophets, presumably with King Ahab's approval. Many of the prophets who didn't end up dead fled. They packed up and left to preserve their life. Still others were hidden in caves under Obadiah's care. Elijah seemed fearless. He appeared and disappeared and reappeared in Israel.

When Elijah told Obadiah to go get Ahab, he said, "But as soon as I leave you, the Spirit of the Lord will carry you away to who knows where. When Ahab comes and cannot find you, he will kill me" (1 Kings 18:12). Elijah assured Obadiah he would not flee. And he didn't. The next scenes show Elijah with Ahab calling a showdown with the false prophets. Again, Elijah seemed fearless—until he wasn't.

Eventually even Elijah, who confronted the false prophets who ate at Jezebel's table, ran from Jezebel. Consider Elijah's mistake. After defeating the false prophets at the showdown at Mount Carmel, he succumbed to Jezebel's witchcraft (see 2 Kings 9:22). Jezebel sent a messenger to Elijah with a death threat and he ran for his life. He fled and went into hiding like his modern-day counterparts. But hiding from Jezebel never turns out well.

I believe part of Elijah's assignment was to take Jezebel down, but he could not stand against the witchcraft and abandoned his post for a cave. His experience in the cave marked the beginning of the end of his ministry. God told Elijah to anoint Jehu to take Jezebel down and to anoint Elisha as prophet in his place.

Think about it for a minute. Elijah had no problem confronting the false prophets, but he hid from Jezebel. Prophets can't afford to hide from Jezebel, but must confront this spirit. There's strength in numbers. I believe Elijah missed it partly because he did not have the support of other prophets. He didn't have a company of prophets to pray for him when Jezebel's witchcraft attacked his mind. Elijah needed a prophetic company to run to like the apostles had in the Book of Acts.

— *Prayer* —

Father, in the name of Jesus, give me the courage never to run and hide from a demon spirit, especially Jezebel. Give me the strength to stand against the wiles of Jezebel and surround me with those who have a warrior spirit who will not tolerate this prophet-killing demon.

Escape Religion's Muzzle

"Woe to you! For you build the tombs of the prophets, and your fathers killed them" (Luke 11:47 NKJV).

Jezebel is credited with murdering prophets in her day, but religion is as much an enemy to the prophets as Jezebel is. Jesus, the Prophet, made religious leaders' skin crawl. His message was revolutionary. His power was undeniable. His following was growing, and it threatened their prominence.

The religious spirit influenced the Pharisees to look for ways to trap Jesus in His own words. Luke 11:53-54 tells us, "As Jesus was leaving, the teachers of religious law and the Pharisees became hostile and tried to provoke him with many questions. They wanted to trap him into saying something they could use against him."

Once, the Pharisees set Jesus up by bringing Him a woman caught in the act of adultery to see how He would judge the case. Another time they watched Him continuously, looking to see if He would heal on the Sabbath. Luke 20:20 tells us, "Watching for their opportunity, the leaders sent spies pretending to be honest men. They tried to get Jesus to say something that could be reported to the Roman governor so he would arrest Jesus."

More than once, the Pharisees accused Jesus of being demon-possessed. Matthew 12:24 reveals the words of the religious leaders: "This Man does not cast out demons, except by Beelzebub the ruler of the demons" (MEV). Ultimately, it was the Pharisees who hatched a plan to have Jesus murdered. They insisted to Pilate that Jesus be crucified.

The religious spirit will try to muzzle you like it did the prophets and apostles. After Jesus was crucified and rose again, the religious leaders threatened Peter and John and insisted they speak no more in the name of Jesus. Their reply: "We must obey God rather than any human authority" (Acts 5:29). Prophet, if you are part of a denomination that doesn't believe in prophets, you have the same choice: Will you obey God or man? Don't let religion muzzle you.

— *Prayer* —

Father, in the name of Jesus, free me from religion's muzzle. Deliver me from legalistic structures that seek to silence my voice and trap me in my words. Rid my heart of religiosity that peppers my prophetic voice with condemnation rather than love.

Carrying the Lord's Burden

"My heart, my heart—I writhe in pain! My heart pounds within me! I cannot be still. For I have heard the blast of enemy trumpets and the roar of their battle cries" (Jeremiah 4:19).

I live in Ft. Lauderdale where there are plenty of palm trees. When the city plants palm trees for new developments and roads, they use three stakes of wood to hold the tree steady until the skinny palms are rooted and grounded in the soil. Those stakes bear the burden of the tree. When we intercede for people or places—whether we know what we are praying for or not—we stake ourselves to them and work with the Holy Spirit to remove what doesn't belong there.

Jeremiah felt the burden of the Lord throughout his ministry. He was a burden-bearer for the Lord. All true prophets are. What is a burden? It's a load that we carry. It's a duty, a responsibility. Part of how we fulfill the Galatians 6:2 mandate to bear one another's burdens is through the ministry of prophetic intercession. However, with prophets the burden is often greater than a single individual. The prophet's burden may be for a city, state, nation, or people group.

Sometimes we don't know how to pray as we ought (see Rom. 8:26-27). Sometimes we may know exactly what we're praying for but we don't know how to pray. The key to fruitful intercession—to effective burden-bearing for the Lord—is to cooperate with the Holy Spirit. The Holy Spirit feels the same burden. He is sharing His burden with you so you can work with Him to bring His will to pass over people, situations, and even nations. Pray in the Spirit as much as you can and you'll develop greater discernment to recognize the burden of the Lord.

When the burden of the Lord comes upon you, you may feel the weight of oppression, hear the enemy's accusations, or experience various negative emotions seemingly out of the blue. That's not you! Learn to quickly discern the call to pray against a thing rather than coming up under it.

— *Prayer* —

Father, in the name of Jesus, help me to discern the burden of Your Spirit to make intercession. Teach me to separate between my own emotions and Your emotions so that I can rise up in effective prayer that brings the result You have in Your heart for the people You love.

Footholds and Strongholds

"Anger gives a foothold to the devil" (Ephesians 4:27).

We have to be careful, as prophets, that the fire is in our bones and not in our soul. There's a difference between righteous indignation and man's anger. The anger of man does not produce the righteousness of God (see James 1:20).

James, the apostle of practical faith, offered this advice: "Understand this, my dear brothers and sisters: You must all be quick to listen, slow to speak, and slow to get angry" (James 1:19). I've seen prophets prophesy out of an angry soul rather than out of a cool spirit. Paul put it this way: "Don't sin by letting anger control you...for anger gives a foothold to the devil" (Eph. 4:26-27).

How do you know if you are an angry prophet? If you think God is angry, you are probably an angry prophet. If your words condemn instead of edify, you are probably an angry prophet. If you are argumentative on social media, you probably have an anger problem. If you struggle with chronic frustration, you may be an angry prophet.

Yes, Jesus, the Prophet, demonstrated righteous anger when He turned over the tables of the money changers in the temple. Your anger is righteous only when what is making you angry makes God angry. But Jesus was angry with the injustice and the sin and was still a friend of sinners. Jesus did not have an anger problem.

David understood this. In Psalm 39:1-3, David related, "I said to myself, 'I will watch what I do and not sin in what I say. I will hold my tongue when the ungodly are around me.' But as I stood there in silence—not even speaking of good things—the turmoil within me grew worse. The more I thought about it, the hotter I got, igniting a fire of words." When these words describe your emotions, it's better to remain silent. You don't want to be that angry prophet.

— *Prayer* —

Father, in the name of Jesus, deliver me from anger, sarcasm, distemper, resentment, and fury. Teach me to discern between Your righteous anger and my own soulish anger so I don't misrepresent Your kind spirit. Help me when I am angry not to sin against Your heart.

Think Like a Prophet

"For My thoughts are not your thoughts, nor are your ways My ways,' says the Lord" (Isaiah 55:8 NKJV).

When you are a doctor, you think like a doctor. When you are an athlete, you think like an athlete. When you are a prophet, you think like a prophet—at least to the extent that your mind is renewed to Word and ways of God in prophetic dimensions.

Even before you recognized your calling to the office of the prophet, people may have told you there was something different about you that they can't put their finger on. That difference is a heavenly perspective that helps you see the world through God-colored glasses.

Prophets have a different way of seeing than other fivefold offices. Instead of seeing through the eyes of an evangelist looking for souls, we see prophetically through the eyes of God. Likewise, prophets have a different way of thinking than other fivefold offices. Instead of thinking in natural terms how to break down the Word of God like a teacher, we think in supernatural terms how to relate what God is saying now prophetically.

As you mature in the prophetic, God trains you to think more and more like Him so you can prophesy with greater accuracy. He trains and renews your mind to His way of thinking, His way of moving, and His way of speaking. He trains you to look for the gold instead of the dirt. He trains you to look for the redeeming value in a difficult situation. He trains you to see the purpose in the pain.

At some point in your journey, you'll find yourself thinking more like God without having to try. His thoughts become your thoughts. I believe David tapped into this awareness, as he once said, "How precious to me are your thoughts, O God! How vast is the sum of them!" (Ps. 139:17 ESV). David also said, "How deep are your thoughts" (Ps. 92:5).

Yes, God's thoughts will always be higher than our thoughts. We can't comprehend the depth of God's end-from-the-beginning thinking. But as you walk with Him, you will think like a prophet. And when you think like a prophet, you walk worthy of your vocation.

— *Prayer* —

Father, in the name of Jesus, help me think like You think. Inspire me to seek the higher thoughts of Your Spirit. Show me where to focus my Word studies so I can renew my mind in the areas that will help me think more like You.

Withstanding Enemy Attacks on Your Eyes

"So the Philistines captured him and gouged out his eyes..." (Judges 16:21).

Seers, sages, and mystics have been under attack for thousands of years. From Bible days to modern days, the enemy is afraid of the seeing eye because the seeing eye discerns, exposes, and rallies an army to defeat his plans in the earth. As God begins to emphasize the eyes of the Body, we can expect the attacks against seers and seeing people to continue and even escalate.

This was a strategy of disgrace in Old Testament times. Speaking of Nahash, 1 Samuel 10:27 reads:

> *...He gouged out the right eye of each of the Israelites living there, and he didn't allow anyone to come and rescue them. In fact, of all the Israelites east of the Jordan, there wasn't a single one whose right eye Nahash had not gouged out....*

Why did Nahash gouge out the right eye? Part of the strategy was to make one unable to resist enemy attack. In warfare, soldiers held the shield with the left hand and swung the sword with the right hand. Without a right eye, they were not as accurate with depth perception and at a major disadvantage on the battlefield.

Remember, Philistines gouged out both Samson's eyes after Delilah tempted and nagged him to expose the secret of his great strength:

> *So the Philistines captured him and gouged out his eyes. They took him to Gaza, where he was bound with bronze chains and forced to grind grain in the prison. But before long, his hair began to grow back* (Judges 16:21-22).

The Delilah spirit is still working against seers and seeing people today, luring them in, betraying their hearts, and blinding their spiritual eyes. Delilah defiles the discernment of the discerners who should see through the deception but are tempted with a desire to look at what seems good to their natural eyes.

Today, gouging—or blinding the seer's eyes—sometimes comes through rejection, persecution, and misunderstanding. Keep looking at Jesus. He will restore your eyes even after the fiercest of attacks.

— *Prayer* —

Father, in the name of Jesus, heal my eyes from the gouging tactics of Delilah and other demon powers who want to blind me before I see them. Anoint my eyes to see again what You are doing and how the enemy is working to thwart You so I can wage war in the earth for Your will.

When the Lord Tests Your Character

"Until the time came to fulfill his dreams, the Lord tested Joseph's character"
(Psalm 105:19).

Some believe that just because they can prophesy an accurate word, God doesn't mind their angry outbursts at home. Or because people are slain in the Spirit when they lay hands on them, God is pleased with the way they treat their friends. Or because a gift of healing is present, God is giving them a pass on that drinking problem, sexual sin, or whatever else is hidden behind closed doors. That's called religion. And it's ugly. Character matters.

No, we don't have to be perfect to prophesy a perfectly accurate word. We don't have to have a flawless character to minister at the altar. We don't need to be absolutely sinless to lay hands on the sick and see them recover. To suggest so would also be called religion. And that would be ugly. Nevertheless, character still matters.

So, what am I saying? We need to stop confusing gifts and callings with maturity and character. God can use a stubborn mule to prophesy, and he can use a stubborn believer to prophesy too. That doesn't mean God endorses stubbornness, which is like the sin of idolatry (see 1 Sam. 15:23). It just means that God needed a vessel to deliver the prophetic word to a person who desperately needed to hear it. That prophecy—or powerful altar call or gifts of healings or working of miracles—isn't about puffing up or glorifying the vessel. It's about edifying the church and glorifying God.

If God called you into ministry, He isn't going to revoke that call or the gifts that go with it the first time (or even necessarily the tenth or twentieth time) you act out or sin. Ultimately, it's we who turn our backs on our ministry when we repeatedly disobey God like Saul did. God is so slow to anger and abounding in mercy (see Num. 14:18) that it may seem like we're getting away with our poor behavior and behind-the-scenes sin. God is just giving us space to repent.

— *Prayer* —

Father, in the name of Jesus, help me to embrace character-building as a priority. I don't want my anointing to take me where my character can't keep me and fall headlong into sin like so many others. Please, develop in me Christ's character and help me choose what is right.

Is the Lord Hiding Something from You?

..."Let her alone; for her soul is in deep distress, and the Lord has hidden it from me, and has not told me" (2 Kings 4:27 NKJV).

There have been times when people I am close to are going through trials or warfare—or just having a bad day—and the Lord will put it on my heart to pray for them. There have been times, though, when someone I am close to is going through trials or warfare—or just having a bad day—and I am oblivious. I only find out when they text me or tell me a day later what they were dealing with.

I used to wonder why I didn't pick up on the issue. I used to wonder how I missed that in the spirit. But as much as prophets love to quote Amos 3:7—"The Sovereign Lord never does anything until he reveals his plans to his servants the prophets"—the reality is sometimes God hides things from us.

When I came across this passage in 2 Kings 4:25-27, it really set me free. In this scene, a woman who bore a son after a prophetic word from Elisha faced a tragedy. When the young boy died in an accident, she ran back to Elisha.

> *So it was, when the man of God saw her afar off, that he said to his servant Gehazi, "Look, the Shunammite woman! Please run now to meet her, and say to her, 'Is it well with you? Is it well with your husband? Is it well with the child?'"*
>
> *And she answered, "It is well." Now when she came to the man of God at the hill, she caught him by the feet, but Gehazi came near to push her away. But the man of God said, "Let her alone; for her soul is in deep distress, and the Lord has hidden it from me, and has not told me"* (NKJV).

You only know what God tells you. Yes, we should be cultivating sensitivity to His Spirit, inquiring of Him, and listening carefully. But the prophetic reality is that if He is not showing us, we have no way to know. Don't beat yourself up.

— *Prayer* —

Father, in the name of Jesus, please help me discern Your call to pray for the ones in my life who need my intercession flow. But help me not to be distressed when You hide things from me, trusting that You have a reason for not showing me what I would have wanted to see.

Avoiding Prophetic Malpractice

"And I tell you this, you must give an account on judgment day for every idle word you speak" (Matthew 12:36).

Malpractice gets doctors sued. In fact, medical errors are the third leading cause of death in America by some reports. That concept got me thinking about prophetic malpractice. Certainly, prophetic malpractice is not likely to kill you, though I suppose a directional word could kill your dreams, your marriage, or your career. I always say, the prophetic word you don't judge is the prophetic word that could derail your life.

Malpractice from a medical sense is "a dereliction of professional duty or a failure to exercise an ordinary degree of professional skill or learning...which results in injury, loss, or damage; an injurious, negligent, or improper practice." Beware prophetic malpractice. You don't want to release the enemy's plan over someone's life because you couldn't judge the source of your prophecy, or because of your negligence or poor practice.

Let's get more specific. Applying that to our ministries, prophetic malpractice would be violating our duty to speak only what God speaks when He speaks it—and being sure to speak what God speaks when God speaks it. Prophetic malpractice is racing ahead to prophesy without proper training or prophetic protocols and leading people astray in the process. Prophetic malpractice brings damage to the believer's soul or results in some type of loss in their life, even if it's just the loss of peace. Prophetic malpractice stems from improper practice.

If you stick with the realm of the simple gift of prophecy, you aren't likely to do much damage, but even then your words can cast aspersions on people, and even a kind word spoken publicly can embarrass a private person. Still, directional words seem to cause the most damage when released out of time, out of order—or out of your mouth instead of God's. In other words, when you speak for God when God isn't speaking, nothing good can come of it. And, at worst, you've engaged in prophetic malpractice.

— *Prayer* —

Father, in the name of Jesus, teach me Your protocols for prophetic ministry so that I don't stray beyond the banks of Your prophetic river into error. Help me to avoid prophetic malpractice that hurts the hearers instead of building them up in love.

Entering the Furnace of Affliction

"Behold, I have refined you, but not as silver; I have tested you in the furnace of affliction" (Isaiah 48:10 NKJV).

The people to whom Isaiah had prophesied these words had just gone through a major enemy attack. They were afflicted. Affliction is "a cause of persistent pain or distress, great suffering." It means "anguish, grief, sorrow, heartache, and woe," according to *Merriam-Webster*'s dictionary. There's suffering for what you did wrong and there's suffering for what you did right, but there's also suffering to become who you are supposed to be. God allows you to go through the furnace of affliction to purify you.

I heard the Lord say:

> When you're in this furnace of affliction, if you'll get your mind off yourself and begin to get your mind on Me—if you'll get your mind off yourself and begin to get your mind on others who have it worse than you—you will see a measure of freedom and a self-sacrificing attitude that will bring you out of the furnace of affliction faster than any measure of self-pity ever would or ever could.

> So, begin to see things the way that I see them. And, understand and know that I am refining you. And, although you're miserable and although you feel like you'll never emerge, you will emerge and you'll emerge with more anointing. You'll emerge from the wilderness like Jesus did, with more power. You will emerge and you will rise faster than you ever could have carrying the weight of the seasons of the past. For I am burning away those things which hinder love.

> I am burning off the mindsets and the characteristics that are not of Me. I am taking you to a new level of glory in the furnace of affliction. I am birthing in you a movement of prayer. ...Your first response when you begin to feel the fire will be to cry out to Me—looking for Me; searching for Me; understanding, as David did, that I will never leave you without help, that I will always deliver you because of My kindness. I will always deliver you because I delight in you. I will always deliver you from the furnace of affliction at the right time.

— *Prayer* —

Father, in the name of Jesus, help me remain steady in the furnace of affliction, understanding that You are delivering me from carnal desires and soulish error in the process. Remind me to keep my eyes on the outcome of the purification in the midst of the fire so I can praise You.

Prophesying with Authority

"Having then gifts differing according to the grace that is given to us, let us use them: if prophecy, let us prophesy in proportion to our faith" (Romans 12:6 NKJV).

When I first started out in prophetic ministry, I had very little faith to prophesy. I knew I was hearing from God, but fear was overcoming my faith. I would not prophesy spontaneously because I wanted to take the time to judge every word, find Scripture to back up the prophecy, and, sometimes, even ask others to review it. If I released a prophecy publicly, it was written out and I would read it.

You might say I was a baby prophet. That was OK then—we grow in God from faith to faith (see Rom. 1:17)—but it would not be OK now. As our relationship with God grows, so should our faith. Experience brings confidence in prophetic ministry, but we should still only prophesy according to the measure of our faith.

The Amplified Bible puts Romans 12:6 this way: "If [someone has the gift of] prophecy, [let him speak a new message from God to His people] in proportion to the faith possessed." And the New Living Translation relates, "So if God has given you the ability to prophesy, speak out with as much faith as God has given you."

Again, it takes faith to prophesy. So how do you get that faith? Romans 10:17 gives us one answer: "So then faith comes by hearing, and hearing by the word of God" (NKJV). We think more like God when we renew our mind to God's Word. Although His thoughts are higher than our thoughts, meditating on the Word builds our confidence in hearing His still small voice and helps us dissect His thoughts from our thoughts.

Paul the apostle put it this way: "And since we have the same spirit of faith, according to what is written, 'I believed and therefore I spoke,' we also believe and therefore speak" (2 Cor. 4:13) When you really believe, you'll prophesy with authority.

— *Prayer* —

Father, in the name of Jesus, help my unbelief. Help me cast down voices of doubt and unbelief that hinder my prophetic flow. Show me how to build my faith in this season, not just to prophesy but so I can walk by faith and not by sight in every aspect of my prophetic life.

The Silent Dimension

"Be still, and know that I am God!" (Psalm 46:10)

When I was a child, I broke my leg and landed in the hospital in painful traction for weeks. After traction, I was in a full body cast. Just months after I was healed and liberated from the cast, I broke my leg a second time and was once again bound to a hospital bed for months and confined to a body cast for months more.

During these extended periods of immobility, I sat in silence hour after hour, day after day, week after week, and month after month. While my parents were at work, nurses or other caregivers would check in with me only a couple of times a day. To some, that may sound more painful than broken bones, and at first it was.

But I learned to enjoy silence. I discovered the benefits of silence. I relished the power of silence. In recent years, I've discovered how silence fuels the seer gift. Silence is the absence of sound, but it's also a dimension in the spirit where one receives revelation from the throne room. Learning how to remain quiet in soul and calm in spirit in order to discern what is happening in the spirit world and see what the Lord is saying is vital to navigating seer dimensions.

St. John of the Cross, a major figure in the Spanish Counter-Reformation, was known as a friend of silence. He wrote things like: "Carve out a day every week, or an hour a day, or a moment each hour, and abide in loving silence with the Friend. Feel the frenetic concerns of life in the world fall away, like the last leaves of autumn being lifted from the tree in the arms of a zephyr. Be the bare tree."

It's been said by many mystics and seers that silence is God's first language. Silence can be uncomfortable at times, but it is a powerful pursuit that brings clarity of vision. "Be still, and know that I am God!" (Ps. 46:10). This heart posture will position you to enter the silent realm.

— *Prayer* —

Father, in the name of Jesus, give me an appreciation for absolute silence in a world of hustle, bustle, and constant distractions and demands on my time. Teach me the value of sitting before You in silence, asking for nothing but merely enjoying the reality that You are with me.

Dangerous Doctrines

"So Samuel grew, and the Lord was with him and let none of his words fall to the ground" (1 Samuel 3:19 NKJV).

Samuel was dedicated to the Lord before he was born. His once-barren mother Hannah made a vow to the Lord to give her child over to His service if the Lord would only let her birth a baby of her own (see 1 Sam. 1:11). God heard her vow and she birthed Samuel, who lived as a Nazirite, wholly set apart for the Lord. He grew up in the temple, serving the Lord from boyhood.

In 1 Samuel 2:26 we read that the child grew in stature and in favor with both the Lord and men. In fact, Samuel was still very young when he first heard the voice of the Lord— and when he essentially confirmed a judgment prophecy that an elder prophet released over Eli—a prophecy of judgment on his family line. What a way to start in prophetic ministry!

After that baptism by fire into his calling, 1 Samuel 3:19-20 tells us: "So Samuel grew, and the Lord was with him and let none of his words fall to the ground. And all Israel from Dan to Beersheba knew that Samuel had been established as a prophet of the Lord" (NKJV).

Unfortunately, some in the prophetic movement are taking this as a doctrine, insisting that if one is a true prophet the Lord will never let your words fall to the ground. Put another way, the deception states that since God called the prophet He will back up anything the prophet says and bring it to pass even if it wasn't His way or His thought.

Clearly, this is refuted by the fact that Nathan once told David to do all that was in his heart and God swiftly corrected him (see 2 Sam. 12) and that Paul's arrest did not take place the way Agabus prophesied (see Acts 21).

You've heard the Bible speak of doctrines of demons. Paul uses this phraseology in 1 Timothy 4:1-2: "Now the Spirit expressly says that in latter times some will depart from the faith, giving heed to deceiving spirits and doctrines of demons, speaking lies in hypocrisy, having their own conscience seared with a hot iron" (NKJV). Be careful not to give heed to doctrines of demons. Many more will rise in the years ahead.

— *Prayer* —

Father, in the name of Jesus, if I am believing a doctrine of demons let the entrance of Your Word bring light so the truth can dispel the lies in my soul. Help me to walk circumspectly and to reject prophetic myths and fables like the Samuel Deception.

JULY

..."If there were prophets among you, I, the Lord, would reveal myself in visions. I would speak to them in dreams. But not with my servant Moses. Of all my house, he is the one I trust. I speak to him face to face, clearly, and not in riddles! He sees the Lord as he is..." (Numbers 12:6-8).

The Apostolic Prophet

"So the elders of the Jews built, and they prospered through the prophesying of Haggai the prophet and Zechariah the son of Iddo. And they built and finished it, according to the commandment of the God of Israel, and according to the command of Cyrus, Darius, and Artaxerxes king of Persia" (Ezra 6:14 NKJV).

Although we often associate the building anointing with apostles, prophets have a key role to play in building lives, churches, business, and other Kingdom endeavors. Beyond prophets with an apostolic anointing, prophets can prophesy to the apostles and the builders as they build the vision God gave them.

Imagine the task of rebuilding the temple. That was the task the Jewish elders undertook. It was a monumental task the enemies of Israel had staunchly opposed—and successfully stopped—for years. The Israelites had to fight for the right to build, and they may have been worn down emotionally before the building construction ever started. There probably were not enough qualified workers. Their bodies were surely sore. They were probably discouraged on some days about how little progress they had made in comparison to the scope of the work.

In Ezra, we see Haggai and Zechariah prophesying to the builders. The New American Standard Bible says they "were successful in building through the prophecy" of the prophets. Clearly, the prophets had a part in the building even though they weren't the ones holding tools in their hands. I believe these prophets were keeping the vision before the builders, to help them stay focused on God's will. Haggai and Zechariah were decreeing and declaring God's plan for the nation of Israel despite past opposition.

The enemy always works to tear down what God is building. Prophets have a vital role to play in what God is building through intercession, prophetic declaration, and decrees; exposing the enemy's strategies and sounding the alarm; engaging in spiritual warfare; and prophesying what God is saying at various points of the building process.

In prophetic ministry there is a lot of focus on tearing down, rooting out, overthrowing, and destroying, but remember that prophets are also called to build and plant (see Jer. 1:10). Ask the Holy Spirit to give you prophetic wisdom, strategies, and encouragement for the builders in your life.

— *Prayer* —

Father, in all my rooting out and throwing down, help me to build and plant according to Your blueprint and Your pattern. Help me to walk in a balanced prophetic ministry and to embrace the fullness of the mantle of a prophet. Make me a repairer of the breach.

Don't Feel Sorry for Jezebel

"Take no part in the worthless deeds of evil and darkness; instead, expose them" (Ephesians 5:11).

Yes, blessed are the merciful, but we can't show mercy to a demon. As prophets, Jezebel is our archenemy and, unfortunately, sometimes this spirit works through people to get to you. We must learn how to separate the personality from the principality. In other words, we have to love the people but hate the demon, and that means discerning Jezebel's false tears.

Yes, we show mercy to the person, but we cannot fall for the classic Jezebel trap of evoking your pity. Make no mistake: If you feel sorry for those Jezebel ensnares, she'll play you like a fiddle, take advantage of your kindness, and pull on your heart strings. This master manipulator will seduce you into its web of witchcraft using your soulish compassion as bait.

Jesus has made a pathway for people in bondage to Jezebel to repent—and so should we. But there is no repentance without confrontation. Our soulish compassion will not lead one of Jezebel's puppets to repentance.

Most people operating in a Jezebel spirit have a long, sad story of how they've been sorely abused; how people misunderstand them; how they've been falsely accused; how they've lived a lifetime of sickness; how churches mistreat them—or some other horror story they remind you of as often as you'll listen. Those stories may be largely true, but the motive for sharing them is not to get free. Rather, they want to form a co-dependent relationship with you so you can pet their flesh and wipe their tears.

The entire scene is sad, truly sad. But offering soulish compassion is just a manifestation of tolerating Jezebel. And tolerating Jezebel is dangerous. Consider Christ's words in Revelation 2:22-23:

> *Therefore, I will throw her on a bed of suffering, and those who commit adultery with her will suffer greatly unless they repent and turn away from her evil deeds. I will strike her children dead. Then all the churches will know that I am the one who searches out the thoughts and intentions of every person. And I will give to each of you whatever you deserve.*

Ask the Holy Spirit to help you see through Jezebel's false tears.

— *Prayer* —

Father, in the name of Jesus, help me discern the traps, ploys, schemes, devices, and wiles of the Jezebel spirit working through people to tap into my compassion. Help me always to move in Christ's compassion but not in my soulish compassion, which leads to soul ties with a demon.

Prophesying to the Pre-Believer

"But if all of you are prophesying, and unbelievers or people who don't understand these things come into your meeting, they will be convicted of sin and judged by what you say" (1 Corinthians 14:24).

Our church was in a storefront space many years ago, and people kept walking in randomly thinking we were the retail shop that occupied the space before us. It was distracting. One day, I prophesied that the next person who opened the door would walk in, hear the word of the Lord, and fall down weeping. Two weeks later, it happened.

Paul the apostle reveals the power of prophesying over unbelievers in his first letter to the church at Corinth. Paul took the opportunity to remind his disciples how the gifts of the Spirit could be used to minister to the lost as well as to the saints. In 1 Corinthians 14:22-25, he writes:

> *Therefore, [unknown] tongues are [meant] for a [supernatural] sign, not to believers but to unbelievers [who might be receptive]; while prophecy [foretelling the future, speaking a new message from God to the people] is not for unbelievers but for believers.*
>
> *So then, if the whole church gathers together and all of you speak in [unknown] tongues, and outsiders or those who are not gifted [in spiritual matters] or unbelievers come in, will they not say that you are out of your mind?*
>
> *But if all prophesy [foretelling the future, speaking a new message from God to the people], and an unbeliever or outsider comes in, he is convicted [of his sins] by all, and he is called to account by all [because he can understand what is being said]; the secrets of his heart are laid bare. And so, falling on his face, he will worship God, declaring that God is really among you* (AMP).

When we prophesy, most of us are prophesying over believers in church. Occasionally, we may go on an evangelism outreach and prophesy over someone. We may even low-key prophesy over someone at work. But, let's face it, most of our prophetic ministry is still to the church. We're missing a powerful opportunity and the Holy Spirit is beginning to challenge many prophets to ministry to the lost, or the pre-believers as I like to call them.

— *Prayer* —

Father, in the name of Jesus, inspire my heart to begin to prophesy to the lost so they will know that Jesus is alive—and that Jesus loves them. Help me use my office to edify, comfort, and exhort the ones who don't yet know how good You are so they will hunger for Your love.

The Independent Prophet

"Yes, I am the vine; you are the branches. Those who remain in me, and I in them, will produce much fruit. For apart from me you can do nothing" (John 15:5).

Jonah's experience in the belly of a whale may be a kid's-church favorite, but it offers a serious warning here for New Testament prophets. While the Book of Jonah tells a familiar story, deeper examination demonstrates two spiritual death knells for prophets—rebellion and stubbornness that come out of an independent spirit.

The Lord told Jonah to go to Nineveh and preach against the wickedness of its society. Jonah's immediate response was to run away from the Lord and board a ship that was headed in the opposite direction toward Tarshish. Jonah rebelled against the word of the Lord because he wanted Nineveh to experience the wrath of God instead of the mercy of God. He had an independent spirit. He did not want to submit to the Lord's will.

The Bible tells us the ship was about to be broken into pieces and the sailors were terrified for their lives. Meanwhile, Jonah was down in the hold of the ship taking a nap. Who could take a nap in the middle of such a violent tempest? Is it possible that Jonah's rebellion opened up a door for a spirit of witchcraft to attack him?

Spiritual witchcraft is the power of satan, and fatigue, weariness, and slumber are some of its manifestations. When witchcraft attacks, its victims may feel tired, oppressed, or depressed. What could have caused Jonah to remain fast asleep in the midst of such a life-threatening situation? That's exactly what the ship's captain wanted to know. Prophets who start off walking in God's will but take a detour into an independent spirit fall prey to demonic attacks.

The prophet with an independent spirit refuses to submit to God's command when they don't agree. Independent prophets are carnal prophets who engage in works of the flesh, such as witchcraft. They look spiritual on the outside but they rebel against the Lord. Independent prophets eventually have a hardened heart and cannot hear the Lord. I believe this is one way true prophets turn false. Apart from Christ, we can do nothing (see John 15:5).

— *Prayer* —

Father, in the name of Jesus, would You root out any streaks of independence, rebellion, and stubbornness from my soul? Help me understand that without You I am nothing. Teach me to lean deeply upon Your grace when I feel like I want to run my own race.

God Will Vindicate You

"The Lord judges the peoples; vindicate me, Lord, according to my righteousness and my integrity that is in me" (Psalm 7:8 NASB 1995).

Vindication is the story of my life. Unfortunately, that means injustice has also marked my history—lots of it. If you are a prophet, you will face much injustice, persecution, slander, hatred, rejection, and more. The good news is, God will vindicate you.

In recent years, I released what turned out to be a controversial prophetic word. Many people crucified me because they didn't want to accept its truth. Thousands of people cursed me and unfollowed my ministry. I asked the Lord, "Did I miss it? What should I do?" He said, "You did not miss it. I will vindicate you." And He did. He always does.

If God ever vindicated anyone, He will vindicate you. God is no respecter of persons (see Acts 10:34). If He will restore what the devil stole from me, He will restore what the devil stole from you. I challenge you right now, instead of complaining day and night about what the enemy has done in your life, try praying day and night for God's justice. Are you desperate enough for God's justice in your life that you'll persist in day and night prayer until you see Him move? Remember Christ's words on justice:

> *...Don't you think God will surely give justice to his chosen people who cry out to him day and night? Will he keep putting them off? I tell you, he will grant justice to them quickly! But when the Son of Man returns, how many will he find on the earth who have faith?* (Luke 18:7-8)

Do you believe that God is your vindicator? Is anything too hard for God? (See Jeremiah 32:26-27.)

I don't know who has maligned you, who has done you wrong, or what the enemy has stolen from you. But what I am absolutely confident of is that God is your vindicator. If you believe it and you persist in prayer for justice, day and night, you can assure someone else of our just God's vindicating power too. Only believe. Amen.

— *Prayer* —

Father, in the name of Jesus, help me to forgive those who have wronged me and help me not to take justice in my own hands. Give me the grace to wait upon You to vindicate me and the peace that passes all understanding while I wait on You to make the wrong things right.

Trade Your Horn for a Trumpet

"Let someone else praise you, not your own mouth—a stranger, not your own lips"
(Proverbs 27:2).

It was sad. I tried to teach him. But he wanted to be a famous prophet. He was constantly praising his prophetic accuracy, tooting his own horn, so to speak, on social media. I gently reminded him of Proverbs 27:2, "Let another man praise you, and not your own mouth; a stranger, and not your own lips" (NKJV). But it seems he had something to prove and he wanted to make sure everyone knew he was a prophet.

My gentle corrections eventually caused him to turn on me and break relationship. Eventually, the young man ended up in divination—prophetic witchcraft. Some of the leaders who once praised him for his accuracy were now calling me asking me what went wrong. His insecurity led him into pride, which ended up in his destruction.

In Matthew 6:1-2, Jesus spoke some words that apply to prophets. Look at prophetic words as good deeds, and let these words sink in:

> *Watch out! Don't do your good deeds publicly, to be admired by others, for you will lose the reward from your Father in heaven. When you give to someone in need, don't do as the hypocrites do—blowing trumpets in the synagogues and streets to call attention to their acts of charity! I tell you the truth, they have received all the reward they will ever get.*

Can you imagine? The religious leaders of the day—Jesus called them hypocrites—actually sounded a trumpet to draw attention to their good deeds. Their motive was clearly to look like the hotshots of Israel. And despite how deeply they dug into their pockets, the only reward they would ever get was the attention of man.

Tooting your own horn in the prophetic is childish because whatever gift we have, it comes from God. We can't take credit for a public prophecy. God wants no part in that pretense. Humility is key to the prophet. If you feel you have something to prove, sit down and heal before you prophesy. Trade your horn for a trumpet and be the voice God called you to be.

— *Prayer* —

Father, in the name of Jesus, heal me of heart issues that cause me to toot my own horn. Deliver me from insecurities. Deliver me from rejection. Deliver me from pride. Help me overcome my carnal nature to take credit for the prophetic words You give me. I glorify You.

Stewarding Difficult Prophetic Words

"Then the Lord spoke to Gad, David's seer. This was the message: 'Go and say to David, "This is what the Lord says: I will give you three choices. Choose one of these punishments, and I will inflict it on you"'" (1 Chronicles 21:9-10).

More than one person has told me I released a difficult prophetic word to them in a prayer line, privately of course. I don't remember most of those instances and usually didn't know the word was difficult. Sometimes God speaks to people in a language they understand even when the prophet doesn't realize the deeper meaning of words.

I vividly remember a time I prophesied over a young woman, "The Lord is saying no. He has something better." The woman broke down in tears. I later discovered it applied to a relationship with a man she wanted to marry. That woman disappeared for a while and I felt bad because I didn't know what happened. But when she reemerged she was happy that she hadn't married that man.

That was a spontaneous prophecy and I had no idea what I was saying. But sometimes we have to deliver difficult prophetic words and we know those words will be difficult to hear. So what does the prophet do? First, make sure you really heard from God. Judge the prophecy. The enemy can try to talk you out of delivering a difficult prophetic word because it's uncomfortable, so you should know in your spirit you are accurate before speaking out. You won't share it with confidence if you aren't confident.

Next, if you receive a difficult prophetic word pray it through before releasing it. You are praying to make sure you got the entire message from the Lord. Many times people release part of a difficult prophetic word and leave out an important part—even the redemptive part. If it's a difficult prophetic word, you need to make sure you prophesy God's kindness or a positive outcome for obedience.

Pray that you deliver it in the right spirit. Pray for the right timing to deliver the word. Pray for the person to receive the truth. I sometimes wonder how Gad or Nathan felt when they had to deliver prophetic rebukes to David. For the sake of the Kingdom, these prophets must have prayed for wisdom on how to present the prophecies in a way the king would receive them. You may not be prophesying to a king, but your assignment is just as important.

— *Prayer* —

Father, in the name of Jesus, teach me how to steward difficult words. Give me wisdom to handle difficult words in the right spirit, bathing them in prayer and pondering the right delivery system. Use me as an agent of healing and redemption even in the face of hard words.

The Watchman's Charge

"Keep watch and pray, so that you will not give in to temptation. For the spirit is willing, but the body is weak!" (Matthew 26:41)

Some prophets have a strong anointing and grace to watch—hence the name watchman—and to pray about what they hear, see, or otherwise discern in both the spirit and natural realms. Either way, all prophets have a mandate to watch and pray. In fact, all believers have a Christ-given mandate to watch and pray (see Matt. 26:41).

As I write in my book *The Making of a Watchman*, some say the watchman's job is complete after he releases what he sees. Nothing could be further from the truth and is an irresponsible stance. That would be like saying the postman's job is finished when he picks up the mailbag from central headquarters—that he has no responsibility to deliver the mail to the houses on his route. The watchman is called to be part of the solution, to be part of the prayer meeting. And at times, the watchman is the only one praying.

You are probably the most familiar with those last two lines—"I sought for a man among them who would make a wall, and stand in the gap before Me on behalf of the land, that I should not destroy it; but I found no one" (Ezek. 22:30 NKJV). But understanding the context here helps you understand the connection between watching and praying, even when things seem helpless and hopeless.

God is always looking for a man (or woman) to stand in the gap to avert disaster. God doesn't send warnings so we can merely brace ourselves for what's coming. He sends us messages so we can prepare a plan. It's not much different, actually, than the meteorologist who warns of a hurricane in South Florida. We don't go on with life as usual. We stock up on supplies and hunker down—or leave the territory.

God sends us warnings so we can work with His Spirit to prepare a battle plan and shut the enemy out. Even in the midst of Israel's sin, God was looking for a praying watchman. Where's your watchtower?

— *Prayer* —

Father, in the name of Jesus, would You give me a watchman's anointing and show me where my watchtower stands? I want to obey Christ's command to watch and pray. So teach me how to operate in this anointing accurately and to warn with clarity.

Mind Every Jot and Tittle

"And I solemnly declare to everyone who hears the words of prophecy written in this book: If anyone adds anything to what is written here, God will add to that person the plagues described in this book. And if anyone removes any of the words from this book of prophecy, God will remove that person's share in the tree of life and in the holy city that are described in this book" (Revelation 22:18-19).

Many years ago, I received a prophetic word from the Lord during my devotional time. My habit was to write down those words as fast as I got them. Once, I wrote the word "an" instead of "the" and the Lord swiftly corrected me. I was a little surprised.

What difference did it really make? It sounded better with the "an." I was young and a writer by trade and didn't understand that, yes, it makes a difference. We never change one jot or tittle of the word of God.

When I was doing a lot of magazine writing, I once shared a prophetic word and an editor actually wanted to edit God! When they sent me my article to proof, I told them they could not put a period where the comma was. They didn't seem to understand why it would matter. I told them the story and they changed it back.

In Revelation 22:18-19, we see a more serious matter, but my stories illustrate just how particular God is about what He says. Although prophecy is not on par with Scripture, if God said it then God said it. I don't think plagues described in the Book of Revelation will come upon us if we change an "an" to a "the" or put a period where there was a comma, but that's not the point. The point is God does not want us changing what He says.

God does not need an editor. In fact, the only book I've ever read in my life that didn't contain a typo, a run on sentence, or some other grammar error is the Bible. No, I don't believe you'll go to hell for removing words from a prophecy or suffer plagues. But does that mean we should tempt God? God forbid. Again, God doesn't need an editor. He needs a scribe, but not an editor.

— *Prayer* —

Father, in the name of Jesus, help me to say Your truth, the whole truth, and nothing but the truth—holding nothing back and adding nothing to what You say. Teach me to reverence Your prophetic words and avoid the temptation to edit the Spirit of God.

When Warfare Skews Your Vision

"I prayed to the Lord, and he answered me. He freed me from all my fears" (Psalm 34:4).

The enemy hates seers because he hates God. The enemy's way is "eye for an eye" retaliation against the ones who are most likely to see him. The Lord showed me clearly how the enemy has skewed the vision of many seers during a season of warfare:

> You've begun to see things not as they are but as the enemy wants you to see them. ...Whatever the enemy is showing you, just look around the corner, because that is where something better lies. Just look around the corner.

Seers, it's one thing to see what the enemy is doing. It's another thing to allow the enemy to mesmerize you with his evil acts to the point of fear or trauma. If you're going to look and see what the enemy is doing, look in the Spirit and see what God wants to do also. Look in the Spirit and see what God has planned. Press in further and ask the Lord to show you the other side.

Let me put it another way. Some seers only see devils, devils, devils. But God is in there somewhere—God's blessings, God's angels, God's strategy, God's provision. You have to press past the demonic to see clearly the Lord's plan in the matter. Again, ask the Lord to show you the other side.

As I continued praying, the Lord showed me the eyes of some seers have been polluted by what the enemy showed them in their dreams. You didn't choose to see it—but the Lord is healing your eyes. Some of you don't even want to dream anymore because of the terror you see in the nighttime. But the Lord is healing your eyes.

The Lord showed me that many seers stopped expressing their gift because people didn't appreciate it. People actually persecuted them for it because they didn't like what you were seeing. The Lord wants to heal your hearts.

— *Prayer* —

Father, in the name of Jesus, heal my eyes from the trauma the enemy inflicted upon me in my childhood. Cleanse my lens from the worthless things that brought pollution into my heart through my eyes. I want to see what You want to show me. I want to dream accurately again.

After You Eat the Scroll

"The voice said to me, 'Son of man, eat what I am giving you—eat this scroll! Then go and give its message to the people of Israel'" (Ezekiel 3:1).

Ezekiel didn't literally eat the scroll, nor did John the Beloved in the Book of Revelation (see Rev. 10:9). The eating of the scroll was symbolic rather than literal. Ezekiel and John digested the prophetic word into their minds and hearts until it literally became part of them. The prophet became one with the prophecy, the secret counsel in the scroll.

The voice said to me, "Son of man, eat what I am giving you—eat this scroll! Then go and give its message to the people of Israel." So I opened my mouth, and he fed me the scroll. "Fill your stomach with this," he said. And when I ate it, it tasted as sweet as honey in my mouth. Then he said, "Son of man, go to the people of Israel and give them my messages. I am not sending you to a foreign people whose language you cannot understand" (Ezekiel 3:1-5).

Notice how the scroll is at first sweet. It's exciting to hear the secret counsel of God. The knowledge of the future makes one feel empowered. But when the prophet realizes he has to deliver a message nobody wants to hear, the excitement wears off and reality sets in. By that time it's too late. The prophet and the prophecy are one.

The prophet must first apply any difficult word from God to his own life to see if personal repentance is in order before he dares prophesy it to another. The prophet must allow the word to try him before he puts others on trial. The prophet must sorrow over the difficult message before he announces it with confident authority.

True prophets, like Ezekiel, don't get to pick and choose what scroll they eat as if they are at a fancy restaurant with a never-ending menu. True prophets must eat whatever scroll God gives them. They must receive the word with gladness as it is an honor to be chosen by the Father as a messenger. They must internalize the prophecy until enough faith rises up in them to deliver its contents with a boldness that cannot be denied.

— *Prayer* —

Father, in the name of Jesus, give me the courage to eat the scroll You give me, knowing that the assignment may be unpleasant to my flesh. Teach me to embrace Your assignments with joy even when I have to share difficult prophetic words with the church You are building.

JULY 12

Seek the Lord When He Can Be Found

"Seek the Lord while you can find him. Call on him now while he is near" (Isaiah 55:6).

When I lose my keys, I start seeking. It's an intentional seeking. It's a thorough seeking. It's a continued seeking until I find those keys because I can't go anywhere without them. This is the same attitude with which the prophet must seek God.

David understood this. He said, "Early will I seek You" (Ps. 63:1 NKJV). Prophets can't afford to put off seeking God. It must be a matter of priority. He must be first place. The type of seeking Jesus spoke of is not a soaking. It's not a passive seeking. It's an action verb.

The Greek word for "seek" is *zeteo*. According to *The KJV New Testament Greek Lexicon*, it means "to seek in order to find." It also means "to seek [in order to find out] by thinking, meditating, reasoning, to enquire into; to crave, demand something more from someone." This is the prophet's quest, not for a prophetic word to share, but for personal pleasure.

There's a running theme in Scripture about seeking the Lord while He may be found. Deuteronomy 4:29 assures, "If you search for him with all your heart and soul, you will find him." And David wrote, "For this cause everyone who is godly shall pray to You in a time when You may be found" (Ps. 32:6 NKJV).

When can God be found? Is He hiding? We know God is with us all the time. Jesus said He would never leave us or forsake us (see Heb. 13:5). But that same Jesus told us to seek first the Kingdom of God and His righteousness (see Matt. 6:33). There's an art to seeking God. There's no formula, but there is a pattern.

When we sow to the spirit, we reap life. When we diligently seek Him, we will find Him—but the finding is not always immediate. Just like seedtime and harvest in the natural, there's a time of seeking and a time of finding in the realm of the spirit.

The Hebrew concept in Isaiah 55:6 is literally "a time of finding." The Lord is always near. He's a very present help in time of need, but if we want to find—or, put another way, to encounter Him—we have to do the seeking. The encounter is our reward.

— *Prayer* —

Father, in the name of Jesus, You alone are worthy. Help me seek You like the eternal treasure You are. Help me be intentional about my seeking. Grant me a burning desire for more of You that supersedes my physical hunger and my desire to prophesy. You are my great reward.

Beyond the Church's Four Walls

"This pleased Potiphar, so he soon made Joseph his personal attendant. He put him in charge of his entire household and everything he owned" (Genesis 39:4).

"More than 90% of the prophets in the Old Testament never functioned inside the walls of the temple. They never earned their income from 'church' ministry. Most were businesspeople or government officials." That's a quote from my spiritual father Dr. Bill Hamon in his book *The Day of the Saints*.

That should set a lot of prophets free from the religious paradigm that tries to convince us we are not spiritual if we don't have a microphone and a platform. Consider this: Both Joseph and Daniel were administrators. That didn't keep them from prophesying to world rulers. Deborah the prophetess was a judge. Amos was a farmer. Moses was a shepherd. Are you getting the drift?

Your prophetic anointing functions and is needed outside of the four walls of the church. While prophets should attend church, their primary venue of ministry may be in one of the other seven mountains of society. Marketplace prophets, then, may ultimately have more influence than the preaching prophet who travels the conference circuit.

If you are marketplace prophet, look for opportunities to encourage people with prophetic insight from the Lord during challenges. Remember Haggai and Zechariah? They were assigned to a construction site:

> So the Jewish elders continued their work, and they were greatly encouraged by the preaching of the prophets Haggai and Zechariah son of Iddo. The Temple was finally finished, as had been commanded by the God of Israel and decreed by Cyrus, Darius, and Artaxerxes, the kings of Persia (Ezra 6:14).

Marketplace prophets—and, listen, even if you are a house prophet or a prophet to the nations the marketplace is part of your ministry—God may lead you to use your gifts to see into the future, to develop strategies that bring increase in businesses, to call out the injustices in society, to warn of pitfalls in industry and the like.

— *Prayer* —

Father, in the name of Jesus, help me to accept my assignment in the marketplace, knowing You've called me to reach beyond the church mountain into other spheres of society. Help me encourage entertainers, businessmen, teachers, and others who need to hear Your voice.

Continuing Prophetic Education

"...Be a good worker, one who does not need to be ashamed and who correctly explains the word of truth" (2 Timothy 2:15).

We're in the second wave of the prophetic movement, yet many schools of the prophets are training the gift instead of the office. Prophets should already know how to prophesy. What prophets need is continuing prophetic education that keeps them sharp and accountable.

Think about it for a minute. Doctors are required to undergo continuing education. So are lawyers, teachers, and even beauty professionals. It's part of keeping their license. Although the gifts and callings of God are without repentance, prophets who don't continue on a prophetic education path slow their growth.

Samuel launched the school of the prophets in Old Testament days. Some translations say "company of prophets" or "sons of prophets." In 1 Samuel 19:18-24, we see Saul running into one of Samuel's companies prophesying. Seen also with Elijah and Elisha in 1 and 2 Kings, *Easton Bible Dictionary* tells us the schools of the prophets were "instituted for the purpose of training young men for the prophetical and priestly offices."

Of course, these schools of the prophets didn't make someone a prophet. Sure, there were prophets among them. There were also priests who did not prophesy. Think of the Old Testament schools of the prophets as seminaries, of sorts, where those who sensed God's call to service would band together for training.

Reputable schools of prophets can help you discern the voice of God, discover ways He may be speaking with you that you haven't experienced, and equip you in the realm of dreams, visions, and spiritual warfare. Schools of prophets can teach you how to wage war with a prophetic word, wage war with the devil, and wage war against your flesh. Continuing prophetic education can help you develop and refine your prophetic voice, build accuracy, and operate with safeguards that protect your prophetic credibility.

Schools of prophets can't make someone a prophet, but they do challenge prophets and prophetic people to think like God thinks, overcome their biases, exercise their gift with feedback and more. Continuing prophetic education is critical to ascending to the next glory of your gift.

— *Prayer* —

Father, in the name of Jesus, help me to walk in a humility that understands I have not arrived. Help me to adopt a mindset of continual learning no matter what stage of my journey I find myself. Lead me to the right voices and materials to sharpen my prophetic edge.

The Art and Science of Prophetic Stewardship

"God has given each of you a gift from his great variety of spiritual gifts. Use them well to serve one another" (1 Peter 4:10).

Stewarding prophetic words is both an art and a science. Let me explain. Stewardship is a management function. When God gives you a prophetic word for someone, you are charged with managing the revelation. The art of stewardship denotes skill, either through study, experience, or observation and thoughtfulness. The science of stewardship deals with the systems of weighing and releasing the word the right way.

The first decision comes from art. When you receive a word, do you share it? Do you keep it to yourself? Do you pray it through? The Lord has a purpose in everything. He will not tell you something about a person, city, nation—or even yourself—just so you can be "in the know." Knowledge is never for knowledge's sake. It is to be applied. So doing nothing is never good stewardship. Of course, praying is never the wrong move— and praying may be the total assignment.

The art and science of prophetic stewardship is informed by the same Holy Spirit who shared the secret with you. Don't sit and wonder what to do. He told you so you could take action. So ask the Lord how to manage that revelation rightly. For example, wisdom asks the Lord before releasing something He shows you over an individual. That's the art of stewardship. If you get the art wrong, you can get the science wrong.

Sharing what the Lord showed you might not edify, comfort, or exhort that person. It might rather embarrass or make that person feel exposed. If the Lord is showing you a weakness or need a person has, it may very well be that the Lord is showing you so that you can intercede for that person or come alongside to help without uttering a prophetic word.

God has given you a gift from His great storehouse of anointings and graces. Using that gift of prophecy well to serve His people requires learning the art and science of stewardship.

— *Prayer* —

Father, in the name of Jesus, show me what You want me to do with the prophetic knowledge You have shared with me. Do I tell them? If so, when? And how? Help me not to make a rash move or speak prematurely or wait too long to deliver Your message.

Visiting the Potter's House

"The word which came to Jeremiah from the Lord, saying: 'Arise and go down to the potter's house, and there I will cause you to hear My words'" (Jeremiah 18:1-2 NKJV).

Several times in Scripture, God is referred to as a Potter. Isaiah 64:8 reveals, "And yet, O Lord, you are our Father. We are the clay, and you are the potter. We all are formed by your hand." A potter is one who forms, fashions, and frames a work of art. We are God's masterpiece and He forms our prophetic ministry as it suits Him. That requires not just one but many visits to the Potter's House.

When God tells you to go to the potter's house, don't delay. The potter's house is a place where you get revelation you can't get anywhere else. It's a place where God causes you to hear His words. It's usually a place that's outside your normal journey, such as it was for Jeremiah who had to leave the high place and the temple to go down to the potter's house.

An invitation to the potter's house is exciting. It's a place where God teaches and instructs us about His precepts and principles. It's a place where He shares His higher thoughts and His higher ways. It's a place where He explains parables and interprets dreams. It's place where He releases wisdom and understanding for your prophetic ministry.

The New International Version puts Jeremiah 18:2 this way: "Go down to the potter's house, and there I will give you my message." The instruction was probably inconvenient to Jeremiah's daily routine, but the instruction was compelling enough for the prophet to drop everything and go. After all, what's a prophetic messenger without a message? What can you speak if you have not heard the Potter's words?

The invitation to the Potter's House comes with an urgency. The Holman Christian Standard Bible says, "Go down at once to the potter's house; there I will reveal My words to you." It's a summons with importance because the revelation is for now and the message God wants released is pressing. Don't neglect your prompt visits to the Potter's House. They shape your ministry.

— *Prayer* —

Father, in the name of Jesus, help me discern Your call to the Potter's House and I will not delay in visiting You. Give me an urgency to go away with You to hear the prophetic message You need me to relay to Your church. Nothing is more important to me than Your mission.

Practicing His Presence

"Then Jacob awoke from his sleep and said, 'Surely the Lord is in this place, and I wasn't even aware of it!" (Genesis 28:16)

Monks live a simple life—a life of quiet and solitude. Brother Lawrence, a seventeenth-century layman who spent much of his life in the Carmelite monastery in Paris, wrote letters to a friend that became the classic book *The Practice of the Presence of God*. In the book, he shares his secret to a life of peace and joy. Of course, that secret is maintaining an awareness of God's presence even in the most mundane of chores.

Awareness of God's presence is definitely something to be practiced. Although we mentally assent that God is everywhere, we are less aware of God with us and God in us. It takes an intentional turning to the God in us over and over again to develop this awareness. It doesn't happen overnight.

In Genesis 28 we are in the beginning of Jacob's story. He had cheated Esau out of Isaac's blessing and he was running to his uncle Laban for refuge. Along the way, he stopped to rest for the night and had a dream of angels ascending and descending on a stairway to heaven. He had an encounter with God in the dream. When he woke up from the dream, he was awakened to God's presence. The reality is God's presence was there all along.

God wants us to walk in an awakening that makes us aware of His presence not just when we are in a worship service or when we hear His voice or when we have a dramatic encounter. He wants us to be so awakened that we are sensitive to His presence even in the mundane areas of our life, like Brother Lawrence.

When you are awakened to God's presence, you will walk with a confidence that He has gone before you to make a way for you. You will have assurance that He has your back. You will know He is directing your steps into revival, favor, wisdom, and divine appointments. When you are awakened to God's presence, it deepens your prophetic ministry in ways that words can't describe.

— *Prayer* —

Father, in the name of Jesus, help me to crucify my flesh so I can be more sensitive to Your heart. I want to know when You walk into a room and when You leave. I want to be aware of what You are doing in and around me. Help me practice Your presence.

Mirror, Mirror in the Word

"Now we see things imperfectly, like puzzling reflections in a mirror, but then we will see everything with perfect clarity..." (1 Corinthians 13:12).

Jesus is the Door to truth, life, love, and every good and perfect gift. His Word is a lamp to our feet, a light to our path, and a mirror in which we see ourselves as we really are. But there are other doors prophets are tempted to walk through to get what they want even if God doesn't want to them to have it. And the enemy is good at deceiving us with smoke and mirrors.

The Bible warns us over and over about deception. You can't read a chapter in the New Testament that doesn't warn us about being deceived or urging us to test spirits. If Jezebel can deceive you, she's got another trophy for her collection. That's why it's important that if we are going to speak the prophetic word of the Lord, we spend time reading the written Word of the Lord—the Bible—and being careful to do what it says. James 1:22-25 tells us:

> *But be doers of the word, and not hearers only, deceiving yourselves. For if anyone is a hearer of the word and not a doer, he is like a man observing his natural face in a mirror; for he observes himself, goes away, and immediately forgets what kind of man he was. But he who looks into the perfect law of liberty and continues in it, and is not a forgetful hearer but a doer of the work, this one will be blessed in what he does* (NKJV).

Self-deception has got to be the worst brand of deception. When we look in the mirror of the Word of God, we will see that we are called to walk in love with our brothers and sisters. We will see we are not supposed to let any corrupt communication come out of our mouth. We will see who we are supposed to be in Christ and where we need to grow because we will look at ourselves through God's eyes.

Don't deceive yourself. Let the Word of God serve as a mirror. We don't know the end from the beginning as God does. What we do know is all the ways of a man seem pure in his own eyes, but the Lord weighs the thoughts and intents of the heart (see Prov. 16:2). We also know that "the way of a fool is right in his own eyes: but he that hearkeneth unto counsel is wise" (Prov. 12:15 KJV).

Hearken unto the counsel of the Holy Ghost. Hearken unto the counsel of the Word. And hearken unto the counsel of mature leaders who aren't too timid to speak the truth in love.

— *Prayer* —

Father, in the name of Jesus, give me a deep love for Your Word, the Bible. As I read the written Word, help me reflect upon what I read so deeply that it reveals anything in me that is hindering my prophetic ministry. Let Your Word serve as a mirror for my soul.

Wisdom in Application

"If you need wisdom, ask our generous God, and he will give it to you. He will not rebuke you for asking" (James 1:5).

Application, essentially, means putting something to use. But if you put the right thing to the wrong use, it's called abuse. You may have seen women using their high heel shoes to hammer a nail into the wall. That's the wrong application of the shoe, and the heel is likely to break.

When God speaks to you, He wants you to put the prophetic word to use. Put another way, the interpretation should birth an application. God doesn't speak just to hear Himself talk. God's word is alive and it's active. It yields fruit and produces results when applied accurately. The key word is "accurately."

Since most personal prophecy is conditional, the truth in the prophetic word must be applied accurately in order to see God's will come to pass. You can understand this from a personal perspective. When God tells you to do something in your life, such as go to Russia as a missionary, it's up to you to apply that word to your life. It's up to you to get a passport and buy a plane ticket. God is not likely going to supernaturally transport you there. Your part of bringing the prophecy to pass is the application.

But for prophets it goes beyond personal application. Weightier words—such as words over world events or nations—are also typically conditional upon people and circumstances—and timing. So if you get a word of warning about an attack on a city, for example, you have to ask God what the application of that prophecy is. In other words, how do we apply that warning? Do we sound the alarm? Do we pray? If so, how do we pray?

Applying the wisdom of a prophetic word takes God's wisdom. Accurate prophetic words that are wrongly applied can lead to wrong outcomes. Prophetic direction wrongly applied can derail someone's life. When you receive a strong word, seek the Lord for the interpretation but don't stop there. Seek Him for the wisdom in the application.

— *Prayer* —

Father, in the name of Jesus, I hear Your voice clearly but sometimes it's hard to discern the next move. Remind me to ask You for Your wisdom on the application, knowing You will not withhold the next steps in the process to see Your will come to pass.

Facing Down the Tempter

"Now when the tempter came to Him, he said, 'If You are the Son of God, command that these stones become bread'" (Matthew 4:3 NKJV).

Satan has many names—the evil one, the father of lies, the accuser of the brethren. These are all aspects of his wicked character. But one of his names—the tempter—describes the allure of sin in our lives. Consider the great men and women of God who fell to the tempter. Adam, Eve, David, Samson, Judas. The truth is we've all fallen short of the glory of God at the tempter's beckoning. And it's time we face down this demon coaxer once and for all and tell him to get behind us!

The tempter uses what's in us, of course, but let's get beyond the generic discussion about the flesh and the carnal mind. By the same token, let's not go the extreme of sexual sin or white-collar Enron-style embezzlement. Chances are, the tempter comes at you with subtler temptations that tap into soulish insecurities or impatience, especially when you are in a wilderness place. The temptation could be a desire to prove your calling to the world at the wrong time. It could be a temptation to misuse the Word—or take it out of context—for personal gain or to prove a point. It could be a temptation to pursue the wrong kind of power or idolize the wrong god.

Indeed, these are the very strategies the tempter used against Jesus when He was in the wilderness. You've probably heard it said that satan doesn't have any new tricks. Well, I'm here to tell you he doesn't have any new temptations, either. It all boils down to the lust of the eyes, the lust of the flesh, and the pride of life, doesn't it? (See 1 John 2:16.)

Said in different words, wanting our own way, wanting everything for ourselves, and wanting to appear important opens the door to the tempter. I believe if we can expose the tempter we can defeat him. When we think we are beyond temptation—in any area— that is when the devil sneaks in and defeats God's will in our lives.

— *Prayer* —

Father, in the name of Jesus, help me discern the tempter's strategies against my life and ministry. Show me the weaknesses of my soul and lead me to the Scriptures that will help me renew my mind so the enemy cannot slither into my garden.

Building Through Prophecy

"At that time the prophets Haggai and Zechariah son of Iddo prophesied to the Jews in Judah and Jerusalem. They prophesied in the name of the God of Israel who was over them. Zerubbabel son of Shealtiel and Jeshua son of Jehozadak responded by starting again to rebuild the Temple of God in Jerusalem. And the prophets of God were with them and helped them" (Ezra 5:1-2).

I've always loved these verses, and often wondered what Haggai and Zechariah were prophesying as the workers rebuilt the temple. The Bible leaves that to our imagination. Even Bible commentaries don't shed much light, only pointing to the prophesying as exhortations. Exhortation is part of the simple gift of prophecy.

Exhortation implies more than encouragement. It implies a stirring address and a persuasive discourse. I imagine the builders were likely weary of the long-term building project and the opposition from Israel's enemies while they worked. They took on a monumental task amid monumental resistance.

So, what were Haggai and Zechariah prophesying to the Jews who were knee deep in this massive yet divine building project? I believe they were proclaiming words from past prophets about the very work at hand, particularly words from Jeremiah about the deliverance of Israel after a 70-year period (see Jer. 25:12).

What were Haggai and Zechariah prophesying? I believe they were declaring strength to the builders. I believe they were decreeing a finished work. If you read Zechariah and Haggai you can catch the spirit of what they were prophesying to the Jews.

In Zechariah we read, "'Not by might nor by power, but by My Spirit,' says the Lord of Hosts" (Zech. 4:6 NKJV). Haggai actually prophesied God's command to rebuild the temple (see Hag. 1). These prophets received direct revelation from God about His will in that hour and stood with the builders, strengthening them with the prophetic words—with the knowledge of the will of the Lord—through the process.

There's an important principle here: Prophets in the local body need to do more than just prophesy. You need to become an active part of walking out the prophetic word. As Ezra described, "and the prophets of God were with them, helping them." Ask the Holy Spirit to help you find your role in bringing prophetic words from past generations to pass.

— *Prayer* —

Father, in the name of Jesus, teach me the value in standing with the builders after I prophesy to the builders. Show me how I can encourage those who step out in faith to walk in the prophetic word I prophesied so they can finish their course.

Economic Prophets

"...The sinner's wealth passes to the godly" (Proverbs 13:22).

Part of the prophet's marketplace authority deals in the realm of economies. I'm not talking merely about predicting economic crises and famine. I'm not merely predicting the value of the dollar or what stock is going to skyrocket in trading. I'm talking about releasing a word in due season so God's people can defy unpleasant economic realities.

Elijah prophesied it would not rain and it didn't (see 1 Kings 17). The he prophesied it would rain again and it did (see 1 Kings 18). Joseph didn't only predict the famine through the interpretation of Pharaoh's dream. He offered a prophetic strategy that caused Egypt to prosper in a world crisis.

> *Therefore, Pharaoh should find an intelligent and wise man and put him in charge of the entire land of Egypt. Then Pharaoh should appoint supervisors over the land and let them collect one-fifth of all the crops during the seven good years. Have them gather all the food produced in the good years that are just ahead and bring it to Pharaoh's storehouses. Store it away, and guard it so there will be food in the cities* (Genesis 41:33-35).

When Moses led the Israelites out of Egypt, the former slaves left with Egypt's riches. Exodus 12:35-36 reads:

> *And the people of Israel did as Moses had instructed; they asked the Egyptians for clothing and articles of silver and gold. The Lord caused the Egyptians to look favorably on the Israelites, and they gave the Israelites whatever they asked for. So they stripped the Egyptians of their wealth!*

God has given us the power to create wealth to establish His covenant in the earth (see Deut. 8:18). With so many prophesies about impending economic doom, wouldn't it be worth making intercession and seeking God's face about how He plans to transfer the wealth of the wicked to the righteous? (See Proverbs 13:22.)

— *Prayer* —

Father, in the name of Jesus, would You share with me You're Kingdom wealth-creation strategies? Teach me how to use money for Your glory, where to sow it, and how to invest it in a way that brings increase to Your Kingdom to fund the Great Commission.

Shunning Prophetic Gossips

"A gossip goes around telling secrets, but those who are trustworthy can keep a confidence" (Proverbs 11:13).

I got a phone call from a young man indicating he was riding in the car with a prophet who had a word for me. I expected him to connect me with that prophet. Instead, he released the prophetic word himself. The word was dismal.

The young man said the prophet revealed he had a dream about me in which I was on a death bed and that if I didn't make some drastic changes I would lose my health. Needless to say, a spirit of fear started attacking me. That prophetic utterance was not wrapped in faith because God never spoke it. The prophetic utterance was wrapped in fear with an assignment to torment me.

When I finally spoke with the prophet six months later, he indicated the young man did not accurately describe the dream and repented for his prophetic gossip. Anyone can make this mistake, but sometimes it's more innocent than others. In my case, the prophet was just processing out loud. He had no idea the young man would tell me.

However, there are more serious prophetic gossips. You've probably run into one or two—or three. These are the types who share intimate details of personal prophecies with people who have no business knowing. That can cause trouble in many forms. That's why the Bible warns against gossip—and I imagine God frowns even more on prophetic gossip.

If we want God to reveal to us His secrets, we have to avoid prophetic gossip. Prophetic gossip says something about the character of the prophet. Solomon put it this way: "The wise don't make a show of their knowledge, but fools broadcast their foolishness" (Prov. 12:23). Wisdom dictates not sharing what you know about someone with anybody but that someone.

And it's not just sharing prophetic gossip that we need to watch for, but also giving ear to it. Proverbs 20:19 warns, "A gossip goes around telling secrets, so don't hang around with chatterers."

— *Prayer* —

Father, in the name of Jesus, warn me if I am about to engage in prophetic gossip before I open my holy mouth—or open my anointed ears to others. Help me avoid the temptation to share what I know with people who don't need to know.

Going on a Treasure Hunt

"It is the glory of God to conceal things, but the glory of kings is to search things out" (Proverbs 25:2 ESV).

God speaks to you in your dreams as an invitation. You might wonder why God doesn't just make Himself plain. Why does He use parables and symbols in dreams that are sometimes difficult to decipher? Often, only the spiritually curious will conduct due diligence on the dream. Often, only the adventurous will go on a treasure hunt with the Holy Spirit to find the gold in the dream.

Isaiah explained it first, then Jesus quoted the Old Testament prophet in His New Testament discourse. In the parable of the farmer scattering seed, Jesus spoke of seeds that fell on the footpath, on shallow soil, among thorns, and on fertile soil. It seems most people didn't get the drift, but His disciples had something the Pharisees did not—spiritual curiosity, asking, "Why do you use parables when you talk to the people?" (Matt. 13:10). Jesus replied:

> *You are permitted to understand the secrets of the Kingdom of Heaven, but others are not. To those who listen to my teaching, more understanding will be given, and they will have an abundance of knowledge. But for those who are not listening, even what little understanding they have will be taken away from them. That is why I use these parables,*
>
> *For they look, but they don't really see. They hear, but they don't really listen or understand* (Matthew 13:11-13).

Jesus never failed to interpret parables to those who had a desire to understand the interpretation. Much the same, the Holy Spirit will not refuse to help you interpret a dream. But you have to be spiritually curious. You many times have to go on that treasure hunt with Him, searching the Scriptures, praying and meditating on the dream. Solomon put it this way:

> *God conceals the revelation of his word in the hiding place of his glory. But the honor of kings is revealed by how they thoroughly search out the deeper meaning of all that God says* (Proverbs 25:2 TPT).

— *Prayer* —

Father, in the name of Jesus, make me spiritually curious. Inspire in me an inquisitiveness that is not satisfied with a surface-level revelation. Lead me and guide me into the deeper truths in my dreams, layer by layer, as I am diligent to seek out Your glorious truths.

Ask and Keep on Asking

"This is what the Lord says—the Lord who made the earth, who formed and established it, whose name is the Lord: Ask me and I will tell you remarkable secrets you do not know about things to come" (Jeremiah 33:2-3).

Many prophets wait until "the word of the Lord comes unto them saying" to gather prophetic insight into a situation. There is a time to wait and there is a time to inquire. In fact, the inquiring is often followed by waiting, but without inquiring you may be waiting for longer than you'd like. God put a burden on Jeremiah to ask Him about His secrets.

See, you can't just assume God is going to randomly share His secrets while you are in the shower or driving to church. He does, of course, at times interrupt us with revelation. But, even still, I believe those random revelatory interruptions are often a delayed answer to inquiries. And I believe David understood this. Psalm 27:4 reads:

One thing have I asked of the Lord, that will I seek, inquire for, and [insistently] require: that I may dwell in the house of the Lord [in His presence] all the days of my life, to behold and gaze upon the beauty [the sweet attractiveness and the delightful loveliness] of the Lord and to meditate, consider, and inquire in His temple (AMPC).

Look at the spirit in which David was inquiring. He wasn't just inquiring. He was requiring insistently. He wasn't just inquiring for information about his battles. He was inquiring about God's emotions. He didn't just want to hear what God had to say. He wanted to know how God felt about it. This is next level listening.

When we inquire of the Lord and wait on Him for an answer, He will share with us remarkable secrets about things to come that we can't imagine. But if our inquiry stops there, we are stopping short of an encounter with His heart that helps us deliver His truth in love—even when the truth is difficult to hear.

Inquire insistently. Wait patiently. And feel deeply God's emotions in the secrets He is sharing with your heart. In doing so, you truly become one with Him in your prophetic ministry.

— *Prayer* —

Father, throughout Your Word You have invited me to ask and keep asking. Help me make both asking and waiting a habit. Lead me to ask the right questions at the right time so I can advance Your purposes through my prophetic ministry.

Is There Not a Cause?

"Speak up for those who cannot speak for themselves; ensure justice for those being crushed. Yes, speak up for the poor and helpless, and see that they get justice" (Proverbs 31:8-9).

Being a prophet isn't all about predicting the future. That's where some in the modern-day prophetic movement get it wrong. Being a prophet is also about being a voice for the voiceless.

The world can take Kingdom justice to an extreme, but make no mistake—God is the God of justice who loves all people and wants them to be treated humanely even if they don't know Him.

God is raising up Kingdom justice prophets. Some may ask, "What is a Kingdom justice prophet?" If you look at Martin Luther King Jr., you are looking at a twentieth century Kingdom justice prophet. Think of what social justice is—crying out against unfair inequalities in the realms of opportunities, wealth, or rights. Most prophets have a social justice cause, but God has bent some to be major social justice voices and to prophesy into these causes and against oppressors.

Social justice is the view that everyone deserves equal economic, political, and social rights and opportunities. It's the concept of fair and just relations between individuals and society. In America, for example, we say, "One nation, under God, with liberty and justice for all." But that's not the reality. Kingdom justice is perhaps a purer form because it depends on the laws of God and not the laws of man.

True prophets hate what God hates. "For I, the Lord, love justice. I hate robbery and wrongdoing. I will faithfully reward my people for their suffering and make an everlasting covenant with them" (Isa. 61:8). God hates injustice, so prophets hate injustice. God loves justice, so prophets love justice.

Amos was a Kingdom justice prophet, as were many other prophets in the Bible. Amos, though, is consider by many to be a model of the Kingdom justice prophet. Study his life and ministry in the Bible and you will discern the reasons why.

The Kingdom justice prophets need to make more noise, and they will because God will impress upon their spirits the need to cry out—even if the world won't listen. What's your cause?

— *Prayer* —

Father, in the name of Jesus, show me the cause You have called me to champion. Just as David cried out in the face of Goliath's wrath against Israel, "Is there not a cause?"—give me a cause to stand for and to prophesy into. Give me a burning desire for my justice assignment.

The End-Times Prophet

"This is a revelation from Jesus Christ, which God gave him to show his servants the events that must soon take place..." (Revelation 1:1).

The signs of the times are all around us. Some are questioning if we are in the beginning of the Tribulation. Others are sure we're at least at the beginning of sorrows. Still others suggest that some of the trumpets named in the Book of Revelation have already sounded. I don't know about all that, but I do know this: Jesus expects us to discern the signs of the times. As a matter of fact, He rebuked the Pharisees in His day for not discerning the signs of the time (see Matt. 16:3).

It doesn't take a prophet to see the signs of the times and the reality that we're getting closer to the Lord's return, but it does take a prophet to help the Body of Christ navigate the end times. Consider Paul the apostle's prophecy in 2 Timothy 3:1-5:

You should know this, Timothy, that in the last days there will be very difficult times. For people will love only themselves and their money. They will be boastful and proud, scoffing at God, disobedient to their parents, and ungrateful. They will consider nothing sacred.

They will be unloving and unforgiving; they will slander others and have no self-control. They will be cruel and hate what is good. They will betray their friends, be reckless, be puffed up with pride, and love pleasure rather than God. They will act religious, but they will reject the power that could make them godly. Stay away from people like that!

So what is the charge of an end-time prophet? First, let me clarify what the charge is not. The charge is not to pronounce judgment, doom, and gloom on the world. The charge of an end-times prophet, rather, is to pray in agreement with what the Lord is preparing to do in the earth, and then prepare a people for the Lord.

You can fulfill that call by understanding what the prophets in the Bible prayed about the end times so you can rightly divide the word of truth, point people to the nearness of His coming, and share messages of warning mixed with hope that wake up the world and bring an urgency to the church to reap the final harvest. Ask the Holy Spirit to help you navigate the end times with wisdom and grace.

— *Prayer* —

Father, in the name of Jesus, help me discern the signs of the times. Help me discern how You want the Body of Christ to respond to the signs of the times. Equip me to be an end-times equipper, leading the Bride to prepare for the soon coming Bridegroom, King, and Judge.

Being a Faithful Witness

"From Jesus Christ, the faithful witness, the firstborn from the dead, and the ruler over the kings of the earth..." (Revelation 1:5 NKJV).

What's your prophetic reputation? Are you known as the prophet who refuses to water down—or, worse, manufacture—a prophetic word to tickle the ears of those listening, or will you speak the prophecy boldly despite the persecution it may bring you?

Would you be willing to go to jail to maintain the purity of your prophetic ministry? Or would you instead go along with the hundreds of other prophets who give way to spirits of divination, Jezebel spirits, witchcraft, or lying spirits in order to make hearers happy (and keep the offerings pouring in)? Put another way, will you be like Ahab's prophets or like Micaiah?

Ahab's prophets told the king whatever he wanted to hear. Micaiah told him what he never hoped to hear: he would die in battle. And that's when the persecution began. Ahab completely disregarded the true prophetic word, even though the Lord was gracious enough to reveal what was going on behind the scenes.

Zedekiah, son of Kenaanah, slapped Micaiah in the face. Ahab ordered Micaiah put in prison with nothing but bread and water until his safe return. For Micaiah's part, he didn't back down from his God-breathed prophecy, boldly telling Ahab that if he ever returns safely, the Lord had not spoken through him (see 1 Kings 22:24-28).

Of course, Micaiah was right. Ahab was killed in battle. We don't know if the prophet ever got out of prison or not. But Micaiah was a good and faithful witness for the Lord. Even if his earthly fate was to die in prison for his prophetic purity, he gains in eternity. Unfortunately, too many in today's prophetic ministry have a temporal view rather than an eternal view of their calling.

Many would rather hang out in Ahab's house than in caves or prisons eating bread and water. But, modern-day prophets, I urge you to remember Micaiah. He set the example for us. Let the Micaiahs arise in this prophetic generation and be faithful witnesses to the truth!

— *Prayer* —

Father, in the name of Jesus, would You impart to me the bold, uncompromising spirit Micaiah carried? Would You help me to stay the course of the prophetic message You have put on my heart even when it means I could lose everything? I want to be found faithful.

Beware Strange Fire

"And Nadab and Abihu, the sons of Aaron, took either of them his censer, and put fire therein, and put incense thereon, and offered strange fire before the Lord, which he commanded them not" (Leviticus 10:1 KJV).

Kabbalah. Angel worship. Strange fire. These foreign practices have found their way into the Body of Christ and I'm sad to say the prophetic ministry is too often the door opener for the church. It seems instead of prophets getting into the world, the world is getting into some prophets. The danger is false prophecies, false worship, and even false revival.

What is this strange fire? One interpretation of strange fire is violating a sacred office through self-exaltation, pride, and sin. This was the downfall of Nadab and Abihu, who moved in presumption and moved out of God's timing. Nadab and Abihu failed to sanctify themselves and fashioned their own strange offering instead of what was commanded (see Lev. 10:1). God judged them because He would not receive an unholy mixture. Our God is pure and holy.

What is this strange fire? Strange fire is unauthorized fire. Other translations call it the wrong kind of fire, profane fire, and unholy fire. Aaron's sons did not get their fire from the holy altar of God. Strange fire is more than prophesying out of the soul and innocently thinking it's God. Strange fire "implies not only that they did it of their own proper motion, without any command or authority from God, but that they did it against his command," according to *Benson Commentary*.

What of this strange fire within prophetic ministry? The Lord wants our heartfelt worship, our love, and our sincere petitions that demonstrate we are leaning and relying on Him. He rejects strange fire and He will eventually reject prophetic ministries who continue releasing strange fire and refuse to repent.

Numbers 26:61 relates how offensive this was to God: "But Nadab and Abihu died when they burned before the Lord the wrong kind of fire, different than he had commanded." God does not strike people dead today for operating in strange fire, but it's still foul.

— *Prayer* —

Father, in the name of Jesus, inspire my heart to pursue holiness in my personal life so I will not be deceived by strange voices sharing demonically inspired prophetic revelation in my ministry. I don't want to release strange fire. Break deception off my mind.

Unlocking Warfare Strategies

"Tomorrow, march out against them. You will find them coming up through the ascent of Ziz at the end of the valley that opens into the wilderness of Jeruel. But you will not even need to fight..." (2 Chronicles 20:16-17).

One often-overlooked role of the prophet is to bring wisdom for warfare. In other words, prophets can prophesy spiritual warfare strategies for victory to the Body of Christ at large, the local church, or even an individual. We see this specific truth in 2 Chronicles 20. Although 2 Chronicles 20:20 (NKJV) is often used in the context of any prophetic word, "Believe His prophets and you shall prosper" was spoken in the context of warfare.

When King Jehoshaphat was told three kings were planning to attack him, it scared him. But when he sought the Lord, God sent a prophet who issued a heavenly directive that must have seemed like strange strategy for battle. We read it in 2 Chronicles 20:15-17:

"Listen, all you people of Judah and Jerusalem! Listen, King Jehoshaphat! This is what the Lord says: Do not be afraid! Don't be discouraged by this mighty army, for the battle is not yours, but God's. Tomorrow, march out against them. You will find them coming up through the ascent of Ziz at the end of the valley that opens into the wilderness of Jeruel. But you will not even need to fight. Take your positions; then stand still and watch the Lord's victory. He is with you, O people of Judah and Jerusalem. Do not be afraid or discouraged. Go out against them tomorrow, for the Lord is with you!"

It was just as the prophet prophesied. When God's people did their part, He did his part and Jehoshaphat was victorious against the three kings. In my book *Waging Prophetic Warfare*, I list a number of prophetic warfare strategies we find in the battle, including prophetic acts like when Elisha told the king to strike the ground for victory.

That said, we cannot only rely on prophetic warfare strategies from the past for victory today. Prophets need to press into the Lord to discover His wisdom for the right now battle. Seek the Lord for prophetic insight into His way of winning the spiritual wars those in your sphere of influences are fighting.

— *Prayer* —

Father, in the name of Jesus, help me understand my role as a spiritual warfare strategist for the people to whom You've sent me. Give me prophetic insight into the spiritual warfare we are facing and show me how to combat and shut down enemy attacks.

Supernatural Impartations

"For I long to see you, that I may impart to you some spiritual gift, so that you may be established" (Romans 1:11 NKJV).

Impartation is a scriptural concept and an important aspect of prophetic ministry. Prophets receive impartations, but prophets also impart. We see Moses, Samuel, and Elijah imparting anointings in the Old Testament, and Jesus and Paul imparting in the New Testament.

Anointings, including a prophetic anointing, can be imparted many ways, but laying on of hands is the most common in the Bible. Impartation is a divine transfer that releases an ability you didn't have before. You can't learn an impartation. You have to receive impartation by faith. The ministry of impartation is clear in the Bible. Paul told the church in Rome:

> *For I long to visit you so I can bring you some spiritual gift that will help you grow strong in the Lord. When we get together, I want to encourage you in your faith, but I also want to be encouraged by yours* (Romans 1:11-12).

Impart in this context simply means "impart" or "give," according to *The KJV New Testament Greek Lexicon*. *Merriam-Webster* defines *impart* as "to give, convey or grant from as if from a store." God has a great storehouse of gifts and He wants to impart what will strengthen you in your calling. *Young's Literal Bible* translates this "to give a share of."

We can receive impartation from God Himself or from anointed men and women through the laying on of hands. I believe we can also receive an impartation by hearing the Word in a Spirit-charged setting through revelation.

When Moses was overburdened leading the Israelites, the Lord imparted the Spirit on him to 70 elders:

> *So Moses went out and reported the Lord's words to the people. He gathered the seventy elders and stationed them around the Tabernacle. And the Lord came down in the cloud and spoke to Moses. Then he gave the seventy elders the same Spirit that was upon Moses. And when the Spirit rested upon them, they prophesied. But this never happened again* (Numbers 11:24-25).

— *Prayer* —

Father, in the name of Jesus, would You order my steps to the people You have ordained to release the spiritual impartations I need to go further into the prophetic ministry You gave me? Would You impart to me from Your Spirit what I need in this season to succeed?

AUGUST

"Remember [and continue to remember] that I told you, 'A servant is not greater than his master.' If they persecuted Me, they will also persecute you. If they kept My word, they will keep yours also. But they will do all these [hurtful] things to you for My name's sake [because you bear My name and are identified with Me], for they do not know the One who sent Me" (John 15:20-21 AMP).

Ichabod Prophets

"She named the child Ichabod (which means 'Where is the glory?'), for she said, 'Israel's glory is gone'" (1 Samuel 4:21).

We've talked about prophesying in the glory. But there's another side to this: prophesying with no glory. Here we find the Ichabod prophets. I call them Ichabod prophets because they are missing a deep revelation of the glory of God, which is the goodness of God.

Instead of edifying the church, Ichabod prophets prophesy harsh words, pronounce judgments with no room for repentance, release curses on people and nations, and celebrate when their witchcraft comes to pass. They may even trumpet an intimacy message, but bitterness supersedes a glory revelation.

We find mention of Ichabod in 1 Samuel 4:20-21. The Ark of God was captured. Eli died and so did his two evil sons. Phineas' wife immediately gave birth when she heard the news.

> *She died in childbirth, but before she passed away the midwives tried to encourage her. "Don't be afraid," they said. "You have a baby boy!" But she did not answer or pay attention to them. She named the child Ichabod (which means "Where is the glory?"), for she said, "Israel's glory is gone."*

The translation of *Ichabod* is somewhat debated. Some theologians say it simply means "no glory." Others say the name actually poses a question: "Where is the glory?" The question, of course, suggests the glory is nowhere to be found. Yet another translator offers the meaning, "Alas! The glory," an expression of bitter sorrow that God's glory is absent.

Moses, the meekest-ever prophet besides Jesus, understood the glory of God despite his assignment to prophesy judgment on Egypt. He once said, "Please show me your glory" (Exod. 33:18 ESV). God responded and caused His goodness to pass before him and called out His name, Yahweh, before Moses. That experience surely marked him for life.

Ichabod prophets do not stand in the Lord's counsel. Ichabod prophets are missing the revelation of God's heart. They aren't prophesying from the glory because they haven't been in praise and worship. They have not stood in His presence. Don't slip into Ichabod's pit.

— *Prayer* —

Father, in the name of Jesus, deliver me from Ichabod tendencies. Warn me if I ever come close to touching the glory that belongs to You. Help me to glorify Your name with my prophetic ministry, and to cultivate an intimacy with You that prepares me to prophesy in the glory.

Surviving Slander Attacks

"He did not retaliate when he was insulted, nor threaten revenge when he suffered. He left his case in the hands of God, who always judges fairly" (1 Peter 2:23).

The spirit of slander attacks prophets at strategic times. Slander seeks to discredit the prophetic voice and is one of Jezebel's favorite weapons. Slander is to make a false spoken statement that causes people to have a bad opinion of someone, according to *Merriam-Webster*. It means to defame, malign, vilify, and asperse, which is a fancy word for a continued attack on one's reputation.

Take heart in this passage from the Sermon on the Mount:

> *God blesses you when people mock you and persecute you and lie about you and say all sorts of evil things against you because you are my followers. Be happy about it! Be very glad! For a great reward awaits you in heaven. And remember, the ancient prophets were persecuted in the same way* (Matthew 5:11-12).

Prophet, how you respond to mistreatment is one of the most important aspects of your spiritual life. When you respond the right way, you climb higher—or go deeper—in the Spirit. In fact, a season of slander is a sure sign that you are up for a promotion. I've learned over the years to transfer my personal rights to God, knowing He will vindicate me amid the slander—or any other mistreatment. You don't want to be like the accuser of the brethren. And you don't want to swap insult for insult (see 1 Pet. 3:9).

God is the judge. He will make the wrong things right in His way and in His timing. Vengeance is His. He will repay (see Rom. 12:19). Don't allow yourself to be overcome with evil; rather, choose to overcome evil with good. Rejoice when you are slandered, knowing that when you respond the right way, you are blessed. Your first response is to pray for those who slander you. And pray. And pray. And pray some more. It keeps your heart clean.

— *Prayer* —

Father, in the name of Jesus, teach me to respond to slander and criticism the way You did. Heal my heart of hurts and wounds that would cause me to lash out and hit back instead of moving in the opposite spirit of my accusers. Help me walk in love.

Cultivating a Lifestyle of Repentance

"But if we confess our sins to him, he is faithful and just to forgive us our sins and to cleanse us from all wickedness" (1 John 1:9).

I love to operate in the office of the prophet and watch others step into that stream. It's refreshing—and it's the sign of a healthy congregation when the Holy Spirit is moving. Where the Spirit of the Lord is given liberty—when we get out of the way and let Him have His way—He will often manifest His gifts in our midst. Of course, the greatest gift of all is His presence. Ultimately, the most important gift of all.

But there is a gift of the Spirit fewer seem to want to exercise in this hour. It's not one of the nine gifts listed in 1 Corinthians 12, but it's a gift from the Spirit of God just the same. It's the gift of repentance. The truth is, we have all fallen short of the glory of God (see Rom. 3:23). In fact, we all fall short of the glory of God every day. That's why we need a Savior, and that's why we are charged with working out our own salvation with fear and trembling (see Phil. 2:12).

If we're not individually walking in a lifestyle of repentance—if we're not exercising this gift from the Spirit of God—it hinders the fullness of our prophetic expression. Again, God doesn't expect us to walk in perfection. He knew every single sin you'd commit before He saved you. But let's remember Israel lost a war against its enemy because there was sin in the camp (see Josh. 7).

As prophets, part of our mandate is to separate the profane from the holy. We must not tolerate sin in our lives or families—or anywhere. But we need to be willing to let the Holy Spirit lead us into a lifestyle of being quick to repent. Prophet, if we aren't willing to repent on a personal level—to exercise this spiritual gift—we cannot decry the conditions in the church or in society. Let's all model the way.

— *Prayer* —

Father, in the name of Jesus, thank You for convicting me of sin so I can repent and You can cleanse me. Thank You for being willing to show me my transgressions without condemning me. Thank You for helping me develop a righteousness-consciousness so I won't want to sin.

Nobody Wants Your Opinion

"Now concerning the virgins [of marriageable age] I have no command of the Lord, but I give my opinion as one who by the Lord's mercy is trustworthy" (1 Corinthians 7:25 AMP).

This may come as a surprise to you, but in the realm of prophetic ministry nobody wants to hear your opinion at an altar call. Don't let that offend or insult you. It's just the reality—people want to know what God is saying to them, not what you think is best for them. Of course, in the context of close relationships people want to know what you think. But if you are not careful, people will take your opinions as prophecy.

Many years ago, I was talking to a friend in an airport about the antichrist. I was pondering the potential that the antichrist may be alive on the earth today. I was explaining my thought process behind my conclusion that it was very possible that people living on the earth today could see the return of the Lord. She rebuked me and said I needed to be more careful. Specifically, she said people may hear me say that and take it as a prophetic word rather than my personal thoughts and opinions.

She was a little abrupt, but she was right. The reality is if you flow in prophetic ministry, you have to be careful not to accidentally lead people astray by sharing your opinion without a disclaimer—and sometimes even with a disclaimer. Some people, particularly those who don't know you, may take everything you say as prophetic when you never intended it to be so.

Much the same, if people know that you flow in prophetic ministry, they will often seek counsel and often take your words as prophetic in nature even if you're just sharing your opinion from experience or natural wisdom. You could accidentally lead someone astray because they are so desperate for a word from God that they take anything you say as a prophecy.

Take this seriously. Some people already have a tendency to interpret your personal prophecy wrong, hearing what they want to hear instead of what the Lord is actually saying. When you wear the prophet's mantle, you need the prophet's wisdom to differentiate between what says you and what says the Lord. Determine to tap into Holy Spirit for this wisdom.

— *Prayer* —

Father, in the name of Jesus, help me to speak with clarity, differentiating between what says the Spirit of God and what says me. Help me not take it for granted that people will rightly judge when I am speaking on my own accord and when I am speaking for the Lord.

What Do You Need to Forthtell?

"But what did you go out to see? A prophet? Yes, I say to you, and more than a prophet. For this is he of whom it is written: 'Behold, I send My messenger before Your face, who will prepare Your way before You'" (Matthew 11:9-10 NKJV).

We've spent a lot of time in prophetic ministry foretelling, but forthtelling is also part of prophetic ministry. *Forthtell* means "to make public" or to "publish abroad," according to *Merriam-Webster*'s dictionary. You could also say to "tell forth." One aspect of forthtelling is to say what God has already said.

There is so much emphasis on prophetic predictions, and that's valid, but what about forthtelling the prophetic word or prophetic warning God already gave until people actually respond? At times, the Lord will have a watchman release a warning from another watchman that was issued a decade ago to remind them of what's coming.

John Paul Jackson's "Perfect Storm" message is a great example. People are re-issuing his warnings about calamities to come, as well as David Wilkerson's serious warnings about America. God may lead you to forthtell a warning from decades past that has not yet come to pass. He may lead you to decreeing a thing until it lands on ears that hear and respond.

According to *Strong's Concordance*, the Greek word for "prophesy" means to "speak forth" in a divinely empowered forthtelling or foretelling. Both foretelling and forthtelling imply direct revelation from the Lord. In other words, you are not forthtelling what you decide to forthtell in the realm of prophetic ministry. God will tell you what to forthtell.

You will be inspired of God to forthtell just as you are inspired by God to foretell. Forthtelling is speaking again what God has already revealed but is still by the unction of His Spirit. As such, forthtelling can challenge the status quo. Forthtelling reveals God's will about the present rather than the future. What do you need to forthtell?

— *Prayer* —

Father, in the name of Jesus, help me to step into the realm of forthtelling. Teach me the value of forthtelling powerful words from the past as much as I value prophesying a fresh word from Your heart. Inspire me to be a student of prophetic history over my nation.

Beware When All Men Speak Well of You

"Woe to you when all men speak well of you, for so did their fathers to the false prophets" (Luke 6:26 NKJV).

I was at a steakhouse in a high tower in Singapore with the leader of a megachurch there, about a half a dozen of his intercessors, and the son of a British revival legend. I was enjoying the scenery, enjoying the company, and enjoying the steak. A few of the intercessors were singing my praises, so to speak, with kind compliments about my prayer ministry. They sort of went on and on and I was a little uncomfortable, though I knew they were sincerely grateful to connect.

Just then, the son of this British revival legend turned to me and said something completely unexpected in the moment: "Woe to you when all men speak well of you, for so did their fathers to the false prophets" (Luke 6:26 NKJV). Of course, he was teasing and we all had a good laugh, but it got me thinking. See, his father was hated by many when he was alive, and he understood the truth Jesus was speaking at perhaps a deeper level than many.

The Message translation of this verse offers a big ouch: "There's trouble ahead when you live only for the approval of others, saying what flatters them, doing what indulges them. Popularity contests are not truth contests—look how many scoundrel preachers were approved by your ancestors! Your task is to be true, not popular."

Remember, in the Old Testament true prophets tended to be persecuted because they prophesied unpopular truths nobody wanted to hear. By contrast, false prophets tended to be celebrated because they told everyone exactly what they wanted to hear. The false prophets were proven wrong again and again, yet people still preferred their ministry.

Unfortunately, it's not completely different today. The pillow and prosperity prophets are among the most popular whereas the true prophets are more often shunned. I've always said this: If you are not turning over any apple carts or tipping over any sacred cows, you probably aren't speaking the true word of the Lord.

— *Prayer* —

Father, in the name of Jesus, teach me not to give too much of an ear to rejection or praise. Help me keep my eyes on You so I can do what I see You do despite what others think. Give me a humble heart and a thick skin so I can respond rightly to persecution and celebration.

Prophesy Back to the Devil

"Today the Lord will conquer you, and I will kill you and cut off your head..."
(1 Samuel 17:46).

When David faced Goliath at the battle line, Goliath prophesied curses over David's life. Goliath prophesied, "I'll give your flesh to the birds and wild animals!" (1 Sam. 17:44). Goliath's prophetic curses did not phase David's faith. Instead, David prophesied back to Goliath:

"You come to me with sword, spear, and javelin, but I come to you in the name of the Lord of Heaven's Armies—the God of the armies of Israel, whom you have defied. Today the Lord will conquer you, and I will kill you and cut off your head. And then I will give the dead bodies of your men to the birds and wild animals, and the whole world will know that there is a God in Israel!" (1 Samuel 17:45-46)

You know how the story ended. Unfortunately, Elijah didn't learn from David's strategy. When Jezebel sent a messenger to Elijah prophesying a death threat, Elijah didn't prophesy back to the wicked queen. Instead, he ran and hid in a cave. Prophets will always have to contend with Jezebels and Goliaths—and other enemies. Vain imaginations hit the mind, which is the battlefield. One way to victory is to prophesy back to the devil.

As recorded in my devotional *Victory Decrees*, I heard the Lord say:

The enemy loves to prophesy lies to your soul. Prophesy back to the devil. Consider how Goliath prophesied to David. The giant prophesied David's fate was death. David did not run from the battle line in fear and trembling. David prophesied back to the enemy. David prophesied the fate of the devil that would dare to come against his God. David knew My voice and My will. So do you. Prophesy My will to the enemy that's prophesying lies to your soul.

This is a prophetic warfare strategy that works every time. Don't hesitate to try it in your next encounter with the wicked one.

— *Prayer* —

Father, in the name of Jesus, help me war like Christ, declaring to the enemy of my soul what is written in Your Word. Remind me when the enemy is releasing terror prophecies to prophesy his demise by the Spirit of might that rests upon me. I decree my Goliaths will fall.

If You Have a Price, Jezebel Will Find It

"Now therefore, send and gather all Israel to me on Mount Carmel, the four hundred and fifty prophets of Baal, and the four hundred prophets of Asherah, who eat at Jezebel's table" (1 Kings 18:19 NKJV).

Let me say that again. *If you have a price, Jezebel will find it.* The prophets who ate at Jezebel's table had a price, and Jezebel not only found it—she paid it. Little did they know the price they would ultimately pay for the compromise. Jezebel always expects a payback for the paycheck.

Think about it for a minute. While the true prophets of the Lord in 1 Kings 18 had a meager existence living on the bread and water Obadiah fed them while hidden in a cave, the false yes-man prophets of Jezebel were on the government's payroll and living the high life. They had the best food and wine. They were sitting among royalty.

According to *The Dakes*, Jezebel employed 450 prophets of Baal and 400 prophets of Asherah. As I calculate in the pages of my book *The Spiritual Warrior's Guide to Defeating Jezebel*, even if feeding them only cost $15 a day, which is a low estimate, keeping these false prophets on the payroll would cost the kingdom of Israel $12,750 a day. That's $89,250 a week, $357,000 a month, and nearly $4.3 million a year. John warned:

> *Do not love this world nor the things it offers you, for when you love the world, you do not have the love of the Father in you. For the world offers only a craving for physical pleasure, a craving for everything we see, and pride in our achievements and possessions. These are not from the Father, but are from this world. And this world is fading away, along with everything that people crave. But anyone who does what pleases God will live forever* (1 John 2:15-17).

Jezebel paid a high price in a time of famine. In exchange for telling Jezebel and Ahab what they wanted to hear, they were privileged. But they were also compromised. Do you have a price?

— *Prayer* —

Father, in the name of Jesus, deliver me from the lust of the flesh, the lust of the eyes, and the pride of life. Root out anything in me that would cause me to chase after idols. I declare am willing to pay Your price and I am not for sale.

Standing in the Counsel of the Lord

"But if they had stood in My counsel, and had caused My people to hear My words, then they would have turned them from their evil way and from the evil of their doings" (Jeremiah 23:22 NKJV).

"Standing in the council of the Lord" is a buzz phrase in the prophetic movement. The New Living Translation modernizes it a bit, "If they had stood before me and listened to me, they would have spoken my words, and they would have turned my people from their evil ways and deeds" (Jer. 23:22). But let's ponder on the "stood in my council" language for a moment.

The idea of standing here is not a casual one. "Stand" comes from the Hebrew word *amad*. According to *The KJV Old Testament Hebrew Lexicon*, it means to present yourself before the king. It means not only to stand but to take one's stand. It means to endure, to stop moving and stand still, to come to the scene and remain there, to station yourself and stand firm.

Again, this is not a casual meeting. This is an expectant waiting. This is a lingering in the presence of God with a firm resolve to hear His heart. This is a post for watching, seeing, and listening so that you can share God's will with the church. It implies a formal meeting you enter with the attitude of maintaining your position for as long as necessary.

Then there's the counsel, which comes from the Hebrew word *cowd*. It's a secret place that few enter into, perhaps not because it's inaccessible but because of the persistence it takes to enter into that dimension. Entering into the counsel demands a commitment to cultivating intimacy with the Lord.

Before Moses gave the Israelites instruction, he could be found standing in the council of the Lord: "It was Moses' practice to take the Tent of Meeting and set it up some distance from the camp" (Exod. 33:7). "Inside the Tent of Meeting, the Lord would speak to Moses face to face, as one speaks to a friend. Afterward Moses would return to the camp" (Exod. 33:11). The question is, where will you pitch your tent?

— *Prayer* —

Father, in the name of Jesus, give me the wherewithal to stand in Your counsel daily. Help me press past the distractions and the flesh and into the meeting place and just wait. Help me not to rush our meeting. Speak, Lord, for Your servant is listening.

When Prophets Are Too Social

"Let your conversation be gracious and attractive so that you will have the right response for everyone" (Colossians 4:6).

Imagine if the disciples had social media today. John and James, the sons of thunder, would have been posting on Facebook about how Samaria deserved to be blasted with the fire of God for not letting Jesus walk through the region during His travels. Jesus would have told them to take down the post.

After Elisha's prophetic instruction brought healing to Naaman's leprosy, young Gehazi would have been taking a selfie with the army commander as he picked up his reward. When Saul built a monument to himself, he would have had chroniclers there to paint a portrait of the historic event (maybe he did).

Social media is a blessing because it helps us distribute our prophetic words to the masses. We reach people we would never otherwise find with words of life and words of warning. But sometimes social media can be too social. By that I mean we can forget that not everything belongs on social media—and it's not a revenge tool.

Prophetic wisdom on social media doesn't attack and tear other people down with passive-aggressive prophecies that aren't prophecies at all, but veiled curses and threats. Ephesians 4:29 says, "Don't use foul or abusive language. Let everything you say be good and helpful, so that your words will be an encouragement to those who hear them."

Prophetic wisdom doesn't release on YouTube a word the Lord spoke in secret for the purpose of prayer. Prophetic wisdom doesn't puff oneself up with post after post of past prophecies that have come true or stretch news headlines to fit a prophecy that was somewhat obscure. Paul wrote, "When people commend themselves, it doesn't count for much. The important thing is for the Lord to commend them" (2 Cor. 10:18).

Here's the point. Social media can be too social for prophets. It can tempt us to tell what we heard when God didn't say to share. It can tempt us to get into silly arguments over petty controversies. It can hinder our prophetic flow. Is it time for a social media fast?

— *Prayer* —

Father, in the name of Jesus, give me a check in my spirit if I am about to share something on social media channels that glorifies myself instead of glorifying Jesus. Impart to me a wisdom to discern what to share and what to keep between You and me in my prayer closet.

God Is Your Only Source

"...Everything I hope for comes from him..." (Psalm 62:5 MSG).

My first mentor in the prophetic made this truth very clear. I remember her looking at me intensely and saying, "A prophet must get everything they need directly from God." As she said those words, her bony finger pointed up toward heaven. I've never forgotten those words, by which she meant that God is not merely the provider of our finances. God is the prophet's only source of anything—ever.

We can't expect to receive the applause of man, nor should we seek it. Our recognition for ministry well done must come from the Lord. Once we make man our source, we're are setting ourselves up for prophetic compromise. God put it this way to Jeremiah, "Cursed is the man who trusts in man and makes flesh his strength, whose heart departs from the Lord" (Jer. 17:5 NKJV). Dependence on man's praise eventually turns our hearts away from God.

By contrast, "Blessed is the man who trusts in Him!" (Ps. 34:8 NKJV). Prophet, you must trust Him for recognition, promotion, healing, deliverance, confidants, opportunities, platforms, and anything else you need or think you need in order to sustain your life and ministry. Prophet, you can't look to people for anything, though God will send people to help you.

David understood this, saying, "Every good thing I have comes from you" (Ps. 16:2). And again, "Those who trust in the Lord will lack no good thing" (Ps. 34:10). And again, "The Lord is my shepherd; I have all that I need" (Ps. 23:1). Paul summed it all up this way: "And this same God who takes care of me will supply all your needs from his glorious riches, which have been given to us in Christ Jesus" (Phil. 4:19).

Once you renew your mind to this reality, you can relax and be who God called you to be. You will not fear man. You will not strive from a place of ambition. You will not compare and you will not compete. You will enter into His rest and receive His best by faith. This is every truly successful prophet's lifestyle.

— *Prayer* —

Father, in the name of Jesus, give me a deeper revelation of You as my Provider of anything and everything I could need or even hope for. Root me and ground me in Your love that provides not based on my performance but based on my covenant with You.

Forerunner Prophets

"This hope we have as an anchor of the soul, both sure and steadfast, and which enters the Presence behind the veil, where the forerunner has entered for us, even Jesus, having become High Priest forever according to the order of Melchizedek" (Hebrews 6:19-20 NKJV).

If the world ever needed forerunner prophets, it's now. What is a forerunner prophet? According to *Merriam-Webster's* dictionary, a forerunner is one who precedes and indicates the approach of another. Interestingly enough, on Dictionary.com a definition of *forerunner* is simply "John the Baptist." John the Baptist is one example of a forerunner prophet. He was a forerunner to Jesus. Mark 1:4-8 reads:

> *This messenger was John the Baptist. He was in the wilderness and preached that people should be baptized to show that they had repented of their sins and turned to God to be forgiven. All of Judea, including all the people of Jerusalem, went out to see and hear John. And when they confessed their sins, he baptized them in the Jordan River. His clothes were woven from coarse camel hair, and he wore a leather belt around his waist. For food he ate locusts and wild honey.*
>
> *John announced: "Someone is coming soon who is greater than I am—so much greater that I'm not even worthy to stoop down like a slave and untie the straps of his sandals. I baptize you with water, but he will baptize you with the Holy Spirit!"*

Forerunner prophets see first. Forerunner prophets hear first. Forerunner prophets go first. Forerunner prophets speak first. They are the voice and not the proverbial echo. Forerunner prophets are often in the wilderness and rejected. Forerunner prophets are pioneers in the spirit who take risks to share the mind and will of God, not doom and gloom but at times warnings and bold redemptive truth telling.

Forerunner prophets transition first, for John as a forerunner was also a transitional prophet. John built a bridge between the Old Testament and the New Testament. The forerunner prophets are so vital to announcing God's plans on earth and helping God's people transition that other prophets prophesy their entry.

— *Prayer* —

Father, in the name of Jesus, help me embrace the spirit of the forerunner, who is not typically appreciated in his time but paves the way for a greater move of God. Help me to see, hear, say, and pray like a forerunner with a confidence that a great Christ-centered revival is coming!

Tapping Into Your Prophetic Potential

"For we are God's masterpiece. He has created us anew in Christ Jesus, so we can do the good things he planned for us long ago" (Ephesians 2:10).

When God birthed my prophetic ministry I could hardly walk in it. I probably looked to my elders like a baby horse trying to stand up and walk for the first time. (If you've never seen that, check out a YouTube video so you can truly relate!) Between the fear of man and the spiritual warfare, I kept falling down. But I kept getting back up again until I got my legs under me.

See, I had the potential within me to travel to nations and release strategic prophetic words that shifted atmospheres. But before I could rise up in my high calling I had to learn how to tap into the prophetic potential within me. And, honestly, that's an ongoing process. I've discovered I have more prophetic potential than I realized—and so do you.

God wants to share profound revelations with you and through you, but you have to tap into your prophetic potential. Potential is something that is existing in possibility and something capable of development into actuality, according to *Merriam-Webster*'s dictionary. Your potential is your ability. God gave you your prophetic ability. He gave you the potential. But it's up to you to tap into it. Here's what I learned about the process.

You need to set some Spirit-led goals for your prophetic maturity, such as hearing God's voice more clearly, diversifying your prophetic reception, or overcoming fear. You also need to set what I call prophetic priorities. Ask yourself, "What new priorities do you have to set to meet those goals to tap deeper into your prophetic potential?"

The Holy Spirit will give you a plan to tap into your highest and best potential. It's your responsibility to follow that plan. He is your Teacher, but you may need to get continued prophetic education from an elder prophet. He is your Leader, but you may need to submit your ministry to someone who has walked where you haven't walked. What's your prophetic potential?

— *Prayer* —

Father, in the name of Jesus, help me discover my prophetic potential. I want to make full use of the prophetic anointing You put on my life to help as many people as possible. Teach me how to recognize and tap into the depths of my potential. I want to pour out my life for You.

The Gall of Bitterness

"For I perceive that thou art in the gall of bitterness, and in the bond of iniquity" (Acts 8:23 KJV).

Bitter prophets are rising, and some of it is the fault of a church who rejected them. Sometimes they are bitter because of abandonment issues in their childhood. Other times an orphan spirit influences them and they feel prophecy is their road to acceptance. Still others have been betrayed. Regardless of the reason why we're seeing more bitterness polluting the prophetic, it's each individual's responsibility to keep their heart clean.

The Lord impressed these words on my heart:

Beware the bitter prophets releasing bitter curses out of their bitter hearts. Pray for them, because their end will be bitter if they don't repent. They are bringing great harm to My Body with manipulative maneuvers that seduce, deceive, and derail. Don't come into agreement with the bitterness, lest you be defiled also. God shall not be mocked; whatever a man sows he will reap. Bless and do not curse.

The Greek word for "bitter" in James 3:11 means "extreme wickedness; a bitter root, and so producing bitter fruit; and bitter hatred," according to *The KJV New Testament Greek Lexicon*. Bitterness is extremely wicked in the eyes of the Lord and correlates to hatred. It's no wonder that bitterness opens the door to demonic oppression. The bitter heart is a darkened heart. First John 2:11 says, "But whoever hates his brother is in darkness, and walks in darkness, and does not know where he is going, because the darkness has blinded his eyes" (MEV).

Bitterness, then, is connected to spiritual blindness and deception. That's why Paul warns the church at Ephesus to, "Let all bitterness, wrath, anger, outbursts, and blasphemies, with all malice, be taken away from you. And be kind one to another, tenderhearted, forgiving one another, just as God in Christ also forgave you" (Eph. 4:31-32 MEV). If you have bitterness in your heart, you won't discern a bitter divining prophet because you have common ground. Ask the Lord to deal with any bitterness in your heart.

— *Prayer* —

Father, in the name of Jesus, deliver me from the gall of bitterness and a harsh spirit. Deliver me from hostility that causes me to see people as my enemy. Deliver me from hard-heartedness that causes me to speak with words and tones that don't reveal Your goodness.

How to Build Your Prophetic Ministry

"Anyone who listens to my teaching and follows it is wise, like a person who builds a house on solid rock" (Matthew 7:24).

Some prophets build their entire prophetic ministries on supernatural encounters, dreams, visions, and prophecies. Nearly every day, it's a new prophetic prediction, dramatic encounter, or life-changing epiphany. Indeed, some of these purveyors of prophecy seem to walk in more revelation than Paul the apostle himself, except their revelations are antibiblical. Yes, antibiblical not just extrabiblical. These ones are building on the wrong foundation.

Part of the problem is the culture within some camps of charismatic Christianity that values gifts of the Spirit over the Word of God—or at least puts gifts on par with the Word of God as evidence of someone's spirituality. Many don't discern the motive of the minister is merely to gain a following. I call this "platforms and paychecks." This is not new. It's has been going on since Old Testament times.

If you build your ministry on prophecy, supernatural encounters, and anything else beyond the Word of God, it won't last. Hear me, as I speak this truth in love: You can't sustain that level of revelation. You will begin to miss your predictions of world events, and people will catch on even if you bury the wrong prophecy in a slew of "accurate" words. Prophets can make all the excuses in the world why the prophetic word didn't come to pass, but that doesn't mean the word was accurate. There's only one way to build a lasting prophetic ministry. Jesus put it best in Matthew 7:24-27:

"Anyone who listens to my teaching and follows it is wise, like a person who builds a house on solid rock. Though the rain comes in torrents and the floodwaters rise and the winds beat against that house, it won't collapse because it is built on bedrock. But anyone who hears my teaching and doesn't obey it is foolish, like a person who builds a house on sand. When the rains and floods come and the winds beat against that house, it will collapse with a mighty crash."

— *Prayer* —

Father, in the name of Jesus, keep reminding me to build on Your written Word and not just on prophetic words. Teach me to value Your Scriptures, which never fail, above prophecies that can fail. Warn me if I am building my ministry on anything but Your Word.

Keep Pointing to Jesus

"Looking unto Jesus, the author and finisher of our faith, who for the joy that was set before Him endured the cross, despising the shame, and has sat down at the right hand of the throne of God" (Hebrews 12:2 NKJV).

Saul was quite a mess. It was bad enough he was disobedient to the word of the Lord. Making matters worse, he was off building a monument to himself when Samuel came looking for him (see 1 Sam. 15:12). Can you imagine?

Normally, people make statues of heroes after they are dead. So, who would commission a statue of themselves while they are living? Self-idolatry was a mark of Saul's kingdom. If we're not careful, we can set ourselves up as idols or allow others to position us as idols. Deuteronomy 13:1-3 reads:

> *Suppose there are prophets among you or those who dream dreams about the future, and they promise you signs or miracles, and the predicted signs or miracles occur. If they then say, "Come, let us worship other gods"—gods you have not known before—do not listen to them. The Lord your God is testing you to see if you truly love him with all your heart and soul.*

No matter how spectacular the prophecy is, or how deep the supposed encounter in which the revelation came, if the prophet puts their voice, their supernatural experience, their track record, or anything else above the Word of God, Jehovah says don't listen to that prophet.

We can't help it if some people see us as larger than life, but New Testament prophets need to teach the saints that they don't have exclusivity on hearing God's voice or knowing His secrets. We need to keep pointing them back to Jesus.

In the Old Testament, few heard directly from the Lord besides the prophets. But in the new covenant, every believer can hear from God. Hebrews 1:1-2 reads, "God, who at various times and in diverse ways spoke long ago to the fathers through the prophets, has in these last days spoken to us by His Son, whom He has appointed heir of all things, and through whom He made the world" (MEV). What did the Son say to the church? Well, He said, "My sheep listen to my voice; I know them, and they follow me" (John 10:27).

— *Prayer* —

Father, in the name of Jesus, help me resist the temptation to allow people to idolize me and my ministry. Remind me, again and again, to point those who follow my ministry back to the One I follow—Jesus Christ. Help me never to touch Your glory in my prophetic ministry.

Don't Take It So Personally

"But neither King Zedekiah nor his attendants nor the people who were left in the land listened to what the Lord said through Jeremiah" (Jeremiah 37:2).

I've known more than a handful of prophets—and received letters from others—who are frustrated about how their prophetic utterances are received. Some are upset because they can't get an audience with the pastor or the apostle. Others are upset because they aren't given a platform to release a prophetic word. Still others are upset because they release the prophetic word and no one acts on it.

Perhaps Jeremiah was part of this latter group. God gave him an audience with world leaders. But the Bible says no one was willing to hear what he had to say. Sure, they may have heard him. But they weren't doers of the word and ended up deceived (see James 1:22). Jeremiah may have been upset, but if he was it didn't show it. That's because Jeremiah may have been young, but he wasn't immature.

Jeremiah didn't take it personally when people didn't receive his prophetic counsel. And neither should we. Don't take the rejection personally. If you are delivering a true word from the Lord, the people aren't rejecting you. They are rejecting the word of the Lord. Don't be like Ahithophel, one of David's counselors. Second Samuel 16:23 tells us, "For every word Ahithophel spoke seemed as wise as though it had come directly from the mouth of God."

When Absalom ran David out of Jerusalem, Ahithophel joined the traitor son and counseled him as he had counseled David. But Absalom rejected his prophetic counsel. Ahithophel took it so personally he saddled a donkey, took off to his hometown, put his household in order, hanged himself, and died (see 2 Sam. 17:23). What a tragedy!

Remember, if you are prophesying God's mind, people aren't rejecting you. They are rejecting God's word. Don't take it personally. It's our job to release the prophetic word and encourage people to take action in faith. But once we've done that, it's out of our hands. Next time someone doesn't act on a prophetic word you've released, let it go and get on with God. If you have rejection issues, ask God to deliver you so you will not be tempted to hang up your mantle.

— *Prayer* —

Father, in the name of Jesus, free me from every remnant of rejection. Help me take on the right perspective when people reject the word from Your heart that You downloaded into my spirit. Teach me to not internalize the rejection but to reject rejection.

Beware False Prophetics

"Beware of false prophets who come disguised as harmless sheep but are really vicious wolves. You can identify them by their fruit, that is, by the way they act. Can you pick grapes from thornbushes, or figs from thistles? A good tree produces good fruit, and a bad tree produces bad fruit. A good tree can't produce bad fruit, and a bad tree can't produce good fruit. So every tree that does not produce good fruit is chopped down and thrown into the fire. Yes, just as you can identify a tree by its fruit, so you can identify people by their actions" (Matthew 7:15-20).

Jesus' warning at the end of the Sermon on the Mount is certainly a word for our age. I've witnessed the rise of false prophets—and false prophetic operations—and I am sure you have too. You know them by their fruit. False prophets prophesy falsely to manipulate souls. False prophets merchandise the saints to line their pockets with money. False prophets promise miracles that never materialize.

True prophets need to discern false counterparts and counterfeits because we don't want to run in their company. Your prophetic reputation matters. You don't want to accidentally endorse a false prophet by working with one. It can be difficult to discern a false prophet because it takes time for fruit to grow. That's why it's important not to jump into relationships too quickly. You certainly can't control who else appears on a platform with you, but wisdom wouldn't knowingly join a lineup of speakers filled with prophetic phonies.

On the flip side, we need to examine our own hearts for any hint of bad fruit. True prophets don't start out as false prophets. We tend to the narrow path until some sort of temptation—the lust of the eyes, the lust of the flesh, or the pride of life—takes us onto a broad path that leads to destruction. Anyone can be deceived, so we walk in humility and examine ourselves and not just others.

Prophet, frequently ask the Lord to reveal to you any wicked way in your own heart. You take a lot of hits as a prophet and the residue of resentment can build up in your soul without your recognition. Striving in ministry is a danger that can lead you astray. Repent of any bitterness, resentment, or unforgiveness that springs up in your soul, as well any disobedience. Ask Him to strengthen you against temptations that will arise.

— *Prayer* —

Father, in the name of Jesus, I repent for sins of commission and omission. I release all bitterness, unforgiveness, and resentment. I reject all pride and self-ambition and striving. Please, strengthen me against temptations that will arise on my prophetic journey.

Two Sides of the Prophetic Coin

"Let these false prophets tell their dreams, but let my true messengers faithfully proclaim my every word. There is a difference between straw and grain!" (Jeremiah 23:28)

When God called you into prophetic ministry, He gave you an office, a grace, a gift, and an anointing—and He expects you to use them. Whatever your prophetic expression—dreams, visions, hearing the Word of the Lord, etc.—He expects you to use your gifts responsibly to edify people, warn of danger, build the church, and advance the Kingdom. He expects you to be sensitive to His heart so You can communicate His heart.

Indeed, the prophetic mantle comes with a great responsibility. It's irresponsible to prophesy without an unction of the Holy Spirit, and it's also irresponsible not to tell a dream or speak His word faithfully when He gives you that unction. If you rush out ahead of the Lord when He has not told you to speak, or if you timidly hang back in fear when He tells you to release your prophetic utterance, you are in sin because whatever is not of faith is sin (see Rom. 14:23).

Seers must also be careful not to embellish, add to, misinterpret, or misapply a visual revelation. You can have a bona fide seer experience and miss the interpretation. You can have an authentic encounter and misapply it to a situation. Either way, you've got wrong results and may accidentally lead people astray. The Contemporary English Version of Jeremiah 23:28 warns, "But when prophets speak for me, they must say only what I have told them."

I love Hebrews 4:16, which invites us to "come boldly to the throne of our gracious God. There we will receive his mercy, and we will find grace to help us when we need it most." We must take this advice, and I believe when we do we will emerge boldly from the throne of grace to release the prophetic utterance, interpretation, and application with which He has trusted us. Prophets are the voice of God in the earth. Would we dare to allow fear to silence His voice? Or will we boldly declare "thus saith the Lord" in faith?

Commit yourself to accuracy in the spirit not just in hearing the word, seeing the vision, or receiving and recording the dream, but also in boldly broadcasting prophetic discoveries with simplicity so people can walk in the truth that sets them free.

— *Prayer* —

Father, in the name of Jesus, give me courage to use my gift boldly and compassionately. Give me the ability to comprehend what You are saying to the church and the wisdom to apply the revelation to the situation it concerns.

Settling Into Your Office

"Those who are planted in the house of the Lord shall flourish in the courts of our God" (Psalm 92:13 NKJV).

I have an office with a desk in my South Florida church. I rarely use it because I am always in the sanctuary doing ministry or in the green room hanging out with staff. But the office is there. You have an office in your church, too, even if it doesn't have a desk, chairs, and a door you can close for privacy. Let me put it another way: Your office is in the church.

What do I mean by that? Prophets can be some of the most popular itinerant ministers in the Body of Christ. I know from experience, when you travel you are out of your own church most Sundays because you are ministering in other churches. A wise apostle once told me I should commit to being at my church at least three times a month (especially since I lead it!). She was right. Prophets need community and itinerant ministry doesn't fully fulfill that need.

I believe prophets should belong to a church family just like every other member of the Body of Christ. Prophet, you need to do more than ministry—you need to receive ministry. You need to submit your soul to someone who will watch over you and pray for you when you face trials, counsel you when you go through a crisis, and stand with you in warfare.

The apostles in the Book of Acts frequented the temple. Jesus, our prototype prophet, went to church. Luke 4:16 tells us, "When he came to the village of Nazareth, his boyhood home, he went as usual to the synagogue on the Sabbath and stood up to read the Scriptures." Remember, church was Jesus' idea—and the writer of Hebrews knew this, writing:

> *Let us think of ways to motivate one another to acts of love and good works. And let us not neglect our meeting together, as some people do, but encourage one another, especially now that the day of his return is drawing near* (Hebrews 10:24-25).

— *Prayer* —

Father, in the name of Jesus, show me the value of being truly plugged into the church—not just to minister but to receive the benefits of community, personal ministry, and accountability. Remind me in all my extracurricular ministry to root and ground myself in a local body.

When You're Running on Empty

"The Sovereign Lord has given me his words of wisdom, so that I know how to comfort the weary. Morning by morning he wakens me and opens my understanding to his will" (Isaiah 50:4).

When you are running on empty, you may be tempted to prophesy out of your gifting instead of prophesying out of an unction. While we can certainly prophesy out of our gifting, we don't want to habitually prophesy out of our gift alone. We want to prophesy out of a presence. We want to prophesy with an anointing that breaks yokes.

When you are pouring out and pouring out and pouring out—especially prophetically—it's critical to take the time to fill yourself up or you will burn out and dry up. Rather than your prophetic utterances being bathed in the presence of God, they may feel forced. Instead of experiencing a free flow, you will begin to feel like you are grinding out prophetic words on demand. That's too much pressure.

The Spirit brings life and freedom. The Word builds us up. Striving and continually moving beyond the grace of God wears us down and eventually wears us out. So when we feel like we're running on empty, we need to pull off the prophetic highway and refuel. We need to spend time with the Lord allowing Him to fill us up again. We need to meditate on the Word to build up our faith, because faith fuels our prophecy.

Jesus put it this way: "Come to me, all of you who are weary and carry heavy burdens, and I will give you rest. Take my yoke upon you. Let me teach you, because I am humble and gentle at heart, and you will find rest for your souls. For my yoke is easy to bear, and the burden I give you is light" (Matt. 11:28-30). And again, "Jesus stood and shouted to the crowds, 'Anyone who is thirsty may come to me!'" (John 7:37).

It's easy to slip into Martha mode in your prophetic ministry because there are so many people who need a living word from God. But remember, sometimes you have to trade the Martha mantle for the Mary mantle and sit at His feet and learn of Him.

— *Prayer* —

Father, in the name of Jesus, show me when I am nearing the edge of burnout so I do not weary myself out and take on burdens You have not called me to carry. Teach me to walk in Your rhythm of grace and to discern I need to seek Your refreshing presence for my weary soul.

Angels of Revelation

"Then I saw another mighty angel coming down from heaven, surrounded by a cloud, with a rainbow over his head. His face shone like the sun, and his feet were like pillars of fire. And in his hand was a small scroll that had been opened..." (Revelation 10:1-2).

Every time I visit Singapore, I get a renewed worldview. It's as if the spirit realm opens up to me and I see with greater clarity. One of my trips there was especially intense. After waking up one morning to a spiritual battle in my room, I heard the Lord say:

> Ancient angels from the company of revelation are going to visit those in this hour who have been experiencing dreams and visions they do not comprehend and cannot understand. I have released companies of revelation angels to expound and explain those deeper truths that many could not bear and the mysteries that have so far only been partially unlocked to a few over the ages.

> I am releasing these angels with a word of caution to My people: satan disguises himself as an angel of light. Stick close to Me, closer than you have ever drawn, and you will avoid deception and enter into a deeper mode of revelation in your daily walk. The unknown will become known in layers and degrees as you demonstrate consistency in the spirit. I am bringing My seers and prophetic people into a new dimension of the revelatory realm where mind cannot comprehend, but angels can explain.

> Just as I sent angels to Daniel and John to bring understanding of what they were seeing, I am dispatching angels on assignment to bring understanding to those who have been crying out for accurate interpretations of things they see and hear as they lay on their bed or as they walk through their days.

> I am dispatching angels on assignment to bring "aha" moments for the purpose of prayer and intercession that brings My will to pass and My Kingdom into the earth in greater measure. I am calling you to incline your ear to Me, to seek first My Kingdom, and to receive My angels of revelation.

Are you ready to receive ancient revelations?

— *Prayer* —

Father, in the name of Jesus, prepare my heart to receive ancient revelations that are relevant to my generation. Help me tap into present-day truth You want to send me through angelic communications like You did with Daniel, Zechariah, and John. Guard me from deception.

The Rise of Media Prophets

"He sends his orders to the world—how swiftly his word flies!" (Psalm 147:15)

Not all scribes in the Bible are prophets, but the many of the prophets were scribes and chroniclers. For all intents and purposes, Moses was a media prophet. Ezekiel was a media prophet. Samuel was a media prophet.

What do I mean by that? Look at the word *media* and its definition. *Media* is "the means of communication, as radio and television, newspapers, magazines, and the Internet, that reach or influence people widely," according to *Merriam-Webster*'s dictionary. A prophet is a person who speaks for God. Media prophets have a public platform that brings the influence of the One to the many—even the masses.

I'm seeing media prophets break into secular media with an understanding of the times and the seasons and telling the world what God wants to do. I see a mantle of wisdom draping the shoulders of media prophets, so they know what to reveal and to whom it should be revealed. I see media prophets cloaked in diplomacy who don't speak "Christianese" so they are relatable in the world.

I love Christian media, but we need media prophets to break the communication barriers and cross over into the secular world. I see media prophets writing fiction books that tell dramatic stories based on prophetic insight that points to Jesus. I see a media prophet rising up to interpret the news through the lens of the Bible, not just end-times events but other current events. I see media prophets sounding the alarm with credibility through channels that have been so far closed to prophetic people.

I see media prophets having a showdown with the psychics that sit on network television and pontificate divination. There is coming a day when prophets sit behind the news desks at CNN, Fox, and MSNBC to share what the Lord is saying, displacing psychics who have held positions on these media mountains. Will you be one of them?

— *Prayer* —

Father, in the name of Jesus, thank You for the voice You have given me. When I am ready, will You open the door for the message You have put on my heart to travel through different media to reach more people? Will You prepare me to stand as a media prophet?

Why God Hides Prophets

"Go to the east and hide by Kerith Brook, near where it enters the Jordan River" (1 Kings 17:3).

While I have been vocal about prophets coming out of hiding, there are times when God hides prophets in obscure places for good reasons. Let's look at Elijah's journey. Elijah's recorded ministry began with making prophetic declarations to an evil king. Look at 1 Kings 17:1-4:

> *Now Elijah, who was from Tishbe in Gilead, told King Ahab, "As surely as the Lord, the God of Israel, lives—the God I serve—there will be no dew or rain during the next few years until I give the word!" Then the Lord said to Elijah, "Go to the east and hide by Kerith Brook, near where it enters the Jordan River. Drink from the brook and eat what the ravens bring you, for I have commanded them to bring you food."*

God put Elijah in hiding just a short time before the prophet called the showdown at Mount Carmel. And notice how God hid him in Kerith, which means "cutting." Kerith was before the Jordan, the place of crossing over. God often wants to cut away a little more of our flesh before the next exploit. Maybe God is cutting some things away from you that will hinder you from transitioning into your next season. Maybe God is preparing you to be a major voice in the nations.

Maybe you are isolated in a cave because God wants you to learn to be dependent on Him for everything. It takes great faith to believe ravens will feed you. Maybe God is about to use you to release a prophetic word to someone to build their faith in a time of famine, like Elijah did with the widow of Zarephath (see 1 Kings 17:13-14).

After the showdown with the false prophets, Jezebel sent a death threat to Elijah. Elijah ran and hid in a cave. The mighty prophet was hidden after his mighty exploit. Maybe God is letting you rest after a battle. Maybe God is positioning you as a wise mentor for the next generation.

Prophet, wherever you find yourself there is a greater prophetic anointing for you. Sometimes God has to hide you before He can reveal you at a greater level. Just make sure you come out of the cave when He calls you.

— *Prayer* —

Father, in the name of Jesus, hide me if You have to. Hide me from Ahab to prepare me for the showdown with the false prophets. Hide me while You cut away things in my heart that hinder my loving obedience to Your Spirit. Help me wait for You to reveal me at the right time.

Straight Prophetic Fire

"For our God is a consuming fire" (Hebrews 12:29 NKJV).

You've probably heard people say, "That was straight fire!" In prophetic circles, that means the word was powerful. But consider this: Something can't carry God's power if it's not pure. For example, we know God's Word is alive and powerful, sharper than any two-edged sword (see Heb. 4:12). And we know why: God's Word is completely pure. David put it this way, "The words of the Lord are pure words: as silver tried in a furnace of earth, purified seven times" (Ps. 12:6 KJV).

If we want our prophetic ministry to be "straight fire" and carry the anointing that breaks yokes and the authority that sends demons fleeing—if we want to operate in prophetic power—we have to pursue pure prophetic fire. I heard the Lord say:

> A purifying fire is coming to the prophetic ministry—a baptism of fire is coming for those who will embrace it and let My fire do its perfect work. Those who resist the fire will be sidelined in the next season. Those who embrace My fire will be led into new realms of prophetic revelation and new levels of accuracy in the Spirit.
>
> Those who understand the purifying work of My fire—the work of My fire to judge sin in your heart and refine you—will enter in willingly. They will walk into the fire freely, knowing that they are coming closer to My heart in the process. I am bringing My fire to the church. Embrace My fire. Don't resist My purifying work in your heart. I have great things stored up for you in the days ahead, but the path is for those holy hearts to walk on.

Will you embrace the fire?

— *Prayer* —

Father, in the name of Jesus, purify my hands, purify my heart, purify my mouth, purify my imaginations, purify my motives. Father, give me the grace to stand in Your holy fire until You have completed Your purification process in my prophetic ministry. I want to be pure.

Creating a Prophetic Culture

"And you should imitate me, just as I imitate Christ" (1 Corinthians 11:1).

Any local body can choose to cultivate a prophetic culture. At Awakening House of Prayer, my home base where I serve as senior leader, we have labored with the Holy Spirit to create an atmosphere where He feels welcome and can move in power and prophecy. Of course, prophetic culture—or any culture—isn't birthed overnight.

What is a culture? Technically, it's a set of beliefs and behaviors, shared attitudes and values, spiritual goals and practices, vocabulary and family. Prophetic cultures don't look the same in every church. Some prophetic cultures are restrictive, wherein only the house prophet can prophesy. Others are freer, where people can share during worship. Some prophetic cultures place an emphasis on dreams and visions, others on presence and glory.

Sure, prophetic cultures may "just happen," especially if you have a lot of prophetic people in any given congregation. But without proper training and accountability you'll see fruits, flakes, nuts—and abuses in prophetic dimensions. We must cultivate and protect the prophetic in our revival hubs, houses of prayer, training centers, and churches.

If we are mindful and intentional about creating a prophetic culture, we'll open a portal of heaven where people who don't normally prophesy will prophesy easily—even if they never prophesied before they got there or after they leave.

Healthy prophetic cultures are shaped where there is a prophet who actively teaches on the prophetic and equips the saints (see Eph. 4:11) and where people can learn and grow without fear of failure. Healthy prophetic cultures have leadership that seeks first the Kingdom of God and His righteousness (see Matt. 6:33) and where there is consistent encouragement for members to seek intimacy with God.

Healthy prophetic cultures include a strong corporate intercessory prayer and fasting focus and a worship experience that allows the Holy Spirit to lead the way. Healthy prophetic cultures foster a culture of honor and refuse to tolerate strife (see 1 Cor. 14:3). What's your prophetic culture and how does it need to change?

— *Prayer* —

Father, in the name of Jesus, teach me how to create or contribute to the prophetic cultures I walk in. Show me how to forward Your prophetic voice not merely through prophecy but through walking in love and honor with everybody at every level of prophetic ministry.

When the Church Hurts Her Prophets

"Most important of all, continue to show deep love for each other, for love covers a multitude of sins" (1 Peter 4:8).

The church has not always been kind to her prophets. Throughout history, prophets have been rejected, maligned, silenced, and even killed. In modern times, we are less likely to see prophets beheaded, but the pain of rejection is real. Church hurt is just as real for prophets as it is for believers seeking to get prophetic equipping.

Have you been hurt in church? What are you supposed to do? How do you handle it? Leave the church? Confront the issue? Bury it? Lash out at the person who hurt you? When people are hurt by a church or church member, how can this conflict be resolved? What does the Bible say about this and how do you practically walk that out?

The very first action to take is prayer. The hurt you feel is real and pretending like you aren't hurt isn't going to bring healing. Sometimes when we get hurt in church folks like to tell us that we have no reason to feel bad and we just need to get over it. Half of that statement is true. We do need to get over it, but it's not always true that we have no reason to feel bad. If someone is spewing malicious gossip behind your back and you find out about it, it stings.

No matter what kind of hurt you're dealing with, don't rush into a confrontation with the offender. Take it to God in prayer. Psalm 50:15 says, "Call upon Me in the day of trouble" (NKJV). That works for a troubled soul just as well as it does any other trouble. Tell Him how you feel and ask Him to heal your wounds. Unless the Lord directs you, keep it to yourself. Trying to explain your hurt could just lead to more hurt. The Lord is your Healer.

— *Prayer* —

Father, in the name of Jesus, help me to stop stuffing my church hurt and, in doing so, opening myself up to Jezebelic influences. Help me forgive those who hurt me and pray for those who rejected me. Give me the mind of Christ on these matters, because Christ knows how I feel.

When the Grace Narrows

"And when he comes, he will convict the world of its sin, and of God's righteousness, and of the coming judgment" (John 16:8).

When we first get born again, it seems all our prayers get answered—and fast. It seems there is very little, if any, spiritual warfare. It's almost like a honeymoon period in a marriage where everything that can go right goes right.

At some point, though, when you begin to step into your high calling—when you accept the mantle of the prophet and begin to speak for the Lord in His name—you will find the grace narrows. You will discern you are being called to walk a finer line than some of your friends and family—or maybe even other prophets. That's been my continual experience. Maybe you can relate.

Many years ago a friend of mine wanted to come over to watch a movie. She brought a movie that was popular at the time with a famous comedian as the star. I didn't even like the cover. Something hit my spirit wrong, but we put in the DVD and started watching. Within 15 minutes, the main character was mocking God—even pretending to be God. I was a relatively new believer then. I had never heard of a mocking spirit or grieving the Holy Spirit, but my spirit inside me was grieved. In fact, I was so grieved I became physically sick to my stomach.

I told my friend I didn't feel the Lord liked this movie and we should top watching it. She called me religious. I told her to take her movie and go home. She was aggravated. I was still grieved and went into prayer. The Lord was grieved, but He did not want me to judge her for being insensitive to His Spirit. See, I was being called to walk a narrower path than she was. Although the movie grieved Him, He did not convict her about watching it. He was only convicting me.

As a prophet, you will be called to walk in a narrower path. Be careful to obey the Holy Spirit—but be equally as careful not to judge others who don't hold the same convictions.

— *Prayer* —

Father, in the name of Jesus, I want to walk the path You've set before me. I know my walk is different from anybody else's. You know what's best for me. Would You help me to walk that fine line as I pursue the narrow path? Would You warn me when I am heading out of bounds?

Stir Up the Gift in You

"Therefore I remind you to stir up the gift of God which is in you through the laying on of my hands" (2 Timothy 1:6 NKJV).

Paul imparted spiritual gifts to people in the churches he planted. In fact, he explicitly told the Romans he wanted to visit them in order to impart a spiritual gift that would establish them (see Rom. 1:11). Paul also imparted to Timothy. Second Timothy 1:6 reveals we can receive gifts freely through impartation, but it's up to us to stay stirred up.

Some time after the impartation, Paul told Timothy to stir up the gift. Other versions say, "fan into flames the spiritual gift" (NLT). Others say, "kindle afresh the gift of God" (NASB 1995). Still others say, "keep ablaze the gift of God" (HCSB). I like the fire connection because it speaks of being on fire for God and service to God and His people for His glory. Prophets are not exempt from the need to stay stirred up.

The reality is, we can feel rusty if we don't exercise our gifts. If you are used to prophesying frequently and lose the opportunity for live interaction it can feel like taking a bike out of storage you haven't pedaled in twenty years. You feel a bit wobbly when you start. As a prophet, you can't allow dust or rust to settle on your gift. If your opportunities for person-to-person prophecy are slim, look for ways to stir up the gift—to rekindle the flame.

It's no accident the Holy Spirit is often depicted as a flame. When He rushed to the upper room like a mighty wind on the Day of Pentecost, He rested on each disciple in the form of fire. Consider this: The disciples weren't out preaching the gospel. They weren't casting out devils or working miracles in that upper room.

When the Holy Spirit's fire touched them and gifted them, they were waiting with expectation. They were praying in one accord. Fanning into flames the spiritual gift may look like praying in tongues for an hour a day. It may look like sitting in silence in His presence. It may look like making intercession. It may look like worship. What does it look like to you?

— *Prayer* —

Father, in the name of Jesus, inspire me to press into Your heart until I am like a raging fire ready to burn up the enemy's plans and light others up with Your love. Show me how to stir up my gifts when it feels like ministry opportunities are dormant.

Pressing Through the Pressure

"We are hunted down, but never abandoned by God. We get knocked down, but we are not destroyed" (2 Corinthians 4:9).

Prophets go through seasons of walking in what I call "the pressure cooker." The purpose of a pressure cooker is to cook food faster—to get to the end result in a shorter amount of time—using pressure. Here's the dilemma: Just because we can't stand the heat doesn't mean we can get out of God's kitchen. Spiritual pressure is part of your process. If you'll embrace this reality you will handle the pressure better.

One thing I've learned in times of pressure is that there's pressure from the inside—what I call Holy Ghost pressure—and pressure from the outside that comes from people, places, things (and some of those "things" include demons). It's easy enough to resist God in the name of resisting the devil just because you don't like what's happening and assume the assignment came from the pits of hell.

I've seen others lay down and let the devil walk all over them in the name of yielding to the Holy Spirit. Don't do that! Ask the Holy Spirit to show you what is of Him and what is against His will for your life. Yield to God; resist the devil.

Here's another thing I've learned about pressure. Whether it comes from the hand of God or the enemy, if you'll just keep pressing through the pressure you'll not only gain strength, the pressure will eventually let up. Don't give up. God knows how much you can handle and He won't let the enemy press you past what you can bear, either. Through the pressing, you are building spiritual strength and character that will serve you well on the next phase of your journey.

God has purpose for everything He does. Take confidence knowing that He's stretching you so that you can hold more of His power, gain more of His wisdom, more of His character—more of Him. He wants to increase your influence and enlarge your territory. Oil comes from the pressing. Do you want to be an oily prophet?

— *Prayer* —

Father, in the name of Jesus, I say yes to You. I say yes to Your will and Your ways even when I don't understand Your work in my life. Would You enlarge my spiritual capacity, to enlarge my heart to love You more, and to help me surrender all that is getting in the way? Make me oily!

SEPTEMBER

"Let two or three people prophesy, and let the others evaluate what is said. But if someone is prophesying and another person receives a revelation from the Lord, the one who is speaking must stop. In this way, all who prophesy will have a turn to speak, one after the other, so that everyone will learn and be encouraged. Remember that people who prophesy are in control of their spirit and can take turns. For God is not a God of disorder but of peace, as in all the meetings of God's holy people" (1 Corinthians 14:29-33).

Don't Be a Pushy Prophet

"Pride leads to conflict; those who take advice are wise" (Proverbs 13:10).

Have you ever received a prophetic word that you absolutely, 100 percent, clearly, no-doubt-about-it knew was from the Lord—only to have the one you share it with forcibly reject it? If you've been operating in spiritual gifts for any length of time, the answer is likely yes. What you do next will reveal your maturity in the prophetic and how much the Holy Spirit can trust you to rightly exercise His gifts.

If you try to force prophetic words down people's throats, even if they are accurate, you become like one of those telemarketers who won't let people off the phone during dinner—or those pesky car salesmen who won't let you off the lot until you do a test drive and consider their best offer.

God doesn't need you to convince people that the word He gave you is accurate. The Holy Spirit is the Author of the prophecy and the Holy Spirit is also the Convincer. Being a pushy prophet could actually be hindering the Convincer from His convincing work. In other words, you could cause the person to totally shut down instead of leaving the door cracked open just enough for the entrance of His word to bring light.

Consider this: the prophetic word or word of wisdom may be embarrassing to the one receiving it. They may not want to admit it's true for any number of reasons. Let them save face and let the Lord deal with their hearts. Pushing the issue could cause them to push you away instead of coming to you later asking for counsel on the word you shared.

Once again, remember, these gifts are His gifts and He distributes them individually as He wills (see 1 Cor. 12:11). If you consistently misuse a spiritual gift or bring others harm when you exercise prophecy, the Holy Spirit may stop talking to you about other people until you learn how to steward the gift responsibly.

— *Prayer* —

Father, in the name of Jesus, help me do my part and let You do Your part. Teach me how to release the prophetic word with clarity, confidence, and boldness and leave the rest up to the Comforter, Counselor, and the Convincer. I don't want to be a pushy prophet.

When You Don't Know How to Pray

"Likewise the Spirit also helps in our weaknesses. For we do not know what we should pray for as we ought, but the Spirit Himself makes intercession for us with groanings which cannot be uttered" (Romans 8:26 NJKV).

The Holy Spirit helps us pray when we don't know how. In Romans 8:26, Paul offers a revelation that can transform your entire prayer life: "Likewise, the Spirit helps us in our weaknesses, for we do not know what to pray for as we ought, but the Spirit Himself intercedes for us with groanings too deep for words" (MEV).

We may think we know how to pray, and sometimes we do, but many times we don't have a clue what prayer answer we really need. If you are not getting prayer answers, consider what James 4:3 says about "asking amiss." The Greek word for "amiss" in the context of this Scripture means "improperly" or "wrongly." If you are praying wrongly, you won't get the right answers—or perhaps any answer.

The Holy Spirit helps us pray God's perfect will. Paul continues the revelation in Romans 8:27: "He who searches the hearts knows what the mind of the Spirit is, because He intercedes for the saints according to the will of God" (MEV).

The Holy Spirit has the mind of God. He always knows the perfect will of the Father and always gets His prayers answered. Let Him help you pray and you will surely tap into the 1 John 5:14-15 promise: "This is the confidence that we have in Him, that if we ask anything according to His will, He hears us. So if we know that He hears whatever we ask, we know that we have whatever we asked of Him" (MEV).

The Holy Spirit gives us a special prayer language. Paul also shared a marvelous revelation in 1 Corinthians 14:2: "For he who speaks in an unknown tongue does not speak to men, but to God. For no one understands him, although in the spirit, he speaks mysteries" (MEV).

I pray in the Spirit as much as I possibly can. I wake up most mornings and pray at least 30 minutes in the Spirit before doing anything else. I pray in the Spirit while I am in my car. I even broke out in tongues on the treadmill at the gym accidentally—because it's automatic. I'm not telling you this to create a law, but to encourage you to allow praying in the Spirit to become so natural that your immediate response in times of need is to lift up Spirit-led prayers.

— *Prayer* —

Father, in the name of Jesus, teach me to pray the right kind of prayers. Inspire my heart to pray with my heavenly language with confidence that it's the perfect prayer and will bring the perfect answer. Grace me to pray prophetically without ceasing.

Whose Shadow Are You Walking In?

"Even when I walk through the darkest valley, I will not be afraid, for you are close beside me. Your rod and your staff protect and comfort me" (Psalm 23:4).

Every prophet wants to enjoy the view from the mountain top. Fewer care to experience the valleys. Nevertheless, you will experience mountain top breakthroughs and valley challenges throughout your prophetic ministry. There's an ebb and flow as you grow.

Job, who went through what is perhaps the most severe extended trial in the Bible, spoke of the shadow of death over and over and over again. The enemy wants to cast a shadow of death in your life. The Hebrew word translated "shadow of death" in Psalm 23:4 is used poetically for thick darkness (see Job 3:5), as descriptive of hell (see Job 10:21), and figuratively of deep distress (see Job 12:22).

In the valley of the shadow of death there's hopelessness and a lack of revelation. You just don't know what to do or which way to go. In the valley of the shadow of death there is oppression and sorrow. In the valley of the shadow of death there is anxiety and even terror (see Job 24:17).

You may still have to walk through a valley, but you don't have to walk in the enemy's shadow. God invites you to dwell in His shadow. Psalm 91:1 assures, "Those who live in the shelter of the Most High will find rest in the shadow of the Almighty." David prayed, "Guard me as you would guard your own eyes. Hide me in the shadow of your wings. Protect me from wicked people who attack me, from murderous enemies who surround me" (Ps. 17:8-9).

You were translated out of the kingdom of dark shadows and into the Kingdom of God's light. Your salvation casts a shadow of eternal life, healing, deliverance, protection, and provision over your life. You are authorized to live, move, and have your being in God's shadow. God's shadow hides us from the enemy's shadow, but we have to walk closely with Him to stay in His shadow.

— *Prayer* —

Father, in the name of Jesus, deliver me from the shadow of death. Walk with me through the valley and lead me to the mountain top. Help me to make my dwelling in Your shadow so the enemy's darkness cannot overwhelm me in the midst of my valley experience.

Discern Prophetic Witchcraft

"You will go in and take the land from nations that practice magic and witchcraft. But the Lord your God won't allow you to do those things" (Deuteronomy 18:14 CEV).

Discerning and navigating spiritual climates from a prophetic ministry perspective was one of the first lessons I learned. That's because in South Florida the rampant rebellion and idolatry has caused what the Bible calls brass heavens (see Deut. 28:23). South Florida is home to voodoo, Santeria, and many other witchcraft practices.

Many ministers who visit the region tell me they fall asleep reading the Bible and they get attacked in their mind or body during their stay. When you are in a climate where witchcraft is strong you have to be especially careful not to prophesy out of divination. Where rebellion and idolatry rule, there are familiar spirits and many voices competing with God's voice. If you are not careful you will repeat what comes from divination's still small voice thinking it's God.

I'm grateful I learned that lesson early on, because I'm aware of the potential pitfalls and have been able to avoid them. You need to discern it, too, not just so you can avoid falling victim to it but so that you can avoid ministering out of a false spirit.

So what is prophetic witchcraft? As I wrote in my book *Discerning Prophetic Witchcraft*, prophetic witchcraft is false prophecy, but it's the source of the prophecy that is concerning. While prophecy speaks the mind, will, and heart of God for a person, situation, or nation, prophetic witchcraft can oppose the will of God—or at least lead you into a different direction.

Prophetic witchcraft taps into a spirit other than the Holy Spirit, who is the spirit of prophecy. Since the spirit of prophecy is the testimony of Jesus (see Rev. 19:10), prophetic witchcraft can't be the testimony of Jesus—or what Jesus is saying. It may sound like God, but it's not God. There are many voices in the spirit. Beware the voice of witchcraft.

— *Prayer* —

Father, in the name of Jesus, would You grace me to keep my ear to Your chest? Would You teach me to discern the subtle differences between Your still small voice and competing familiar spirits that want to deceive me and others?

Seeing Your Prophetic Blind Spot

"His watchmen are blind, they are all ignorant; they are all dumb dogs, they cannot bark; sleeping, lying down, loving to slumber" (Isaiah 56:10 NKJV).

As you drive your prophetic ministry forward, beware of blind spots. If you drive a car, you're familiar with the danger of blind spots. A blind spot is an area of the road you can't see in the mirrors. If you are not careful, you can get in an accident because the car behind you was hidden in the blind spot. Good drivers know they can't rely completely on a mirror. They need to turn their head to get a better view.

Here's the thing: We all have blind spots, and we can't see our own blind spots. Put another way, you can't see what you can't see. If you don't think you have a blind spot, that is your blind spot! David said, "How can I know all the sins lurking in my heart? Cleanse me from these hidden faults. Keep your servant from deliberate sins! Don't let them control me. Then I will be free of guilt and innocent of great sin" (Ps. 19:12-13).

Jethro served as a mentor in Moses' life when he could not see past the masses of Israelites who wanted constant counseling. Consider the strong words Jethro offered Moses, who was on the brink of burnout. Moses was trying to be the judge of an entire nation. He was doing a good thing, but it wasn't sustainable.

> *When Moses' father-in-law saw all that Moses was doing for the people, he asked, "What are you really accomplishing here? Why are you trying to do all this alone while everyone stands around you from morning till evening?"* (Exodus 18:14)

Moses explained to Jethro why he was doing what he was doing, and his father-in-law replied, "'This is not good!' Moses' father-in-law exclaimed. 'You're going to wear yourself out—and the people, too'" (Exod. 18:17-18).

Moses couldn't see the long-term impact of how he was stewarding his prophetic ministry. It took an objective observer with courage to speak up to help Moses see what he couldn't see. What's your blind spot?

— *Prayer* —

Father, in the name of Jesus, show me my blind spots! I don't want to walk around as a prophetic accident waiting to happen. I don't want to hurt people because I can't see what I can't see. Teach me what I don't know about myself so I can submit my flaws to Your transforming Spirit.

Keeping a Pure Prophetic Flow

"Then the Lord said, 'These prophets are telling lies in my name. I did not send them or tell them to speak. I did not give them any messages. They prophesy of visions and revelations they have never seen or heard. They speak foolishness made up in their own lying hearts'" (Jeremiah 14:14).

Jeremiah 14:14 is quite an indictment about the prophets in his day. I imagine Jeremiah felt pretty lonely with all the false prophets around and about him. Jeremiah was taking a strong stand for God and suffering the persecution that often goes along with taking those strong stands. But Jeremiah also had God's ear, God's trust, and God's heart because he stayed true to God's Word.

Most prophets in our day aren't prophesying downright lies or false visions in His name. But some prophets do go where God has not sent them and speak when God has not spoken to them. It's vital in this hour that you learn to discern when and where the Lord wants you to minister and not to cave in to the pressure to speak a prophetic word when the Lord isn't giving you one. There is a pressure in prophetic ministry that can lead you astray.

God's prophetic promises are completely pure (see Ps. 119:140). God's prophetic direction and commands are pure, enlightening the eyes (see Ps. 19:8). God's prophetic thoughts toward us are true, honorable, just, pure, lovely, commendable, and excellent (see Phil. 4:8). Our prophetic ministry should be marked by love that issues from a pure heart and a good conscience and a sincere faith (see 1 Tim. 1:5).

We maintain prophetic purity by abiding in Matthew 6:33: "So above all, constantly seek God's kingdom and his righteousness, then all these less important things will be given to you abundantly" (TPT). The Amplified Bible puts it this way: "But first and most importantly seek (aim at, strive after) His kingdom and His righteousness [His way of doing and being right—the attitude and character of God], and all these things will be given to you also."

When we seek His Kingdom we won't have time to build our own personal kingdom. When we see His way of doing and being right, adopt His attitudes, and conform to His character, our prophetic flow will be pure.

— *Prayer* —

Father, in the name of Jesus, purify my heart. Inspire me, Lord, to seek Your Kingdom rather than building my own kingdom on the gifts and talents You have given me. I trust You to open doors for my prophetic anointing and prophetic utterance in Your timing.

When the Enemy Tears Your Mantle

"And as Samuel turned about to go away, he laid hold upon the skirt of his mantle, and it rent" (1 Samuel 15:27 KJV).

We know Jesus' mantle is white as snow and His cloak of zeal never wears out, but ours can get damaged. When I stand in a prayer line, many times I see people's mantles. Sometimes they are ripped, torn, slashed, or stained. Yet I see dirty mantles, sometimes tattered, sometimes with holes in them from warfare.

What we see in the spirit is often symbolic and has a connected meaning in the natural dimensions. When I see torn mantles, the Lord often leads me to prophesy new mantles. I'm prophesying new mantles now for those who took hits and heat in the face of religious persecution.

When you serve Saul-style leaders—leaders who are rebellious toward God, operate in the fear of man, and otherwise move in a control spirit—you may eventually find your mantle torn. If you've submitted yourself to Saul, you may find the continual manipulation, restraining and directing influence, ungodly power, intimidation, domination, oppressive oversight, and the like tear your mantle in more than one place.

Saul-like leaders don't want to see you rise up in your anointing, wear your mantle, and pursue God's calling on your life. Saul leaders may also use your gifting to promote their agenda. They make empty promises, manipulate or use fear tactics to keep you under their thumb so you will continue sharing the gifts and revelation they need to succeed. Saul leaders do not want to see you advance beyond their mantle.

Remember when Samuel confronted Saul about his sin against the Lord. Saul did not wipe out the Amalekites, but left the king alive and took the best spoils. Samuel rebuked him and told him God was rejecting him as king over Israel. "As Samuel turned to go, Saul tried to hold him back and tore the hem of his robe" (1 Sam. 15:27).

Has Saul torn your mantle? Did you find your anointing hindered in a controlling ministry?

— *Prayer* —

Father, in the name of Jesus, repair my mantle. Fix the tears Saul-like leaders imposed upon my mantle during my wilderness season. Help me see how the Saul experience made me a better prophet so I won't be a bitter prophet.

Instituting Prophetic Habits

"After sending them home, he went up into the hills by himself to pray. Night fell while he was there alone" (Matthew 14:23).

Every day, I get up at 3:45 a.m. I take a shower, pray in the Spirit, command my morning, read the Word, delve into prophetic education, and do an hour-long prophetic prayer call. All that happens before 7 a.m. I've been doing this for years. These are some of my prophetic habits.

There are foundational habits every prophet needs to adopt. A habit is an acquired mode of behavior or a behavior pattern acquired by frequent repetition, according to *Merriam-Webster's* dictionary. So, have you ever considered your prophetic habits?

We know Jesus had habits. For example, He got up early in the morning to pray. Mark 1:35 tells us, "Before daybreak the next morning, Jesus got up and went out to an isolated place to pray." We know Jesus secluded Himself at times to commune with the Father over important issues, such as choosing His disciples. Luke 6:12 tells us, "One day soon afterward Jesus went up on a mountain to pray, and he prayed to God all night." We know Jesus practiced thankfulness. He rested. He was a good listener, and He was a worshiper. Jesus was very focused on His mission.

Jesus should be our model for prophetic habits, of which the above-listed are just a few. For example, fellowshipping with the Holy Spirit must be a habit. He is the One who is delivering the prophetic words from Jesus to your spirit so you can edify, exhort, and comfort the Body of Christ. You need to stick closely to Him.

What are your prophetic habits? What bad habits do you need to drop to adopt better habits? What good habits do you need to replace with God habits? What patterns in your life need to be disrupted and reset? What in your schedule do you need to rearrange in order to be more focused on your mission? Selah.

— *Prayer* —

Father, in the name of Jesus, help me break the bad habits that are holding me back from my highest calling. Help me replace the negative trends in my life with godly habits that propel me deeper into Your plans and purposes for my life and ministry.

Understand Your Prophetic Strengths

"Each person has a special gift from God, of one kind or another" (1 Corinthians 7:7).

Many years ago, I read *The Wall Street Journal* best-selling book *StrengthsFinder*. The book also offered a quiz that helped me identify my top five strengths. The theory is once you've determined your strengths, play to those strengths. You'll get stronger if you exercise your strengths rather than putting an overemphasis on your weaknesses.

There's no such test for the prophetic ministry, but you can still assess your spiritual life for prophetic strengths. One way you do that is by keeping a track record of how God speaks to you and judging the utterances for accuracy. If you dream a lot but your dreams never come to pass and no one bears witness to future implications, for example, dreaming is not your core prophetic strength.

You can also practically assess your prophetic strengths by exercising in different realms of the prophetic. For example, I have no interest in prophetic dancing, so we can rule that out as a strength. I can't sing, so we can rule out leading prophetic worship. I excel in prophetic writing, but would not have known this if I didn't put pen to paper.

Ask the people in your life what your prophetic strengths are. You might be surprised that their perspective is different—and sometimes more accurate—than yours. You may not realize how accurate or powerful you are in certain aspects of the prophetic.

Once I determined my prophetic strengths—writing, teaching, prophesying, and the like—I gained confidence. As I continued to exercise those strengths they grew, just like your natural muscles grow when you lift weights.

Although we want to improve our prophetic weaknesses, we have to understand God wired us to be stronger in certain areas than others. Our duty is to minister out of our strengths and bear fruit. Jesus said, "To those who use well what they are given, even more will be given, and they will have an abundance" (Matt. 25:29). How much do you want more?

— *Prayer* —

Father, in the name of Jesus, help me see my prophetic strengths so I can lean into the most accurate possible prophetic flow and help the greatest number of people with the prophetic ministry You've called me to steward. Help me step into my strengths with godly confidence.

Discern Your Prophetic Weaknesses

"The human heart is the most deceitful of all things, and desperately wicked. Who really knows how bad it is?" (Jeremiah 17:9)

When I first started walking in prophetic ministry, my biggest weakness was oral presentation of a word. I lacked the confidence to speak with authority, so the prophecy wasn't always so convincing. Another weakness was my bent toward studying everything out before presenting a prophecy. It was a responsible way to judge prophecy, but it held me back from any form of spontaneous prophecy and probably robbed people of a blessing.

There are many types of prophetic weaknesses. Maybe you are weak in the Word. Maybe your discernment is poor. Maybe your timing is off. Maybe you are biased. Nobody likes to admit a weakness, but for the sake of our own prophetic growth—and an accurate utterance—we need to discern and acknowledge our prophetic weaknesses.

Ignoring our prophetic weaknesses and forging ahead in a prophetic realm anyway can lead us into error. We need to understand our weaknesses so we don't overreach our prophetic boundaries. Not everybody is called to prophesy into politics, for example, or over nations. Presumption usually leads to error.

If God doesn't use you in dreams, stop telling people what you see about them in dreams. If your words of knowledge are always wrong, back off that for a season. A weakness can be strengthened, but only according to the giftings the Holy Spirit gave you. In order to function properly we need to develop skills and proficiencies, aptitudes and attitudes.

With that in mind, know this: Some of our prophetic weaknesses are not in the gifting but in the character or in the soul. Weak character and emotional issues can impact our prophetic ministry perhaps more than we'd like to admit. If you have anger issues, it can affect your ability to hear from the Lord and to release what you heard. You can't prophesy by the Spirit, for example, when you are angry. What are your prophetic weaknesses?

— *Prayer* —

Father, in the name of Jesus, help me to recognize my weak spots so I don't start flowing where You're not going. Show me the areas of my character and my soul that I need to straighten out to shore up my natural weaknesses in order to move rightly in the supernatural.

Prophesy to Yourself

"And David was greatly distressed; for the people spake of stoning him, because the soul of all the people was grieved, every man for his sons and for his daughters: but David encouraged himself in the Lord his God" (1 Samuel 30:6 KJV).

Walking in the office of a prophet is not for the faint of heart. It can be discouraging when people don't receive your ministry—or when people attack your ministry. Both are bound to happen. In David's case, he was catching it from all sides. Saul was hunting him down in the wilderness. The Philistine king, whom he had ironically aligned with for safety from Saul, rejected him as a warrior in his army against Israel. And when the dejected prophet went home, he found tragedy waiting.

Three days later, when David and his men arrived home at their town of Ziklag, they found that the Amalekites had made a raid into the Negev and Ziklag; they had crushed Ziklag and burned it to the ground. They had carried off the women and children and everyone else but without killing anyone. When David and his men saw the ruins and realized what had happened to their families, they wept until they could weep no more (1 Samuel 30:1-4).

What a position to be in. Even his own men turned against him. In that moment, the only one for him was the Lord God Almighty Himself. In that moment, David had a decision to make. I believe he chose to prophesy to himself. Remember, David prophesied to the Philistine giant Goliath at the battle line before his great victory. Now, he would prophesy to himself in a moment of utter defeat.

Yes, Scripture says David encouraged himself in the Lord. I believe he did that through prayer and speaking over himself what God was saying rather than what anyone else was saying. Samuel wasn't around anymore. He had to encourage himself.

Remember this when people reject you, won't receive your ministry, or even want to throw stones at you. Prophesy and re-prophesy what God has said about you in the past. Prophesy and re-prophesy those intimate words He spoke to your heart about your mission, mandate, and mantle. Prophesy and re-prophesy what He is saying to your heart right now. Speak the Word and you will find new strength for the battle ahead.

— *Prayer* —

Father, in the name of Jesus, would You remind me of what You told me in past seasons when I have forgotten because of the trials of life? Would You speak words of life to me that I can speak over myself when I am in the midst of a battle that threatens to oppress me?

Pursuing Radical Obedience

"You are my friends if you do what I command. I no longer call you slaves, because a master doesn't confide in his slaves. Now you are my friends, since I have told you everything the Father told me" (John 15:14-15).

Notice here how Jesus relates friendship to obedience. There's a level of intimacy with Jesus that opens up revelation, but many times the entry way to that level is obedience. This is not legalistic. In fact, Jesus gave us one new command: "So now I am giving you a new commandment: Love each other. Just as I have loved you, you should love each other" (John 13:34).

The closer you get to Jesus, the more prophetic you become. Of course, it's your love for God that motivates your obedience, and it's your obedience—not just your sacrifice— that sets the stage for going deeper into intimacy with His heart. And it's that intimacy that leads you to revelation about His Kingdom.

Noah walked in significant revelation. He received from the Lord a specific, detailed blueprint for an ark and a strategy that saved mankind amid a flood. But it required radical obedience to walk in that place. Noah had to obey every detail God gave him, line by line. There was no room for error. It had never rained before!

Abraham walked in the revelation of the Messiah. In John 8:56, Jesus said, "Your father Abraham rejoiced as he looked forward to my coming. He saw it and was glad." That makes me say "wow." But Abraham left the familiar with radical obedience. God said, "Leave your native country, your relatives, and your father's family, and go to the land that I will show you" (Gen. 12:1).

Although we'll never walk in perfect obedience in this age, God sees when we set our heart toward obedience. That's why God, despite David's mistakes, called him a man after His own heart. Make a decision to pursue radical obedience. Choose to trust God when He tells you to go or speak. Be willing to do anything He asks! Die to your own ways and comfort. Radical obedience paves the way to deep revelation. It's yours for the taking.

— *Prayer* —

Father, in the name of Jesus, give me the grace of obedience as I set my heart to follow You fully. Help me resist the temptation to go my own way and do my own thing. Teach me to walk in lock step with You every day and in every way.

The Making of a Prophet

"...So after you have suffered a little while, he will restore, support, and strengthen you, and he will place you on a firm foundation" (1 Peter 5:10).

When I was pregnant with my daughter there was a must-have book. It was called *What to Expect When You Are Expecting*. The book was so helpful because it laid out everything I should know in various aspects of the birthing process, month to month and through delivery. Honestly, some of it severely scared me, and not everything they said would happen in the book happened (thank God!).

Although my pregnancy was different in some ways from other women I knew, there is a generally established process for birthing and what it does to the body. Much the same, every prophet's making is a bit personalized to the gifts, callings, and issues in a prophet's life that need to be refined, but there is a generally established process for the making.

So what can you expect during the breaking process? As I wrote in my book *The Making of a Prophet*:

> Simply put, whatever it takes to mold you into a prophetic vessel of honor suitable for the Master's use. My character flaws are different than yours. Your strengths are different than mine. But broadly speaking, you can expect to suffer and you can expect to learn patience during the making process. Only after you've died to contaminating and corrupting influences and developed the godly character traits you are lacking can God trust you to be His spokesman on the largest platforms.
>
> You may need to die to a pursuit of recognition and develop your faith. You may need to die to pride and develop the virtue of humility. You may need to die to a know-it-all attitude and develop true biblical knowledge. You may need to die to lust and develop self-control. You may need to die to a quitter's attitude and develop perseverance. You may need to die to unholy habits and develop godly ones. You may need to die to a sharp tongue and develop kindness. Or you may need to die to selfishness and learn to walk in love.

The making of a prophet never really ends. Where are you in the process?

— *Prayer* —

Father, in the name of Jesus, I know You have customized a making process just for me. Make me sensitive enough to Your Spirit that I can embrace rather than resist the process. I want to work with You, not against You, as You continue to make me the prophet You want me to be.

Carrying the Anointing with Humility

"When they went from one nation to another, and from one kingdom to another people, He permitted no man to do them wrong; yes, He rebuked kings for their sakes, saying, 'Do not touch My anointed ones, and do My prophets no harm'" (1 Chronicles 16:20-22 NKJV).

This is a popular Scripture among prophets and those who defend the prophetic anointing. However, we need to examine this Scripture in the context of humility for an accurate understanding of how to apply it in our era.

For starters, the idea in 1 Chronicles draws partly from the record of God's communication to King Abimelech in a dream: "Now return the woman to her husband, and he will pray for you, for he is a prophet. Then you will live. But if you don't return her to him, you can be sure that you and all your people will die" (Gen. 20:7). God was looking out for the prophet Abraham. First Chronicles 16:22 was never intended to be a license to make prophets immune from the humility of accountability.

Prophets are not above making mistakes. New Testament prophets and prophecy are fallible as modern-day prophets are not oracles of God. Prophets are not above sinning. The only prophet who ever walked the face of the earth without sin was Jesus.

Prophets are not above correction or rebuke. Accountability is just as appropriate for prophets as any other believer. Prophets are not better than, more anointed than, or more spiritual than anyone else. Prophets are merely standing in an office God prepared for them. Prophets have to be especially careful to walk in humility because knowledge puffs up (see 1 Cor. 8:1).

We need to consider both sides of this issue. Yes, Christians should remember that: "He who receives a prophet in the name of a prophet shall receive a prophet's reward" (Matt. 10:41 NKJV). On the other hand, prophets need to remember not to demand respect and honor and special treatment just because God has given you a prophetic gifting and anointing.

Unfortunately, some prophets have used 1 Chronicles 16:22 as a means of control, wielding that sword to cut through objections and opposition to what they want, regardless of whether it's what God wants.

Prophets, guard your heart from the temptation to think of yourself more highly than you ought (see Rom. 12:3). Pride comes before the fall (see Prov. 16:18). Ask the Holy Spirit to help you to carry the anointing with humility and resist any tendency toward control.

— *Prayer* —

Father, in the name of Jesus, help me guard my heart from control, pride, and a haughty spirit so I don't trip over my own ego. Remind me that everything I am and everything I have comes from Your generous Spirit. Apart from You, I am nothing.

The Nazirite Prophets

"Work at living in peace with everyone, and work at living a holy life, for those who are not holy will not see the Lord" (Hebrews 12:14).

Samuel was set apart from his mother's womb. He was a Nazirite indeed. John the Baptist claimed the same legacy. God is raising up Nazirite prophets in this era who will war against the Delilah spirit, gaining retribution for the blinding attacks on seer eyes.

A Nazirite is one who takes the Numbers 6:1-21 vow. In essence, the seer who takes a Nazirite vow separates themselves unto the Lord. It means no drinking. It means a lifestyle of repentance. It means offering your life as a drink offering to the Lord. It means making sacrifices in obedience to God. It means being a sold-out prophet—a consecrated prophet.

Consecration is pulling away from something to move toward something. As prophets laboring as unto the Lord, we must purposely pull away from anything and everything that will dull our spiritual senses to God's voice. That may mean no exposure to media, entertainment, or other worldly inputs. It may mean fasting.

Prophet, if you want to attract the Holy Spirit into your life, you need to consecrate yourself more and more. Cut out the activities that don't please Him and don't edify you. It's not just a matter of cutting out sin, it's putting away childish things. Paul said, "All things are lawful for me, but not all things are helpful; all things are lawful for me, but not all things edify" (1 Cor. 10:23 NKJV). Paul also wrote these challenging words:

> *Beloved friends, what should be our proper response to God's marvelous mercies? To surrender yourselves to God to be his sacred, living sacrifices. And live in holiness, experiencing all that delights his heart. For this becomes your genuine expression of worship.*
>
> *Stop imitating the ideals and opinions of the culture around you, but be inwardly transformed by the Holy Spirit through a total reformation of how you think. This will empower you to discern God's will as you live a beautiful life, satisfying and perfect in his eyes* (Romans 12:1-2 TPT).

— *Prayer* —

Father, in the name of Jesus, show me how to consecrate myself. Show me the little things that hold me back from a fuller revelation of Your generous Spirit. Tell me what to put away and I will remove it far from me. You are my only good.

Cultivating Sensitivity to His Heart

"We have much to say about this topic although it is difficult to explain, because you have become too dull and sluggish to understand" (Hebrews 5:11 TPT).

God is careful about who He shares the most intimate part of His heart with. While He is open to all, only those who are sensitive to His heart experience the deeper things of God. While the invitation is standing for all His sons and daughters, few venture to go into the deep because of the price of admission. But, prophet, He expects you to go deeper.

Yes, God is careful about with whom He shares the deepest things of His heart. It's not that God can't deal with hurt feelings. He's not emotional in the way we are emotional. And we probably grieve His Spirit more than we know and He is long-suffering. Our heavenly Father is not sensitive like someone who is easily offended, though we can and probably do vex Him at times. Deep relationships demand sensitivity.

Some prophets are more sensitive than others because they have intentionally cultivated a sensitivity to His heart. That requires time, communication, study of His Word and His emotions, and developing a God-on-the-inside mindset that pulls our thoughts to Him when the world is working to distract us. Paul put it this way: "Yes, feast on all the treasures of the heavenly realm and fill your thoughts with heavenly realities, and not with the distractions of the natural realm" (Col. 3:2 TPT).

When you are sensitive to someone, you choose to do things that please that person. Your impulse is to cater to what they desire. Paul wrote, "Those who are motivated by the flesh only pursue what benefits themselves. But those who live by the impulses of the Holy Spirit are motivated to pursue spiritual realities" (Rom. 8:5 TPT).

The Holy Spirit is always at work in you, teaching you, convicting you, comforting you, leading you, guiding you, drawing you into prayer, revealing things to come, and wooing you to Jesus. When you cultivate a sensitivity to His heart, you hear more from Him, you tap into secrets and mysteries, you become more prophetic, and you serve Him better.

— *Prayer* —

Father, in the name of Jesus, help me do what only I can do—be intentional about pleasing You. Teach me what You like and tell me what grieves Your heart so I can be purposeful about bringing a smile to Your face. I want to be sensitive to Your kind heart.

Embracing Your Baptism of Fire

"I baptize with water those who repent of their sins and turn to God. But someone is coming soon who is greater than I am—so much greater that I'm not worthy even to be his slave and carry his sandals. He will baptize you with the Holy Spirit and with fire" (Matthew 3:11).

You've probably heard people in the business world use the phrase "baptism *by* fire." That means the difficulty or pain of a new, unfamiliar experience. The baptism *of* fire is similar but altogether different. Jesus came to baptize us with the Holy Spirit and with fire, but many prophets have only experienced the first half of the baptism. The Lord knows what you can handle and when you can handle it.

The Passion Translation adds a lot of color to the second half of Matthew 3:11: "He will submerge you into union with the Spirit of Holiness and with a raging fire!" The Greek word for fire in that verse is real deep—*fire*. *Help's Word Studies* says:

> In Scripture, fire is often used figuratively—like with the "fire of God" which transforms all it touches into light and likeness with itself. God's Spirit, like a holy fire, enlightens and purifies so that believers can share more and more in His likeness. Indeed the fire of God brings the uninterrupted privilege of being transformed which happens by experiencing faith from Him. Our lives can become true offerings to Him as we obey this imparted faith from God by His power.

If you want an expedited ticket to your next prophetic glory, embrace the baptism of fire—the spirit of burning (see Isa. 4:4). Let God purge you and burn away everything that hinders love. John the Baptist was filled with the Holy Spirit from his mother's womb, but I believe he was also baptized in fire in the wilderness. That's why he burned and shone (see John 5:35).

Sixteenth century mystic St. John of the Cross had a special name for Jesus: The Living Flame of Love. His poem by the same name went like this: "O living flame of love that tenderly wounds my soul in its deepest center! Since now You are not oppressive, now Consummate! If it be Your will tear through the veil of this sweet encounter!"

— *Prayer* —

Father, in the name of Jesus, baptize me with Your fire. Immerse me in the Living Flame of Love and burn away the impurities of my soul. I know the fire may burn, but it's a good burn. It will leave me refined, purified, and able to better represent Your heart to the world.

Rejecting Prophetic Mixture

"You adulterers! Don't you realize that friendship with the world makes you an enemy of God? I say it again: If you want to be a friend of the world, you make yourself an enemy of God" (James 4:4).

The Lord gave the prophet Moses specific instructions for making the anointing oil. Moses had to collect and mix a specific blend of pure myrrh, fragrant cinnamon, calamus, and cassia with olive oil. It was a holy, not a hybrid perfume.

Today's prophetic ministry is seeing hybrids and mixtures and blends that God has not sanctioned. Prophets, you must reject such prophetic mixtures or God will reject your prophetic ministry. God's prophetic anointing is pure and holy, just as He is holy. Discern and reject the syncretistic blends that manifest as profane fire in disguise. Reject syncretism that, to many, sounds like God and uses biblical language, but it's a hybrid anointing that can't heal.

Maybe you've never heard the word *syncretism*. Syncretism is a blend of different religious, cultures, or schools of thought. Syncretism defies logic, often mixing contradictory beliefs in the name of unity. The New Age movement is syncretistic, blending various religions, relying on various gods, and crediting the "universe" with power it doesn't have. Some of the prophetic movement is syncretistic, too, as the New Age has blended into some utterances.

Don't be fooled. Just because something has Christian elements doesn't make it Christian. In his letter to the church at Philippi, Paul points to "enemies of the cross" (Phil. 3:18). Islam is not a friend of the cross. Buddha was not a friend of the cross. Leaders of false religions are not friends of the cross. And we cannot reconcile the enemies of the cross to the Christ who hung upon a tree to pay the price for their sin if we compromise the gospel and essentially worship their god.

How does God feel about syncretism? "You must worship no other gods, for the Lord, whose very name is Jealous, is a God who is jealous about his relationship with you" (Exod. 34:14). Jesus said, "If you love me, obey my commandments" (John 14:15). Jesus said, "Anyone who isn't with me opposes me, and anyone who isn't working with me is actually working against me" (Matt. 12:30).

— *Prayer* —

Father, in the name of Jesus, help me avoid counterfeit anointings. Make me holy even as You are holy. Purify my heart so I will have a pure prophetic voice. Teach me to discern mixtures in my midst so I can avoid coming into agreement with hybrid anointings that violate Your Word.

The Pen of a Ready Writer

"My heart is overflowing with a good theme; I recite my composition concerning the King; my tongue is the pen of a ready writer" (Psalm 45:1 NKJV).

Early in my walk with God, someone prophesied over me that my tongue was the pen of a ready writer. In a way, it seemed like an obvious prophecy. I mean, I was a professional journalist at the time and was quite prolific writing for many newspapers and magazines.

When I looked into it a little more in Scripture, I promptly decided I didn't like the prophetic word because I was more comfortable using my pen than my tongue. I didn't care to involve my mouth in the prophetic process. My pen worked just fine, thank you. But the pen-of-a-ready-writer prophecy was true. Today, my tongue is just as prolific as my pen.

What if I told you that God wanted you to be prolific with both your tongue and your pen? Many prophets in the Bible were writers. David was one of the most prolific, but Moses, Samuel, Jeremiah, Daniel, Isaiah, and many other prophets wrote books filled with revelation for current and future generations. In fact, many of these prophets may have written more than they spoke.

I love what *Benson's Commentary* says about this verse: "I will recite what I have composed with so much fluency, as shall equal the style of the most skillful and diligent writer. Or, rather, he means, I am but the pen or instrument in uttering this song. It has another and higher original, namely, the Spirit of God, by whose hand this pen is guided."

Think about that for a minute. When you set out to write, the same Holy Spirit who guides your mouth will guide your pen. And when you set out to speak, the same Holy Spirit who guides your pen will guide your mouth. Whether you are more comfortable writing or speaking prophecy, the Holy Spirit is guiding you, so stretch yourself.

— *Prayer* —

Father, in the name of Jesus, help me be willing to move outside my comfort zone in delivering the revelations You share with my heart. Help me not to shrink back from writing, speaking, singing, or any other means of sharing the message You inspire me to release.

Liberating Nations

"Then by a prophet the Lord brought Jacob's descendants out of Egypt; and by that prophet they were protected" (Hosea 12:13).

Prophets and deliverance ministry go hand in hand. Moses delivered an entire nation out of the oppressive bondage the Israelites suffered in Egypt. When David played the harp that sent away the evil spirit plaguing Saul, it was the prophetic anointing on the young boy's life that manifested through music. When Jesus was casting out devils, He was functioning in the office of the prophet.

Although deliverance ministry is not reserved for prophets—any believer can cast out devils in the name of Jesus by the power of the Holy Spirit—prophets have a unique gift mix that sets the stage for freedom. There is something about the prophetic anointing that stirs up devils—and can make them flee. It's been said prophets bring warfare, but prophets also bring deliverance.

Of course, it's not all about casting out devils. A deliverance mindset goes beyond expelling demons in the name of Jesus. A deliverance mindset may include intercession that breaks deception off the minds of people, prophetic preaching that releases powerful truth that sets the captives free, prophetic worship that enthrones God and invites the Spirit of the Lord to bring freedom in an atmosphere. Whatever your prophetic expression, understanding the deliverance anointing and adopting a deliverance mindset will cause your ministry to be more fruitful.

If you're operating in a prophetic anointing, ask the Lord for other spiritual gifts that will ready you for deliverance ministry, such as the word of knowledge and the discerning of spirits. But keep in mind sometimes the assignment is broader. Some prophets, like Moses, are called to facilitate the healing—the deliverance—of nations. You can't just decide to deliver a nation, but you can prepare your heart for God to use you as a deliverer in whatever capacity He chooses.

— *Prayer* —

Father, in the name of Jesus, use me as a deliverer. Teach me the principle of deliverance and the authority that I carry to cast out demons from people, cities, and even nations. Make me bold as a lion, shrewd as a snake, and gentle as a dove as I seek to liberate Your people.

With All Your Getting

"Wisdom is the principal thing; therefore get wisdom: and with all thy getting get understanding" (Proverbs 4:7 KJV).

When I received an epic vision of the war room in heaven, I did not immediately release the particulars of the encounter. I had visual revelation but I didn't have enough understanding in my heart about the deeper meanings of the vision, who to share it with, how to apply it, or when to release it. I waited two years to publish *Decoding the Mysteries of Heaven's War Room*, which was the first time I shared the vision publicly.

Solomon offered critical words for prophets. I like how the Amplified Bible parses out the deeper meaning of Proverbs 4:7, "The beginning of wisdom is: Get [skillful and godly] wisdom [it is preeminent]! And with all your acquiring, get understanding [actively seek spiritual discernment, mature comprehension, and logical interpretation]" (AMP).

Prophets see, hear, and say. But it's important to understand enough of what God is showing you before you open your holy mouth and prophesy something that's going to lead people in the wrong direction. In other words, it's important to understand first that you've heard from the Lord—to judge the revelation you receive as divinely inspired—and ask the Lord what He is saying. This entire process can take place in seconds or take months like it did with my epic vision of heaven's war room.

Remember, prophetic revelation can have more than one layer of meaning. Some prophetic revelation is rife with metaphors that take Bible understanding to open up. Some understanding only comes through prayer and meditation on the prophetic revelation.

At times, you will be tempted to release revelation without understanding and there may be times when God will have you do that. But, generally, without an unction wisdom presses in for interpretation. Interpretation means understanding. We must be careful not to speak rashly. Proverbs 12:18 says, "There are those who speak rashly, like the piercing of a sword, but the tongue of the wise brings healing" (AMPC).

— *Prayer* —

Father, in the name of Jesus, help me to chew on what You are saying and showing me so I can release prophetic revelation that hits the mark and encourages Your people to act according to Your will. Warn me if I am tempted to speak too soon what I don't yet understand.

Set Your Heart to Pay the Price

"For I swear, dear brothers and sisters, that I face death daily. This is as certain as my pride in what Christ Jesus our Lord has done in you" (1 Corinthians 15:31).

You can't earn—or buy—spiritual gifts, but there is a price to pay. Beyond prayer, fasting, and study, there is the intentional developing of your character. As I said in my book *The Making of a Prophet*, "If there is a cost to being a true disciple of Christ, then how much more is the cost to be His mouthpiece in an age of culture wars and the persecuted church? Be realistic about what you may have to give up in order to cooperate with where the Spirit wants to take you."

You may pay the price of persecution or rejection, but the costliest part of pursuing an accurate prophetic ministry is crucifying your flesh. Again, this is the call of every Christian, but how much more those who are called to walk in prophetic ministry, claiming to speak for a holy God? Consider these Scriptures:

"My old self has been crucified with Christ. It is no longer I who live, but Christ lives in me. So I live in this earthly body by trusting in the Son of God, who loved me and gave himself for me" (Gal. 2:20). And again, "Those who belong to Christ Jesus have nailed the passions and desires of their sinful nature to his cross and crucified them there" (Gal. 5:24).

Jesus said in Luke 9:23, "If any of you wants to be my follower, you must give up your own way, take up your cross daily, and follow me." If that wasn't challenging enough, He also said, "I tell you the truth, unless a kernel of wheat is planted in the soil and dies, it remains alone. But its death will produce many new kernels—a plentiful harvest of new lives" (John 12:24). And He added, "Don't be afraid of those who want to kill your body; they cannot touch your soul. Fear only God, who can destroy both soul and body in hell" (Matt. 10:28).

— *Prayer* —

Father, in the name of Jesus, as I set my heart to pay the price to walk in the prophetic anointing, help me. Teach me how Paul continued to crucify his flesh day after day until the day he left his body behind to meet You in heaven.

The Parabolic Prophet

"When the Lord first began speaking to Israel through Hosea, he said to him, 'Go and marry a prostitute, so that some of her children will be conceived in prostitution...'" (Hosea 1:2).

God commanded the prophet Hosea to marry a prostitute named Gomer. Sounds strange, I know. But God had a purpose in this painful experience. He was demonstrating to Israel how he felt about His chosen people committing spiritual adultery by serving other gods. Hosea represented God, his wife Gomer represented Israel, the prophet's willingness to stay married despite her prostitution represented God's love. Hosea 3:1-5 reads:

Then the Lord said to me, "Go and love your wife again, even though she commits adultery with another lover. This will illustrate that the Lord still loves Israel, even though the people have turned to other gods and love to worship them."

So I bought her back for fifteen pieces of silver and five bushels of barley and a measure of wine. Then I said to her, "You must live in my house for many days and stop your prostitution. During this time, you will not have sexual relations with anyone, not even with me."

This shows that Israel will go a long time without a king or prince, and without sacrifices, sacred pillars, priests, or even idols! But afterward the people will return and devote themselves to the Lord their God and to David's descendant, their king. In the last days, they will tremble in awe of the Lord and of his goodness.

You've heard of parables, but have you heard of parabolic prophets? Parabolic prophets become the word or message they release. They don't just carry the message, they live it as an example to God's people, to encourage them to respond to God's words and ways. Hosea is the epitome of a parabolic prophet, following God's directions to name his first daughter with Gomer "Not loved" and his first son "Not my people."

Parabolic prophets have to endure some harsh realities at times. It's beyond a prophetic act; they become the prophetic act. It's beyond prophesying; it's becoming the prophecy. As a parabolic prophet, Hosea deeply felt God's pain and prophesied with deep passion a message of repentance. What message are you living out?

— *Prayer* —

Father, in the name of Jesus, help me appreciate the assignment of parabolic prophets. Help me understand the extent to which I may have to go to put forth Your prophetic message to a rebellious people in my generation. Help me accept the challenge, if You give it.

Prophetic Disillusionment

"When you arrive at Gibeah of God, where the garrison of the Philistines is located, you will meet a band of prophets coming down from the place of worship. They will be playing a harp, a tambourine, a flute, and a lyre, and they will be prophesying. At that time the Spirit of the Lord will come powerfully upon you, and you will prophesy with them..." (1 Samuel 10:5-6).

Like Bible promises, most personal prophecy is conditional. There's almost always an "if-then" with personal prophecy because the promise is dependent on the recipient's obedience to the instruction. In other words, as with God's yes-and-amen promises to us in His Word, personal prophecies rely on us doing our part. When we do our part, God will always do His part. We can't do His part, but He won't do our part.

For example, if I prophesy to someone God is sending them to China as a missionary, God is (most likely) not going to miraculously translate them in the spirit to China. They will have to get a passport, save money for the trip, book airline tickets, learn about the culture, and so on. Those sorts of conditions are implied and so obvious they don't have to be prophesied.

Of course, some personal prophecy will happen based on faith alone. At times, faith is the only condition. But most personal prophecy demands we cooperate with the grace of God. So consider this: If we don't explicitly prophesy conditions God reveals, our failure to prophesy the divine instructions can lead people into prophetic disillusionment.

Without explicit conditions on a bold word, people may even call you a false prophet, lose faith in the prophetic, and stop trusting God because they assumed the manifestation was automatic. I know that sounds dramatic but I've seen it happen. It would be like sending someone IKEA furniture without the instructions on how to assemble it. It's frustrating and people may give up before the cabinet is complete.

We prophesy according to the proportion of our faith, but we need to prophesy in a way that doesn't leave people despising prophecy because we fail to release the divine instructions that go along with the word. Think about it for a minute. If Samuel hadn't given Saul instructions, he wouldn't have had a heart change (see 1 Sam. 10:1-8).

— *Prayer* —

Father, in the name of Jesus, help me to always be careful to release any and every divine instruction You offer with the prophetic word I utter. Teach me to keep listening for the fullness of Your prophetic message before I say amen.

The Prophet's Grief

Isaiah called Jesus "a man of sorrows" (Is. 53:3). Likewise, the prophet is, at times, a person of sorrow seemingly walking down a narrow road many simply cannot fathom. The prophet grieves deeply over what grieves the Spirit of God. He is touched by the Holy Spirit's emotions. He mourns and is miserable when God's will is violated.

As Abraham J. Heschel wrote in his perennial classic *The Prophets:* "Their breathless impatience with injustice may strike us as hysteria. We ourselves witness continually acts of injustice, manifestations of hypocrisy, falsehood, outrage, misery, but we rarely grow indignant or overly excited. To the prophets even a minor injustice assumes cosmic proportions. They speak and act as if they sky were about to collapse because Israel has become unfaithful to God."

To Heschel's point, Jeremiah—also known as the weeping prophet—prophesied these words: "Be astonished, O heavens, at this, and be horribly afraid; Be very desolate," says the Lord. "For My people have committed two evils: They have forsaken Me, the fountain of living waters, and hewn themselves cisterns—broken cisterns that can hold no water" (Jer. 2:12-13).

Surely Jeremiah felt the Lord's grief over the state of Israel. The prophet grieves because he hates what God hates and sees that the wages of sin are death (see Rom. 6:23). Psalm 97:10 tells us, "You who love the Lord, hate evil!" Psalm 119 shows us how the prophet hates "every false way" and "vain thoughts." The prophet "abhors lying" (see Psalm 119:163).

The New Testament prophet may not be grieving over Israel, but rather the state of the modern-day church. The Holy Spirit within a prophet can, at times, be so grieved that the prophet becomes overtaken with spiritual sorrow for a people or nation who rejects the way of God. The prophet's spirit can be vexed as the Holy Spirit is blasphemed, tempted, quenched, resisted, and lied to.

That grief can, at times, turn into travailing prayer. Paul described travailing prayer as "groanings too deep for words (see Rom. 8:26-29). Travailing prayer is laboring with pain, severe toil or exertion. Prophets enter into travail by the Spirit of God—not through their own grief but through His sorrow over a situation and His heart to restore people to the King. When you find yourself grieving over what grieves the Lord, pray until that burden lifts knowing that God is moving through that grief to bring forth His will.

— *Prayer* —

Father, in the name of Jesus, would you help me discern when the grief and sorrow I feel is my heart picking up on Your emotions? Would you inspire me to yield to the prayer burden in cooperation with the Holy Spirit so I can be a prophetic change agent in the earth?

Mastering Mortification

"For if ye live after the flesh, ye shall die: but if ye through the Spirit do mortify the deeds of the body, ye shall live" (Romans 8:13 KJV).

It sounded morbid. It was almost scary. A Word of Faith preacher-turned-apostle was preaching a strong and convincing message about crucifying the flesh. But he didn't use the word *crucify*. He used the word *mortification*. Put plainly, I was mortified. Crucifying the flesh I could handle, but mortification sounded like death—and that's because it is.

King James puts it harshly in Romans 8:13, using the word *mortify*. Colossians 3:5 piles it on: "Mortify therefore your members which are upon the earth; fornication, uncleanness, inordinate affection, evil concupiscence, and covetousness, which is idolatry" (KJV). That's intense, but it's biblical.

Mortification isn't merely to embarrass in this context. Mortify means to put to death, slay, deprive of power, and destroy the strength of, according to *The KJV New Testament Greek Lexicon*. Mortifying the flesh means to starve it to death, to deprive it of the pleasures it craves, and to reject its carnal appetites. And that's where the war begins.

It's been said the battle is in the mind but make no mistake—your flesh is at war with the Spirit of God. Paul assured us, "The sinful nature wants to do evil, which is just the opposite of what the Spirit wants. And the Spirit gives us desires that are the opposite of what the sinful nature desires. These two forces are constantly fighting each other, so you are not free to carry out your good intentions" (Gal. 5:17).

Mortification is a lifestyle that leads to power. Walking in the highest levels of prophetic realms without falling headlong into carnal desires demands mortification. You may ascend to the holy hill with clean hands and a pure heart, but if you don't practice mortification your success will embolden your flesh and the pride of life could lead you to destruction. Like they say, the higher they go, the harder the fall. The good news is the Holy Spirit will help you die daily.

— *Prayer* —

Father, in the name of Jesus, would You give me the grace to crucify—to mortify my flesh? Would You teach me to die daily, to slay carnal desires, to deprive my carnal appetites of their desires? Thank You, Lord, for strengthening my spirit to rise above my flesh.

SEPTEMBER 27

The Making of a False Prophet

"They have wandered off the right road and followed the footsteps of Balaam son of Beor, who loved to earn money by doing wrong" (2 Peter 2:15).

I don't believe false prophets start off as false prophets. I believe they start off on the right track, with zeal and fervor for righteousness, with a hunger to hear and share His voice, and with a determination to build the Kingdom of God. Unfortunately, some genuine, God-called prophets end up on the road of deception. Remember, a false prophet is not merely someone who delivers an inaccurate word. A false prophet is someone who sets out to deceive and is himself deceived.

In reality, some who call themselves prophets were never called to begin with. They took on the title because they coveted the calling, or because someone erroneously prophesied them into an office God didn't have in mind, or even because they truly felt God called them (but were wrong). Many false prophets never understood true prophetic ministry and never operated in the true prophetic anointing, which goes well beyond personal prophecy.

While minor character flaws may merely cause you to prophesy less accurately than you otherwise could—and that's a shame in and of itself—more serious character issues left unaddressed can lead the true into false realms. Balaam is perhaps a familiar example. But let us not get so familiar with his mistake that we overlook the warnings within it. God recorded his story so that we can learn from his missteps, not merely so we can judge Balaam for his error.

Balaam didn't start out as a false prophet. He was one of the greatest prophets of his time, according to Josephus. That says a lot considering he lived in the days of Moses. But it just goes to show you the anointing may take you where your character can't keep you. Don't ever let that happen. Get your character straight so you can use the anointing God has given you to bless and curse not. Balaam was disobedient toward God, going to prophesy for King Balak without permission and later giving Israel's enemy ammunition to lead them into immorality.

— *Prayer* —

Father, in the name of Jesus, help me not to let any little foxes spoil my prophetic vine. Show me if I have opened the doorway to prophetic deception. Fine-tune my character and conform me to Christ the Prophet so I can stay true to Your purpose for my life.

Examine Me, O Lord

"But if we would examine ourselves, we would not be judged by God in this way" (1 Corinthians 11:31).

It's a running theme in Scripture for a reason. The living Word of God exhorts us to examine ourselves over and over again. It's a practice prophets must embrace in order to keep the clean hands and pure heart that qualifies them to ascend to God's holy mountain for revelation. David understood this and cried out to the Lord, "Examine me, O Lord, and prove me; try my mind and my heart" (Ps. 26:2 NKJV).

The apostle Paul warned the Corinthians to examine themselves before they took communion, "So anyone who eats this bread or drinks this cup of the Lord unworthily is guilty of sinning against the body and blood of the Lord. That is why you should examine yourself before eating the bread and drinking the cup" (1 Cor. 11:27-28). Paul didn't stop there. He went on to say that "For if you eat the bread or drink the cup without honoring the body of Christ, you are eating and drinking God's judgment upon yourself" (1 Cor. 11:29).

I like *The Message* translation of 2 Corinthians 13:5-9:

> *Test yourselves to make sure you are solid in the faith. Don't drift along taking everything for granted. Give yourselves regular checkups. You need firsthand evidence, not mere hearsay, that Jesus Christ is in you. Test it out. If you fail the test, do something about it. I hope the test won't show that we have failed. But if it comes to that, we'd rather the test showed our failure than yours. We're rooting for the truth to win out in you. We couldn't possibly do otherwise.*

Do you hear the Holy Spirit? Examine yourself from time to time. Make sure your faith is solid. Greed is not the only character issue for which you are looking. Examine yourself top to bottom with the Holy Spirit's help. If you fail the test, do something about it. Repent. Change your way of thinking. Change your life. The Father, Son, and Holy Spirit are rooting for you—and so am I.

— *Prayer* —

Father, in the name of Jesus, show me if there is any wicked way in me. Show me if I am in error or pride that will lead me into destruction. Convict my heart of what is out of order with Your Kingdom. I repent and turn to You. Cleanse my hands. Purify my heart.

Meditation Mandate

"But they delight in the law of the Lord, meditating on it day and night" (Psalm 1:2).

Meditation on the Word is a doorway to prophetic realms—and to greater accuracy in the prophetic. Entering into God's presence through this door renews your mind so you can divide between soul and spirit, builds your faith to prophesy, and helps you decipher what the Lord may show you through parables.

When you enter prophetic realms through the door meditating on the Word, you are flooding your soul with light. You are not in danger of entering prophetic realms through a loophole, back door, or perverted portal of darkness. Even though satan disguises himself as an angel of light (see 2 Cor. 11:14), meditation on the Word of God makes you more sensitive to the Holy Spirit, who leads and guides you into accurate prophetic expressions. You are less likely to be deceived if you meditate on and obey the Word (see James 1:22).

Meditation on the Word is a safe gate into prophetic realms because Jesus is the Word made of flesh (see John 1:14). And we read:

> In the beginning the Word already existed. The Word was with God, and the Word was God. He existed in the beginning with God. God created everything through him, and nothing was created except through him. The Word gave life to everything that was created, and his life brought light to everyone. The light shines in the darkness, and the darkness can never extinguish it (John 1:1-5).

The Word of God is alive and it is a spirit (see Heb. 4:12). Meditating on the Word renews your mind to God's possibilities, but it also positions your spiritual eyes to see and your spiritual ears to hear more accurately. You may see Bible scenes come alive from the pages of Scripture, or you may find yourself in a seer swirl where suddenly you are having simple visions, open visions, or ecstatic encounters. Ask the Lord to give you revelation through the gate of meditation on the Word.

— *Prayer* —

Father, in the name of Jesus, help me to meditate on Your Word day and night. Help me see through the lens of Your Word. Help me see it as active and alive in the prophetic dimensions. Give me a hunger and thirst for Your Word and the grace to meditate on Your Word.

When God Gives You an Unusual Prophetic Act

"Then the Lord said, 'My servant Isaiah has been walking around naked and barefoot for the last three years. This is a sign—a symbol of the terrible troubles I will bring upon Egypt and Ethiopia'" (Isaiah 20:3).

If you lean toward the intercession side of the prophetic, you've probably poured water over a rock or thrown salt in a river. I haven't done that, but we did march around a building seven times and shout *à la* Joshua 6, and I did climb over a fence on the Navajo Nation to put a healing cloth in a witchcraft monument known as Window Rock. (Don't tell anybody.)

The Bible is full of prophetic acts—which I define in *The Seer's Dictionary* as an action God asks one to take in order to illustrate a principle or act out His will in a situation. That should give us a clue as to one of the important ways God likes to use people in the earth realm as a point of contact through intercessory prayer and action in spiritual warfare.

Isaiah 20 tells us the prophet walked around naked for three years as a prophetic sign. No thank you! God had Moses lifting up his staff while Joshua led the Israelites to defeat the Amalekites. When Moses' staff was lifted up, Joshua would win. When he let his arms down, the enemy would advance (see Exod. 17:8-13). Elisha told a king to get a bow and some arrows and shoot them, then later to pick up the arrows and strike the ground. The number of strikes prophetically determined the measure of the king's victory (see 2 Kings 13:15-18).

But beyond Isaiah, Ezekiel perhaps lived through the strangest prophetic act we see in the Bible. He laid on his left side for the sin of Israel for 390 days, then on his right side for 40 days for the sin of Judah. God told the prophet, "I will tie you up with ropes so that you cannot turn from one side to the other until you have finished the days of your siege" (Ezek. 4:8 NIV). He even had to cook his food over dung. Would you be willing to go to such extremes for a prophetic word?

— *Prayer* —

Father, in the name of Jesus, help me see the value in prophetic acts—even when others around me find them foolish. Use me as a point of contact in the earth to demonstrate Your will, even if it the actions humble my soul.

OCTOBER

"So one night the king of Aram sent a great army with many chariots and horses to surround the city. When the servant of the man of God got up early the next morning and went outside, there were troops, horses, and chariots everywhere. 'Oh, sir, what will we do now?' the young man cried to Elisha.

"'Don't be afraid!' Elisha told him. 'For there are more on our side than on theirs!' Then Elisha prayed, 'O Lord, open his eyes and let him see!' The Lord opened the young man's eyes, and when he looked up, he saw that the hillside around Elisha was filled with horses and chariots of fire" (2 Kings 6:14-17).

Pressing into Multiplied Visions

"I have also spoken by the prophets, and have multiplied visions; I have given symbols through the witness of the prophets" (Hosea 12:10 NKJV).

God is pouring out His spirit on all flesh, and with that outpouring come prophetic operations such as prophecy, dreams, and visions. God is the God of multiplication and He is multiplying visions for seer prophets with clean hands and a pure heart. God is multiplying visions as a way of literally showing us things to come, as promised in John 16:13.

The English Standard Version puts Hosea 12:10 this way: "I spoke to the prophets; it was I who multiplied visions, and through the prophets gave parables." And the New American Standard Bible translates the verse like this: "I have also spoken to the prophets, and I gave numerous visions, and through the prophets I gave parables."

The key in this verse is to understand what the Lord means by the word *multiplied*, which comes from the Hebrew word *rabah*. According to *The KJV Old Testament Hebrew Lexicon*, that word means "be or become great, be or become many, be or become much, be or become numerous." It also means "multiply, have many, to increase greatly or exceedingly."

Visions are mentioned in the Bible far more than dreams, yet we have largely focused on dreams for the past several decades. God is giving power seers great visions, many visions and numerous visions, and exceedingly increased visions. You might wonder why. One reason is because of the times we are in. Times of acceleration demand more rapid revelation.

The Book of Revelation is essentially an example of multiplied visions. The purpose of these multiplied visions was stated in Revelation 1:1, to reveal "the things that must soon take place" (ESV). Multiplied visions are being released to reveal things that must soon take place, to guide us in how to respond, and to show us how to prepare. We are living in the last days and have entered the end times. The signs of the times are all around us. Ask the Lord to open up your eyes to multiplied visions.

— *Prayer* —

Father, in the name of Jesus, multiply my visions. Teach me to explore this seer dimension with Your Spirit so I can better discern the times and seasons. Help me understand what I see in the great visions You show me so I can prepare Your people for what's next.

Being a Prophet of One Thing

"One thing I have desired of the Lord, that will I seek: that I may dwell in the house of the Lord all the days of my life, to behold the beauty of the Lord, and to inquire in His temple" (Psalm 27:4 NKJV).

David was a prophet who spent a lot of time in both the wilderness and the secret place. In fact, I believe David found his own personal secret place in the wilderness. I believe David could enter the secret place even while on the run from Saul because he was a prophet of one thing.

David likely discovered how to enter into the secret place while he was a young boy tending sheep. His preparation in the secret place during his youth prepared him for his future public conquests. Indeed, David discovered a secret to sustaining his ministry through the warfare, the trials, and the victories. That secret is gazing upon the beauty of the Lord.

The Hebrew word for "behold" is *chazah*. According to *The KJV Old Testament Hebrew Lexicon*, it not only means to see, perceive, look, and behold, it also means to see as a seer in the ecstatic state and to prophesy. Did you get that? Prophets who are intentional about gazing upon His beauty will unlock multiplied visions of things to come. Let that sink in! This word *behold* is truly among seer mysteries few have understood—but King David perceived its power. He was a prophet of one thing.

Prophet, when you behold the beauty of the Lord, it leads you to make the right inquiries. Put another way, when you gaze upon Him in the secret place as a priority, He leads you to ask the right questions and you will walk out with answers, secrets of His heart, revelation about your life—and whatever else you need.

The Passion Translation of Psalm 27:4 offers an even more intimate understanding of David's heart:

Here's the one thing I crave from Yahweh, the one thing I seek above all else: I want to live with him every moment in his house, beholding the marvelous beauty of Yahweh, filled with awe, delighting in his glory and grace. I want to contemplate in his temple.

— *Prayer* —

Father, in the name of Jesus, give me such a deep hunger for Your presence that I prioritize my life in such a way that You are always first. Help me escape the hectic pace of life and go away with You to the secret place where I find life and love that sustain my heart.

When Believers Hate Your Guts

"And all nations will hate you because you are my followers"... (Matthew 10:22).

There are some people who downright hate my guts—or at least hate what I stand for. Some people believe women can't preach, much less prophesy. A particularly hateful reader called me a false teacher and accused me of blasphemy because I am a woman. That should qualify as hate speech. Here's a snippet of what he wrote:

> God is very clear in His word regarding the positions that women may hold in the church, and what positions they may not hold in the church. Miss LeClaire's attempt to dismiss God's Word (and by extension God Himself) as somehow wrong or old fashioned or whatever, by emphasizing her own personal belief as more authoritative than God and His Word is arrogantly blasphemous, and demonstrates her position as a false teacher. Repent, Miss LeClaire. Repent and turn to the Lord God Almighty seeking His forgiveness.

Beyond rejecting the reality of modern-day prophets, some heresy hunters hate prophets with a passion. Hate is a strong word. It's an intense hostility and aversion usually deriving from fear, anger, or a sense of injury, according to *Merriam-Webster's* dictionary. None of this should surprise us. Jesus said:

> *"If the world hates you, remember that it hated me first. The world would love you as one of its own if you belonged to it, but you are no longer part of the world. I chose you to come out of the world, so it hates you"* (John 15:18-19).

Jesus said, "And all nations will hate you because you are my followers. But everyone who endures to the end will be saved" (Matt. 10:22). Jesus said, "Then you will be arrested, persecuted, and killed. You will be hated all over the world because you are my followers" (Matt. 24:9). And John the Beloved said, "So don't be surprised, dear brothers and sisters, if the world hates you" (1 John 3:13). Don't be surprised when people hate you. Rejoice that you are suffering hatred for Christ's sake.

— *Prayer* —

Father, in the name of Jesus, teach me how to turn the enemy's hateful word curses into blessings by praying for the ones who hate me and what I stand for. Grace me to walk in love with people who call themselves Christians but don't represent Your heart.

Putting on Your Prophetic Armor

"Therefore, put on every piece of God's armor so you will be able to resist the enemy in the time of evil..." (Ephesians 6:13).

God has issued prophetic armor to every spiritual warrior—to every warring prophet. I call it prophetic armor because, well, it's not flesh-and-blood armor and we dress ourselves in it as a prophetic act. We understand the prophetic symbolism of the armor and how embracing it prophetically gives us victory.

Paul describes this spiritual outfit in Ephesians 6:12-17:

> *For we are not fighting against flesh-and-blood enemies, but against evil rulers and authorities of the unseen world, against mighty powers in this dark world, and against evil spirits in the heavenly places.*
>
> *Therefore, put on every piece of God's armor so you will be able to resist the enemy in the time of evil. Then after the battle you will still be standing firm. Stand your ground, putting on the belt of truth and the body armor of God's righteousness. For shoes, put on the peace that comes from the Good News so that you will be fully prepared. In addition to all of these, hold up the shield of faith to stop the fiery arrows of the devil. Put on salvation as your helmet, and take the sword of the Spirit, which is the word of God.*

As I wrote in my book *Waging Prophetic Warfare*, Jesus paid the price for our prophetic armor, but it's up to us to put it on. If you disregard any piece of your battle array, you are open to attack.

Prophets may have a tendency to focus more on the sword of the Spirit, which is the Word of God, above all else. But we must also be intentional about our identity in Christ beyond our prophethood and the necessity to stand on the truth in faith in the midst of an attack. After all, Paul said when you've done all you can do to stand. But stand armored up.

— *Prayer* —

Father, in the name of Jesus, remind me to put on the whole armor or God in my prophetic battles against unseen forces. Give me a confidence that Your armor is impenetrable by my spiritual enemies and Your sword is sharp enough to sever all attacks when I swing it.

Governing in the Spirit

"My Kingdom is not an earthly kingdom. If it were, my followers would fight to keep me from being handed over to the Jewish leaders. But my Kingdom is not of this world" (John 18:36).

I always tell people, "I'm a governmental prophet, not a political prophet." We've seen a growing number of political prophets in recent years. Political prophets predict presidential elections and legislation and all manner of events in the political realm.

Political prophets have, in recent years, become controversial. If we're as honest, usually there are as many who are wrong as there are those who are right. With a fifty-fifty chance of being right and so much political bias in the Body of Christ, this is not a surprise.

That said, I am not one who believes prophets should stay out government. We see prophets in the Bible dealing with kings and governors. Samuel's mission revolved around two kings: Saul (see 1 Sam. 10:1) and David (see 1 Sam. 16). He anointed them both with his horn of oil and advised them in their kingship for a season. After Samuel died, God raised up more prophets to advise King David, including Gad and Nathan.

Jesus wasn't a political prophet. He didn't prophesy who would become the next Caesar in Rome, but He did support paying taxes to Caesar (see Matt. 22:17-21). Jesus was a governmental prophet. He prophesied about Kingdom government rather than natural government. He prophesied about a Kingdom that is not of this world (see John 18:36).

We are citizens of heaven. This world is not our home. While political prophets are concerned with speaking into the rulership of the earth, governmental prophets are more concerned about prophesying into what is going on in the Kingdom and what God wants to do to bring His will to earth as it is in heaven.

It's been said the government of the world takes place in the prayer rooms of the earth. Governmental prophets do more than predict election outcomes, then—they make intercession for the governments of the earth from a seat of governing authority in Christ. And the latter is typically more effective in bringing God's ultimate will to pass.

— *Prayer* —

Father, in the name of Jesus, speak to my heart if I am tempted to get too involved in politics, which is governing the affairs of man, and pull me back into the government of God, which is concerned with establishing Your Kingdom on the earth. Help me stay above the political fray.

Evading Controversy and Scandal

"Have nothing to do with foolish, ignorant controversies; you know that they breed quarrels" (2 Timothy 2:23 ESV).

Prophets—and the prophetic words they release—tend to be somewhat controversial at times. Just look through the pages of Scripture and you'll see most of Israel did not want to hear anything the Old Testament prophets had to say.

Indeed, both ancient and modern prophets often have a prophetic view and a prophetic word that runs opposite and even confronts the status quo—and they aren't shy about sharing it. Jesus was the most controversial prophet of all, dismantling religious regulations in presenting a new covenant. For that, He was crucified.

Although the truth can be controversial at times, you want to be known for truth, not controversy. Put another way, it's one thing when a true word is controversial. We should never back down from that type of controversy or the persecution that results in prophesying the sure word of the Lord. But we should avoid personal controversy like the plague.

Through the years there have been several high-profile prophetic controversies, from financial scandals, to moral failures, to heated theological debates that have separated people who once walked together. It's tempting to take sides in controversies and taint our prophetic ministry by association. That's why it's wise to pay no attention to them, save for the purpose of prayer.

Paul spoke of those who have "an unhealthy interest in controversies and quarrels about words that result in envy, strife, malicious talk, evil suspicions and constant friction between people" (1 Tim. 6:4-5 NIV). Controversies always breed strife, and strife kills the anointing. If you can't be a peacemaker, let your tongue cleave to the roof of your mouth. And, by all means, guard your heart so you don't fall into financial scandals, moral failures, and theological error.

— *Prayer* —

Father, in the name of Jesus, help me resist the temptation to be controversial for the sake of being seen. Deliver me from any tendency to be loud and proud for the sake of gaining attention. Help me avoid stepping into controversies that lead to deadly strife.

Put Away the Feather Prophecies

"For a time is coming when people will no longer listen to sound and wholesome teaching. They will follow their own desires and will look for teachers who will tell them whatever their itching ears want to hear" (2 Timothy 4:3).

Many people want to hear a thrilling prophetic word from a prophet. Some sit in audiences hoping on the inside God will speak a life-changing word to them through the prophet on the platform. The reality is prophets don't and shouldn't always say what people want to hear. Prophets must only speak what God says.

Some in the church today—yes, the church today—just want you to tickle their ears. Some will bring in prophets to offer personal prophecy over people looking for a cheap thrill from God. God doesn't offer cheap thrills and He's not in the ear tickling business. Nevertheless, ear tickling motives are not a new phenomenon. Paul wrote in 2 Timothy 4:3:

> *For the time will come when people will not tolerate sound doctrine and accurate instruction [that challenges them with God's truth]; but wanting to have their ears tickled [with something pleasing], they will accumulate for themselves [many] teachers [one after another, chosen] to satisfy their own desires and to support the errors they hold* (AMP).

God is not pleased with ear-tickling prophets who say what people want to hear so they can be popular with the masses. If you don't believe me, look at these words from Jeremiah 6:13-15:

> *Because from the least of them even to the greatest of them, everyone is given to covetousness; and from the prophet even to the priest, everyone deals falsely. They have also healed the hurt of My people slightly, saying, "Peace, peace!" when there is no peace. Were they ashamed when they had committed abomination? No! They were not at all ashamed; nor did they know how to blush. Therefore they shall fall among those who fall; at the time I punish them, they shall be cast down* (NKJV).

In this case, Jeremiah was prophesying a very unpopular word. In fact, Jeremiah was prophesying judgment. These false prophets were prophesying the opposite of the true word of the Lord to tickle ears and fill their pockets with money. God called it an abomination. That's just how serious it is.

— *Prayer* —

Father, in the name of Jesus, help me avoid the temptation to compromise my prophetic ministry by substituting sugar-coated words for the sober words You have told me. Give me a backbone of steel to stand up in opposition to the twisted ear-tickling voices of my generation.

Your Prophetic Lineage

"Jacob was the father of Joseph, the husband of Mary. Mary gave birth to Jesus, who is called the Messiah" (Matthew 1:16).

Lineage is clearly important, or the Bible would not offer us all the "begats" in Scripture. In the Book of Genesis, the first book in the Old Testament, we see the descendants of Adam, which is where we read of Enoch and Noah (see Gen. 5). Then in Matthew, the first book in the New Testament, we see the genealogy of Jesus, the Prophet, starting with Abraham (see Matt. 1).

In today's language, we call this a family tree. You get genes and traits from your family line, like the color of your hair, freckles, and other natural features. But you also get spiritual traits, such as generational blessings and generational curses.

When you look at a prophetic lineage, you are, in a sense, exploring your prophetic family tree. This may or may not include your blood relatives. It does include prophetic spiritual mothers and fathers in your Christian descent. When exploring your prophetic lineage, you aren't just looking at your spiritual mother and father, but their spiritual mothers and fathers and their spiritual mothers and fathers. Some may also call this a prophetic pedigree.

For example, Bishop Bill Hamon is my spiritual father. That means his anointing flows over my life, since I am submitted to his covering. It means I can access part of the mantle that he carries, which is prophecy and equipping, as well as deep revelation about times and seasons in the church.

Like you, there are other people in my prophetic lineage who have imparted to me along my journey. They are also part of my prophetic lineage. It's important to look at your prophetic lineage so you can understand the rich spiritual heritage in your spiritual family line. Just as you have a natural genealogy, you have a spiritual genealogy from which you can attain generational blessings.

— *Prayer* —

Father, in the name of Jesus, help me as I journey to discover my prophetic lineage so I can appreciate the diverse anointings and mantles that are influencing my ministry. Show me the generational blessings that belong to me.

When You're in Transition

"Do not be afraid or discouraged, for the Lord will personally go ahead of you. He will be with you; he will neither fail you nor abandon you" (Deuteronomy 31:8).

I've always told people, "I live in transition." Most prophets do. John the Baptist must have felt that way. Being a transitional prophet from the old covenant to the new covenant, there was tremendous tension—tension beyond anything we will probably ever experience. Still, prophets who live in transition live in an almost perpetual sense of tension between what is and what will be.

As prophets, we have to be experts at transition. And let's face it, transitions can be a little scary even if someone prophesied it! That's why God told Joshua, "This is my command—be strong and courageous! Do not be afraid or discouraged. For the Lord your God is with you wherever you go" (Josh. 1:9). Remember, God gave Joshua this word right after Moses died as He charged him with transitioning Israel out of the wilderness and into Promised Land.

Here's the thing: Many shifts—even shifts that bring increase and blessing into our life— can stretch us beyond our natural limits. They can take us far beyond our comfort zone. Trusting God means walking by faith and not by sight (see 2 Cor. 5:7). We can't see God with our natural eyes, but we can discern Holy Spirit's leading and follow Him in child-like faith, knowing even if we misread Him, He's got our backs.

Then there's the warfare during transition. No worries, James 4:7 tells us, "So be subject to God. Resist the devil [stand firm against him], and he will flee from you" (AMPC). Yielding to the Spirit of God won't eliminate all warfare in your shift, but it will produce peace in the storms that often come in times of transition.

Transitioning isn't easy and there will be the temptation to quit and give up. Determine in your heart ahead of time that nothing will stop you from walking in God's will. And remember Galatians 6:9, "So let's not get tired of doing what is good. At just the right time we will reap a harvest of blessing if we don't give up."

— *Prayer* —

Father, in the name of Jesus, help me embrace the reality of transition in my life and ministry and to become an expert at it, never bucking and fighting against Your leadership even when it seems everything is falling apart or when the enemy is pressing me to quit.

Your Words Carry Weight

"They are a stubborn and hard-hearted people. But I am sending you to say to them, 'This is what the Sovereign Lord says!' And whether they listen or refuse to listen—for remember, they are rebels—at least they will know they have had a prophet among them" (Ezekiel 2:4-5).

The prophet's job is not to make people repent. Forced repentance is not true repentance and, after all, it's the kindness of God that leads people to repent (see Rom. 2:4). Repentance is a gift that comes in the wake of the Holy Spirit's conviction and is willful. The prophet's job is to make the call to repentance, releasing Spirit-inspired words that set the stage for conviction, which precedes breakthrough.

By the same token, the prophet's job is not to make people obey the word of the Lord. Forced obedience is not true obedience. True obedience comes from loving God more than loving self and is willful. The prophet's job is to declare the word of the Lord with passion and purity. The prophet is not responsible for whether or not people obey the prophetic word.

In other words, you just need to be obedient to God. You cannot control the outcome. You cannot make people obey the word, but by your obedience some may be saved. Don't let the enemy tempt you to believe your prophetic ministry was ineffective because you don't see immediate results from the words you deliver.

Remember, you are sowing the seed of the Word of God and making intercession for the people to whom God is sending you. That seed might not bear immediate fruit, and it might not bear fruit at all. Either way, you've done your part, God has done His part, now the people need to do their part in responding to Him.

In my book *The Heart of the Prophetic*, I discuss many functions of prophetic ministry. When you function in the office of a prophet—whether you call yourself a prophet or not—people will know there has been a prophet among them because your words carry weight. You don't have to try to make it known. You don't have to declare it. Just obey God.

— *Prayer* —

Father, in the name of Jesus, help me stay mission-minded and not be tempted to feel like I've failed because the prophecy didn't produce change. Remind me that Your word never fails and never returns void. Just because I don't see the fruit doesn't mean my ministry wasn't effective.

Expanding Your Prophetic Authority

"Though your beginning was small, yet your latter end would increase abundantly" (Job 8:7 NKJV).

I've always been fiery, but I haven't always carried the authority to prophesy—or even write—certain things. I wrote an article once quoting Jesus calling the Pharisees white-washed tombs full of dead men's bones. It was a hard-hitting article about the religious spirit and I thought the language was appropriate. I thought the article was strong.

My apostle thought it was strong, too. But he thought it was too strong. I couldn't understand his reasoning at the time. After all, I was quoting Jesus. Jesus was the One who called out the hypocrites, frauds, and imposters. Jesus was the One who compared their hearts to rotting corpses. I was just quoting Jesus.

It wasn't that my words were not true. It's that I didn't have the prophetic authority to say them. I didn't have the stature in prophetic circles to speak into certain things. I didn't have the credibility or the respect, but more than that I hadn't paid the price. I was a novice with a fiery heart and a burning pen. I had the truth in my spirit but lacked the leadership experience.

Over the years, God has expanded my prophetic authority. When I wrote the article I mentioned, it was for a church magazine that I started—and which had some success. Although that magazine ultimately died when I left the church, it was a training ground for my next exploit—becoming editor of the largest charismatic Christian magazine in the world—*Charisma*.

God expanded my prophetic authority little by little. I can say things now I could not say twenty years ago. And twenty years from now I can say things that I can't say today. The prophets Samuel and Jesus both grew in favor with God and man (see 1 Sam. 2:26). Neither one started out with the authority they ended up with. Remember that and choose your words wisely. Just because it's true doesn't mean you're the one to say it.

— *Prayer* —

Father, in the name of Jesus, help me stay in the bounds of the authority You have established for me in this season. I don't want to step into dimensions of the prophetic that You have not authorized. I don't want to prophesy out of turn.

Your Prophetic Ranking

"The high priest has the highest rank of all the priests..." (Leviticus 21:10).

If you know anything about the medical field, you know there's a ranking. You have the chief of surgery at the top, then attendees, residents, and finally interns who do the scut work as they learn and grow. In the military, we see generals, colonels, captains, corporals, privates, and so on. In other words, there's a rank.

It works the same way in the spirit realm. We know demons have a hierarchy. Paul describes the ranks, in part, in Ephesians 6:12: "principalities, against powers, against the rulers of the darkness of this age, against spiritual hosts of wickedness in the heavenly places" (NKJV). God's angels also have ranks. There are archangels, angels, cherubim, seraphim, and so on.

Likewise, prophets have different levels of authority or rank. As I describe in *The Seer's Dictionary*, rank in the spirit is someone's position or degree of authority in the spirit realm. This is seen clearly among David's mighty men. Second Samuel 23 describes their ranks.

> *These are the names of David's mightiest warriors. The first was Jashobeam the Hacmonite, who was leader of the Three—the three mightiest warriors among David's men. He once used his spear to kill 800 enemy warriors in a single battle. Next in rank among the Three was Eleazar son of Dodai, a descendant of Ahoah* (2 Samuel 23:8-9).

The list goes on with "next in rank" appearing several times.

A newly born-again believer with a prophetic gift has a different level of authority in the spirit than one who has been pursuing the Lord and walking in his office for decades. But even seasoned prophets have different ranks in the spirit.

A good example of this is how the Israelites recognized Jesus was walking in a greater authority than other teachers of His day. Mark 1:22 notes, "And they were astonished at His teaching, for He taught them as one having authority, and not as the scribes" (NKJV). What's your rank in the spirit?

— *Prayer* —

Father, in the name of Jesus, help me discern rankings in the spirit so I can submit myself to proper prophetic authority. Teach me not to battle above my rank, prophesy above my authority, or be presumptuous in my prophetic ministry.

Breaking Word Curses

"So Jezebel sent this message to Elijah: 'May the gods strike me and even kill me if by this time tomorrow I have not killed you just as you killed them.' Elijah was afraid and fled for his life. He went to Beersheba, a town in Judah, and he left his servant there" (1 Kings 19:2-3).

When I wake up most mornings, I break word curses, hexes, vexes, spells, incantations, potions, and every expression of witchcraft coming against me, my family, my finances, my businesses, my ministries, and everything I put my hand to, in Jesus' name. Why do I do that? Because with an international ministry, I am getting hit with all this mess constantly. I don't even have to discern it. It's on social media and in my e-mail inbox.

Remember, Proverbs 18:21 says the power of death and life are in the tongue. A word curse is a form of witchcraft that taps into the power of death that's in your tongue—or someone else's tongue. This spirit of Jezebel can work through people to release word curses—and we can word curse ourselves.

Have you ever really thought about what a curse is? The word "curse" in that Scripture means "to make despicable, to curse, to make light, to treat with contempt, bring contempt, or dishonor," according to *The KJV Old Testament Hebrew Lexicon*. You might say, "Well, Proverbs 26:2 says a causeless curse shall not land."

"Causeless" in Proverbs 26:2 comes from the Hebrew word *chinnam*. One of *The KJV Old Testament Hebrew Lexicon* definitions of this word is "for no purpose." Every curse carries a purpose. A curse of poverty intends to see its victim poor. A curse of sickness intends to see its victim infirmed. A curse of death intends to see its victim in the grave. Just as blessings are wrapped in faith, I believe curses are wrapped in witchcraft.

Curses—or at least the associated witchcraft—will land if we don't break it first. According to the *International Standard Bible Encyclopedia*, "A curse was considered to possess an inherent power of carrying itself into effect." Jezebel released a word curse against Elijah and it released witchcraft, fear, and thoughts of death. It landed. What if Elijah had broken that word curse and, instead of running, went back to Jezreel and confronted the witch? Don't let word curses send you into a cave.

— *Prayer* —

Father, in the name of Jesus, would You give me a deep revelation of the power of death and life in words? Would You help me discern if the root of my warfare is really a word curse that's simple to break? While they curse me, I will yet praise You.

Prophet, Receive a Word

"And as we stayed many days, a certain prophet named Agabus came down from Judea. When he had come to us, he took Paul's belt, bound his own hands and feet, and said, 'Thus says the Holy Spirit, "So shall the Jews at Jerusalem bind the man who owns this belt, and deliver him into the hands of the Gentiles"" (Acts 21:10-11 NKJV).

In one season, people I hadn't heard from in months emerged with vivid dreams about my present condition and my future hope. Others I just recently met had spectacular open visions of what the Lord was calling me to do next. Indeed, a river of personal prophecy was flowing into my life from many streams.

At first, I found it strange that so many people—even random strangers who sent me Facebook messages—were having so many dreams, visions, and prophetic words concerning my ministry. I thought, "Dear Lord, it's so weird that all these random folks are dreaming about me."

The river soon started flowing over the banks and turned into a flood. Folks I had never met before and would never see again started delivering massively directional words. These words were so specific and so bold these saints must have been super-sure they were hearing from the Lord. They would be foolish to come up to me and proclaim such things in His name. It was enough to make my jaw drop.

At the same time, I was having dream after dream and getting word after word directly from the Lord about crossing bridges, mega provision, relational deaths, spiritual assignments against me, turning points, and big decisions. Add it all up, and it's a prophetic deluge that was undeniable.

There comes a time when the collective of prophetic voices becomes so loud and so confirming we have to extend our faith to believe God for what sounds impossible. There comes a time when we have to get out of our minds and into His heart. You may prefer to hear it all yourself, but humility demands that even prophets receive prophetic ministry.

Prophets, let somebody prophesy to you. Just because you hear from the Lord doesn't mean you're hearing everything God wants to say to you personally. The Bible says, "Believe His prophets, and you will succeed" (2 Chron. 20:20 MEV). That verse is as much for you as it is about you.

— *Prayer* —

Father, in the name of Jesus, help me never to take on pride in hearing. Teach me to walk in humility so that I can receive a prophetic word from even the most unlikely source and treasure it in my heart. I want to hear Your message through any messenger You choose.

When You Feel Like Giving Up

"Listen to my prayer, O God. Do not ignore my cry for help! Please listen and answer me, for I am overwhelmed by my troubles. My enemies shout at me, making loud and wicked threats. They bring trouble on me and angrily hunt me down" (Psalm 55:1-3).

If you're like me, there are times when you feel like God just isn't listening. Mean voices are rising with guilt and condemnation or angry slander against you. You feel like you've prayed your guts out. You're battling fear. You just want to fly away, to escape the trial. You want to run off to a cabin in the woods. You need a break from the stormy weather—and you need it now. You've tried everything and nothing changes.

I know all too well what it feels like to want to give up. I know all too well the temptations to revert to the world's comfort in the midst of a trial. I know all too well the emotions that come with a raging storm against your family. But quitting is simply not an option. If we lay our weapons down, the devil won't just forfeit his position and pursue someone else. If we lay our weapons down, we just become an easier target for the enemy. The devil will keep attacking until he's robbed us of our faith to believe in the goodness of God.

When we feel like giving up, we can take our complaints to God. He can certainly handle it. Like David, we can take our deep sighs to God dusk, dawn, and noon. But ultimately, we have to come to the conclusion that God does hear us (see Ps. 116:1), that He is working on the situation (see Rom. 8:28), and that His grace is sufficient for us (see 2 Cor. 12:9).

Ultimately, we have to conclude God is trustworthy (see Ps. 9:10). Ultimately, we have to keep on our whole armor of God so we are able to withstand the attacks of the enemy against our mind and, having done all, stand (see Eph. 6:13).

Pile your troubles on God's shoulders. If He carried the prophet David's load and helped David out—and He did—then He won't fail you. As trite as it sounds, set your heart to trust in God, and you will not be disappointed (see Rom. 10:11). Don't give up.

— *Prayer* —

Father, in the name of Jesus, strengthen me in my inner man so my outer man—my flesh—can't tag team with my weary soul to override what Your Spirit within me really wants. Give me a supernatural endurance so I won't stop running the race before I cross the finish line.

Joy in the House of Prayer

"I will bring them to my holy mountain of Jerusalem and will fill them with joy in my house of prayer. I will accept their burnt offerings and sacrifices, because my Temple will be called a house of prayer for all nations" (Isaiah 56:7).

In 2012, the Holy Spirit told me to make prayer my life's work. I launched Awakening House of Prayer in the Fort Lauderdale area with a mandate for day-and-night prayer, equipping the saints for the work of the ministry, standing for unborn life, exercising the gifts of the Spirit, and pursuing holiness. Today, we have hundreds of prayer houses, hubs, and churches around the world. That can only be God.

The irony is, I never enjoyed prayer. It was drudgery—and I was scared to pray publicly. In fact, as a young Christian, when corporate prayer meetings were going on, I would hide in the bathroom, hoping the leader wouldn't call on me to make intercession. Prayer was boring, and I wasn't sure how effective it was despite James' argument that the effective, fervent prayer of a righteous person makes tremendous power available (see James 5:16).

Today, I pray fervently over an hour a day—many hours some days. When you realize God is not mad at you—that He actually likes you and takes delight in your weak prayers—it changes your perspective on prayer. Instead of begging and pleading with a faint hope that He might hear you, you are confident that He not only hears you but will answer you (see 1 John 5:14-15).

Praying in the Spirit is an essentially part of enjoyable prayer. Prophet, you need to build yourself up in your most holy faith (see Jude 20), and praying in the Spirit unlocks revelation. Spontaneous singing also makes prayer enjoyable. Paul said he would sing with the Spirit and his understanding (see 1 Cor. 14:14-15).

Then there's spiritual warfare. Putting God in the center means we are agreeing with God and His Word rather than hyper-focusing on talking to the devil; this makes prayer more enjoyable. There are times to rebuke the devil, but agreeing with and declaring God's promises is more fruitful and enjoyable than screaming at the devil. Find a way to make prayer more enjoyable, and you'll enter into deeper prophetic realms.

— *Prayer* —

Father, in the name of Jesus, help me enjoy prayer and intercession. Help me set a schedule, give me a prayer burden, and help me pray in a way that I see fruit from the effort. Lord, teach me to pray and give me joy in the house of prayer.

When Jezebel's Witchcraft Attacks

"Now it happened, when Joram saw Jehu, that he said, 'Is it peace, Jehu?' So he answered, 'What peace, as long as the harlotries of your mother Jezebel and her witchcraft are so many?'" (2 Kings 9:22 NKJV)

When witchcraft—the power of the enemy—is particularly heavy in the spiritual climate, my eyes actually burn. Everything seems like a much bigger deal than it really is because witchcraft works to take your eyes off Jesus by magnifying the problem. The enemy can use people to release witchcraft against you through word curses, but this spiritual force seems to sometimes hang over your head like a dark cloud.

Eventually, witchcraft couldn't get me by day. I was ready for the onslaught. So instead, witchcraft attacked me at night—in my sleep. I had some of the worst nightmares I ever had in my entire life. Of course, these witchcraft nightmares left me exhausted. Don't you know it's so much more difficult to work with one hand and battle with the other when you are physically exhausted?

The devil wants your thoughts and words because then he can sway your actions. Thankfully, I discerned what was going on, and I'm changing my battle plans. I've spent many, many hours in worship and prayer seeking revelation on how I can better gird up the loins of my mind.

When it comes to witchcraft, we have to withstand it. The Amplified Bible, Classic Edition says to "be firm in faith [against his onset—rooted, established, strong, immovable, and determined]" (1 Pet. 5:9). If worship doesn't break the witchcraft, take authority over it in the name above all names. Witchcraft has to bow at the name of Jesus.

But make sure you don't have any common ground with the enemy. Repent for any rebellion in your heart and surrender your will anew to God. Remember, we are more than conquerors in Christ, and no weapon formed against us can prosper—not even witchcraft. Our job is to be spiritually discerning enough to catch the devil at his onset, resist him, rebuke him, and praise God for the victory.

— *Prayer* —

Father, in the name of Jesus, teach my hands to fight and my fingers to war. Grant me greater discernment in dealing with Jezebel's witchcraft attack and all the power of the enemy. Show me the path to victory and I will follow it.

When Judas Sells You Out

"For Jesus knew who would betray him..." (John 13:11).

Jesus, our prototype Prophet, was betrayed more than once—and He actually knew ahead of time who would betray Him. Jesus, our prototype Prophet, also modeled how to respond. While we don't want to live in prophetic paranoia, we have to understand that if Jesus had a Judas, so will we. While we don't always see them coming—sometimes it's a blindside—we should expect it.

After all, Jesus said that in the end times many "will be offended, will betray one another, and will hate one another" (Matt. 24:10 NKJV). I believe it often happens in that order. Someone isn't going to betray you unless they first take satan's bait of offense. And no betrayal stings worse than a knife in your back wielded by someone who was supposed to have your back.

People outside your inner circle persecute and malign you—but they can't really betray you because betrayal implies trust. People inside your inner circle—those you've trusted and invested yourself in—can and sometimes do betray you, then persecute and malign you to disguise their dirty deeds. Sometimes they repent, but usually not until later— much later. Of course, we have to forgive them whether they repent or not.

Prophet, when you are betrayed, you have two choices: You can sink to your hater's level and enjoy the temporary satisfaction of attacking them in the same spirit that attacked you, or you can decide to move in the opposite spirit—the Spirit of Christ—and allow Him to prepare a table before you in the presence of your enemies (see Ps. 23:5).

I've discovered that when I do things God's way, He restores what the enemy stole and promotes me to another level of influence in my prophetic ministry. It happens every time. You just have to hang on to the Word and move on with your life—forgiving your betrayer, opening your heart to receiving God's healing, then forgetting what lies behind and expecting God to move on your behalf.

— *Prayer* —

Father, in the name of Jesus, help me to walk in love even with those who are secretly working against me. Give me Christ's heart for the Judases in my life so I can pray for their restoration. Teach me not to take the betrayals personally, even though they feel personal.

When the Prophet Is Fully Awake

"For you are all children of the light and of the day; we don't belong to darkness and night. So be on your guard, not asleep like the others. Stay alert and be clearheaded" (1 Thessalonians 5:5-6).

I wake up before 4 a.m. almost every morning. When I first hear the alarm, I am not fully awake. I've learned to thank God when I first wake up, stretch a bit, and then begin praying in tongues in a divinely hot shower so I can become fully awake before I get into the Word and prayer. In other words, there is a transition from slumbering to awake to fully awake. (I don't think I'm fully awake until after the hot shower and the coffee!)

There are spiritual parallels here for the prophet. Although God can and does speak to us in our dreams while we sleep in the natural, in order to walk in our highest calling we need to be fully awake. That's when we see the glory of God. That's when we can prophesy in the glory.

You are probably familiar with the passage in Luke 9 where Jesus was talking with Moses and Elijah on the Mount of Transfiguration. Somehow, during this expedition with Jesus, the three apostles fell asleep. It seems they were always falling asleep when they should have been praying. But that's another story.

> *Peter and the others had fallen asleep. When they woke up, they saw Jesus' glory and the two men standing with him. As Moses and Elijah were starting to leave, Peter, not even knowing what he was saying, blurted out, "Master, it's wonderful for us to be here! Let's make three shelters as memorials—one for you, one for Moses, and one for Elijah"* (Luke 9:32-33).

Catch that. Even the apostle who walked with Jesus fell asleep at a critical moment. But when they were fully awake, they saw God's glory. They saw something they couldn't have possibly perceived while they were asleep and couldn't fully appreciate until they were fully awake. A personal awakening will open your eyes to the glorious warrior God, the Bridegroom King and Judge Jesus so you can prophesy the fullness of what God is saying in the glory.

— *Prayer* —

Father, in the name of Jesus, wake me up! Wake up my heart. Wake up my ears. Wake up my eyes. I want to be fully awake so I can see and hear everything You say no matter how You say it. Help me not to sleep and slumber when I should be watching and praying.

The Teaching Prophet

"Among the prophets and teachers of the church at Antioch of Syria were Barnabas, Simeon (called "the black man"), Lucius (from Cyrene), Manaen (the childhood companion of King Herod Antipas), and Saul" (Acts 13:1).

I can prophesy boldly, but I can also teach plainly. It's a gift-mix that God is emphasizing in this hour. In the past, prophets would travel across the nation prophesying life-changing words to people, churches—and even over cities and nations—and then move on to the next ministry stop with yet another life-changing word.

The problem is, many of those life-changing words never changed anyone, any church, any city, or any nation because the hearers of the prophecies didn't understand what to do next. In other words, the people who received the prophecy with joy didn't know how to apply the word and the enemy snatched the seed before it took root.

In response, God is emphasizing teaching prophets who not only prophesy a life-changing word but expound on the word to help people apply what God said and see divine results. Prophets who don't have a teaching grace are partnering with teachers who have a prophetic bent to break down the prophecies into actionable steps that are easy to obey.

Jesus modeled the way. Jesus was a teaching prophet. When He shared His Sermon on the Mount, He wasn't hard-core preaching. He was teaching. Jesus did prophesy at times, but Jesus taught more than He prophesied. Jesus taught His disciples to pray. Jesus taught us about the Father. Jesus taught us to forgive and much more.

Remember, they called Jesus a prophet but they also called Him teacher (see Luke 13:10). Often left to pastors, teaching is a gift that every prophet should cry out for. Teach others how to hear the voice of God according to the Ephesians 4:11 mandate. Teach people what to do with the prophetic word you just released. Teach people to pray. When you do, you're being like Jesus, the teaching prophet.

— *Prayer* —

Father, in the name of Jesus, would You give me the grace and anointing to teach Your people? Show me how to break down prophetic words in practical steps so Your people can apply the truth in the prophecy to the situation at hand and see Your will come to pass.

Breaking Evil Decrees Against You

"God blesses you when people mock you and persecute you and lie about you and say all sorts of evil things against you because you are my followers. Be happy about it! Be very glad! For a great reward awaits you in heaven. And remember, the ancient prophets were persecuted in the same way" (Matthew 5:11-12).

Persecution is part and parcel of prophetic ministry. If you are operating in the office of the prophet, you are going to make people uncomfortable at times and angry at other times. While we should never seek to offend, we should not hold back on true prophetic utterances for fear of offending. While we should not intentionally stir the pot, we should not shrink back from releasing hard utterances aimed at setting people free from deception.

Old Testament prophets were sawed in half, jailed, and mocked. John the Baptist was beheaded. Jesus was crucified. If you are going to walk in prophetic ministry you need to develop tough skin. It's not likely that you'll be sawed in half, jailed, or beheaded, but you will meet with religious systems that despise the truth you carry. You will see doors shut in your face if you boldly proclaim the word of the Lord.

Most of the persecution you face as a prophet will be in the form of words. When you find out someone is persecuting you in the form of gossip, slander, or word curses, you have two choices: You can react in the same wicked spirit as your persecutor, or you can resist the temptation to act like the accuser of the brethren and respond like your Father in heaven instead. In the Sermon on the Mount, Jesus said:

> But I say, love your enemies! Pray for those who persecute you! In that way, you will be acting as true children of your Father in heaven. For he gives his sunlight to both the evil and the good, and he sends rain on the just and the unjust alike (Matthew 5:44-45).

Pray that God would forgive your persecutors, for even if they know what they are doing they don't understand the impact of the seed they are sowing. Pray God would give them a spirit of wisdom and revelation in the knowledge of Jesus (see Eph. 1:17-19). Pray for God to root them and ground them in love (see Eph. 3:17-19). Pray for God's love to abound in them (see Phil. 1:9-11). Ask the Holy Spirit to remind you to make intercession when the sting of persecution tries to blind your eyes to love.

— *Prayer* —

Father, in the name of Jesus, prepare my heart for the persecution. Help me remember that my mandate is to please You, not man. Teach me to reject the political man-pleasing spirit that will lead me into a pit of compromise and deception. I break word curses, in Jesus' name!

Entering the Prophetic Swirl

"As they were walking along and talking, suddenly a chariot of fire appeared, drawn by horses of fire. It drove between the two men, separating them, and Elijah was carried by a whirlwind into heaven" (2 Kings 2:11).

As prophets, we're always on. The prophetic wind, so to speak, is always blowing when we're standing in our office ministering under God's anointing. But sometimes you'll notice you're not just in a prophetic moment—you're in a prophetic swirl. When it happens, it's undeniable.

A prophetic swirl, in my definition, is when you are carried into a state of spiritual awareness where everything waxes prophetic. In other words, everywhere you go you're picking up prophetic significance. You see the same numbers over and over again, and you know God is speaking to you or confirming something on your heart. You think about your friend and your friend calls five minutes later. You go to a hotel and the room number matches the Scripture you read that morning.

Prophetic swirls draw me in at times. You might also call it prophetic rain. It brings more than revelation; it brings understanding. It brings clarity. It brings confirmation. It brings an awareness that God is intervening through natural events, places, people, songs, billboards, and other means to emphasize a message or open my eyes to a new thing.

Don't neglect the prophetic swirl. Thick clouds swirl around God in the vault of heaven (see Job 22:14). And there was always a swirl of activity around Jesus (see Mark 6:31). Prophetic swirls can also bring healing: "For an angel of God periodically descended into the pool to stir the waters, and the first one who stepped into the pool after the waters swirled would instantly be healed" (John 5:4 TPT). Anything can happen in a prophetic swirl.

When you are in a prophetic swirl, stay close to God. Understand that personal prophetic swirls usually precede mega transition or mega revelation. God is trying to keep your attention. Don't miss a word He is saying.

— *Prayer* —

Father, in the name of Jesus, help me not to miss the prophetic swirls but to jump in with both feet and reap all the revelation You have for me. Show me how to navigate the prophetic swirls so I can capture what You pour out and share it with Your beloved ones.

Discerning the Ways of God

"He made known His ways to Moses, His acts to the children of Israel" (Psalm 103:7 NKJV).

It's one thing to know the Word of God. It's another level to also understand the ways of God. Both are a life-long process. God told the prophet Isaiah:

"My thoughts are nothing like your thoughts," says the Lord. "And my ways are far beyond anything you could imagine. For just as the heavens are higher than the earth, so my ways are higher than your ways and my thoughts higher than your thoughts" (Isaiah 55:8-9).

The ways of God are the mannerisms of God, the habits of God, the methods of God, the behavior and moral character of God. We progress in our understanding as our relationship with God deepens. Our search to understand the ways of God should include asking for a revelation of His habits, methods, behavior, and character.

Moses wasn't shy about asking. Not only did Moses ask God to reveal His glory, the prophet asked God for a revelation of His ways: "If it is true that you look favorably on me, let me know your ways so I may understand you more fully and continue to enjoy your favor" (Exod. 33:13).

David, who is known to be a student of God's emotions, was also a searcher of His ways. Over and over again David petitioned God to learn of His ways.

"Show me Your ways, O Lord; teach me Your paths," he cried (Ps. 25:4 NKJV). And again, "Teach me Your way, O Lord, and lead me in a smooth path, because of my enemies" (Ps. 27:11 NKJV). And again, "Teach me Your way, O Lord; I will walk in Your truth; unite my heart to fear Your name" (Ps. 86:11 NKJV). Not only was David curious about the ways of God. He wrote, "I will meditate on Your precepts, and contemplate Your ways" (Ps. 119:15 NKJV).

Prophet, when you begin to understand the ways of God, you will understand deeper meaning of prophecies, dreams, and visions. When you contemplate His ways, you will receive a greater revelation of His love. And that makes all the difference.

— *Prayer* —

Father, in the name of Jesus, teach me Your ways and show me Your paths. I want to adopt Your habits, Your methods, and Your moral character. I want to understand what moves Your heart and what spurs You to action.

Prophesy in the Glory

"The priests could not continue ministering because of the cloud; for the glory of the Lord filled the house of God" (2 Chronicles 5:14 NKJV).

Ruth Ward Heflin, the great glory intercessor with a prophetic anointing who often led people into spontaneous worship, is known for saying this: "Praise until the worship comes, worship until the glory comes, then stand in the glory."

I've always loved that quote. One day, the Holy Spirit inspired me to add a line for prophets and prophetic people. So my adapted version reads like this: "Praise until the worship comes, worship until the glory comes, stand in the glory—then prophesy in the glory." In reality, it's prophesying from the glory.

What do I mean by that? I mean prophesying from your position seated in heavenly places in Christ Jesus (see Eph. 2:6). I mean prophesying from heaven's perspective. Prophesying in the glory is prophesying from a place in His Spirit that you don't get to casually. It comes out of a lifestyle of praise and worship—a lifestyle of seeking first the Kingdom.

Second Chronicles 5 speaks of a time when the first temple for God—the temple Solomon built based on the blueprints his father David gave him—was completed. Solomon was dedicating the temple to the Lord. They were standing on holy ground. Second Chronicles 5:13-14 tells us:

> *Indeed it came to pass, when the trumpeters and singers were as one, to make one sound to be heard in praising and thanking the Lord, and when they lifted up their voice with the trumpets and cymbals and instruments of music, and praised the Lord, saying: "For He is good, For His mercy endures forever," that the house, the house of the Lord, was filled with a cloud, so that the priests could not continue ministering because of the cloud; for the glory of the Lord filled the house of God* (NKJV).

When we abide in Him, we can prophesy from the glory without the minstrel. Christ in us is the hope of glory (see Col. 1:27). It's a different perspective and one few find.

— *Prayer* —

Father, in the name of Jesus, teach me the principles of prophesying in Your glory. Inspire my heart to cultivate the lifestyle of a glory dweller who understands how to deliver life-changing throne room revelation to Your Bride.

Your Season of Pruning

"I am the true grapevine, and my Father is the gardener. He cuts off every branch of mine that doesn't produce fruit, and he prunes the branches that do bear fruit so they will produce even more" (John 15:1-2).

In a vision, I saw the Lord standing over a great bush with pruning shears. The silver shears were glistening as light bounced off the blade. He opened and closed the shears quickly, almost as if to send an audible signal to the bush that He was about to perform an unwanted surgery.

In the vision, the Lord began to prune the bush, carefully clipping here and there and then standing back to examine His work. The bush wound up flat on top, like a carefully sculpted work of art, but He didn't stop there. He looked at the base of the bush, the thick woody part that was thrust into the soil. He saw weeds round and about it.

With gardening gloves on, He pulled each weed with precision, pulling up the entire root of the weeds but leaving the base of the bush intact. He then packed fertilizer around the base of the bush and almost instantly it started sprouting beautiful blooms from the top.

Prophets must be pruned. Pruning is not necessarily a sign that you've done something wrong. In fact, pruning often precedes promotion. I'll always remember when I heard the Lord say:

I am indeed pruning your life. I am pruning your relationships. I am pruning away those things that hinder growth in your life. I am pulling out the weeds and dealing with the little foxes that spoil the vine. As I am cutting them away you may feel the pain of loss, but understand that the joy of growth will follow the adjustment.

I have taken out My pruning shears to cut away things that hinder so that you will bear fruit that remains for My glory. So submit to the pruning because, like ripping off a Band-aid, the pain is temporary. Greater joy is coming. Greater peace is coming. Greater productivity is coming as a result of this season of pruning.

— *Prayer* —

Father, in the name of Jesus, I welcome Your pruning even though it doesn't feel good at the moment. I trust You, the vinedresser, to shape me the way You see fit. I trust You to clip away things from my life that are holding me back from my prophetic destiny.

Preparing for Your Prophetic Promotion

"Humble yourselves in the sight of the Lord, and He will lift you up" (James 4:10 NKJV).

I heard the Lord say: "I am promoting My faithful ones in this season to positions in My Spirit and in the natural that defy human reasoning. My faithful ones have prayed and sought My face and walked in My will with the little things, and I am making them rulers over more in My Kingdom."

Here's some advice. Don't chase the promotion—chase the God who gives the promotion and He will promote you at the right time. No man on earth and no devil in hell can stop what God wants to do in your life—but you can make a big mess trying to make it happen.

Manipulating situations may get you somewhere more quickly, but it won't keep you there long. Remember, whatever you do to get somewhere, you'll have to keep doing to stay there. You will never have to force anything that's truly meant to be. Don't promote and exalt yourself. That's God's job.

Don't look to man to make it happen. What man gives you, man can take away. If you look to man to make it happen for you, you'll be tempted to compromise. You'll be expected to do things God may not have called you to do. Some Christians have sold their soul to man for a quick promotion instead of selling out to God and trusting His timing.

If you were ready to handle the promotion now, God would give it to you now. Many times, we need to develop the character that will keep us where the anointing takes us. Romans 5:3-5 tells us patience produces character. Ask the Holy Spirit to show you areas of your life that need work—and then ask for the grace to get to the next glory.

Humility has no rights. And the Word tells us plainly: "Therefore humble yourselves under the mighty hand of God, that He may exalt you in due time" (see 1 Pet. 5:6 NKJV).

— *Prayer* —

Father, in the name of Jesus, teach me to wait on You to promote me to my next level, trusting that You will lift me up at the right time. Teach me how to avoid that hasty spirit that tries to work the prophetic system and build a ministry without Your blessing.

The Green-Eyed Prophet

"...You are jealous of one another and quarrel with each other. Doesn't that prove you are controlled by your sinful nature? Aren't you living like people of the world?"
(1 Corinthians 3:3)

Early in my prophetic ministry, a major prophet I admired came to minister at our church. He started prophesying to various people in the audience, and I was hoping—and praying—that he would prophesy over me. But he didn't. Instead, he prophesied over a friend of mine—and it wasn't just any prophecy.

The mighty prophet of God released a prophetic word over my friend, announcing his calling into the office of the prophet and decreeing how God would use him. I was so mad. I was jealous. I felt like he got my prophecy, and he didn't even want it! About ten years later, that same mighty prophet prophesied over me in front of over 50 nations, ordaining me under his covering.

I didn't know it then, but I had no reason to be jealous. I didn't realize my time would come. Jealousy can be a problem among prophets. We see Miriam and Aaron were jealous of Moses and started complaining, "They said, 'Has the Lord spoken only through Moses? Hasn't he spoken through us, too?' But the Lord heard them" (Num. 12:1). Uh-oh. Miriam ended up with leprosy, at least for a few days.

Don't be jealous of what other prophets carry or how God uses them. God won't promote a jealous heart. Remember, jealousy is a work of the flesh (see Gal. 5:20). Think about it for a minute. Saul was jealous of David—and tried to kill him. Joseph's brothers were jealous—and tried to kill him. Cain was jealous of Abel—and did kill him. When you allow jealousy into your heart, you are tapping into a murderous spirit that will ultimately kill your prophetic anointing. James 3:14-16 says:

> But if you are bitterly jealous and there is selfish ambition in your heart, don't cover up the truth with boasting and lying. For jealousy and selfishness are not God's kind of wisdom. Such things are earthly, unspiritual, and demonic. For wherever there is jealousy and selfish ambition, there you will find disorder and evil of every kind.

— *Prayer* —

Father, in the name of Jesus, show me if there is any jealous way in me. Deliver me from any roots of jealousy and envy in my heart. Free me from the selfish ambition that would cause me to covet the anointing on another prophet.

OCTOBER 28

Honor's Reward

"Honor all people..." (1 Peter 2:17 NKJV).

There's a lot of talk in prophetic circles about the prophet's reward, but the prophet would do well to pursue honor's reward. Honor is essentially respect. Respect is holding someone in high regard. I heard the Lord say:

Honor releases My blessing, My anointing, and My great rewards. Many have sown dishonor, disrespect, and discord and are seeing the fruit of unrighteousness in their life. They have not understood or recognized the glory that comes from walking in honor.

You will see greater peace in your life when you honor My commands. Things will go well with you when you sow honor. Honor is the humble road, not just when you give honor to whom honor is due but when you extend honor to those who have used you, abused you, and worked to defile you with the words of their mouth and the actions of their heart.

When you walk in honor with all men, you will experience a greater understanding of My Kingdom principles and you will unlock blessings that were once unseen and unknown to you. Choose humility. Choose honor. I promise you it's worth it.

Honor the elders in the prophetic who came before you. They plowed through persecution to pave the way for you. They pioneered what you're walking in now. Honor your pastors and leaders. When you honor your spiritual leaders, you receive more from them—more wisdom, more impartation, more trust, and more opportunities to use your gifts.

The enemy sets us up to dishonor our leadership so we can't receive the grace that's on their lives. Honor your fellow prophets with kind words. Honor those to whom you prophesy by walking in love.

This will help you: You don't have to agree with someone to honor them. You can respect their position without respecting their belief. God does not show partiality and we shouldn't either. If we're not honoring people, we're not honoring God.

— *Prayer* —

Father, help me develop a culture of honor in my life and ministry, first honoring everything You've done for me, then honoring my forerunners, my contemporaries, my leaders, and those I minister to. Let honor mark my prophetic ministry.

When You Need a Friend

"No longer do I call you servants, for a servant does not know what his master is doing; but I have called you friends, for all things that I heard from My Father I have made known to you" (John 15:15 NKJV).

Jesus is the Friend who sticks closer than a brother. But, let's face it, prophets have a hard time finding flesh-and-blood friends. After all, you don't have time for Judas and Jezebel—two spirits that love to work through people to attack prophets and prophetic ministries. You need a true, God-sent, covenant friend. You need a friend you can trust.

A true covenant friend is someone you can trust with anything. Once violated, trust can be difficult to earn back. True friends have tight lips, have your back, and have the integrity not to share your personal life with others or break your boundaries. True friends are consistent and don't merely say the words but do the actions to back them up.

A true covenant friend will tell you what nobody else will. Proverbs 27:6 says, "Wounds from a sincere friend are better than many kisses from an enemy." Friends should lift you up, but sometimes the Lord will use them to help you root out wrong behaviors and mindsets.

A true covenant friend will get into agreement with you. Amos 3:3 says, "Do two people walk together, if they have not agreed?" (MEV). That doesn't mean that true friends will agree on every little thing, but it does mean that they won't break relationship over disagreements.

A true covenant friend will stand up for you and fight alongside you. In 1 Samuel 18–20, Saul tried to kill David a dozen times. Jonathan, Saul's son, had a covenant relationship with David and stood with him through the assaults. Even though Jonathan was next in line for the throne of Israel, he helped David escape his father's wrath (see 1 Sam. 20). That's a self-sacrificing friend.

Prophet, treasure your covenant friends like gold. Cherish them with all of your heart. Respect and honor them at all times. You can't make a true covenant friendship happen but you can ask God for them—and you can work on being the best friend you can possibly be.

— *Prayer* —

Father, in the name of Jesus, You know how hard it is to find true friends. Everyone scattered from Jesus when the persecution came. Help me discern those who are called to walk with me, even if they don't walk in prophetic ministry. Help me develop godly friendships.

Ride the Wind

"The wind blows wherever it wants. Just as you can hear the wind but can't tell where it comes from or where it is going, so you can't explain how people are born of the Spirit" (John 3:8).

"There's wind on that!" It's a popular saying in prophetic circles. Wind is a symbol of the Holy Spirit, so when we say there's wind on a thing it means the Holy Spirit is moving in it. We need to discern the wind and ride it.

As a prophet, when you discern the grace of God on something you have to let that wind blow until it shifts. When you ride the wind, you are in a Holy-Ghost flow and you gain mass momentum. You're in that sweet spot where you've got crazy favor with God and man. We can ride the wind of blessings. We can ride the wind of increase. We can ride the wind of change. We can even ride the wind of adversity for His glory.

We were born of the Spirit, but sometimes we want to live out of our heads instead of our hearts. We need to determine in our hearts we're going to ride the wind of the Spirit no matter what our reasonings say, no matter what the naysayers say, and no matter what the devil says.

Sometimes we need a fresh baptism of the Spirit. Sometimes we need a fresh baptism of fire. Instead of moaning and groaning in the flesh, sometimes we need to start travailing in the Spirit for that new thing He wants to birth in our lives.

Of course, to cooperate with the wind we have to discern the type of wind blowing. Sometimes the winds of refreshing are blowing. Other times it's the winds of intercession or the winds of reconciliation. In this season, the winds of change are steadily blowing.

If we don't discern the wind, we may resist God, thinking it's the devil because the Holy Spirit is trying to take us to a new place. Most of us don't want to follow the Comforter to that uncomfortable place of change. We want to stay in the comfort of familiarity. We have to discern the winds of change—the winds of transition.

— *Prayer* —

Father, in the name of Jesus, help me discern Your presence—Your wind, Your grace, and Your blessing—on a thing. Even if I can't hear You or see You, help me discern the wind of Your Spirit moving so I can cooperate with what You are doing in the earth and in the spirit realms.

False Confirmation

"Indeed, we all make many mistakes. For if we could control our tongues, we would be perfect and could also control ourselves in every other way" (James 3:2).

Confirmation! It's rare I see anyone release a prophetic word on social media without scads of people responding, "Confirmation!" What does *confirmation* mean, really? *Merriam-Webster* defines the word as, "confirming proof," such as finding proof of a theory or "the process of supporting a statement from evidence."

Be careful. Confirmation bias can water down the all-important quality of discernment in your prophetic ministry. In fact, confirmation bias negates discernment in favor of a common belief. Confirmation bias, then, is "a bias that results from the tendency to process and analyze information in such a way that it supports one's preexisting ideas and convictions," according to Dictionary.com.

Put another way, confirmation bias happens when your own personal desire affects what you believe. It's like wishful thinking, which is a form of self-deception, and there's nothing prophetic about that.

Confirmation bias leads to a potentially dangerous error when applied to the prophetic. That's because confirmation bias opens the door to a spirit of error to flow over a people group—not just the compromised prophet but also the people who believe the prophecy. Confirmation bias can cause us to lose our objectivity, miss the truth God is speaking, and lead others into error.

Applied to the prophetic, it looks like this: One prophet prophesies about a person, place, or thing. That prophet is cheered on, getting thousands of likes and shares. Another prophet agrees with that prophecy and suddenly "hears the same thing." The second prophet confirms the first prophet's word.

Suddenly, people everywhere begin to prophesy the same thing. They are all hearing the same prophetic word, or some variation of that prophetic word. Others start reporting dreams and visions in line with that prophetic word. And pretty soon anybody who doesn't agree with that prophecy is on the outside looking in at the confirmation bias. Anyone who doesn't agree is called faithless or Jezebel. Finally, when it looks like the prophecy is not going to come to pass, more spectacular prophecies and theories emerge.

— *Prayer* —

Father, in the name of Jesus, help me avoid confirmation bias like the plague on prophetic ministry it is. Help me discern any tendencies in my heart to get into agreement with what I hear just because it fits my desires. Deliver me from confirmation bias.

NOVEMBER

"He delivers me from my enemies. You also lift me up above those who rise against me; You have delivered me from the violent man. Therefore I will give thanks to You, O Lord, among the Gentiles, and sing praises to Your name" (Psalm 18:48-49 NKJV).

Eyes Wide Open

"...I kept looking..." (Daniel 7:4 NASB 1995).

When God gave me an epic vision of the war room of heaven that I shared in my book *Decoding the Mysteries of Heaven's War Room*, there was so much to see. It was at the same time breathtaking and mesmerizing. It was difficult to absorb everything, but I took a page out of Daniel's prophetic playbook and kept on looking.

Daniel was a persistent prophet. He seemed determined not to miss anything God was showing him. Daniel had an epic vision, too. His was the vision of the four beasts documented in Daniel 7. He was minding his own business when he saw the four winds of heaven stirring up the great sea. Four beasts were coming out of the sea. One looked like a lion with eagles' wings. That would have been enough to cause many seers to stop and stare, but not keep looking at everything else swirling around. Daniel kept on looking.

"I kept looking until its wings were plucked, and it was lifted up from the ground and made to stand on two feet like a man; a human mind also was given to it. And behold, another beast, a second one, resembling a bear" (Daniel 7:4-5 NASB 1995). What a sight! But Daniel kept on looking. He saw a leopard with four bird wings on its back and four heads. It must have been scary! Some seers would have turned away, but Daniel persevered through the vision. The vision just kept getting scarier, but Daniel kept looking and finally saw the glory of God.

We have to be careful not to stop short as seers and seeing people. Many times we see a flash. We see an impression. We see a glimpse. We see a light and we stop looking. We can be so enthralled by the first fruits of our experience in the seer dimensions—the quick visual—that we don't press all the way in to see the full view. Or, we stop looking because what we are seeing in the spirit scares us. Some have even shut down the gift because of fear of what they see. Keep looking.

— *Prayer* —

Father, in the name of Jesus, help me embrace fully the seer gift and the responsibility that comes with it to, at times, see unpleasant aspects of the netherworld. Give me a persistent eye that keeps on looking until I've captured the details You want me to see.

When Your Prophetic Words Expire

"Is anything too hard for the Lord? I will return about this time next year, and Sarah will have a son" (Genesis 18:14).

I remember ministering to woman at my church during altar time. She was grieving because her grandmother just died—and she was very close to her grandmother. She was also somewhat estranged from her daughter, who was going through a life trial.

Before I could even think about it, I prophesied how the death of one would be the rebirth of another and there would be a significant shift within 30 days. It seemed impossible, if you looked at the natural circumstances. But, like I said, the words didn't come from my mind—they came from God's heart. Before the thirty-day time period was up, the daughter came home.

Some prophecies don't have expiration dates. God is longsuffering and He waits for us to meet the conditions of some prophetic promises He makes. They are, in a sense, open ended. However, when you put a date on the prophecy, well, you've given it an expiration date (even if God didn't).

There are times when the Lord will specifically give you a date or season or time—for example, "in the next 10 days" or "before the end of summer." But be sure it's the Lord before you start prophesying dates. Many times, putting a wrong date on a right prophecy can cause someone to dismiss a true word just because it didn't happen in the time frame prophesied.

Unlike the expiration date on that yogurt in the refrigerator, when you put an expiration date on a prophecy and it doesn't come to pass you position yourself to look like you missed God. Like rotten milk, it may leave some people with a bad taste in their mouth. In reality, you may have only missed the timing.

It's not always necessary to reveal the timing, even if you know it. You have to discern what exactly the Holy Spirit is leading you to share in the moment. Some of this comes through experience. By contrast, sometimes it's vital that you release the timing with the word or people will not feel the urgency of heaven on the utterance. Pray for discernment.

— *Prayer* —

Father, give me discernment into Your timing on the prophetic words You put in my mouth to share with Your people. Help me not to be presumptuous and put an expiration date on an open-ended prophecy and help me to boldly share timelines when urgency demands it.

The Price of Outpacing God

"The best way to live is with revelation-knowledge, for without it, you'll grow impatient and run right into error" (Proverbs 19:2 TPT).

Moses sensed a call of God on his life but he made mistakes in his zeal. Put another way, he outpaced God and it got him into trouble. In fact, getting ahead of God led him into the wilderness for forty years for additional training. Exodus 2:11-14 gives us the backstory:

> *Many years later, when Moses had grown up, he went out to visit his own people, the Hebrews, and he saw how hard they were forced to work. During his visit, he saw an Egyptian beating one of his fellow Hebrews. After looking in all directions to make sure no one was watching, Moses killed the Egyptian and hid the body in the sand.*
>
> *The next day, when Moses went out to visit his people again, he saw two Hebrew men fighting. "Why are you beating up your friend?" Moses said to the one who had started the fight.*
>
> *The man replied, "Who appointed you to be our prince and judge? Are you going to kill me as you killed that Egyptian yesterday?" Then Moses was afraid, thinking, "Everyone knows what I did."*

Moses was called as a deliverer and he sensed that calling strongly, but he was out of God's timing. He stepped out into a God-ordained ministry too soon. He made a life in the wilderness and was probably rather content until his burning bush moment. God was calling him not just to deliver one Israelite from one Egyptian, but to deliver an entire nation from Egyptian rule. In his youthful zeal, he was ready to deliver. In his aged wisdom, he was hesitant.

Moses was in process in one wilderness so he could lead millions through another wilderness. God morphed him from a murderer to a deliverer, from impatient to intercessor, from insecure to bold in God. God will make you into the prophet He's called you to be. But keep the process in mind. Getting ahead of God may seem like a good idea, but it usually sends you back to the Potter's House.

— *Prayer* —

Father, in the name of Jesus, help me stay in lock step with Your timing, plans, and purposes for my life and ministry. Warn me if I about to turn to the right or to the left. Prevent me from running ahead of Your grace.

The Cure for Prophetic Leprosy

"As long as the serious disease lasts, they will be ceremonially unclean. They must live in isolation in their place outside the camp" (Leviticus 13:46).

When I first realized my call into prophetic ministry, my mentor asked my best friend, "How is she doing?" She was really asking if I was getting puffed up. Paul said aptly, "Knowledge puffeth up, but love edifieth" (1 Cor. 8:1 ASV). I was anything but prideful. I was humbled. But another prophet in the church who started rising shortly after me stepped into prophetic leprosy, or spiritual pride.

The first and worst cause of error that prevails in our day is spiritual pride. So said Jonathan Edwards, a preacher, theologian, and missionary to Native Americans who lived in the 1700s. Edwards went on to say that spiritual pride is the main door by which the devil comes into the hearts of those who are zealous for the advancement of Christ—the chief inlet of smoke from the bottomless pit to darken the mind and mislead the judgment, and the main handle by which satan takes hold of Christians to hinder a work of God. Powerful words!

If that was true in Edwards' day—and it was—then how much more is it true in our day? I call spiritual pride among prophets spiritual leprosy because it's like a plague that defiles the pure prophetic flow in which God wants us to minister. Prophetic leprosy is so deceptive that the one who walks in it is too proud to consider that he may be suffering from this deplorable disease. In fact, spiritual pride mistakes the favor of man for the favor of God.

Edwards concluded that until the disease of spiritual pride is cured, medicines are applied in vain to heal all other diseases. The good news is spiritual pride can be cured. The prescription is a strong dose of conviction, repentance, and humility—and I might say an ongoing effort to cooperate with the grace of God to walk in the fear of the Lord.

— *Prayer* —

Father, help me see if there is any hidden pride in my heart. If I start puffing up, remind me that there is no good thing in my flesh and that every good and perfect gift comes from the Father of lights. Deliver me from the darkness of pride.

A Scary Proposition

"And if a prophet is deceived into giving a message, it is because I, the Lord, have deceived that prophet. I will lift my fist against such prophets and cut them off from the community of Israel. False prophets and those who seek their guidance will all be punished for their sins" (Ezekiel 14:9-10).

As prophets, we need to be students of the Word and rightly divide the Word of truth (see 2 Tim. 2:15). If we don't rightly divide the Word of truth, how can we be lovers of the truth? Indeed, we might fall in love with a lie if we aren't searching the Scriptures, especially where it relates to hard passages about the prophetic ministry.

This passage in Ezekiel has always troubled me. It should trouble you, too. No one wants to be deceived, and these verses appear to say that the Lord Himself is deceiving the prophet. How can these things be so? Let's look at some other translations of Ezekiel 14:9 as we act like good Bereans. Ezekiel 14:9 speaks of a prophet prophesying to idolaters.

[The prophet has not been granted permission to give an answer to the hypocritical inquirer] but if the prophet does give the man the answer he desires [thus allowing himself to be a party to the inquirer's sin], I the Lord will see to it that the prophet is deceived in his answer, and I will stretch out My hand against him and will destroy him from the midst of My people Israel (AMPC).

"If a prophet gives a false message, I am the one who caused that prophet to lie. But I will still reject him and cut him off from my people" (CEV). "If a prophet is tricked into giving a prophecy, it is I, the Lord, who tricked the prophet" (GW). "If a prophet is deceived and tells these idolaters the lies they want to hear, I, God, get blamed for those lies. He won't get by with it. I'll grab him by the scruff of the neck and get him out of there" (MSG).

Again, these verses trouble me. What's the takeaway? In this case, the prophet compromised himself. The prophet entered into idolatry of a person's heart and said what that person wanted to hear instead of what the Lord wanted to say. A wrong motive—usually a motive to gain something through the false prophecy, such as applause or financial gain, favor with man, or invitations to larger platforms—is at the root of this behavior.

Motives matter. It's easy for people to get caught up in the expectations of people and seduced by the promise of promotion. But remember, all true promotion comes from God, not man. Ask the Holy Spirit to purify your motives so you don't pollute your prophetic.

— *Prayer* —

Father, in the name of Jesus, I don't want to be used to prophesy to the idolatry in someone's heart. Purify my motives so I don't pollute my prophetic and enter into the sin of the people I'm called to lead into repentance. Save me from myself, Lord.

Your Prophetic Role Model

"...A great prophet has risen up among us"; and, "God has visited His people" (Luke 7:16 NKJV).

Many prophets want to be like Elijah and call fire down from heaven, or like Elisha and have a double portion anointing that sees miracle after miracle manifest in their midst. Others want to be like Samuel and revel in the reality that none of their words fall to the ground, or walk in the diplomacy of Nathan, who had the uncomfortable task of rebuking a king. Still others see themselves like a John the Baptist, a forerunner prophet, or a Jeremiah-like weeping prophet.

There's nothing inherently wrong with that. There is much to admire about the lives of these great men of God who suffered at the hands of religion and Jezebel. But we shouldn't want their mantles or anointings. We should want Christ's mantle and anointing, and indeed that's what we're walking in as fivefold prophets.

If we model our prophetic ministry after any prophet it should be Christ the Prophet. Christ is clearly superior to the Old Testament prophets we admire. He is, in fact, the Prophet all the other prophets prophesied about. Moses said, "The Lord your God will raise up for you a prophet like me from among your fellow Israelites. You must listen to him" (Deut. 18:15).

Jesus is our prototype Prophet. He is the One with Whom we should compare ourselves and the One by Whom we should measure our ministries. While we'll never be perfect like the Son of God, we can allow God to perfect us and move us from faith to faith so we can prophesy with greater accuracy. The more we become like Jesus, the more we can speak His testimony through the spirit of prophecy.

Here's the bottom line: When we model our ministries after Old Testament prophets, we're in danger of prophesying out of an old covenant. We can admire Samuel's accuracy and John the Baptist's boldness. We can wonder at Elisha's miracles and Elijah's zeal for God. But the prophetic ministry shifted when Jesus came on the scene. Look to Jesus.

— *Prayer* —

Father, remind me that Jesus is my role model so I won't be tempted to adopt the ways and styles and methods of man. Conform me into the image of Christ so I can serve as an ambassador of hope in His everlasting Kingdom.

Your Governing Authority

"Here are some of the parts God has appointed for the church: first are apostles, second are prophets, third are teachers, then those who do miracles, those who have the gift of healing, those who can help others, those who have the gift of leadership, those who speak in unknown languages" (1 Corinthians 12:28).

Ephesians 4 fivefold prophets, along with apostles and teachers, are part of the government of God. The government of God is the rule of God manifested through the church. The government of God is not conducted in the castle or a white house. A government is a body of people, or rulers, that has governing authority in the church.

The government of God ensures the Ruler of rulers—the head of the Church, Jesus Christ—is glorified in the assembly. That includes providing direction to the local body under His leadership, ordaining fivefold ministers, sending out teams to evangelize or plant churches, bringing correction and discipline within the church, and otherwise setting the proper order so the Holy Spirit can move freely.

We see this model in the church at Antioch, whose presbytery included Barnabas, Simeon, Lucius, Manaen, and Saul (Paul)—all these men were apostles, prophets, and teachers submitted to the Holy Spirit's leadership. While pastors and teachers can serve on a presbytery at the discretion of apostolic and prophetic leadership, the government of God as set in New Testament order includes prophets. This combination brings increase to the Kingdom.

Isaiah 9:7 tells us, "Of the increase of His government and peace there will be no end, upon the throne of David and over His kingdom, to order it and establish it with judgment and justice from that time forward, even forever. The zeal of the Lord of hosts will perform this" (NKJV).

God advances His heavenly Kingdom through His government on earth, which is responsible for building churches that reach out and preach the gospel, win the lost, and equip believers for the work of the ministry (see Eph. 4:11). Even if you don't sit on a church presbytery, you are still part of the government of God in the earth.

Ask the Holy Spirit where your territory is and who He's called you to equip for the work of the ministry. Ask Him to send you to a people who need the gift mix He's put in you to rise up and increase God's government on the earth.

— *Prayer* —

Father, in the name of Jesus, would You give me a deep revelation of the government of God? Renew my mind to the principles of Your government, justice, legislation, and judgment. Help me shake off worldly concepts of government and embrace Kingdom government.

Walking in Abraham's Shoes

"Finally, Abraham said, 'Lord, please don't be angry with me if I speak one more time. Suppose only ten are found there?'" (Genesis 18:32)

God is weary of the doom and gloom prophets. We're seeing a tipping point in heaven as a response to the Jonah prophets who delight in judgment. God is promoting Abrahamic prophets who are willing to stand in the gap for people and nations that are on the wrong side of God for mercy's sake.

You know the story in Genesis 18. Abraham got wind of God's plans to destroy Sodom and Gomorrah, especially wicked cities indeed. But Abraham stood in the gap. Listen to the intercession of Abraham in Genesis 18:23-26:

> *"Will you sweep away both the righteous and the wicked? Suppose you find fifty righteous people living there in the city—will you still sweep it away and not spare it for their sakes? Surely you wouldn't do such a thing, destroying the righteous along with the wicked. Why, you would be treating the righteous and the wicked exactly the same! Surely you wouldn't do that! Should not the Judge of all the earth do what is right?" And the Lord replied, "If I find fifty righteous people in Sodom, I will spare the entire city for their sake."*

Abraham kept interceding until he got down to the 10-person mark. Although he understood God is the God of judgment, he also understood that He is also the God of mercy. This is why he cried out: "O Lord, I have heard Your speech and was afraid; O Lord, revive Your work in the midst of the years! In the midst of the years make it known; in wrath remember mercy" (Hab. 3:2 NKJV). Let's all remember, "Mercy triumphs over judgment" (James 2:13 NKJV).

Prophets who take pleasure in seeing judgment fall do not have the heart of God. God does not delight in judgment. It's not His will that any shall perish, though we understand some will. Judgment is a reality of the Kingdom, but in this decade God is going to change the hearts of some of the judgment prophets with mercy encounters. If you delight in judgment, ask the Holy Spirit to encounter your heart with His love.

— *Prayer* —

Father, in the name of Jesus, would You give me the intercessory prayer anointing of Abraham—an anointing that dares to keep on asking for mercy when judgment is clearly deserved. Teach me the principle that mercy triumphs over judgment.

The Prophetic Purge

"Purify my conscience! Make this leper clean again! Wash me in your love until I am pure in heart" (Psalm 51:7 TPT).

Every prophet goes through seasons of purging. *Merriam-Webster's* dictionary defines *purge* as "to clear of guilt; to free from a moral or ceremonial defilement; to cause evacuation from; to make free of something unwanted; to get rid of."

Could it be possible that something you're holding on to, won't get rid of, or keep tolerating is preventing you from advancing to the next level? I know from experience that, yes, it's more than possible.

That's why, from time to time, we need examine our lives and see what we need to get rid of. It may be time to stop tolerating the wrong and start embracing the right. It may be time to get free of demons that bind us. It may be time to move out of toxic relationships. It may be time to purge our lives of idols and ideologies that don't forward the Kingdom of God through our prophetic ministry.

David said in Psalm 51:7, "Purge me with hyssop, and I shall be clean; wash me, and I shall be whiter than snow" (NKJV). That needs to be our first cry. Before we seek to purge people and things from our lives, we need to ask God to purge us. Paul once offered this advice:

> *Therefore, since these [great] promises are ours, beloved, let us cleanse ourselves from everything that contaminates and defiles body and spirit, and bring [our] consecration to completeness in the [reverential] fear of God* (2 Corinthians 7:1 AMPC).

Before Isaiah could step into the fullness of God's promises to him, he was purged. Isaiah 6:6-7 tells the story:

> *Then one of the seraphim flew to me, having in his hand a live coal which he had taken with the tongs from the altar. And he touched my mouth with it, and said: "Behold, this has touched your lips; Your iniquity is taken away, and your sin purged"* (NKJV).

Ask God what He wants you to purge—and what He wants to purge from your life. Once you've completed the purge, you'll make room for the promotion.

— *Prayer* —

Father, in the name of Jesus, purge me from prophetic pollution that is contaminating my flow. Purge me from wrong mindsets, theologies, and ideologies that are clouding my prophetic perspective. Sever the ties that bind me to the old so I can embrace the new.

Advancing Prophetic Wisdom

"If you need wisdom, ask our generous God, and he will give it to you. He will not rebuke you for asking" (James 1:5).

I pray for many things every day. I pray for my family, my friends, my ministry, my nation—and, of course, myself. I pray for protection. I pray for a deeper revelation of God's love and over my life. I pray for grace. But there's one thing I've been praying for more and more lately—and I am convinced that if we would pray more for this one thing we would make better use of our time, live happier lives, and ultimately see more answers to our prayers.

What is this one thing I've been praying for more and more lately? Prophetic wisdom. I believe if we pray more for prophetic wisdom—even if it means praying less for natural needs—we'll receive more wisdom and our natural needs will be more than met. Proverbs 3:13-18 reads:

> *Joyful is the person who finds wisdom, the one who gains understanding. For wisdom is more profitable than silver, and her wages are better than gold. Wisdom is more precious than rubies; nothing you desire can compare with her. She offers you long life in her right hand, and riches and honor in her left. She will guide you down delightful paths; all her ways are satisfying. Wisdom is a tree of life to those who embrace her; happy are those who hold her tightly.*

Wisdom begets wisdom—and we need more wisdom in our prophetic operations than perhaps ever before. We're in a new prophetic era with multiple generations of believers, some of whom have never heard of prophecy before and others who abuse it. Prophetic wisdom will help us build our ministry God's way (see Prov. 24:3). Prophetic wisdom will help us be more cautious about our associations (see Prov. 14:16). Prophetic wisdom will give us favor (see Eccles. 10:12). Prophetic wisdom will lead us to honor (see Prov. 3:35). It will keep us and guard us if we love it (see Prov. 4:6-7).

You have a prophetic anointing. You have prophetic armor. What you may need more than anything in the coming days is wisdom in how to operate in your prophetic mantle.

— *Prayer* —

Father, in the name of Jesus, give me wisdom from above, which is first pure, then peaceable, gentle, open to reason, full of mercy and good fruits, partial, and sincere. Teach me to operate in wise prophetic principles beyond my years.

Prophets of Hope

"Let Your mercy, O Lord, be upon us, just as we hope in You" (Psalm 33:22 NKJV).

I once prophesied these words to the head intercessor at a church I attended: "You are a prophet of hope." I didn't know at the time that I was comparing her ministry to Isaiah's. Despite pronouncing judgment upon judgment, Isaiah goes down in Bible history as a prophet of hope. His judgment prophecies were terrifying, but his hope prophecies still speak to our hearts today.

Isaiah prophesied things like, "He will make a highway for the remnant of his people, the remnant coming from Assyria, just as he did for Israel long ago when they returned from Egypt" (Isa. 11:16). And again, "I—yes, I alone—will blot out your sins for my own sake and will never think of them again" (Isa. 43:25). And again, "For I am about to do something new. See, I have already begun! Do you not see it? I will make a pathway through the wilderness. I will create rivers in the dry wasteland" (Isa. 43:19).

And again, "But in that coming day no weapon turned against you will succeed. You will silence every voice raised up to accuse you. These benefits are enjoyed by the servants of the Lord; their vindication will come from me. I, the Lord, have spoken!" (Isa. 54:17).

Zechariah follows suit, prophesying, "Come back to the place of safety, all you prisoners who still have hope! I promise this very day that I will repay two blessings for each of your troubles" (Zech. 9:12). And Jeremiah, the weeping prophet, also had a bright message for Israel, even in the midst of judgment: "'For I know the plans I have for you,' says the Lord. 'They are plans for good and not for disaster, to give you a future and a hope'" (Jer. 29:11).

No matter how troubling the Lord's words, keep listening. God is the God of hope and He has a message of hope in the midst of a crisis. Determine to put your heart to the chest of Jesus and be a living, breathing prophet of hope. You'll be in good company.

— *Prayer* —

Father, in the name of Jesus, infuse my soul with hope. Help me hear through the ears of hope and see through the eyes of hope so I can communicate even the most troubling messages through the filter of a future hope.

The Spirit of the Prophets

"Remember that people who prophesy are in control of their spirit and can take turns" (1 Corinthians 14:32).

Do not prophesy without permission. What do I mean by permission? If the meeting is not yours, you do not have the authority to prophesy without the permission of the person who is holding the meeting. Let me give you an example.

I've been in meetings with zealous prophets who don't follow this protocol. They are given the mic for a moment to pray and they take over the meeting with prophecy after prophecy after prophecy. This is out of order and makes the prophet look reckless and irresponsible. First Corinthians 14:40 tells us to do all things decently and in order.

Some will claim they had fire shut up in their bones and could not help it. But the rule of decency and order must prevail. Just eight verses before the "decency and in order" instruction Paul, inspired by the Holy Spirit, also said this: "The spirits of the prophets are subject to the prophets" (1 Cor. 14:32 NKJV).

The Message says it like this: "Take your turn, no one person taking over. Then each speaker gets a chance to say something special from God, and you all learn from each other." We must submit to the authority of the meeting. If we are not given permission to prophesy, then we don't prophesy. If the meeting leader misses it or is being disobedient to God, that is between God and that leader. If it's not your meeting, you should not usurp the authority of the leader. If God wants your prophetic message released, He will make a way—even if it's not the way you think. Remember, God's ways are higher than our ways. Trust Him and stay decent and in order and you will gain respect.

— *Prayer* —

Father, in the name of Jesus, help me develop a spirit of self-control so I don't overstep my bounds. Season me so I am able to hold my peace when others have something to say. Help me to remember that everything You tell me doesn't need to be shared in the moment.

Watch Your Mouth

"And among all the parts of the body, the tongue is a flame of fire. It is a whole world of wickedness, corrupting your entire body. It can set your whole life on fire, for it is set on fire by hell itself" (James 3:6).

Way back in 2005 during Hurricane Wilma power outages I had a lot of time on my hands. I took that time to really press into the Lord. I asked Him what my biggest problem was. (In case you don't know, that's a dangerous question that you shouldn't ask if you don't want the answer.)

I expected Him to tell me I needed to pray more or read the Word more—or do something more. His answer made my jaw drop: "Your mouth, the very thing I've called you to use." What? He reassured me my mouth was my biggest weakness during that season. I released the power of death too often. I complained too often. It was an uncomfortable truth, but I knew it was the truth.

What did I do? I did what any prophet should do. I asked the Lord to set a guard over my mouth and started studying what the Bible says about the mouth, to renew my mind to the wisdom about the benefits and dangers of using my mouth correctly.

Proverbs 21:23 tells us, "Watch your words and hold your tongue, you'll save yourself a lot of grief" (MSG). Proverbs 6:2 warns, "You are snared by the words of your mouth; you are taken by the words of your mouth" (NKJV). And Proverbs 18:6, "A fool's lips enter into contention, and his mouth calls for flogging" (MEV).

Meditate on these Scriptures for a while. Maybe the Lord didn't tell you that your biggest problem is your mouth. Maybe your biggest problem is something else. But whatever your biggest problem is, your mouth is in the mix somewhere. I guarantee your mouth is part of the problem.

Proverbs 13:3 tells us, "He who guards his mouth preserves his life, but he who opens wide his lips will have destruction" (NKJV). And Proverbs 15:23, "A man has joy by the answer of his mouth, and a word spoken in due season, how good it is!" (NKJV). Ask the Lord to help you get control over that little member in your mouth—that tongue that sets your ministry on fire.

— *Prayer* —

Father, in the name of Jesus, help me to watch my mouth! Help me to be slow to speak. Help me discern when not to speak at all—or prophesy at all. Teach me the wisdom of heaven with regard to how I use my mouth, not just to prophesy but to edify in my everyday speech.

The Anna Anointing

"...She never left the Temple but stayed there day and night, worshiping God with fasting and prayer" (Luke 2:37).

People with an Anna anointing have a lifestyle of prayer—a consecrated life of intercession. It's something that may not come natural to our flesh, but the spirit of the prophet longs for this ongoing dialogue with God that shifts natural circumstances with power from on high.

Available to both men and women, the Anna anointing is an anointing for prophetic intercession, or praying prophetically. Praying prophetically is when the Spirit informs your prayer by what He tells you to pray or when the Spirit seems to take over and you pray what's on His heart directly without ever hearing it. It just flows out of your mouth.

The Anna anointing will help you stay constant in prayer and pray in diverse ways. It is part of every praying prophet's gift mix. The Anna anointing is combined with a grace to spend long hours in prayer and fasting for many years. Anna dedicated her life to prophetic intercession, which is praying with the heart and mind of God. Luke 2:36-38 describes her:

> *Anna, a prophet, was also there in the Temple. She was the daughter of Phanuel from the tribe of Asher, and she was very old. Her husband died when they had been married only seven years. Then she lived as a widow to the age of eighty-four. She never left the Temple but stayed there day and night, worshiping God with fasting and prayer. She came along just as Simeon was talking with Mary and Joseph, and she began praising God. She talked about the child to everyone who had been waiting expectantly for God to rescue Jerusalem.*

Anna the prophetess fulfilled the command, "to pray without ceasing" in 1 Thessalonians 5:17 (NKJV). She prayed day and night and night and day. She fulfilled the command in Ephesians 6:18, "And pray in the Spirit on all occasions with all kinds of prayers and requests" (NIV). With prophetic intelligence, she prophesied about Jesus before John the Baptist did. Before Jesus and John the Baptist were born, she was prophesying about the Messiah.

— *Prayer* —

Father, in the name of Jesus, let the Anna anointing mark my ministry. Help me to become the praying prophet You've called me to be. Let the ministry of prayer infuse my prophetic utterances that break open atmospheres.

Living a Fasted Lifestyle

"But when you fast, comb your hair and wash your face. Then no one will notice that you are fasting, except your Father, who knows what you do in private. And your Father, who sees everything, will reward you" (Matthew 6:17-18).

Jesus gave His disciples instructions for when they fast—not *if* they fast, but *when* they fast. He said not to look gloomy like the hypocrites do but to keep their fasting to themselves. If you brag about your fasting, He said, you've got your reward.

There are many rewards to fasting—and to living a fasted lifestyle. Fasting is abstaining from food or some activity to focus on God. A fasted lifestyle, by contrast, is a disciplined lifestyle in which we steward our spirit, soul, and body in a way that glorifies God.

South African writer, pastor, and teacher Andrew Murray wrote: "Prayer is reaching out after the unseen; fasting is letting go of all that is seen and temporal. Fasting helps express, deepen, confirm the resolution that we are ready to sacrifice anything, even ourselves to attain what we seek for the kingdom of God."

When the Holy Spirit leads you to fast, it could be for a number of reasons, such as spiritual warfare, breaking a yoke of bondage, or overcoming some carnal behavior. But He may also lead you to fast just to gain more sensitivity to His Spirit and thereby sharpen your spiritual eyesight.

In that way, fasting—and a fasted lifestyle—is a gate into the prophetic dimensions. Fasting doesn't change God, but it does change you. Remember, Peter was on the roof, hungry, and waiting for food when he fell into a trance (see Acts 10:10). When the Holy Spirit leads you to fast, ask Him to open your eyes and ears a little wider.

Basil, bishop of Caesarea (AD 330–379) once said, "Fasting begets prophets and strengthens strong men. Fasting makes lawgivers wise; it is the soul's safeguard, the body's trusted comrade, the armor of the champion, the training of the athlete."

Of course, your fasting should be Spirit-led or you won't have grace to last through the fast. But when He leads you, prepare your heart for revelation. Set aside time to feast on the Word and prayer. A fasted lifestyle will lead you into new levels of the prophetic.

— *Prayer* —

Father, in the name of Jesus, lead me to fast when I need to put my flesh under. Help me to gain a greater sensitivity to Your Spirit while fasting. Help me deepen the resolution that I am ready to sacrifice anything to see what You want to show me.

What's Your Rep?

"Let this mind be in you which was also in Christ Jesus, who, being in the form of God, did not consider it robbery to be equal with God, but made Himself of no reputation, taking the form of a bondservant, and coming in the likeness of men" (Philippians 2:5-7 NKJV).

I've seen many prophets throughout my journey who built reputations on their accurate prophecies. Jesus built a reputation based on His character. Sure, He was known for signs and wonders and that's why many people followed Him when He was alive. But we remember Him best for being the sinless Savior, for dying on a cross to pave the way for our eternal life. That's His claim to fame.

Jesus made Himself of no reputation. He wasn't trying to make a name for Himself. He gave up His divine privileges. He emptied Himself. He demanded nothing and gave everything. He ministered tirelessly. He was a friend to sinners. His eternal reputation is love, and as prophets so should ours be.

When we try to make a name for ourselves, we usually end up with a compromised name. Discerning people can see when we are striving for the blessings of God instead of resting in His promises and waiting for His promotion. They can see when we're trying to make something happen instead of trusting the God we claim speaks through us. Trying to make a reputation for ourselves actually hurts our reputation.

Discerning people can tell when we sell out for money instead of selling out for souls, like Jesus did. Proverbs 22:1 tells us, "Choose a good reputation over great riches; being held in high esteem is better than silver or gold." God will provide the needs of the modern-day prophet just like He provided for Elijah through ravens, widows, and angels.

Ecclesiastes 7:1 tells us a good reputation is more valuable than costly perfume. Our conduct behind the scenes is as important as our conduct under the spotlight. Paul put it this way in 1 Peter 2:11-12:

Beloved, I beg you as sojourners and pilgrims, abstain from fleshly lusts which war against the soul, having your conduct honorable among the Gentiles, that when they speak against you as evildoers, they may, by your good works which they observe, glorify God in the day of visitation (NKJV).

Prophet, you will get enough persecution for doing what is right. Let's avoid the persecution that comes from doing what's wrong and preserve our reputations for integrity.

— *Prayer* —

Father, in the name of Jesus, help me to be less concerned about my name and more concerned about glorifying Your name in the earth in my prophetic ministry. Help me avoid the temptation to build my reputation instead of Yours.

Pursue the Prophetic Release

"...Since you are so eager to have the special abilities the Spirit gives, seek those that will strengthen the whole church" (1 Corinthians 14:12).

When I was younger in the ministry I was not eager to prophesy, and that was wrong. Paul, inspired by the Holy Spirit, plainly tells us to desire to prophesy (see 1 Cor. 14:39). Some translations actually say "earnestly desire" or even "covet to prophesy." This is not just any desire; it's a strong desire.

There's a good reason for Paul's instruction. Prophecy does so many things in the spirit realm. We should be asking God what's on His heart and mind and be eager to release the life-giving words. Paul put it this way in 1 Corinthians 14:1-5:

> *Let love be your highest goal! But you should also desire the special abilities the Spirit gives—especially the ability to prophesy. For if you have the ability to speak in tongues, you will be talking only to God, since people won't be able to understand you. You will be speaking by the power of the Spirit, but it will all be mysterious. But one who prophesies strengthens others, encourages them, and comforts them. A person who speaks in tongues is strengthened personally, but one who speaks a word of prophecy strengthens the entire church.*
>
> *I wish you could all speak in tongues, but even more I wish you could all prophesy. For prophecy is greater than speaking in tongues, unless someone interprets what you are saying so that the whole church will be strengthened.*

Notice how Paul, out of all the gifts of the Spirit, emphasized prophecy. That's because prophecy strengthens, comforts, exhorts, encourages, and builds people up. Prophecy demonstrates that Jesus is alive. Prophecy brings healing to bodies and deliverance to souls. Prophecy helps restore marriages and so much more.

The enemy is always prophesying to people falsely. Through true prophecy, God's truth dismantles the enemy's lies. God's truth builds up what the enemy is tearing down. Be eager to prophesy.

— *Prayer* —

Father, in the name of Jesus, give me an earnest desire to prophesy. Help me continually stand in Your presence with wide open ears and eyes to hear and see what You want to tell me about Your people so I can edify, comfort, and exhort the Bride.

God Is Launching Fiery Prophets

"John was like a burning and shining lamp, and you were excited for a while about his message" (John 5:35).

I heard the Lord say:

> I'm about to ignite the prophets. Many have ignored the prophetic voices in this hour, but I'm about to set them on fire so the world can watch them burn with the message that's on My heart. Many have forsaken My prophetic voices in the season, but I'm about to raise them up in an undeniable way so that all can see that I have a voice, and I have a say, and I have a plan, and I have a purpose for My people and for this nation in the season.

> So embrace My fire now as I pour it out upon you and understand that I am doing a new thing in the prophetic ministry. Some of the old ways are no longer working because they were seasonal. The new way will be fire, fire, fire. The new way will be intimacy with Me that demonstrates and manifests My love in the midst of the hard days.

> I will give you hard words, but they will be laced with fire and they will burn through the opposition. Some will still oppose you, yes, but many will begin to hear because as they see and they sense what is happening in the world they will need verbiage and words to understand and describe what it is they are coming into.

> The prophets and prophetic voices in the land will not only give heed to what I'm saying, but they will express it with clarity. They will sound the alarm. They will blow the trumpet. They will understand what is on My mind and what is on My heart because they have spent time in My counsel. I am bringing them out of the wilderness places even now, and I am setting them on a watch tower, and I am setting them in a military formation to go forth and lead an army of prophetic saints into the battlefield to overtake the wicked one in Jesus' name.

Are you ready for God to ignite you?

— *Prayer* —

Father, in the name of Jesus, light me up. Set me on fire. I want to burn and shine for You like John the Baptist. I want to release prophetic utterances that cause people to burn for Your presence and Your holiness.

When the Revelation Is Progressive

"This is what the Lord, the God of Israel, says: Write down for the record everything I have said to you, Jeremiah" (Jeremiah 30:2).

Do you journal? In recording the prophetic words God has spoken over my life, I've unlocked additional revelation—and additional application. I noticed that at least some of these revelations played out a little differently—or maybe a lot differently—than I expected. We don't always see the fullness of God's prophetic intent when we receive words for ourselves or others.

When you experience progressive application of a prophetic revelation, you're essentially growing into the prophetic word. At first you didn't have the capacity to walk in the completeness of what the Lord was saying, so you enter into a training ground that allows you to apply the principles of the prophetic word on a smaller scale.

One of the best examples I can offer from my personal life is what I now affectionately refer to as the "Ezra revelation." In Ezra 5 we discover the work on the house of God in Jerusalem ceased after much resistance and opposition. After some time, the restoration of the temple resumed with prophets playing a key role. Ezra 5:1-2 tells us the prophets encouraged the builders.

When I saw this Scripture, the Lord spoke to my heart about the role of prophetic ministry in building—or rebuilding, as it were—God's house. I was convinced the application was a weekly meeting with prophets in our congregation during which we could pray and seek the Lord for prophetic strategies about building the local church. That wasn't wrong, but 10 years later I saw the prophetic revelation God was pouring into my heart was about more than one local church—it has to do with an awakening in America.

Record the prophetic words, dreams, and visions you receive and seek to put the truth within them into practice today. But don't stop there. Refer back to your journals over time, and you may see clearly how the Lord has shifted dynamics to bring you into a deeper application of that prophetic revelation.

— *Prayer* —

Father, in the name of Jesus, help me discipline myself to journal so I can recall what You've said in every season and review where I am on the journey to Your great and precious promises. Help me apply Your revelation to my life accurately for Your glory.

Pre-Meditated Prophetic Curses

"...bless, and curse not" (Romans 12:14 KJV).

"If you leave this church you will walk around wandering with no anointing for the rest of your life. You will not fit in anywhere. Any anointing you have is because of me." That prophetic curse was released over my life in 2010. But his word curse had the opposite effect of what was intended.

The apostle thought I would stay put, subservient to his control. Instead, I soon left that church, forgave, broke the curse, and walked into continual increase. The apostle who released the prophetic curse, by contrast, diminished in influence. God doesn't bless people who curse, yet too many prophets lay out curses instead of blessing God's people.

James, the apostle of practical faith, says the tongue is restless and evil, full of deadly poison.

> *Sometimes it praises our Lord and Father, and sometimes it curses those who have been made in the image of God. And so blessing and cursing come pouring out of the same mouth. Surely, my brothers and sisters, this is not right! Does a spring of water bubble out with both fresh water and bitter water? Does a fig tree produce olives, or a grapevine produce figs? No, and you can't draw fresh water from a salty spring* (James 3:9-12).

That's a mouthful! Many people point to Paul cursing the sorcerer who was standing between him and the proconsul to whom he was ministering with temporary blindness (see Acts 13:8). Paul also called down a curse on false teachers with false gospels (see Gal. 1:8-9). Clearly, these were not curses veiled in prophecy to believers. These were Holy Spirit-inspired judgments in the early days of the church when Christianity was being established. You never see Paul cursing a believer—or just the general population of persecutors.

God is not cursing believers, so prophets who release curses are not speaking for God. You probably aren't cursing people in your prophetic utterances, either. But is your flow as pure as it could be?

— *Prayer* —

Father, in the name of Jesus, I want the rivers of water that flow from my heart to be pure, not tainted by disappointment, bias, or bitterness. Cleanse me from all unrighteousness, God, so I can represent Your generous Spirit to the world.

Your Burning Bush Moment

"...Take off your sandals, for you are standing on holy ground" (Exodus 3:5).

I'll always remember my burning bush moment. Well, actually, the bush was smoking. I was heading into the back door of my condo building when I noticed a bush in the garden was smoking. I stopped to look because it was more smoke than a cigarette—or even two cigarettes—could muster. I examined the bush careful and could not see any natural source of smoke.

I must have looked foolish, and that may have been the point. God was trying to get my attention. He was trying to show me something that I wasn't seeing. He was trying to tell me something I wasn't hearing. He got my attention at the smoking bush and shared truth with me soon after that helped me break through to the next level.

Moses had an encounter with God at the burning bush and it changed his life. Like me, Moses passed by a burning bush and said, "This is amazing. ...Why isn't that bush burning up? I must go see it" (Exod. 3:3). What the Bible says next is also amazing: "When the Lord saw Moses coming to take a closer look, God called to him from the middle of the bush, 'Moses! Moses!'" (Exod. 3:4).

Think about it for a minute. What if Moses hadn't stopped to look? Burning bushes actually were not all that uncommon in the desert. But this one caught Moses' attention and he turned aside. If he had kept on walking—if he was not sensitive to the Spirit—he would have walked right past this life-defining encounter.

In that encounter, Moses heard the voice of the God of Abraham, Isaac, and Jacob. He heard the God who created the world. He heard the God who was greater than the gods of Egypt. He heard God call His name and say, "Moses, Moses, I will be with you." Moses was called. He was commissioned. He was promoted. He was sent. Don't miss your burning bush moments.

— *Prayer* —

Father, help me not to walk right by my divine encounters. Make me sensitive to Your Spirit so that I can see what You are saying in everyday circumstances. Tune my heart to Yours so completely that I will never miss a moment in Your manifest presence.

Extreme Prophetic Makeover

"So all of us who have had that veil removed can see and reflect the glory of the Lord. And the Lord—who is the Spirit—makes us more and more like him as we are changed into his glorious image" (2 Corinthians 3:18).

Makeover shows are some of the hottest reality TV titles in entertainment today. But sometimes we need to do more than makeover our hair, our clothes, or our homes. Plastic surgery, Lasik for our blurry vision, personal trainers, and interior decorators can make things look good on the outside, but all true change and beauty starts in the spirit. Sometimes, if we get caught up in the ways of the world, we need an extreme prophetic makeover.

The prophet's makeover process never ends. God remakes and remodels and brings us into new glories throughout our lives. Our heart posture should cooperate with the grace of God rather than resisting His touch ups. Imagine a makeup artist trying to get you ready for a photoshoot while you're resisting the powder that keeps the shine down. Imagine a dentist trying to put a filling in your tooth with your mouth clamped shut. Imagine getting a haircut and refusing to sit still.

In order to see an extreme prophetic makeover in your life, you need to yield to the Holy Spirit. He is the makeover agent. He is the power of God dwelling on the inside of us. He works in us through the Word of God, accelerating the renewal of our mind so we can reject sinful thoughts and habits and see transformation in our lives. He works through conviction, showing us what we're doing wrong and helping us do what is right.

Ultimately, the Holy Spirit's greatest work in our life is not giving us prophecy but making us more like Christ. *The Passion Translation* puts it this way, "We are being transfigured into his very image as we move from one brighter level of glory to another. And this glorious transfiguration comes from the Lord, who is the Spirit" (2 Cor. 3:18).

Yield to the Holy Spirit's extreme prophetic makeover. It may be uncomfortable, but it will bring forth fruit in your soul, fruit in your spirit, and fruit in your prophetic ministry.

— *Prayer* —

Father, in the name of Jesus, help me to submit to the extreme prophetic makeover. Do what You have to do in me so You can do what You want to do through me and for me. Only You can do it, so I surrender all that I am to You.

The Snare of Self-Righteousness

"...When we display our righteous deeds, they are nothing but filthy rags..." (Isaiah 64:6).

When Elijah walked the earth, Jezebel was murdering the prophets. Many of them fled Israel. Some were hiding in caves. Elijah was roaming about. Apparently, God transported him from one place to another without warning. When Elijah appeared to Obadiah and told him to tell the king to come meet with him, Ahab's servant got nervous.

And now you say, "Go and tell your master, 'Elijah is here.'" But as soon as I leave you, the Spirit of the Lord will carry you away to who knows where. When Ahab comes and cannot find you, he will kill me... (1 Kings 18:11-12).

Elijah wasn't grounded in a company of prophets. He didn't see any other prophets in Israel, so he thought he was the only one.

Elijah was so confident in his unmatched fervor for the Lord, the prophet actually told God: "I have zealously served the Lord God Almighty. But the people of Israel have broken their covenant with you, torn down your altars, and killed every one of your prophets. I am the only one left, and now they are trying to kill me, too" (1 Kings 19:10).

In these three sentences, we see what was going on in Elijah's heart and how dangerous it is. Elijah had taken on a self-righteous mindset. This is a precarious temptation for prophets, especially those who are wholeheartedly pursuing holiness in a corrupt world. But we have to remember that our own righteousness is like filthy rags to the Lord (see Isa. 64:6). Our righteousness comes from our faith in Christ alone.

The Lord set Elijah straight, making it clear there were 7,000 others who had not bowed a knee to Baal or kissed him. It's easy to fall into the self-righteousness trap when we feel like we're the only ones standing for God, but this mindset will ultimately lead us into pride and pride comes before a fall.

— *Prayer* —

Father, in the name of Jesus, give me deeper revelation of who I am in Christ, but also give me an understanding that apart from Him I can do nothing. You alone are righteous and just. You have preserved a remnant, and I will not think more highly of myself than I ought.

A Thankless Job, but a Thankful Heart

"Be thankful in all circumstances, for this is God's will for you who belong to Christ Jesus" (1 Thessalonians 5:18).

Being a prophet can be a thankless job. There's the idea that prophets don't exist today. There's rejection. There's persecution. There's suffering. But prophets aren't in the office for man's reward. Prophets are standing in the office at the pleasure of the King.

Regardless of the thankless job, prophets who cultivate a thankful heart stay pure. Consider the suffering, for example. We don't thank God for the suffering, but we can thank God in the suffering and endure it with courage. First Thessalonians 5:18 admonishes us to "Be thankful in all circumstances, for this is God's will for you who belong to Christ Jesus."

Daniel the prophet modeled the way for us in the midst of difficult circumstances. Administrators in Babylon were jealous of Daniel and tricked King Darius into signing a decree they knew Daniel would not agree with—anyone who prayed to anyone but the king for 30 days would be thrown into the lion's den.

> But when Daniel learned that the law had been signed, he went home and knelt down as usual in his upstairs room, with its windows open toward Jerusalem. He prayed three times a day, just as he had always done, giving thanks to his God (Daniel 6:10).

Thanksgiving was part of Daniel's lifestyle and he refused to stop thanking his God even if it meant death. How many of us could do the same?

You know what happened next. God sent an angel to shut the lions' mouths so they would not harm the prophet. I wouldn't doubt it at all if Daniel was thanking God for the breakthrough before the angel arrived. There is power in thanksgiving. It seems the prophet understood Philippians 4:6-7 before it was written:

> Don't worry about anything; instead, pray about everything. Tell God what you need, and thank him for all he has done. Then you will experience God's peace, which exceeds anything we can understand. His peace will guard your hearts and minds as you live in Christ Jesus.

— *Prayer* —

Father, in the name of Jesus, help me remain thankful. Help me to cultivate an attitude of gratitude amid the suffering, slander, and serious attacks. You are worthy of thanksgiving, praise, and honor. I know You are able to make me stand.

When You Feel Like You're Standing Alone

"Don't be afraid, for I am with you. Don't be discouraged, for I am your God. I will strengthen you and help you. I will hold you up with my victorious right hand" (Isaiah 41:10).

The prophet's life can be a lonely one at times. The prophet often watches in the spirit alone and often makes decrees alone. The prophet often eats the scroll alone and then releases a warning that lands on deaf ears alone. The prophet often sounds the alarm to a sleeping church alone and makes intercession alone while the saints are snug in their beds without a care in the world. The prophet's burden in prayer is often severe, and so is the feeling of being alone.

Despite all the talk of companies of prophets, there are indeed times when the prophet has to walk alone. John the Baptist walked alone in the wilderness for many years. Samuel walked alone before he started his schools. Elijah was convinced he was walking alone. He once told the Israelites, "I am the only prophet of the Lord who is left, but Baal has 450 prophets" (1 Kings 18:22). And after defeating the false prophets on Mount Carmel, twice Elijah told the Lord, "I am the only one left, and now they are trying to kill me, too" (1 Kings 19:10,14).

Paul knew what it was like to stand alone. He once told his spiritual son, Timothy: "The first time I was brought before the judge, no one came with me. Everyone abandoned me" (2 Tim. 4:16). David knew what it was like to walk alone. He fought the lion alone. He fought the bear alone. And he was the only one among the Israelites who wasn't afraid to stand up to Goliath alone (see 1 Sam. 17).

Sometimes you may walk alone. But many times it just feels like you are standing solo. Elijah, for example, had a wrong perspective. When you feel like you're walking alone, get your mind off yourself and get your mind on God. He will never leave you or forsake you even to the end of the age (see Heb. 13:5). You are not alone.

— *Prayer* —

Father, in the name of Jesus, help me shift my mindset. Help me accept the times when I have to walk through seasons without anyone who really gets where I am going. Remind me that You are the Friend who sticks closer than a brother—and that You understand my plight.

Casting Down the "Persecution" Complex

"...I have become a laughingstock all day long; everyone mocks me" (Jeremiah 20:7 NASB 1995).

Jeremiah was the most persecuted prophet of the Old Testament. He was cursed, beaten, and thrown into prison. He once said, "What sorrow is mine, my mother. Oh, that I had died at birth! I am hated everywhere I go. I am neither a lender who threatens to foreclose nor a borrower who refuses to pay—yet they all curse me" (Jer. 15:10).

That's intense. It's no wonder God promised him in the early days of his ministry to make him strong like a fortified city that can't be captured (see Jer. 1:18). He had to be strong to endure the persecution. Toward the latter part of his ministry we read, "They were furious with Jeremiah and had him flogged and imprisoned in the house of Jonathan the secretary. Jonathan's house had been converted into a prison" (Jer. 37:15).

We don't know how Jeremiah finally died, but many historians believe he was stoned to death. Now that's persecution! You may find yourself the subject of vile accusations, slander, and maligning that have no basis in truth—but words can't hurt you unless you let them. Don't fall to the persecution complex. If Jeremiah withstood sixty years of attacks without hiding in his cave and having a bad attitude, so can you.

As recorded in my *Victory Decrees* devotional, I heard the Lord say, "Let me deal with your persecutors. Let me deal with your detractors. Let me deal with your abusers. Don't you do it. Take your hands off this. I will vindicate you. Take your mouth off them. I will show them to be in the wrong. Don't tie my hands with a vengeance mind-set. Vengeance is mine. I will repay. I know it's tempting. I know your flesh rises up when you see their success at your expense. Let My Spirit rise up and defend you. Let Me make it right for you. Your payback is in Me. Let's do this My way. My ways are higher than your ways. Trust Me."

— *Prayer* —

Father, in the name of Jesus, help me handle persecution the way Jesus did. Help me not to throw myself a pity-party or take on a victim mentality. Teach me to let the persecution and attacks roll off my back.

Come Up Here

"Then as I looked, I saw a door standing open in heaven, and the same voice I had heard before spoke to me like a trumpet blast. The voice said, 'Come up here, and I will show you what must happen after this'" (Revelation 4:1).

God is inviting you to come up higher. Prophesying generic words to "somebody" that could be for anybody and everybody may be edifying but there's a higher level—a deeper level. It's time for prophets to press into the supernatural like Elijah, to see in the spirit with clarity like Elisha, to know details and directions. It's time to raise your prophetic water level.

We know water levels ebb and flow. If your prophetic water level is ebbing, that means you're like the low tide. The water level has receded. Low tide is the opposite of overflow. You can walk on a sandbar in low tide. You need to refill yourself with the water and the word so you can flow again.

By contrast, high tide is when the water is at its highest point. You can't live in high tide, but you shouldn't live in low tide either. If you are living in low tide, you need to do something to raise your prophetic water level. I get this concept from Ezekiel 47:1-5:

> *In my vision, the man brought me back to the entrance of the Temple. There I saw a stream flowing east from beneath the door of the Temple and passing to the right of the altar on its south side. The man brought me outside the wall through the north gateway and led me around to the eastern entrance. There I could see the water flowing out through the south side of the east gateway.*
>
> *Measuring as he went, he took me along the stream for 1,750 feet and then led me across. The water was up to my ankles. He measured off another 1,750 feet and led me across again. This time the water was up to my knees. After another 1,750 feet, it was up to my waist. Then he measured another 1,750 feet, and the river was too deep to walk across. It was deep enough to swim in, but too deep to walk through.*

What's your prophetic water level?

— *Prayer* —

Father, in the name of Jesus, stir in me a holy fervor to go deeper into the prophetic. I don't want to release shallow prophecies in Your name. I want to get into the minute details of the instructions You want to share with Your people. Deepen my water level.

Looking Through Berean Eyes

"And the people of Berea were more open-minded than those in Thessalonica, and they listened eagerly to Paul's message. They searched the Scriptures day after day to see if Paul and Silas were teaching the truth" (Acts 17:11).

As prophets, we need to embrace a Berean spirit. The Bereans were first open-minded. They wanted to learn new things. They didn't camp out in the last move of God, set in their ways and rejecting present-day truth. They were hungering and thirsting after righteousness—and they were continually filled.

As prophets, we need to embrace a Berean spirit. They were biblically curious. They didn't just read the Scriptures; they searched the Scriptures. They didn't just search the Scriptures randomly; they were searching with the intent of confirming truth. Put another way, they were lovers of the truth and able to rightly divide the word of truth (see 2 Tim. 2:15). They were students of the Word.

As prophets, we need to embrace a Berean spirit. The English Standard Version of Acts 17:11 says they examined the Scriptures daily. They examined the Scriptures so they could hold fast to that which is good (see 1 Thess. 5:21). They set out to discern whether what they heard matched up with what God had already said. They were judging a righteous judgment (see John 7:24).

As prophets, we need to embrace a Berean spirit. The Bible says they had noble character and were fair-minded. The International Standard Version calls them receptive. They were intelligent, open to conviction, teachable, and less biased than the rest. They were diligent, searching the Scriptures daily.

As prophets, we need to embrace a Berean spirit. Before Paul wrote 2 Timothy 3:16-17, the Bereans embraced it: "All Scripture is inspired by God and is useful to teach us what is true and to make us realize what is wrong in our lives. It corrects us when we are wrong and teaches us to do what is right. God uses it to prepare and equip his people to do every good work."

— *Prayer* —

Father, in the name of Jesus, give me the grace that was on the lives of the Bereans. Give me a hunger for Your Word and a love of the truth that discerns error and rejects heresy. Help me make Scripture study a top priority so I can better discern Your will.

Out of Your Head, Into His Heart

"Trust in the Lord with all your heart, and lean not on your own understanding" (Proverbs 3:5 NKJV).

When I was younger in prophetic ministry, I would try to wrap my mind around what God was saying prophetically. I didn't know then what I know now: Sometimes we don't understand everything we prophesy. And sometimes, if we're not careful, we can reason ourselves right out of delivering what would be a life-changing word to someone desperately in need.

When I got out of my head and into God's heart, I prophesied things that seemed unlikely to my mind but they came to pass with pinpoint precision. When I got out of my head and into His heart, I learned how much higher God's thoughts are than mine. Maybe you can relate. Prophecy doesn't always make sense, and it doesn't have to make sense to be true.

We see Peter struggling with this. An expert fisherman, he had worked all night in the Sea of Galilee and caught nothing. Jesus was there preaching on the shore, and when He finished His message He gave Peter a prophetic instruction: "Now go out where it is deeper, and let down your nets to catch some fish" (Luke 5:4).

The prophetic words made no sense to Peter's mind. He was the expert fisherman. Jesus was just a carpenter. At first, Peter spoke from his head:

"Master," Simon replied, "we worked hard all last night and didn't catch a thing" (Luke 5:5).

But Peter quickly transitioned out of his head and into God's heart. Peter didn't just catch a boatload of fish; he got a revelation that when we hear His words we must act from the heart even if we don't understand in our minds.

It's tempting to lean on your own understanding, not because you don't trust the Lord but because you don't trust that you heard Him right. The reality of the prophetic dimension is we are not always going to understand what God means by what He says, but the ones we're prophesying to will. It's not always for us to understand. Our job is to stay out of our head and get into His heart—and trust.

— *Prayer* —

Father, in the name of Jesus, help me stop reasoning out prophetic words to the point that I doubt what You said. Teach me to get out of my head and into Your heart so I can edify Your people with Your life-giving words.

Risky Faith

"...And I swear in his name that it won't rain until I say so. There won't even be any dew on the ground" (1 Kings 17:1 CEV).

Shawn Bolz interviewed me for his podcast once and asked me about risky prophetic words. He wanted to know the riskiest prophetic word I ever released. My answer? It had to do with the outcome of a presidential election. When I shared it, he told me he remembered the word and was praying for me! That's how risky it was.

If I were wrong, that presidential prophecy would have impacted my credibility. Credibility is important, but our credibility with God is more important than our credibility with man. As prophets, we have to be willing to take risks. We have to be ready to prophesy words that are uncomfortable to release because—even though we're sure we heard from God—what if we didn't?

When I think of risky prophecies, I think of Elijah. Elijah prophesied—to the wicked King Ahab no less—"As surely as the Lord, the God of Israel, lives—the God I serve—there will be no dew or rain during the next few years until I give the word!" (1 Kings 17:1). What a prophecy! I wonder what went through the prophet's mind after he so boldly prophesied a drought to the face of the king.

We know from the Book of James that Elijah was praying! James 5:17 says, "Elijah was as human as we are, and yet when he prayed earnestly that no rain would fall, none fell for three and a half years!" I imagine he was praying earnestly. He released the word and then he started praying for its fulfillment. You know the story. It didn't rain for thirty-nine months. Israel was in drought.

If that were the end of the story, that would be memorable. But Elijah prophesied another risky word: "Then Elijah said to Ahab, 'Go get something to eat and drink, for I hear a mighty rainstorm coming!'" (1 Kings 18:41). There was no rain in sight. So Elijah climbed to the top of Mount Carmel and bowed to the ground and prayed. He kept on praying until he finally saw the first sign of the prophecy's fulfillment—a cloud the size of a man's hand.

— *Prayer* —

Father, in the name of Jesus, give me the courage to extend my faith to prophesy in risky situations. Help me not to keep my mouth shut when You're trying to open it wide so You can fill it. Show me when to take the leap and when to use godly caution.

DECEMBER

"Go out and stand before me on the mountain," the Lord told him. And as Elijah stood there, the Lord passed by, and a mighty windstorm hit the mountain. It was such a terrible blast that the rocks were torn loose, but the Lord was not in the wind. After the wind there was an earthquake, but the Lord was not in the earthquake. And after the earthquake there was a fire, but the Lord was not in the fire. And after the fire there was the sound of a gentle whisper. When Elijah heard it, he wrapped his face in his cloak and went out and stood at the entrance of the cave..." (1 Kings 19:11-13).

Developing Eagle Eyes

"He had been taught the way of the Lord, and he taught others about Jesus with an enthusiastic spirit and with accuracy..." (Acts 18:25).

Prophets and seers, it's critical that you test your visual accuracy. Put another way, it's important to test your visual accuracy in the spirit just as you would test your visual accuracy in the natural. If your natural vision is not strong, you need a prescription to fix it so you can see clearly and avoid accidents. If your spiritual vision is dim or you are seeing wrongly, the prescription is the Word and the Spirit.

Your holy imagination might show you a picture—even a good picture—but it doesn't mean it's a God picture. There are a lot of good things in your mind and your spirit that aren't necessarily coming from God. Your unholy imagination can also show you pictures. Paul tells us clearly to cast those down (see 2 Cor. 10:5). But if you can't discern the difference, you could deceive yourself or others.

The Lord speaks of prophets who "are telling lies in my name. I did not send them or tell them to speak. I did not give them any messages. They prophesy of visions and revelations they have never seen or heard" (Jer. 14:14). And again, "Do not listen to these prophets when they prophesy to you, filling you with futile hopes. They are making up everything they say. They do not speak for the Lord!" (Jer. 23:16).

I believe these were false prophets knowingly offering false visions. In your case, you are working to discern whether what you are seeing is from the Lord or just your imagination running wild—or even the wicked fantasy. And you must do so with strong due diligence. Remember, a vision from God will not violate Scripture but should somehow glorify God by showing you His will, revealing the enemy's plans, or spurring you to press into Him or pray.

— *Prayer* —

Father, in the name of Jesus, help me divide between vain imaginations and divine imaginations. If my visual accuracy is off, please give me the prescription to correct my eyesight so I can see clearly what You are trying to show me in the seer dimensions.

Where's the Way of Escape?

"The temptations in your life are no different from what others experience. And God is faithful. He will not allow the temptation to be more than you can stand. When you are tempted, he will show you a way out so that you can endure" (1 Corinthians 10:13).

When I was very young in prophetic ministry, I was surrounded by apostles and prophets. It was to my benefit, at least most of the time. There were a few instances where elder prophets didn't teach me through their successes but through their mistakes. Any of us, even seasoned prophets, can make mistakes.

In this instance, an elder prophet whom I deeply respected prophesied over me in a prayer line. I was so happy he was going to minister to me, until after he released the word. The prophecy essentially predicted I was about to go through a dark night of the soul and during that darkness I would want to quit the ministry. I would wonder if I was even called at all, he prophesied, and I would be discouraged.

Well, suffice it to say I was devastated and it scared me! I knew he was accurate and I thought I was doomed! I went to my apostle and shared the word with him in hopes of getting some advice on how to make it through this gut-wrenching trial that would apparently start any minute. He listened carefully and offered some sound advice.

The apostle told me the prophet's word was accurate, but that he forgot to offer the way of escape—he forgot to prophesy the outcome of the trial. The apostle then told me the part I needed to hear so I could hold on to a promise in the midst of the ordeal I was about to walk through.

Here's the lesson: Prophesying a warning or hard word without any way of escape or edification is a misuse of prophetic ministry. God does not want people to feel overwhelmed or afraid or condemned. If you get a warning for someone, press in until you get the positive side of the word.

— *Prayer* —

Father, in the name of Jesus, help me not to prophesy in part when the part would leave someone discouraged and depressed. Teach me to wait on You to give me the full story before I open my mouth in Your name so my ministry leaves people edified in the face of a warning.

The Feeler Prophet

"...But Paul was greatly annoyed, and turned and said to the spirit..." (Acts 16:18 NASB 1995).

Our heavenly Father is a master communicator with diverse communication manifestations. Like all believers, prophets are in what I call communications training. God is intent on teaching us to receive His communication in all its diversity. One of those modes of communication is feeling. And feeler prophets are rising.

Simply put, a feeler prophet is one who feels in the spirit realm and can articulate what God is showing them through this prophetic sense. Being a feeler prophet is like having a spiritual antenna, a sensory organ that you can't see. That antenna receives information from the Holy Spirit like antennas on old-fashioned TVs helped viewers pick up better visual reception of programs. This spiritual antenna gives you a special sensitivity or receptiveness.

The spiritual sense of feeling is often tied in with the gift of discernment, but a feeler prophet discerns with feelings and sensations, not just with dreams, visions, and audible revelation. In this context, feeling is like an impression, but it's stronger than an impression. Most impressions are faint. Feelers have stronger impressions rather your typical "check in the spirit."

Another way to put it is feelers have spiritual sensations. At times, this can manifest as a sudden unexplainable pain in your body, which would signal someone else has pain. Some circles have called this a manifestation of the word of knowledge, which it is, but it comes in tactile form. Likewise, feelers can be moved with strong emotion, but it's not their emotion.

Paul operated in this in Acts 16. A girl with a spirit of divination was following him, shouting about their mission. "This went on day after day until Paul got so exasperated that he turned and said to the demon within her, 'I command you in the name of Jesus Christ to come out of her.' And instantly it left her" (Acts 16:18).

Start paying attention, prophet: What do you feel?

— *Prayer* —

Father, teach me to move in the feeler dimensions. I want to receive prophetic revelation and insight in any mode or means You want to deliver it. Help me not to ignore sudden feelings but to press in to see if You have something to say or show me.

Nurturing Prophetic Children

"Then, after doing all those things, I will pour out my Spirit upon all people. Your sons and daughters will prophesy. Your old men will dream dreams, and your young men will see visions" (Joel 2:28).

I see the eyes of children opening. You may not have children, but you may know people who do. I believe prophets need to take a greater interest in the youngest of generations, teaching them principles of seeing in the spirit through the door of Jesus because they are going to begin to prophesy through dreams and visions.

I heard the Lord say:

> Don't be concerned when some of your children start falling into trances. Don't take them to the doctor because it's Me, and they will come out of that trance and they will have prophetic insight, wisdom, and knowledge on things to come because I'm showing them things that eye has not seen nor ear heard.

> Encourage the young ones, encourage the children. Encourage them. Don't push them away. Don't tell them, "Later on I'll talk to you," but take the time even now because in this season I'm pouring out My Spirit on all flesh, but I have a special eye on the young ones who have not yet been corrupted and polluted by the ways of the world. And I want to use them as pure voices and pure visionaries in their generation.

> So encourage them, teach them, show them the way. I am the Way and you will see and know that I will activate even the very young ones in these gifts and the gifts of My Spirit, and they will see with clarity and know and understand, even be able to articulate things that their human capacity could not possible comprehend, says God.

Some children have strong prophetic bents, but we think they are just operating out of the realm of the imagination. We could be unintentionally quenching the Spirit of God working through them. God forbid! Luke records people were even bringing infants to Jesus to receive an impartation (see Luke 18:15-17). It's never too early to begin exposing children to prophetic life.

— *Prayer* —

Father, in the name of Jesus, would You give me the opportunity to equip the parents of children how to respond to their prophetic protégés? Help me be mindful and intentional about helping to raise up the next generation.

The Warrior Prophet

"Endure suffering along with me, as a good soldier of Christ Jesus. Soldiers don't get tied up in the affairs of civilian life, for then they cannot please the officer who enlisted them" (2 Timothy 2:3-4).

When we got saved, we essentially enlisted in Heaven's Army, a saints-and-angels army in which we are armored up, spiritual weapon-carrying soldiers. Perhaps you never thought of it that way, but that's exactly how Paul put it to Timothy.

I remember a time when there was so much going on that I lost sight of the source. The Lord told me plainly, "You are in a war." I wrote in big letters on my wall calendar, "I am in a war" so I would never forget it again. Prophet, whether you recognize it or not, you are in a war.

Although every prophet—just like every believer—has to fight the good fight of faith, some prophets are what I call warrior prophets. Part of the warrior prophet's responsibility is to lead the charge to war and to equip believers to battle the powers of darkness. Warrior prophets tend to have a gift mix that includes discerning of spirits. Warrior prophets have a forehead like flint and may also carry a breaker anointing that plows through spiritual opposition.

As I wrote in my book *The Making of a Prophet*, David is probably the strongest example of a warrior prophet—he actually led God's army into battle. God told David he was a "man of war" (1 Chron. 28:3 NKJV). This is a characteristic of the Lord Himself. Exodus 15:3 says, "The Lord is a man of war; the Lord is His name" (NJKV). Although the prophet David was also a psalmist and a man of prayer—prophets typically flow in multiple manifestations of the prophetic anointing—God made his name great through warfare, beginning with the defeat of Goliath.

Of course, it's not just the men who lead spiritual battles. Women can take a cue from Deborah the prophetess and judge of Israel (see Judg. 4). Deborah had a prophetic word for Barak, the commander of the army, about victory in battle, but he didn't have it in him to walk in the word. He actually said, "If you will go with me, then I will go; but if you will not go with me, I will not go!" (Judg. 4:8 NKJV). Deborah, then, actually led the charge.

— *Prayer* —

Father, in the name of Jesus, help me adopt a warrior mentality so I can be part of the prophetic solution to the battles Your people face, leading them when You charge me and equipping them to overcome with Your name, Your Word, and Christ's blood.

When Prophetic Speculation Goes Awry

"Some believers have been led astray by teachings and speculations that emphasize nothing more than the empty words of men" (1 Timothy 1:6 TPT).

Speculation has found its way into the prophetic ministry, but it must not find its way into your heart. Just think of how many people have predicted the date of Christ's return by speculating as to the timelines of biblical prophecy.

One man speculated Christ would return in 1988 and gave nearly 100 reasons why he was right. Another had repeated speculations and each time he missed it he came out with another speculation with a revised date and time of Christ's Second Coming. These prophetic speculators have been wrong time and time again and have caused controversies in the church.

Of course, not all prophetic speculation has to with the day and hour of the Second Coming of Christ—or about whether or not the antichrist is alive and well on the earth today or any number of other end-times events.

Prophetic speculation is when we develop theories based on outward circumstances alone without input from the Holy Spirit. Prophetic speculation is an opinion based on the natural senses rather than unadulterated prophetic insight. Prophetic speculation is based on an unproven theory, not a Holy Ghost knowing. Prophetic speculation has no real evidence behind its assertion, and it's not discernment.

Even though prophetic speculation may be accurate at times, it is not inspired by the Holy Spirit. Like speculating in the stock market, prophetic speculation is risky business. When you miss it, it can be costly. You can lose credibility and damage your reputation. Prophetic speculation is not prophecy and can lead us into serious error—and lead others astray. As prophets, we're responsible for our utterances.

Beware of looking for too many prophetic signs. Jesus said we would recognize the signs of the times. We don't have to dig them out of news cycles to match our prophecies. Signs should be following you rather than you seeking them to prove a revelation that's really speculation. Ask the Holy Spirit to help you avoid prophetic speculation.

— *Prayer* —

Father, in the name of Jesus, help me see any areas where prophetic speculation has seeped into my ministry. Help me not to look for outward signs but to rely on the inner witness to understand and confirm the truth You are sharing with my heart.

Jezebel's Master Plot

"Therefore, I will throw her on a bed of suffering, and those who commit adultery with her will suffer greatly unless they repent and turn away from her evil deeds" (Revelation 2:22).

I went to college for journalism, but I really wanted to be a filmmaker. I wanted to write, produce, and edit movies. When the credits would roll in the movie theater, I would stick around and envision my name on the screen. Over the years, I've dabbled in film, especially the writing side.

I remember thinking through the life of Jezebel and what a scripted movie would look like. How would the plot summary read? What would be the storyline? I shared this imaginary plot summary in a book, *The Spiritual Warrior's Guide to Defeating Jezebel*:

> A wicked spirit that has roamed the earth for thousands of years seeking some-one to entice into sin, Jezebel is more than a spirit of control and manipulation that many make it out to be. Jezebel is a spirit of seduction that works to woo people into immorality and idolatry—but it doesn't work alone.

> With the help of Ahab, false prophets, and faithful servants, Jezebel has been sinking its seductive teeth into society for ages—and has infiltrated the pulpit and the pews of the church. Since few see Jezebel for what it, this spirit contin-ues to seduce the hearts and minds of those who claim Jesus as their first and true love. Will Jezebel ultimately lead the church into a great falling away or will the church wake up to this perversion before it's too late?

Jesus summed it up in Revelation 2:20, "Nevertheless I have a few things against you, because you allow that woman Jezebel, who calls herself a prophetess, to teach and seduce My servants to commit sexual immorality and eat things sacrificed to idols" (NKJV).

Catch this: Jezebel can't seduce you unless you let her. Jezebel can't teach you unless you let her. Jezebel can't force you into immorality. Jezebel cannot coerce you into idolatry. When you give Jezebel an inch, she will take a mile. You have to nip Jezebel's operations in the bud or her seeds will turn into a tree with deep roots.

— *Prayer* —

Father, in the name of Jesus, help me to stop tolerating Jezebel in my midst. Help me to stop making excuses for Jezebelic behavior and dulling my senses to her seduction. Show me how to confront people operating in this spirit with grace and truth that sets them free.

The Zealous Prophet

"If you are faithful in little things, you will be faithful in large ones. But if you are dishonest in little things, you won't be honest with greater responsibilities" (Luke 16:10).

I was zealous to pray for nations, but I didn't have the authority to intercede at the level at which I was aiming. I felt a prayer burden, but I was assigning it to the wrong nation. Let me explain. I felt I was a prophet to the nations (and I was, in the making) and I decided (notice, I decided) I wanted to pray for America.

I cried out to the Lord in prayer, "Lord, give me Your heart for America. Give me a burden for America. Help me pray for America." I went on like that for a few minutes before the Lord interrupted me. "I have not assigned you to pray for America in this season. Pray for Antigua and Barbados."

He was speaking of the nations Antigua and Barbuda and Barbados. I had no idea where those nations were. So I looked on the map that hung over my bed (all real prophets have a map over their bed) and I couldn't find them. I searched high and low. Finally, I saw little specs on the map representing those tiny nations. God was starting me out small.

It reminded me of Jesus' words in Luke 16:10, "The one who faithfully manages the little he has been given will be promoted and trusted with greater responsibilities. But those who cheat with the little they have been given will not be considered trustworthy to receive more" (TPT).

I was a little disappointed, but I set out to pray for these two nations as if my life depended on it. That paved the way for God to expand the stakes of my tent, so to speak. He enlarged my territory over time, giving me America and then later Europe. Here's the point. God will increase your authority in the prophetic and in prayer as you are faithful to execute in obedience your assignment at the level where you are.

— *Prayer* —

Father, in the name of Jesus, give me a faithful spirit and help me be a faithful witness in my prophetic ministry. Teach me how to follow Your training program for me and grace me to steward well what You have put in my hand so I can graduate to the next level for Your glory.

Standing in the Office

"This is a true saying, if a man desire the office of a bishop, he desireth a good work"
(1 Timothy 3:1 KJV).

You've probably heard the phrase, "standing in the office of the prophet." Have you ever thought about what that really entails on a day-to-day basis? The Bible does speak of the office of a bishop, and we know the fivefold ministry gifts are, essentially, offices. So what is an office? It's a special duty, a charge, or a position. It's a service, a responsibility, a function.

Sometimes the functioning part is not difficult but the standing can be challenging. The word *stand* means "to perform the duty of; to take up or maintain a specified position or posture; to maintain one's position; to be in a position to gain or lose because of an action taken or a commitment made; to endure or undergo successfully; to tolerate without flinching; to bear courageously," according to *Merriam-Webster's* dictionary.

Can you see the suffering in there? There's obviously resistance to standing in the office of the prophet or else you wouldn't have to endure, tolerate without flinching, and bear courageously. So to stand in the office of the prophet in the broadest sense is to walk worthy of the vocation to which you were called, to endure the hardship that comes along with it like a good soldier, to be bold and unmovable in the face of opposition.

If you are going to stand in the office of the prophet, then you have to be prepared to stand and withstand the spiritual warfare that the anointing on your life is going to stir up. The devil won't wait for you to engage him. And we shouldn't be looking for the devil. We should be looking for God. The devil will surely find you, and if you're walking with God you will see him.

Nevertheless, while standing in the office of the prophet you can fully expect to be engaged in warfare with principalities and powers that want to keep your anointed mouth shut so that you don't do damage to the kingdom of darkness. Just remember, when you've done all you can do—stand!

— *Prayer* —

Father, in the name of Jesus, give me the strength to stand in my office, walk worthy of my calling, and battle the demonic forces trying to move me away from Your will. Help me not to take any matter into my own hands, but to acknowledge Your wisdom and lean into Your grace.

The Jehu Anointing

"...It must be Jehu son of Nimshi, for he's driving like a madman" (2 Kings 9:20).

I believe Elijah was supposed to take down Jezebel, not just her false prophets. He had the boldness to call the showdown at Mount Carmel, but when Jezebel put the heat on he melted. Although Elijah finished well, he didn't finish off Jezebel—but he did prophesy her demise and God used him to commission a new king who would incite her eunuchs to throw Jezebel violently to her death. His name was, of course, Jehu.

Everybody wants that Elijah mantle. But we have to know when to wear the Elijah mantle and when to wear the Jehu mantle. We need to dress for the occasion. Conquering Jezebel demands a Jehu anointing. The Elijah anointing will deal with the false prophet operations in the land, but the Jehu anointing will deal with the Jezebelic operations in the land.

Keep in mind, Jehu was not a prophet. He never prophesied to kings like Elijah did. He was a warrior who was anointed king to take over where Elijah left off. Elijah ran from Jezebel and threw himself down in a cave. Jehu ran to Jezebel and commanded she be thrown down to her death. Elijah prophesied about Jezebel, "The dogs shall eat Jezebel by the wall of Jezreel" (1 Kings 21:23 NKJV). Jehu was the agent to fulfill Elijah's prophetic word.

Let this encourage your heart, prophet. In Scripture, the first time Jezebel was confronted, Jezebel was defeated. Although the spirit of Jezebel will never go away until Jesus comes back, we don't have to tolerate Jezebel's witchcraft in our lives. We can ask the Lord for that Jehu anointing that carries the vigor and authority to see Jezebel thrown down. We can push back Jezebel's witchcraft in the name of Jesus. But we must not run away from Jezebel. We must be willing to confront it.

— *Prayer* —

Father, give me the Jehu anointing—the boldness to confront Jezebel and her witchcrafts in my life. Help me not to wince and walk in the opposite direction when a Jezebel attack comes but to run toward the confrontation with an assurance that Jezebel will fall.

Prophets in the Fire

"...He commanded that the furnace be heated seven times hotter than usual. Then he ordered some of the strongest men of his army to bind Shadrach, Meshach, and Abednego and throw them into the blazing furnace" (Daniel 3:19-20).

I was on audition for God on my way to the next level of prophetic ministry. Of course, I didn't know that. All I knew was the fire seemed to be seven times hotter than any fiery trial I'd ever experienced. It almost seemed as if a new trial started before the last trial ended. I was fighting off overwhelm because the fire seemed too hot to handle. I'm convinced the fire is hotter for prophets.

Maybe you can relate. But remember this: No matter how hot the fire, we have no excuse to forsake our prophetic calling. How can we edify, comfort, and exhort people when we're curled up in a fetal position and hiding from the world like a caterpillar who envelops itself in a cocoon while it changes? The testing of our faith works endurance in us. These character-building seasons are as precious as gold; they bring the dross to the surface and purify our souls.

Shadrach, Meshach, and Abednego were thrown into the fire suddenly, fully dressed. They went into the fire in bondage. And the evil king demanded the heat be turned up seven times. No one could possibly survive such a trial. The roaring flames were all around them—and there was a fourth Man in the fire.

Prophet, when you are in the midst of a fiery trial Jesus, the Prophet, is in there with you. The Deliverer is in the fire with you. He wants to deliver you from the bondages of the enemy. He wants to free you from demonic chains. He wants to liberate you from trust issues. You will come out of the fire without shackles and fetters. This will be your story:

...Shadrach, Meshach, and Abednego stepped out of the fire. Then the high officers, officials, governors, and advisers crowded around them and saw that the fire had not touched them. Not a hair on their heads was singed, and their clothing was not scorched. They didn't even smell of smoke! (Daniel 3:26-27)

— *Prayer* —

Father, in the name of Jesus, teach me not to resist the fiery trial but to allow You to burn away everything that hinders love. Help me see how the fiery trial is perfecting my faith and breaking enemy bondages off my mind.

Prophets of Innovation

"And I will give you treasures hidden in the darkness—secret riches. I will do this so you may know that I am the Lord, the God of Israel, the one who calls you by name" (Isaiah 45:3).

Prophets of innovation are rapidly rising. You are well-positioned for innovations—new ideas, methods, and devices—when you incline your ear to wisdom and prudence. Proverbs 8:12 tells us, "I wisdom dwell with prudence, and find out knowledge of witty inventions" (KJV).

I see innovations throughout the Bible in the form of inventions, which are tied to our creator God's wisdom impartations. The Bible speaks of Jubal, the first of those who played the harp and flute (see Gen. 4:21), and Zillah, the forger of all instruments of bronze and iron (see Gen. 4:22). Second Chronicles 26:15 speaks of Uriah who made engines of war invented by skillful men.

In modern times, many inventors credit God with their innovations. George Washington Carver, who invented at least 300 products from peanuts—including paper, soap, glue, and medicines—said, "The Lord has guided me," and "without my Savior, I am nothing." Mary Hunter, an award-winning chef, insists all her recipes come from heaven: "I don't have a cookbook. God gives me my own. Prayer is where I get ninety-nine percent of my recipes."

Gary Starkweather, an engineer who invented the laser printer, said: "I believe that to a great extent, the creativity we possess is because the Creator put it there. God put things [in us] as tool developers and creative individuals and I think it has to please Him when He sees us use those faculties to make something completely new."

I agree with Starkweather's revelation and we need to embrace this pure wisdom from above. God is a Creator, an Innovator, and an Inventor and we were created in His image and in His likeness. John 1:3 proclaims, "All things were created through Him, and without Him nothing was created that was created" (MEV). I believe this is still true and that witty inventions, technologies, scientific breakthroughs, and other innovations that make a positive impact on society are inspired by His Spirit, even if the inventor does not yet know Him.

Prophets are positioned to lead the way on the innovation front—and not just in the church but beyond the church. Are you ready to incline your ear to wisdom and prudence?

— *Prayer* —

Father, in the name of Jesus, help me press past the distractions and stop settling for the status quo in the church and in the marketplace. Impart to me the wisdom to see what others cannot so I can bring innovative solutions to a world You love.

Discovering Prophetic Portals

"But he commanded the skies to open; he opened the doors of heaven" (Psalm 78:23).

I've spent a good deal of time in Moravian Falls. There, I discovered prophetic portals. A prophetic or spiritual portal is an entry point to the supernatural world. In a way, it's a fancy word for door or entrance. It's a gateway into prophetic dimensions.

Portals are biblical. David declared in Psalm 24:7, "Open up, ancient gates! Open up, ancient doors, and let the King of glory enter." And noted in Psalm 118:20, "These gates lead to the presence of the Lord, and the godly enter there."

One day at my church, I saw angels coming through windows carrying glory gifts. I call them as glory gifts because these boxes with bows appeared to be glowing with the glory of God. These windows were portals. We know there are windows in heaven because Malachi 3:10 speaks of them—not just a single window but more than one. Of course, we don't know how many. We know the angels go through windows of heaven based on Jacob's experience in the wilderness: "As he slept, he dreamed of a stairway that reached from the earth up to heaven. And he saw the angels of God going up and down the stairway" (Gen. 28:12).

Jacob had a life-changing encounter in this portal. God could have spoken to Jacob anywhere. But He directed him to a specific place with an open heaven. He may do the same with you. Other times, He stirs on your heart to pray until you break through the hard heavens where you are and in response He rends the heavens. Isaiah prayed, "Oh, that you would burst from the heavens and come down! How the mountains would quake in your presence!" (Isa. 64:1).

Only God can open the portals of heaven, but He often does so at our request. God responds to faith, but He responds to hungry faith. Solomon described this hungry faith, "Joyful are those who listen to me, watching for me daily at my gates, waiting for me outside my home!" (Prov. 8:34).

— *Prayer* —

Father, in the name of Jesus, teach me how to discern heavenly portals. Show me how to press past flesh and demonic resistance to enter into the portals that You are calling me into so I can receive a fresh word from Your heart.

Following Prophetic Breadcrumbs

"But when the Father sends the Advocate as my representative—that is, the Holy Spirit—he will teach you everything and will remind you of everything I have told you" (John 14:26).

I hadn't received a significant personal prophecy from the Lord in years—nor was I looking for one. While I used to crave prophetic words as a young Christian, I've learned not look to man as a mediator to deliver messages from God. Nevertheless, out of nowhere, I started having dream after dream and getting word after word directly from the Lord about crossing bridges, mega provision, relational deaths, spiritual attacks, turning points, and big decisions.

Add it all up, these prophetic breadcrumbs were undeniable. But I still had no idea what was going on. It was almost troublesome because it was clear that whatever was about to happen was a huge "suddenly" I never saw coming. That makes sense, of course, since Paul taught us that we know in part and we see in part (see 1 Cor. 13:9-12).

Each prophetic word I received from Father's heart—every dream, every vision, and every angelic encounter—served as a puzzle piece that was slowly bringing into view the big picture. If anyone had told me what that picture looked like in a single prophecy, my mind and emotions would have rejected it. God in His wisdom trickled out bits and pieces of information like breadcrumbs on a hiking trail. And I followed.

Through this I learned that many suddenlies are not suddenlies at all. God changes us from glory to glory, and we move from faith to faith. He prepares our hearts, sometimes for years in advance, for the next breakthrough. He sees the end from the beginning and sends messengers we know and messengers we don't to drop prophetic breadcrumbs on the path to our destiny.

When you find yourself flooded with prophetic revelation about yourself or others, don't ignore the breadcrumbs. When you follow them they will lead you to the truth the Holy Spirit is trickling out. If you are spiritually curious, you will run right smack dab into a revelation that will inspire your heart.

— *Prayer* —

Father, in the name of Jesus, help me not to miss the prophetic breadcrumbs You are dropping on my path. Give me a heart that is sensitive to what You are saying and doing in my life so I can get into agreement immediately with Your good, perfect, and acceptable will.

Breaking Inner Vows

"But I say, do not make any vows!" (Matthew 5:34)

I had just been sorely rebuked by an elder prophet for something I did not even do. I was completely innocent, and yet I was being vehemently cursed on my voicemail. It was beyond hurtful and I took it especially hard. So hard that I climbed up in my loft bed and cried my eyes out.

Suddenly, I heard a voice saying, "I will never let them hurt me again." I didn't recognize the voice. Indeed, it was not the still small voice of God. It was the voice of a stranger. It startled my spirit and I sat up in my loft bed and shouted, "No!" I had no idea at the time, but it was Jezebel trying to get me to speak out an inner vow so this spirit could be my protector.

Inner vows are ungodly promises we make ourselves. They become self-fulfilling prophecies when we voice them out loud or meditate on them too long in our mind. Inner vows usually start with "always" or "never" statements. If I had uttered the words I heard, I would have come under the influence of a Jezebel spirit.

At the time, I didn't know anything about inner vows. Thank God, He alerted my spirit and I rejected the imagination. God takes vows seriously, and a prophet's anointed mouth can do himself a lot of damage with these unwise promises.

"But I say, do not make any vows! Do not say, 'By heaven!' because heaven is God's throne. And do not say, 'By the earth!' because the earth is his footstool. And do not say, 'By Jerusalem!' for Jerusalem is the city of the great King. Do not even say, 'By my head!' for you can't turn one hair white or black. Just say a simple, 'Yes, I will,' or 'No, I won't.' Anything beyond this is from the evil one," Jesus warned in Matthew 5:34-37.

Do you need to break inner vows?

— *Prayer* —

Father, in the name of Jesus, show me if I have uttered inner vows that are holding me back from Your best plan for my life. Help me remember the always-never statements I made that are causing me harm and keeping me trapped in old patterns.

Fruit-Bearing Gifts

"But the fruit of the [Holy] Spirit [the work which His presence within accomplishes] is love, joy (gladness), peace, patience (an even temper, forbearance), kindness, goodness (benevolence), faithfulness, gentleness (meekness, humility), self-control (self-restraint, continence). Against such things there is no law [that can bring a charge]" (Galatians 5:22-23 AMPC).

When I was a kid, Lifesavers® candy was popular. The red ones were my favorite. I wasn't a big fan of the pineapple flavor but I ate them anyway because, well, they were fruity treats. You are probably wondering how this relates to the prophetic. Let me catch you up: Lifesavers® are fruity gifts. Prophets, too, should be fruity gifts—or, put a better way, fruit-bearing gifts.

You can be the most accurate prophet who ever walked the face of the earth, but if you don't develop the fruit of the Spirit in your life you may not have fruit that remains. In other words, your legacy might be that you were an accurate jerk. Surely, you've heard of famous ministers who have had tantrums backstage or affairs behind the scenes. They were gifted, but the fruit of the Spirit was lacking.

Galatians 5:22-23 lists the fruit of the Spirit: "But the Holy Spirit produces this kind of fruit in our lives: love, joy, peace, patience, kindness, goodness, faithfulness, gentleness, and self-control. There is no law against these things!"

If you want something to grow, you have to feed it and water it. Reading the Word and praying in the Spirit waters the seed of the fruit of the Spirit the Holy Ghost brought with Him when He came to live on the inside of you. When you walk in the Spirit you will not give in to the ways of the flesh (see Gal. 5:16). What you starve and dehydrate dies. When you sow to the Spirit, you reap fruit that remains.

I love *The Passion Translation* of this verse: "But the fruit produced by the Holy Spirit within you is divine love in all its varied expressions: joy that overflows, peace that subdues, patience that endures, kindness in action, a life full of virtue, faith that prevails, gentleness of heart, and strength of spirit. Never set the law above these qualities, for they are meant to be limitless." Meditate on that.

— *Prayer* —

Father, in the name of Jesus, give me a hunger to cultivate the fruit of the Spirit alongside the gifts of the Spirit so my ministry will see lasting influence. Grace me to seek first Your Kingdom and Your righteousness so I can model a Christ-like prophetic ministry.

DECEMBER 17

Exploring Your Dream Language

"'In the last days,' God says, 'I will pour out my Spirit upon all people. Your sons and daughters will prophesy. Your young men will see visions, and your old men will dream dreams'" (Acts 2:17).

I'm a seasonal dreamer. By that I mean I dream in batches. My prophetic dream activity is sporadic, with many dreams over a few months and then none for a few months. Through tracking my prophetic dream patterns, I've also been able to explore my dream language.

While there's a generally accepted dream language based on biblical symbols and numbers, I've discovered dream interpretation dictionaries can sometimes be more harmful than helpful. That's because God sometimes speaks to us in a way that is uniquely relevant or emotional to us.

Case in point: If you got bit by a dog when you were a kid, a dog showing up in your dream carrying a message may not be a positive image for you. If you are a dog lover, that same dog with the scroll in his mouth may thrill you and send you on a treasure hunt with the Holy Spirit to unlock the contents of the scroll. As I wrote in my book *Decoding Your Dreams*:

> God knows our emotional makeup better than we do. God knows our knowledge base. God knows our personal experiences. And He knows we're going to filter any and all communications through a uniquely-colored lens. While we must always turn to the Bible for interpretation, sometimes the interpretation is more subjective than biblical—but will never violate Scripture.
>
> Dreams, then, are not only symbolic and parabolic, at times they are subjective. When you are interpreting dreams other people have—whether it's about you or about something related to your own life—you can't filter it through your own dream code. Our heavenly Father speaks to us in a way that is intimate between us and Him.

Now, if you are dreaming as a prophet it's a different story. God may not speak to you in a language you understand but in a language that makes sense to the masses. Not every dream you have is just for you, and not every dream you have is for the Body of Christ. What is God saying to you in your dreams?

— *Prayer* —

Father, in the name of Jesus, help me to decode my dreams, knowing that the interpretation belongs to You and I labor in vain to understand without Your grace. Help me discern the difference between a personal dream and a corporate dream so I can walk in truth.

Walking Through Dry Seasons

"The boy Samuel ministered before the Lord under Eli. In those days the word of the Lord was rare; there were not many visions" (1 Samuel 3:1 NIV).

Samuel rose up as a prophet in Israel during a dry season. The Amplified Bible emphasizes just how dry it was, "The word of the Lord was rare and precious in those days; visions [that is, new revelations of divine truth] were not widespread." The Good News Translation says, "There were very few messages from the Lord, and visions from him were quite rare."

This was not the only time Israel went through a dry season. Asaph laments, "We no longer see your miraculous signs. All the prophets are gone, and no one can tell us when it will end" (Ps. 74:9). And Amos prophesied a prophetic word of famine in Amos 8:11, "'The time is surely coming,' says the Sovereign Lord, "when I will send a famine on the land—not a famine of bread or water but of hearing the words of the Lord.'"

That means every prophet in the land was walking through a dry season. God wasn't giving them prophetic messages to share, or at least not many. There was no great revelation coming to them, so they were relatively silent. I wonder if they understood why the revelation dried up. Did God tell them what He was doing and why, or did the flowing river just cease without explanation?

Either way, we all walk through dry seasons prophetically. That can be extremely uncomfortable and even distressing, especially when you are accustomed to flowing prolifically. I've learned to stay consistent in dry seasons. I may not have the word of the Lord, but I can still make intercession. I may not have dreams and visions, but I can still spend time with Him. I may not have a fresh encounter, but I can still read my Bible.

The point is, we can still be doers of the Word when we're not hearing the prophetic word. We can keep pressing into His presence, studying His emotions, and learning His ways even if He's not speaking. Sooner or later, the dry season will end and you will still be well watered.

— *Prayer* —

Father, in the name of Jesus, teach me to discipline myself to walk in Your Word and with Your Spirit even when I am not hearing, seeing, or feeling anything. Give me the grace to dig my prophetic well deeper during a famine so I will be prepared for the abundance of rain.

The Comparison Pit

"...They compare themselves to one another and make up their own standards to measure themselves by, and then they judge themselves by their own standards. What self-delusion!" (2 Corinthians 10:12 TPT)

I only fell into the comparison pit once in decades of ministry—and I never want to do that again. I was traveling the nation with a powerful preacher—probably the best preacher of our generation. We tag teamed a lot because of the tremendous synergy between us. People stood and shouted when he held the mic. But I am more of a teacher than a preacher. While I can preach at times, my gift is breaking down the Word in a way people can apply it.

After one conference I remember taking the enemy's thought, "You're not as gifted in the pulpit." I thought about it and agreed. My mind was under attack for a few days, and I started feeling bad about my own ministry. Then the Lord's still small voice suddenly got very loud. He told me I was equally as gifted, but the manifestation of my gifting was different and carried a different Kingdom purpose. That's what made the partnership so powerful.

In the age of social media, it can be especially tempting to compare your prophetic words with others'. But remember, everything looks slick on social media. You're seeing the polished version of other prophets most of the time. Comparison makes us discontent with what God gave us instead of content to be used for His glory. Comparison kills our confidence in who God called us to be. Comparison creates contempt for others whom we deem better—or lesser.

That's why Paul the apostle said, "In all this comparing and grading and competing, they quite miss the point" (2 Cor. 10:12 MSG). The Amplified Bible puts it this way, "When they measure themselves by themselves and compare themselves with themselves, they lack wisdom and behave like fools." Don't fall into the comparison pit.

— *Prayer* —

Father, deliver me from the comparison pit. Help me to keep my eyes on the Bridegroom, the Prophet, the Lord of my ministry. Teach me to value what You have given me like the treasure it is and to never covet another's unique prophetic expression.

The Contemplative Prophet

"Be still, and know that I am God!" (Psalm 46:10)

Every time I teach on contemplative prayer, people enter into prophetic dimensions they've never experienced before. Every day saints are seeing Jesus, receiving profound revelation, and coming out of the prayer closet refreshed through this practice.

Sometimes called centering prayer or soaking prayer, contemplative prayer opens your spiritual eyes and spiritual ears in ways some other prayer types don't because it leads you into a deeper awareness of God, the Source of all revelation. Contemplative prayer is centuries old and is actually rooted in monks, hermits, and nuns. I do not agree with some of the doctrines of the Catholic Church, but the reality is those who set themselves apart in His presence live from the inside out.

Contemplative prayer is biblical. King David was a prime practitioner: "My heart has heard you say, 'Come and talk with me.' And my heart responds, 'Lord, I am coming'" (Ps. 27:8). David understood, "You will show me the way of life, granting me the joy of your presence and the pleasures of living with you forever" (Ps. 16:11). And he spoke of a generation who seeks God's face (see Ps. 24:6).

Contemplative prayer is essentially being still and knowing He is God. It's not petitioning. It's waiting. I remember when I taught this practice at my prophetic training school in London. For the first five minutes, everyone was fidgeting. They settled after about 10 minutes. By the fifteen-minute mark some people were smiling, others were weeping, and others were writing down prophetic words in their journals. It never fails.

Andrew Murray, a twentieth-century South African pastor and author, wrote, "Here is the secret of a life of prayer. Take time in the inner chamber to bow down and worship; and wait on Him until He unveils Himself, and takes possession of you, and goes out with you to show how a man can live and walk in abiding fellowship with an unseen Lord."

— *Prayer* —

Father, in the name of Jesus, help me arrange my schedule to find pockets of time when I can draw near to You, so You will draw near to me. Help me prioritize Your presence over Your prayer answers, knowing that all I need is there in Your presence all along.

Prophetic Disagreements and Divorces

"Then the contention became so sharp that they parted from one another..." (Acts 15:39 NKJV).

There will likely come a time in your ministry when you experience a prophetic divorce. A prophetic divorce is a harsh separation with a ministry partner based on a sharp disagreement. You see this happen with some of the greatest men in the Bible, including Paul and Barnabas. Acts 15:36-41 chronicles the prophetic divorce for our benefit:

> *After some time Paul said to Barnabas, "Let's go back and visit each city where we previously preached the word of the Lord, to see how the new believers are doing." Barnabas agreed and wanted to take along John Mark.*
>
> *But Paul disagreed strongly, since John Mark had deserted them in Pamphylia and had not continued with them in their work. Their disagreement was so sharp that they separated. Barnabas took John Mark with him and sailed for Cyprus. Paul chose Silas, and as he left, the believers entrusted him to the Lord's gracious care. Then he traveled throughout Syria and Cilicia, strengthening the churches there.*

How you handle a prophetic divorce is vital. Paul and Barnabas had a strong disagreement and went their separate ways, but these two men of God didn't try to tear one another's ministries down. In fact, Paul later told the church at Corinth Barnabas' ministry was worthy of support (see 1 Cor. 9:6). Paul later told the church at Colossae to welcome John Mark if he showed up in their midst (see Col. 4:10). And Paul even requested John Mark's presence in his second letter to Timothy, though Bible scholars say this was likely a decade later after Mark matured (2 Tim. 4:11).

Likewise, when Abraham and Lot separated, they didn't try to destroy one another's reputations with secret statements and not-so-secret phone calls casting aspersions of wrongdoing on innocent hands. No, Abraham actually went to war to rescue Lot from danger (see Gen. 14) and later interceded for his life when God set out to destroy Sodom (see Gen. 18:22–19:29). This is true love. Strife is an abomination. Walk in love.

— *Prayer* —

Father, help me steward my relationships well. Help me stay faithful to covenant friendships, but if splits and separations must take place, give me the grace to walk in humility and keep my mouth off the people who I feel wronged me. Help me bless friends who become enemies.

Submitting to the Breaking and Making

"Does not the potter have power over the clay, from the same lump to make one vessel for honor and another for dishonor?" (Romans 9:21 NKJV)

When I was young in the prophetic ministry, I heard a lot about the breaking and humiliation of prophets. It scared me to death. People told stories of how the Lord stripped them bare before He launched them out. One time, in a small group of prophets, an elder prophet started praying, "Lord, break us, bend us, mold us, shape us." I made it clear to the Lord I was not in agreement with those prayers! I was terrified of what might happen.

Fear never comes from God and you don't have to be afraid of what the Lord will do as part of your making process. Yes, you will have to be broken in some areas so He can reshape you into the image of His Son. If you resist the making process, God will break you anyway and it will only hurt worse and take longer. Your best route is to submit to the breaking and the making, which really never ends. Consider this Scripture:

> I went down to the potter's house, and there he was, making something at the wheel. And the vessel that he made of clay was marred in the hand of the potter; so he made it again into another vessel, as it seemed good to the potter to make (Jeremiah 18:3-4 NKJV).

Look at it like this: You are the lump of clay and God is the Potter. God is actively molding you to fulfill your prophetic destiny. He is molding you into a vessel of honor, but you have a part to play in the molding. Paul explained it this way:

> But in a great house there are not only vessels of gold and silver, but also [utensils] of wood and earthenware, and some for honorable and noble [use] and some for menial and ignoble [use]. So whoever cleanses himself [from what is ignoble and unclean, who separates himself from contact with contaminating and corrupting influences] will [then himself] be a vessel set apart and useful for honorable and noble purposes, consecrated and profitable to the Master, fit and ready for any good work (2 Timothy 2:20-21 AMPC).

Ask the Lord to help you submit to this life-giving process.

— *Prayer* —

Father, in the name of Jesus, break off of me the fear of the breaking. You have not given me a spirit of fear and You will not allow more to come upon me than I can bear. Teach me to trust You in the midst of the shaping, molding, and even breaking You've prepared for me.

Multiply Yourself

"You have heard me teach things that have been confirmed by many reliable witnesses. Now teach these truths to other trustworthy people who will be able to pass them on to others" (2 Timothy 2:2).

I know how easy it is to lose sight of the Ephesians 4 equipping mandate of the New Testament prophet amid the harried pace of life. After all, you have to invest in Bible study, your prayer life, your church attendance, and perhaps your itinerant ministry—and that's on top of the mundane issues of life. But there comes a time when you've matured enough to carry the responsibility of reproducing yourself—and you must.

Christian International (CI) is my ministerial alignment. One of the seven anointings on CI is to reproduce reproducers who reproduce reproducers. Paul put it this way: "And all that you've learned from me, confirmed by the integrity of my life, deposit into faithful leaders who are competent to teach the congregations the same revelation" (2 Tim. 2:2 TPT). And the Amplified Bible draws it out:

> *The things [the doctrine, the precepts, the admonitions, the sum of my ministry] which you have heard me teach in the presence of many witnesses, entrust [as a treasure] to reliable and faithful men who will also be capable and qualified to teach others.*

The first command God gave to mankind was not about the Tree of the Knowledge of Good and Evil. The first command God gave to mankind was to be fruitful and multiply. As a matter of fact, the Bible calls it a blessing: "Then God blessed them and said, 'Be fruitful and multiply'" (Gen. 1:28). One key to advancing a pure prophetic movement is to multiply ourselves, to pour our lives out as a drink offering into the next generation.

Here's the catch: You have to identify faithful people. Opportunists will surely come. Platform-chasers will want you to give them immediately what it took you years to build. You'll need great discernment to identify the right ones to pour your life into. But it's worth it. Imagine if Elijah hadn't poured his life into Elisha? What if Paul hadn't poured his life into Timothy?

When you are in your prophetic prime, you may not want to stop and reproduce yourselves in others. But that's the best time. Don't delay on the Ephesians 4 mandate. How are you raising up?

— *Prayer* —

Father, in the name of Jesus, show me who to pour my life into just like You showed Jesus the twelve disciples. Help me identify the hungry ones and teach me how to prioritize equipping the next generation in accuracy and purity.

Build Yourself Up

"But you, my delightfully loved friends, constantly and progressively build yourselves up on the foundation of your most holy faith by praying every moment in the Spirit" (Jude 20 TPT).

When I was in missions in Nicaragua, I was carrying a heavy load of cameras to document what the Lord was doing in our midst. It was about 110 degrees and I was beyond overheated, so when an apostle asked me to come sit with him I didn't think twice. I thought he was just inviting me for a rest, but in reality he would share a secret to his success.

He shared with me the importance of praying in the Spirit, which would not only release the perfect prayer and utter mysteries by the spirit but also build me up. See, prophets get torn down. Persecution is a frequent reality to the uncompromising prophet. Misunderstanding is part and parcel of the prophet's ministry. Words can hurt.

Jude offers keen advice for the prophet, "But you, beloved, build yourselves up on [the foundation of] your most holy faith [continually progress, rise like an edifice higher and higher], pray in the Holy Spirit" (Jude 20 AMP). *The Message* puts it this way:

But you, dear friends, carefully build yourselves up in this most holy faith by praying in the Holy Spirit, staying right at the center of God's love, keeping your arms open and outstretched, ready for the mercy of our Master, Jesus Christ. This is the unending life, the real life! (Jude 20-21)

In some seasons I pray in the Spirit more than others. I like to pray in the Spirit at least 30 minutes a day. I'm not telling you this to create a law, but to encourage you to allow praying in the Spirit to become so natural that you don't even have to think about it. Part of the prophet's role is to build people up. Sometimes, the only one around to build you up is the Holy Spirit. Let Him utter words through your mouth that leave you edified.

— *Prayer* —

Father, I surrender full control of my life to You. I ask You even now to fill me to overflowing with Your Spirit, just as You have promised to do if I ask according to Your will. I ask this in the name of Jesus and believe that You are pouring out Your Spirit upon me right now.

Let Your Gift Make Room for You

"A man's gift makes room for him, and brings him before great men" (Proverbs 18:16 NKJV).

Jesus is the greatest gift ever, but God's gifts to mankind didn't stop there. Not only do we have access to the throne of grace, the right of using the name above all names, the blood of the Lamb, the living Word, our spiritual weapons of warfare, and the whole armor of God, we also have the Holy Spirit, who shares the testimony of Jesus we prophesy.

Prophet, you have gifts. You may feel, at times, like no one sees your gift. You may feel like no one recognizes who you are—that you are hidden. Listen, if you are hidden you are hidden for a reason. Paul the apostle was extremely gifted both spiritually and naturally, but almost immediately after he was called he was hidden for several years in Arabia. He was hidden until the Holy Spirit led Barnabas to bring him forward.

Be assured of this: Your gift will make room for you at the right time. You will be recognized at the right time and in the right season. In the meantime, develop your gift through study and exercise. Yes, function in your gift in appropriate contexts. Use your gift to serve people whether anyone recognizes you are a prophet or not (see 1 Pet. 4:10).

Let me put it another way. You don't need a title, a platform, or a microphone to function in your gift. Instead of asking people for opportunities, let your gift do the talking for you. When you operate in your gift with integrity, accuracy, and consistency as unto the Lord and not unto gaining opportunity, your gift will make room for you.

First Kings 20:41 reads, "Then the prophet quickly pulled the bandage from his eyes, and the king of Israel recognized him as one of the prophets." Sometimes God lets you stay hidden from those who could promote you. But I assure you, the same Jesus who gave you the gift and the office will open up the eyes of those who can make room for you at the right time.

— *Prayer* —

Father, in the name of Jesus, help me cultivate the gift mix You have given me whether or not anyone ever notices. Strip me of the craving for the approval and applause of men and teach me how to find my identity and worth in You and You alone.

The Competition Trap

"Don't push your way to the front; don't sweet-talk your way to the top. Put yourself aside, and help others get ahead. Don't be obsessed with getting your own advantage. Forget yourselves long enough to lend a helping hand" (Philippians 2:3 MSG).

Don't fight and war with your brothers and sisters over titles and promotions and other blessings. Where there is unity, I will command a blessing that you cannot contain. I will command a blessing that forces you to cooperate with another to reap that harvest because there is more than enough for all My children. Dare to believe Me today and to stretch yourself further than you did yesterday. Understand and know you can overcome whatever is facing you down when you work with your spiritual family. You will overcome together.

Those are words from the Holy Spirit in my devotional *Victory Decrees*. And they are still as true now as when the Holy Spirit first spoke them to me. The competition trap is real for emerging prophets—and sometimes even seasoned prophets can fall headlong into it. But competition is not Kingdom and prophets who engage in this practice are hindering their anointing.

Paul warned, "Let nothing be done through selfish ambition or conceit, but in lowliness of mind let each esteem others better than himself" (Phil. 2:3 NKJV). Competition comes from a spirit of self-promotion. That's why I like *The Passion Translation* of this verse: "Don't allow self-promotion to hide in your hearts, but in authentic humility put others first and view others as more important than yourselves."

Notice how it says don't allow this into your hearts. Jesus tells us we speak out of the abundance of our heart (see Luke 6:45). That's a scary thought when it comes to prophetic ministry because that translates to prophesying out of a spirit of competition, trying to look more prophetic or more accurate than someone else. It's a dangerous pit.

I've been to too many prayer meetings and prophetic roundtables and seen too many people competing for mic time, pushing their way to the front, and sweet talking their way to the top. While the spirit of competition may convince you this will propel you forward, in God's Kingdom it only holds you back. Be assured, any short-term gains we see will be wiped out with long-term losses.

— *Prayer* —

Father, help me to honor my brothers and sisters in Christ. Help me to help them do what they are called to do and avoid all striving, for Your glory. I decree strife cannot make its way into my relationships. I declare I am one with my brothers and sisters in the Lord.

Deliverer, Deliver Thyself

"You are my hiding place; You shall preserve me from trouble; You shall surround me with songs of deliverance. Selah" (Psalm 32:7 NKJV).

Moses was the deliverer of a nation. David delivered Saul from evil spirits by playing his harp. And Jesus cast out devils everywhere He went. Indeed, prophets and deliverance ministry work together like a hand and a glove. That's because many prophets also operate in a strong gift of discernment. But what happens when the prophet needs deliverance?

David, the deliverer of Saul, shows us the way. David cried out to God for deliverance time and time again. It wasn't always deliverance from demons as we know them today. Sometimes it was deliverance from demon-inspired people. I can only imagine how the spirit of fear gripped David at times. And we see his story is riddled with rejection experiences, betrayal, and grief.

David, though, understood God as deliverer. Nobody was around to play a harp for him in the wilderness while he was on the run from Saul, but the future king turned to the King of glory and described the outcome: "I sought the Lord, and He heard me, and delivered me from all my fears" (Ps. 34:4 NKJV). David also said, "You are my help and my deliverer; do not delay, O my God" (Ps. 40:17 NKJV). And again, "Be pleased, O Lord, to deliver me; O Lord, make haste to help me!" (Ps. 40:13 NKJV).

Here's the point. Prophets get rejected. Prophets get persecuted. Prophets get wounded. Left unresolved, these wounds and fears open the door to the enemy—one of them being Jezebel. Jezebel would love to add you to her trophy collection. Jezebel would love to add you to her yes-man prophet list and use you like a puppet.

If you walk in fear, rejection, addictions, or any other challenge you can't overcome on your own—if you've hit a wall you can't break through, find your way around, or go over or under—you need help. Maybe there's no one around to help you, but there is One who is your Helper and He is your Deliverer. Cry out to Him like David did and He will deliver you from whatever is holding you in bondage.

— *Prayer* —

Father, in the name of Jesus, deliver my soul from evil. Father, deliver my eyes from worthless things. Deliver my ears from twisted truths. Deliver my mind from vain imaginations. Deliver me from every tie that binds so I can move in the Spirit with accuracy.

Avoid Prophetic Conspiracies

"Don't call everything a conspiracy, like they do, and don't live in dread of what frightens them. Make the Lord of Heaven's Armies holy in your life. He is the one you should fear. He is the one who should make you tremble" (Isaiah 8:12-13).

As a prophet, you want to be known for prophetic integrity, not worldly conspiracy. Prophetic integrity is a soundness that comes from submitting to prophetic ethics and protocols. Prophetic conspiracy, on the other hand, is prophesying about secret plans that have been proven false—and continuing to insist you were right despite the facts that prove you wrong.

When you buy into and refuse to let go of a conspiracy, you lose your integrity.

Since God started restoring prophets to the church, there have been several high-profile prophetic conspiracy theories circulating the Body of Christ. There was the Three Days of Darkness Catholic prophecy that caused thousands of believers not to go to church over Easter weekend 2021. This prophecy pulls from Exodus 10 when horrible darkness plagued Egypt. The prophetic conspiracy went viral online. Other prophetic conspiracies point to famines and tsunamis that God never spoke about. Still other prophetic conspiracies claim the government is going to insert chips into our bodies and control our minds.

These prophetic conspiracies breed fear in the hearts of men. People begin to ask: Should we be stocking up food? Heading for Canada? Taking all our money out of the bank? Hiding in underground bunkers with big guns and plenty of ammunition? How should we respond to the many conspiracy theories and prophetic predictions of doom, gloom, destruction, and disaster? What does a blood-bought, Bible-believing, Holy Spirit-filled, tongue-talking saint do at such a time as this?

I found the answer in Isaiah 8:12-13: "Don't believe their every conspiracy rumor. And don't fear what they fear—don't be moved or terrified. Fear nothing and no one except Yahweh, Commander of Angel Armies! Honor him as holy. Be in awe before him with deepest reverence!" (TPT).

A spirit of error and strong delusion is rising in the earth and more prophetic conspiracies will rise in the years ahead. Prophet, be careful not to get caught up in conspiracy rumors and re-prophesy something God never said and, in doing so, sully your reputation.

— *Prayer* —

Father, in the name of Jesus, help me avoid the deception of conspiracy theories. Help me keep my ear clear of fallacies so I can hear Your warnings and sound the alarm while never breeding fear in the hearts of those who follow my ministry.

Re-Prophesying the Prophecy

"But when the Father sends the Advocate as my representative—that is, the Holy Spirit—he will teach you everything and will remind you of everything I have told you" (John 14:26).

We love to prophesy, but we see the concept of re-prophesying throughout the pages of the Bible. John the Baptist re-prophesied the words of Isaiah to announce his calling and assignment to Israel: "Listen! It's the voice of someone shouting, 'Clear the way through the wilderness for the Lord! Make a straight highway through the wasteland for our God!'" (Isa. 40:3).

Much the same, Jesus re-prophesied the psalmist's words about Himself: "Bless the one who comes in the name of the Lord. We bless you from the house of the Lord" (Ps. 118:26). And Peter re-prophesied Joel's words on the Day of Pentecost:

> *Then, after doing all those things, I will pour out my Spirit upon all people. Your sons and daughters will prophesy. Your old men will dream dreams, and your young men will see visions. In those days I will pour out my Spirit even on servants—men and women alike* (Joel 2:28-29).

God may lead you to re-prophesy any prophetic word that hasn't yet come to pass. Sometimes He will lead you to re-prophesy a word that is about to come to pass or is happening as you speak it. In this sense, re-prophesying can serve as confirmation and announcement at the same time.

Think about it. Prophetic messages from late generals like Smith Wigglesworth are still circulating the Internet hoping to land on people with ears to hear and faith to pray it through. Many are re-prophesying Wigglesworth's prophecy about a Word and Spirit revival in the end times. Others are re-prophesying the late David Wilkerson or Kenneth Hagin or Lester Sumrall's prophecies.

Re-prophesying isn't done on a whim. Like any prophetic utterance, the Holy Spirit inspires us to re-prophesy what He wants to emphasize. In other words, God will show you a prophecy from the past and give you an unction to re-prophesy it in the present to impact the future. God's Word never returns void, but sometimes we must prophesy it more than once.

What do you need to re-prophesy?

— *Prayer* —

Father, in the name of Jesus, help me see the value in picking up ancient swords—or swords from the generation before me—and prophesying again and again until they come to pass. Show me what to re-prophesy and I will faithfully proclaim Your Word.

Seer Misfocus

"Your eye is like a lamp that provides light for your body. When your eye is healthy, your whole body is filled with light. But when your eye is unhealthy, your whole body is filled with darkness. And if the light you think you have is actually darkness, how deep that darkness is!" (Matthew 6:22-23)

It seems there's never any lack of drama or controversy in the church. As much as I try to create a no drama zone in my life, sometimes dramatic theatrics find their way into my sight. People love to tell me when other people are talking about me—and I shut that down immediately. I don't want to know. I don't need another prayer assignment. God is my Vindicator.

Still, now and then the temptation comes to look at the drama broiling over a controversial issue. Usually, the drama spreads like wildfire on social media and you almost can't help but to catch wind of it. "You won't believe the brawl on Johnny's Facebook page, and what he said about Sarah. They are going in," someone once told me. The intense report was hard to believe. I was curious, so I set out to look for myself. That's when I heard the Lord say, "Every time you look at these things you are diminishing your ability to see in the spirit."

Wow! I stopped dead in my tracks and decided it wasn't worth it. Maybe the Lord hasn't said those words to you, but that doesn't make them any less true for you. Seers have to be careful to guard their eye gates. We can defile our eye with seer misfocus. What we focus on impacts our soul and can skew our spiritual vision.

The Passion Translation of Matthew 6:22-23 puts it this way:

The eyes of your spirit allow revelation-light to enter into your being. If your heart is unclouded, the light floods in! But if your eyes are focused on money, the light cannot penetrate and darkness takes its place. How profound will be the darkness within you if the light of truth cannot enter!

Anything you focus on that allows darkness into your soul is dangerous to your spiritual vision. Once you pollute your eyes, it's more difficult to discern between a true vision and a vain imagination. Once you compromise your eye gates you've invited the enemy access into your soul. Is it really worth it?

— *Prayer* —

Father, help me not to look at the drama that can traumatize my eyes and blur my spiritual vision. Give me the self-control to stay above the fray of the theatrics that tempt me to engage in ungodly opinions. Teach me to avoid the strife.

A Kairos Time in Your Prophetic Ministry

"So let's not get tired of doing what is good. At just the right time we will reap a harvest of blessing if we don't give up" (Galatians 6:9).

"Stay calm. Be patient. Your time is coming." In 2001, during a critical turning point in my life, the audible voice of the Lord woke me up from a deep sleep speaking these prophetic words. Like young Samuel, I did not know it was the audible voice of the Lord at the time. I had no idea what God meant, but I never forgot what He said. I hid His words in my heart and, during especially difficult trials, the Holy Spirit brought the life-giving utterance to my remembrance. The prophecy seemed to echo in my soul and encouraged me to keep going.

Paul wrote, "And don't allow yourselves to be weary in planting good seeds, for the season of reaping the wonderful harvest you've planted is coming!" (Gal. 6:9 TPT). I found out firsthand how true those words are. About fifteen years after the audible voice of the Lord spoke to me, I had a second encounter. Seemingly randomly, while I was in worship, the Lord said, "Your time is now." I am walking in my kairos time.

As a prophet, if you keep your hand to the plow, keep prophesying by His unction, and keep walking in obedience, you will see your kairos time—your right time, your opportune time. You will see your season of reaping. You will see the fruit of your prophetic ministry. You will see changed lives. You will see atmospheres shift. You will see nations healed. You will see the recognition of your ministry. You will see a good reputation. You will see an increase of influence. Yes, you will see your kairos time.

Walking in prophetic ministry can be wearisome. There's a lot of warfare. Most people have no idea the struggles the prophet faces in the making process that never ends. Your prophetic words are seeds, whether people hear them or receive them. Sow your prophetic ministry as unto the Lord. Do it for His glory. When you do, you'll find more opportunities than you can accept to walk in your high calling.

— *Prayer* —

Father, in the name of Jesus, help me stay steady and faithful as I run my race for Your glory. Help me not to push my way into an opportunity that I'm not ready for. Teach me to discern my times, which are in Your hands.

ABOUT JENNIFER LECLAIRE

Jennifer LeClaire is senior leader of Awakening House of Prayer in Fort Lauderdale, Florida, founder of the Ignite Network, and founder of the Awakening Prayer Hubs prayer movement. Jennifer formerly served as the first-ever female editor of *Charisma* magazine and is a prolific author of over 50 books. You can find Jennifer online or shoot her an email at info@jenniferleclaire.org.